D0913197

Scooter

THE BIOGRAPHY
OF
PHIL RIZZUTO

by
Carlo DeVito

TRIUMPH
BOOKS

Library of Congress Cataloging-in-Publication Data
DeVito, Carlo.
    Scooter : the biography of Phil Rizzuto / by Carlo DeVito.
        p. cm.
        Includes bibliographical references and index.
        ISBN 978-1-60078-165-0
        1. Rizzuto, Phil, 1917-2007. 2. Baseball players—United States—
    Biography. 3. New York Yankees (Baseball team) I. Title.
    GV865.R5D48 2009
    796.357092--dc22
    [B]
                                                                    2009049515

This book is available in quantity at special discounts for your group or organization. For further information, contact:

Triumph Books
542 South Dearborn Street
Suite 750
Chicago, Illinois 60605
(312) 939–3330
Fax (312) 663–3557
www.triumphbooks.com

Printed in U.S.A.
ISBN: 978-1-60078-165-0
Design by Sue Knopf

All photos courtesy of AP Images unless otherwise indicated

"The Diamond Dude" by Ogden Nash copyright 1955 by permission of Curtis Brown Ltd. and the Estate of Ogden Nash

This book is dedicated to my grandfather,
Philip Vincent DeVito,
who loved Tony Lazzeri, Frank Crosetti, Joe DiMaggio,
and Phil Rizzuto, and who instilled his love of baseball
and the Yankees through three subsequent generations.
And to his great-grandsons,
Dylan and Dawson DeVito,
the All-Stars in our family.

CONTENTS

III: The View from the Booth

PROLOGUE

A small group of local leaders, noticeable for its diversity, Jews, Sihks, and other ethnicities, gathered near the backstop of one of the baseball diamonds at Smokey Oval Park in Queens. It was a relatively warm, overcast day in mid-October. There was a slight breeze.

"Welcome everyone and welcome to Richmond Hill and Smokey Oval Park. Thank you for being here today," said Rory I. Lancman, the Queens Assemblyman. "Today we have the opportunity to both honor and remember a great American and a great New Yorker, Phil Rizzuto, as well as pay honor and tribute and show sensitivity to a new generation of New Yorkers and that's the South Asian Community and in particular the Sikh community here in Richmond Hill. We're standing here in front of what is currently called Smokey Oval Park at Atlantic and 125th Street."

As with any event, the city did not stop its constant sea of noise and distraction. Cell phones beeped, airplanes roared overhead, an occasional horn blared. It was all a reminder of the city of the man they were honoring. It was the city he loved.

"Phil Rizzuto, the Scooter, played his high school baseball here in Richmond Hill. It's where he learned to become a great baseball player and where we like to think he learned to become a great American and a great New Yorker. Richmond Hill is also home to a large South Asian community, including a Sikh community, and one of the things I learned in getting to know the Sikh community better is that the concept of smoking is offensive, and sacrilegious even, to Sikhs.

"With Phil Rizzuto's passing, we're presented with an opportunity to remember Phil Rizzuto and to remember him here in a part of Queens that had such an impact on his life and where he as a Yankee, and he as a Yankee broadcaster, had such a tremendous impact on the people in this community.

"Just as Phil Rizzuto was a child of immigrants, immigrants who came to this country to give their children a better life and a better opportunity, an opportunity which Phil Rizzuto seized and went onto a long and wonderful and important life. Today the children of immigrants in this community use and enjoy this park to fulfill their parents' dreams to get a good education to be all that they can be in this great country of ours."

While the crowd that watched was small, it respectfully listened to all those were assembled to speak. Among them were reporters from some of the best-known papers of the region—an odd collection of newspapers for such a community-specific purpose. But it spoke volumes about how Phil Rizzuto had been regarded.

"If people in Queens have their way, one of the more peculiar names on the roster of city parks will soon be history. Smokey Oval Park, a cluster of ball fields and playgrounds in Richmond Hill, gets its name from deposits of soot and ash that passing trains used to dump on the area, according to the Parks Department," wrote John Sullivan of the *New York Times*. "The ash heaps are long gone, but the name has lived on to baffle visitors to the neighborhood. Mr. Rizzuto…lived in nearby Glendale but played high school baseball in Richmond Hill, which gives the neighborhood sufficient reason to honor the Hall of Famer. (There was some support for another former resident, Jack Kerouac, but Mr. Lancman said the beat writer could not compete with the shortstop.)"

"There are certain things about Phil Rizzuto that makes it especially appropriate," Lancman said, following a news conference at the site that morning. "He embodied the spunk and decency of New Yorkers."

And of course, it was especially funny, and a testament to Rizzuto, that the park be named after a Yankee, right in the backyard of the Mets, who had just suffered a late-season collapse. The irony of it was lost on no one, especially the Assemblyman.

"Mr. Lancman is also bowing to the will of a large group of his constituents. Two of the city's largest Sikh temples are located near the park, he said, and smoking is banned by the Sikh religion. He said delegates from the community approached him and asked to change the name," continued Sullivan.

"It sounds like a place for smoking and drinking and things like that," said Raghbir Singh, a founder of one of the temples, the Makhan Shah Labana, and chairman of the 25th District's Democratic club. "When we print up fliers, we have to say we are having an activity in nearby Smokey Park."

The proposal was backed by Community Board No. 9, the Queens Jewish Community Council, and the leaders of the local Sikh community.

All through the conference, two Sikh men, respectful, well-dressed with their dark, bushy, well-kept beards and traditional turbans, stood in stark contrast on either side of a sepia print photo of Rizzuto in a well-used baggy gray-flannel baseball uniform dating all the way back to his youth. The photo stood testament to a version of this city that no longer existed. But it also stood testament to the kind of endearment garnered for the more than half-century of service by one man to a city that loved him, and to the sport he gave his life to.

INTRODUCTION

"To know Scooter was to love him," wrote veteran sportswriter Phil Pepe, who covered the Yankees for decades. "To know that I will never see him again, never hear him again, never spend time with him again, never poke fun at him again, never laugh at his idiosyncrasies again, leaves a void that can never be replaced."

This seems to be a classic and genuine sentiment among people who knew Scooter. For there is one thing that can be said of Phil Rizzuto—he was well-liked. Even beloved. But once you start to really spend time with Rizzuto, you begin to understand he had more depth of quality, more general chutzpah, and more moxie than most people.

"Everyone was pretty much in agreement that Rizzuto was a sweet, funny, lovable little guy who said enough nutty things to fill a shelf of books," wrote sportswriter and journalist Allen Barra. "Phil Rizzuto was tough, feisty, sharp, and opinionated; he took shots, both verbal and physical, and gave back as good as he got. He held grudges. He was a hard-headed businessman. No one who shilled for The Money Store should ever be called 'innocent;' no one hip enough to do cameo appearances on *Seinfeld* or *Arli$$* or lend his voice to a Meat Loaf video is 'pure.' Acknowledging these facts makes Rizzuto no less admirable—on the contrary, it gives him depth and dimension."

That is the Phil Rizzuto you will find in these pages. Plagued by phobias of all kinds, hindered by his slight stature, driven by ego and grudges, he was the epitome of the old rubric, "It is not the size of the dog in the fight, but the size of the fight in the dog."

He played the innocent when it suited him. He was tough enough when it counted. He was shrewd enough when he had to be. He was slick enough when he wanted to be.

"He didn't get a thing out of life by being cute and lovable; Rizzuto succeeded by ignoring other people's evaluations of him," Barra added. "Whether you were talking about his difficulties breaking into the major leagues or into the broadcast booth, each step for Rizzuto was hard fought and fairly won. He was dismissed by both the Dodgers and the Giants before he gained a toe-hold with the Yankees. He worked for years in the broadcast booth with men who openly criticized him and dismissed him. He won seven World Series as a player and was the longest-serving broadcaster in Yankees history."

For any metropolitan-area Yankees fans, the voice of summer, with all its promise and glory, was embodied by Phil Rizzuto. He was the unmistakable voice of the New York Yankees, much longer than the fabled Mel Allen. So Rizzuto's foibles were well known to all. But few today saw him play. Those that did were in awe.

He was considered by many who played with him as the best, or one of the best bunters in the history of the game. He had speed enough to steal bases when running the base paths, and he was quick enough to rob hits and lead the league in double-play combinations.

Roger Angell once wrote in his book, *Five Seasons*, that he watched the early 1970s Yankees, trying to gain an appreciation for them, "but when I come home from the Stadium and go to bed, what I see before I sleep is Phil Rizzuto laying down a drag bunt, suddenly dipping the bat down by his belt buckle to tap the ball, then whirring away down the line…"

Red Smith, when he wrote an article about the appreciation of baseball, pointed to the Scooter "to enjoy the thrill of appreciation that anybody must feel seeing…Phil Rizzuto scoop up a grounder and get rid of the ball in one fluid motion."

But there was more grit than poetry. Rizzuto was the backbone of the Yankees for 13 seasons. The New York Yankees could hit home runs, but they were mainly built on pitching and defense. Home runs died in Joe DiMaggio's center-field glove, and sharp grounders and line drives found their way into

Rizzuto's flashy hands. Rizzuto was the backbone of that defense. Teammates such as DiMaggio, Keller, and Henrich said so then and insisted the same in later years.

"Rizzuto batted .273 and drove in 562 runs and scored 877 runs for 13 years? What about Reese? Batted .269 with 885 runs batted in and 1,338 runs scored in 16 years? That's a lot more power for Reese, but, holy cow, Rizzuto did everything the Yankees asked of him. Stole 149 bases, sacrificed, held the infield together from the DiMaggio years to the Mantle years," George Vecsey wrote in the *New York Times*.

He also played more games than any other Yankee between the years 1947 and 1954. And not by a little bit, but by a lot. Much more than DiMaggio. Much more than Mantle. More than even Berra.

YEAR	NO. OF GAMES, PLAYER		
1946	149 C Keller	131 DiMaggio	125 Rizzuto
1947	153 Rizzuto	148 Snuffy Stirnweiss	144 McQuinn
1948	153 DiMaggio	146 Henrich	141 Snuffy Stirnweiss
1949	153 Rizzuto	128 Coleman	116 Berra
1950	155 Rizzuto	153 Coleman	151 Berra
1951	144 Rizzuto	141 Yogi Berra	131 McDougald
1952	152 Rizzuto	151 Yogi Berra (tie with McDougald)	
1953	149 Billy Martin	141 McDougald	137 Berra
1954	151 Berra	146 Mantle	130 Collins

Between 1949 and 1953, the Yankees won five straight World Series titles. Rizzuto was a major part of those championships.

He belonged in the Hall of Fame.

He belonged in the Hall of Fame as a player. And he belonged in the Hall of Fame as a broadcaster. For a man of such short stature, he cast a giant and remarkable shadow over baseball.

"People born in the 1860s, like Connie Mack was, they saw Phil Rizzuto play baseball," said Marty Appel, who knew Phil Rizzuto for more than 38 years on MLB radio. "And people who will still be living in the 2060s will still have remembered him as a broadcaster."

Other people will remember him for his platinum-record performance with the singing sensation Meat Loaf, while others will remember him as the older bespectacled man shouting on and on about second mortgages and low, low interest rates.

Phil Rizzuto had one of the most remarkable lives anyone could ask for. But it wasn't handed to him. He earned it the hard way.

I

LEARNING
THE
INFIELD

1

Bridge of the Future and the Trolley Dodgers

The Conductor's Son

Construction of the Brooklyn Bridge began on January 3, 1870. It was completed thirteen years later and was opened for use on May 24, 1883. The future of the bridge's viability was put in doubt when, on May 30, a rumor that the bridge was unsafe and in danger of collapsing caused a panic, resulting in a stampede that crushed and killed twelve people. One year later, on May 17, 1884, the brilliant P.T. Barnum helped to squelch any lingering concerns about the bridge's stability—while publicizing his famous circus—when one of his most famous attractions, Jumbo the Elephant, led a parade of 21 elephants over the Brooklyn Bridge.

The bridge was designed by German-born John Augustus Roebling, whose iron works were in Trenton, New Jersey. Roebling had earlier designed and constructed other smaller suspension bridges across the country. During the surveying for the East River Bridge project, Roebling's foot was badly injured by a ferry that pinned it against a pylon; within a few weeks, he died of a series of worsening infections. His son, Washington, succeeded him, but in 1872 he was stricken with caisson disease (decompression sickness, commonly known as "the bends") due to working in compressed air in caissons. Washington's wife, Emily Warren Roebling, became his aide, learning engineering and communicating his wishes to the on-site assistants. When the bridge opened, she was the first person to cross it. Washington Roebling rarely visited the site again.

Despite these tragedies, the bridge became a beacon of technology and wonder for the rest of the world, as the bridge's towers remained the tallest constructed objects in the Western hemisphere for many years to come, and the bridge proved stalwart beyond its needs. The neighborhood around its Brooklyn approach was bustling with immigrants.

"It was an area already peopled with a good number of immigrants from Italy," wrote sports announcer and biographer Gene Schoor. "New York was, and still is to a great extent, an amalgamation of ethnic enclaves, each enclave a Little Poland, a Little Hungary, a Little Italy. Coming to a new land, the immigrants felt more secure with others who had come from the same country in Europe, spoke the same language, observed the same customs."

"While a section of lower Manhattan has boasted of its Little Italy, we had ours here in Brooklyn along the waterfront where many God fearing Italians lived at peace among their neighbors, Irish, Scotch, German, and Jewish," wrote James A Mannix in a Letter to the Editor of the *Brooklyn Eagle*, c. 1940.

"Only recently, I noticed laborers covering Trolley car rails with asphalt and this brought back memories," Mannix continued. "How many people recall the days when so many men of Italian origin laid trolley rails along many streets when they worked for the old B.R.T.? Came noon time and they would knock off on a very hot day and after seating themselves on the sidewalk under an awning, they would undo their packages of lunch and wash their lunches down with a bottle of beer, milk, or coffee."

• • •

Philip Rizzuto Sr. and Rose Angotti were both born in 1892 into the Italian ethnic neighborhood that found itself under the shadow of the Brooklyn Bridge. The Brooklyn Bridge and the newly dedicated Statue of Liberty were modern marvels of turn-of-the-century America. They were two symbols of the power of the ideals of the United States. One of those ideals was that America was the great melting pot and that advancement was attainable to all who came together here. Phil Rizzuto Sr. believed in that dream. Philip was one of seven children. He had two brothers and four sisters.

In earlier biographies and even in many newspapers at the time of his death, the Scooter's parents were identified at immigrants. And in several stories, "Papa" Rizzuto was saddled with a heavy Mediterranean accent. Early Rizzuto biographies and newspaper stories attribute the same speech patterns, pointing to this version of Rizzuto's parentage. But nothing could have been further from the truth. While his language or inflection might have been influenced by the neighborhood he grew up in, "Papa," and "Mama" for that matter, both attended New York public schools. Philip Rizzuto was a lifelong fan of the Brooklyn Dodgers. He was devout in his following of the team and all its trappings and well versed in its history.

Philip and Rose married in 1913 and continued to live in this same neighborhood. According to the National Bureau of Economic Research, Inc., there was a recession that extended from January 1913 to December 1914. In this difficult climate, Rizzuto Sr. took on any number of jobs, including working as a day laborer, a ditch digger, and a road worker. They always had a roof over their heads and food on the table, even as their family grew. In 1914, they welcomed their first child, a daughter they named Mary. A few years later, Rose gave birth to a second daughter, who was also named Rose.

In the early months of 1917, Rizzuto Sr. took a job as a trolley car conductor for the Brooklyn Rapid Transit Company (BRT). The BRT was incorporated January 18, 1896. By 1900, it was a highly regarded rapid transit system, having acquired many local systems throughout Brooklyn and virtually all of the rapid transit and streetcar operations in its target area. In 1913, it acquired one of the last remaining independent systems, the Coney Island and Brooklyn Railroad. BRT existed as a holding company, leaving the acquired or newly formed companies to carry out the actual operation of the system, provide power and services for the system, and even design and acquire rolling stock. In 1913 the BRT also signed the Dual Contracts with the City of New York to construct and operate new subways and other rapid transit lines to be built or improved under these contracts. This was a large and well-established company, and the pay and working conditions of a trolley conductor were considerably better than that of a day laborer.

Still, Rizzuto Sr. worked anywhere from 10- to 14-hour days in a time when there was no workers union. Paychecks were regular and reliable, provided the employee showed up for work.

Long before buses became a large part of the city's public transportation system, Brooklyn's trolleys were so prevalent that eventually they influenced the name of the borough's most famous sports team, then the Superbas, which was later changed to the Brooklyn Trolley Dodgers and eventually shortened to the Dodgers.

Rizzuto Sr.'s trolley route took him from Richmond Hill, Brooklyn, to Ridgewood, Queens. While Brooklyn of the era was one of the largest and most bustling cities in America, Queens was an area in transition. Ridgewood is a neighborhood in the borough of Queens that borders the neighborhoods of Maspeth, Middle Village, and Glendale, as well as the Brooklyn neighborhood of Bushwick. Historically, the neighborhood straddled the Queens-Brooklyn boundary.

The majority of the neighborhood covers a large hill, more than likely part of the glacial moraine that created Long Island. Major streets in Ridgewood include Forest Avenue, Fresh Pond Road, Myrtle Avenue, and Metropolitan "Metro" Avenue. All of these streets are narrow two-lane roads (with parking lanes), and the high volume on these streets can cause traffic tie-ups during rush hour. The intersection of Fresh Pond and Metropolitan is especially notorious for being a bottleneck. The main shopping areas are on Myrtle Avenue and Fresh Pond Road. Other smaller shopping strips are located on Metropolitan Avenue, Forest Avenue, and Seneca Avenue.

Ridgewood is a densely settled neighborhood, with housing stock ranging from six-family buildings near the Brooklyn border to two-family and single-family row houses deeper into Queens. Most of Ridgewood was developed block-by-block around the turn of the 20th century.

Today, Ridgewood's land area lies within Queens County. However, its political boundary with Brooklyn causes confusion and debate about where the western boundary of Ridgewood truly lies and whether part of Ridgewood is considered to be actually part of Brooklyn. It is interesting to note that until the late 1970s, Ridgewood and neighboring Glendale (Queens) were entirely served by the Brooklyn post office in Bushwick.

In 1917, the same year he had taken a job with the BRT, Rizzuto Sr. purchased a home in Ridgewood. "They settled in a frame house on a little street named Dill Place. It wasn't much of a house—one of six others which were so constructed that the front entrance was on an alley," wrote veteran *New York Daily News* sports scribe Joe Trimble in his biography of Rizzuto in 1951.

There, Philip Francis Rizzuto Jr. was born on September 25, 1917, though for most of his public life he was listed as being born on that same date in 1918 due to common concerns of the baseball profession when players were concerned with being aged out or retired due to their advanced years—professional sports were a young man's game. His brother, Alfred, was born a few years later in 1920.

Life for the Rizzutos, like many folks of the period, was difficult, but the family did not go without. There was always plenty of food on the table, birthday parties, family celebrations (when Phil and Rose's brothers and sisters would visit from Brooklyn and Queens), and always wine enough for Phil Sr. There were also occasional Saturday morning movies. "The kids didn't feel deprived or underprivileged," Schoor wrote.

The Rizzutos went to school at Public School 68 in Ridgewood. They were a religious family who went to church every Sunday. There was no missing church. The kids had to find inexpensive ways to amuse themselves. The girls skipped rope and played hopscotch. "The boys played ball, nearly all year round, either baseball, softball, stickball, or touch football in the streets. Even in the winter, Phil would go out with another ball-crazy youngster and have a 'catch,'" Trimble wrote. Phil Sr. had given Phil Jr. a bat, ball, and glove by four years of age. He was too little to lift the toy bat.

"They were always thinking of some kind of ball," Rose Rizzuto said. "Phil was always the little fellow in the games, but he also was the fastest runner. I used to look out the window and see them playing 'association' on the street during the football season. That's touch football with four or five on a side. He could run away from the bigger boys every time.

"In the spring and summer it was baseball, baseball all the time. His father was a fan and my brother Dominick, who lived near us, was too. Pop and Dom and the boys talked about the big leaguers—mostly about the Dodgers, of course. We didn't think too much about the Yankees and the Giants in those days. They seemed so far away and the Dodgers were Brooklyn, our team. Every night at supper time the girls and I had to keep quiet while Phil and Al and Pop listened to the scores on the radio."

To Phil and Al, the Yankees were generally not given much thought, since they were in the American League. It may as well have been another country. But the Giants in those days were the enemy, the hated rival. They were across town, and they were in the same league.

Some of the Public Schools had baseball teams that participated in the Public School Athletic League (PSAL). However, PS 68 did not have a team. And so Phil did not participate early on in community-organized sports. Instead, he was baptized, like many boys of his era, in the world of sandlot sports. And like many boys of his time, the sandlots were claimed and cleared by the boys themselves. Dirt, rocks, broken glass. All they needed was enough space.

Without a team to belong to, his mother made him a baseball uniform when he was eight years old. One day, he returned home with the uniform torn. "We couldn't find a place to play, so we cleaned up a lot. Didn't get it very clean, though, and I guess there was lots of rocks and pieces of glass around," Rizzuto told Trimble.

Every once in a while, Phil was entrusted with bringing lunch to his father. This was especially important because on the $40 a week Phil Sr. made, eating lunch out was a rare exception.

"Be careful," Rose would admonish her little son.

"I'll be careful," Phil would wave her off, and race out to the appointed corner. Phil had made a game of waiting for his father. The trolleys made an awful racket, and their approach was easy to hear. Phil would put his foot on the rails, awaiting the vibration that would announce his father's approach. When his father's trolley came to a stop, Phil would jump aboard and ride a few blocks, watching as his father inspected the contents of his meal. Then he would jump off and go home.

However, these games soon came to an end. In 1927, it seemed like all of America was making more and more money, and Phil Sr. wanted to make more money, too. He quit his senior conductor status to take a job as a foreman in home construction. Despite Wall Street's downfall in late 1929, Phil Sr. and Rose had saved up enough money to put a down payment on a house at 78-01 64th Street in Glendale, Queens. It was a two-family stucco dwelling situated on a corner lot. With two teenage daughters (Mary was sixteen and Rose was fourteen) and two growing sons, Rose insisted they needed a bigger house. They rented out the upstairs and refurbished the basement as a bedroom for the boys. They boys were especially thrilled since the room also held a pool table.

According to Trimble, "[The girls] would soon be having boyfriends and it wasn't nice to have suitors calling for the girls at the old clapboard house where they had to walk down an oft-littered community alley to get to the front door."

Life for a short period was very good. However, the failing health of a once-robust economy felled their dreams. In a few years, Phil Sr. was out of a job, and things got tight. Phil went back to the BRT. He had given up his seniority and was only offered part-time work with entry-level salary. Rose took in sewing, and everyone in the house chipped in, including Phil Jr., who donated the money he earned from his paper route. Like many families, the Rizzutos fell victim to the Great Depression. They were forced to accept Home Relief.

According to the Tenement Museum, "A precursor of welfare, Home Relief provided a small amount of funds, as well as goods, to families suffering under Depression-era unemployment. Those on relief received $13 a month for rent. In many cases, though, this proved to be insufficient: the average rent on the Lower East Side in 1930 was $18 a month. Along with rent money, home relief also provided a clothing allowance. In 1935, the allowance was roughly 27 cents a month, which could buy jellyroll skirts and crocodile pants."

"Roughly 210,000 New York City families were dependent upon the program in late 1934. By 1939, little had changed: studies of Jews living on the Lower East Side at that time found two-thirds of them on some form of public relief and one-third on Home Relief. This large-scale reliance on government aid wrankled some Americans. Critics of the program wanted to see people work rather than live off hand-outs. In turn, critics faulted the government's inability to find satisfactory work for employable relief recipients. Some also criticized recipients, deriding them as 'spoiled' louts who abused the system," the Museum continued.

Regardless, the Depression endured. Many recipients were simply unable to live without this support. As Special Investigator Wayne W. Parrish wrote in a 1934 Home Relief report, "The temper of the client in New York is such that it would take machine guns to cut off relief." Rizzuto told Trimble years later that his mother always had a look of relief and gratitude when the checks arrived.

Still, sports, and especially baseball, continued to occupy young Phil Jr. He continued to hone his athletic skills, making the most of his speed. Once place where he honed those skills was Smokey Oval Park near Richmond Hill.

From the time this park opened in 1938, it has been known locally as Smokey Oval Park. In 1987, Parks officially named it Smokey Oval. The name refers to the park's location, across from a Long Island Railroad (LIRR) terminus, which once made it a landing area of soot and ash from the railway. It is also inspired by the oval-shaped mound at the front of the park. Back when Phil Rizzuto played here, it was just an unused lot owned by the LIRR.

"When he was at Richmond Hill, what was now Smokey Oval Park was not a park. It was a sandlot.… And that was where my father used to play all the time. I have pictures of him from the age of four, with a bat in his hand," Patricia Rizzuto said.

"Richmond Hill was a very important place to him, because he played both baseball and football. How he played football I don't know," Patricia Rizzuto told Assemblyman Rory I. Lancman (D-Queens). "He was at Richmond Hill because of the coach he was working with. He actually had college scholarships offered to him…He decided not to go that way."

"This is a real matriarchal family. His mother pushed him and pushed him. And he was out there every day, in the sandlot, playing ball," Patricia Rizzuto continued. "We had a house in Brooklyn. Two…four…six…eight… all the relatives. Uncles, aunts. They'd come out with the mandolins and ohhhhh.…This is where he grew up. This was his neighborhood. This is where he got his start. This is where the family owned the house until 2002.

He never forgot about this place. We used to come here for the holidays. And grandmom and grandpop would make a big pot of gravy…my grandfather also had a hand-wrung sausage machine and that would go into the gravy… there were a lot of kids on his side of the family and it was great…. He never forgot this neighborhood."

• • •

Along with the other boys of the area, Phil often played baseball or stickball in the street. Pearl Meyer Suss, who lived on the same block as the Rizzuto family, became closely acquainted with the ball games the boys were playing because the balls kept smashing through her front windows. This infuriated her mother. "In those days the neighborhood was largely German, and a row of women appeared in front of their houses every Friday to scrub their front stoops by hand," wrote Ellen Barry in the *New York Times*. Suss admitted years later that Phil did not particularly stand out to her at the time. There were so many boys playing ball all the time. However, a few years later the broken windows were something the Meyers could brag about.

"We felt, 'Oh, boy, we really knew him,'" Mrs. Suss said when she was 83. "We were high class."

"One of the best things we had," Phil recalled, "My mother, she got a baseball, took it apart, stuffed it with stuff from pillows and—me!—you could really throw it, and curves, and hit it, and it didn't go hard enough to break the pane of glass. That was a great idea. On the corner is where we lived: four corners and four poles. We played everything; racquetball, football. All day long, I'd be outside."

"He was very small even when he was in Richmond Hill, but he was very fast. And he wasn't as powerful a hitter as some of the other guys on the team. So that's when he started this bunting thing. It goes all the way back to Richmond Hill High School…. It was the perfect play for him because he could lay down the bunt and he could just take off. And he was really fast."

Phil looked everywhere he could to find a game to play in. He would even play against boys much older than him. Phil would play baseball anywhere, "in the streets, then in whatever leagues I could get into," he said. "They had the Standard Union League, the Brooklyn Eagle League—I got more experience playing on those bad fields with rocks all over the infield."

Rizzuto's first sandlot team was called the Ridgewood Robins. The Robins, at one point, was one of the many early references to the Brooklyn Dodgers. The little league team earned that moniker because of its manager during the period between 1914 and 1931 whose name was Wilbert "Uncle Robbie" Robinson, a legendary Hall of Famer.

Robinson was born in Massachusetts and played in the major leagues from 1886 to 1902, catching 1,316 games. He was one of the anchors of a Baltimore Orioles dynasty that won three straight titles from 1894–96. His friend and former teammate, John McGraw, enticed Robinson to be his pitching coach with the New York Giants from 1903 to 1913, during which the Giants won five National League pennants. Robinson donned his manager's cap for the first time in 1914, when he took over the Brooklyn franchise in the National League. The team was known by various nicknames including Bridegrooms, Superbas, and Dodgers, but during Robinson's managerial tenure, which lasted until 1931, the club was as often referred to as the Robins.

In a promotional stunt on March 13, 1915, at spring training in Daytona Beach, Florida, Robinson attempted to set a new record of sorts by trying to catch a baseball dropped from a passing areoplane. The record attempt was 526 feet. However, outfielder Casey Stengel allegedly convinced the pilot to drop a grapefruit instead of a baseball, and when the fruit splattered, Robinson was sure he was covered in blood until he heard the screams of laughter from players and fans alike.

These were the kinds of stories that Phil and other young fans of the Dodgers grew up with. These were the heroes of his father's childhood. For the young Rizzuto, there must have been no greater honor for a boy his age in that neighborhood than to play on a team named for the legendary manager.

The manager of the Robins was Mr. Willenbucher. Willenbucher had sold the Rizzutos their house in Glendale. The Willenbuchers were a pair of brothers, George of Brooklyn and Peter of Queens. Peter Willenbucher's sons, Peter G. Willenbucher Jr. and Frederick W. Willenbucher, were on the team.

"What do you play?" Willenbucher was supposed to have asked the little Rizzuto boy.

"I'm an outfielder," Rizzuto said confidently.

"I can see you can cover the outfield. You're like a cricket," said the older man. However, his teammates, as children are wont to do, were less kind, riding the diminutive Phil. They chided him out loud in front of the coach. Words like "midget" and "runt" were the baseline of the insults. The older man wavered, and then relented. "Okay, let's see what you've got."

In his first time in the batter's box during the first practice, little Rizzuto hit one ball after another, lining shots through the infield for sure base hits. And when they placed him in the field, he ran down everything. He was fast!

"You're all right," Mr. Willenbucher relented. However accepting of their new teammate the players were, it did not stop them from riding their newest and smallest player. In a little while, their jibes turned into terms of endearment, as the little kid proved himself again and again.

That year the *Standard Union*, a Brooklyn newspaper, sponsored a sandlot tournament, whose championship game would take place at a major league park—Ebbets Field. It was every Brooklyn little leaguer's dream. The Robins swept through the tournament and landed in the championship game. The Rizzuto household could not have been more excited. Given his father's and uncle's passion for the Brooklyn franchise, playing at Ebbets Field was a dream come true!

"I was about 4' high then and playing left field," Rizzuto later told Arthur E. Patterson of the *New York Herald Tribune*.

In the championship game, the Robins faced the Coney Island Athletics.

It was at Ebbets Field that Mr. Willenbucher pulled Rizzuto off to the side. "Look here, Phil. You want the team to win, don't you?" Willenbucher asked the excited child. Rizzuto nodded in the affirmative readily. "You do what I tell you then?" Again, the child assented eagerly. Then Willenbucher lowered the bomb. "Okay, every time you get up, you just stand there."

"Just stand there?" asked the confused boy.

"Yeah. Just stand there. Don't swing your bat. Whatever they pitch you, just take it." The young boy was only more confused. "See, you're only 4' tall. They can't possibly pitch you. Every time you get up, they'll walk you. We need men on base to win the game, kid. Don't you see?" The crestfallen child nodded his head. He couldn't talk. He was devastated. Finally, he was here at Ebbets Field, in a championship game, and the coach didn't want him to swing.

The first time he got into the batter's box, he stood there, and sure enough, he took his base on balls. In the field, as big an infield he had ever seen in his life, he felt really small for the first time. But Phil rose to the occasion and made his plays routinely, covering ground well and making no errors.

"Mr. Willenbucher wouldn't let me swing at all. First I'd bat left-handed and then I'd bat right-handed, but I wasn't allowed to swing. I walked the first four times up," Rizzuto remembered years later. "On the fifth time the pitcher got two strikes on me so I had to swing. I fouled the ball and I was so low down that it rose up and hit the umpire right in the Adam's apple. Boy, was he sore."

The umpire called Phil every name in the book as he struggled with his pain. After the umpire restarted the game, Phil didn't move in the batter's box. He was frozen and luckily the pitcher threw wide, so Rizzuto walked for the fifth and final time.

Ridgewood won the game, and the Robins were the champions of Brooklyn.

2

AL KUNITZ

In 1931, Phil Rizzuto Jr. enrolled at Richmond Hill High School, which was a bit further away than he was used to going, but it was the closest high school in the area. It was the high school children from his neighborhood attended.

"If the city politicians were lax in providing playgrounds, they were grossly negligent in building and staffing sufficient schools. All the high schools were overcrowded, and there was no money to build new ones," wrote *Daily News* sportswriter Joe Trimble.

The good news for young Phil was that the trolley route to and from school was his father's route. If he were lucky and caught it just right, he could catch his father's train and save the nickel fare, riding the train for free and then put the coin to use later.

"Every nickel counted back there in 1932, because those were the pre-New Deal times when nearly every corner had a man standing on it—selling apples," Trimble remembered.

Rizzuto was out of his element now. Some of the boys he had played with were at other schools and, like many children, he was intimidated by the older and bigger boys of his high school. Phil was used to being teased about his smallish 4'11" stature. But that was on a sandlot, where he knew the boys and where he could answer with his bat or his glove. Here, in high school now, he became painfully aware of his lack of height. Usually confident and self-assured, Phil shrank from attention and was quiet if not withdrawn.

In the spring of 1932, he reported for the first baseball tryout with his childhood friend Johnny Zimmerlich. But Zimmerlich's grades were poor, and thus he was declared academically ineligible. When Zimmerlich got cut, Rizzuto, still shy and self-conscious, quit the team. It was not a sign of protest against the school. It was the opposite. Rizzuto's lack of confidence kept him from participating. At that point, he preferred the camaraderie of the sandlot boys he knew to the possible exposure to ridicule by older and bigger boys he did not know.

Phil struggled in school. He was smart enough, but he was easily bored in classes. While he loved organized athletics, he did not think much of classroom learning and was easily distracted. As a result his grades suffered, and his academic standing was a constant concern for his mother and father, who were convinced at the time that Phil would have a hard time in the world. This withdrawal only made him feel more out-of-sorts.

"He never thought about anything but baseball when he was in high school," his mother said. "He studied just about enough to pass and no more. His father and I were convinced that he wasn't going to become a well-educated man. Like most parents, we hoped he might go on and get the college education we had been unable to get. But he just wasn't one for the books." In his subsequent years in high school, it became apparent that the only reason he worried at all about his academic standing was so that he would stay eligible for athletics.

Nevertheless, the spring and summer of 1932 saw Rizzuto plying his trade on the Smokey Oval, as it was known then, and other sandlots around the area.

In the spring of 1933, Phil was a little more assured of himself. That, and Johnny Zimmerlich had also upped his grades, and the two answered the call for baseball tryouts.

The coach of Richmond Hill High School was Al Kunitz, who was an experienced baseball man.

"Al Kunitz served as a Yankees batboy…and Kunitz enjoyed a close relationship with Lou Gehrig," according to George Godwin, a Gehrig aficionado and ALS authority. Kunitz later went to Columbia University with Gehrig's help and played catcher for the varsity team. His weight during those playing days was 135 pounds, so that might have created some affinity for the young Rizzuto. Despite his size, Kunitz was regarded as one of the best catchers in the college game during that era. He played some minor league ball, and later became a teacher.

Kunitz was well-respected by all his students. Approximately 10 years after Phil Rizzuto left Richmond Hill, a young Walter S. Gray enrolled at High School of Music and Art. By then, Al Kunitz was chairman of the physical education department there.

"Kunitz was a precise and demanding teacher, tolerant of our too-often less-than-enthusiastic approach to physical education but unremitting in his efforts to assure that we escaped terminal nerdhood," Gray wrote.

"Mr. Kunitz," a budding violinist would ask, "do I have to climb the ropes today? The concert's tomorrow, and I don't want to get rope burns on my hands."

"That's all right, sonny. Climb the ropes."

Around the time Rizzuto was a freshman, there was a gifted young pitcher Kunitz had coached and promoted heavily named Marius Russo.

Russo, who would later become known as "The Kid from LI," was born in Kings Park, New York. He played baseball for Richmond Hill High School. He later attended Brooklyn College and Long Island University in Brooklyn. Eventually he would go on to play for the Newark Bears and the New York Yankees.

Kunitz taught the young pitcher control, and he was rewarded for his efforts. Kunitz's relations with the Yankees were well known, and he had been known to get a tryout or two for young, remarkable players.

On his first day, Kunitz winced when he saw the young, slight, and small figure of Rizzuto.

"What position do you play?" Kunitz asked.

Rizzuto sheepishly replied he played outfielder. He let Rizzuto take a practice in the large outfield and shook his head.

"Fortunately, the coach at Richmond Hill…had a little more foresight about Rizzuto's size and ability," veteran sportswriter Bill Madden once wrote.

"You'll never be an outfielder, kid," Kunitz said. "You're too small. But with a pair of hands and an arm like you've got, what a shortstop you'll be! Rabbit Maranville was a midget, but he got by for 20 years in the big leagues."

"I don't know. I never played the infield," said the reluctant young sophomore.

"I'll teach you. You want to learn?"

"You saying I can't make this team as an outfielder?" asked the boy.

"Nope," answered Kunitz.

"Okay. I'll play infield."

"That said, Kunitz switched Rizzuto to shortstop and began teaching him the intangibles of the game that would help him more than compensate for his lack of size. Perhaps most importantly, Kunitz taught Rizzuto how to bunt—which became the staple of his 13-year Yankee career," Madden said.

"When I made the team, he took me as a special assignment," Rizzuto later said. "He really worked on my bunting and stealing. I owe it all to Al Kunitz. He made me realize my limitations and my potential."

Ralph Benzenberg, who played shortstop, was the star of that first team Rizzuto played on. Benzenberg was the team captain. The second baseman was Jimmy Castrataro. Benzenberg was good enough to earn himself a minor league contract, but he later settled for a more stable lifestyle rather than sit out life in the bushes. But at the time it was another feather in Kunitz's cap, having shipped off another player to the minors and a contract.

Kunitz tried Rizzuto at third base in the beginning. He already had an experienced and solid double-play combination at short and second, so Rizzuto found himself on the hot corner. Kunitz worked closely and tirelessly with Rizzuto. Rizzuto warmed to the task and proved an eager if not sometimes quick learner. Kunitz showed him how to pivot, how to set up, how to take hot grounders, and how to remember where to throw. He hit him grounders and line drives and pop-ups. Kunitz never showed favoritism. He drove Phil hard. There were no short cuts. Kunitz was trying to mold a real ballplayer. Kunitz had had some success as a baseball coach and was tough and driven to succeed. With time, Rizzuto took on the duties of third base, and the coach's personal attention paid off.

However, that was only half of Rizzuto's initial education. Kunitz was brutally honest with Rizzuto where his batting was concerned as well.

"Let's face it. You're never going to be another Babe Ruth," Kunitz confronted the youngster. "You're not built to be a long-ball hitter. Instead of fighting your size, you've got to learn to take advantage of it. You're a small target. Crowd the plate and develop the patience to wait out the pitchers for walks. They're as good as base hits. Choke up on the bat a little, learn to place the ball. And by all means develop the bunt. Become an expert at it. It can become one of the best weapons for a little guy like you."

"A ballplayer has to hit the ball on the nose three times in a game to get one good base hit, on the average," Kunitz continued. "A well-placed bunt will make up for all of those well-hit balls that land right in the glove of an outfielder."

"He got me to practice the bunt, waiting to the last second and not tipping it off like a lot of kids do today. He also taught me to steal bases, and everything a little guy could do," Phil said. "He was as tall as I was. He taught me the pitfalls of a little man in the big leagues, or in any professional sport."

Kunitz also taught Rizzuto the technique behind the hit-and-run play. This teaching was both valuable in the batter's box and also out on the diamond, as well.

"The man on first will break for second as the pitcher winds up," Kunitz told his young pupil. The second baseman or the shortstop will head for the base to make the put out. Kunitz then pointed out that the situation afforded the batter more space to hit behind the runner between second and first or second and third, depending who went for second. "Got it?" Kunitz asked. Phil nodded. Phil Rizzuto became one of the consummate hit-and-run experts in the majors, and he used his knowledge in the field to try to cut runners down when he saw the tell-tale signs of a hit-and-run being set up against him.

Kunitz also had a profound effect on another facet of young Rizzuto's life. One day during a game, Rizzuto caught a bad call and lost his cool. It almost cost the team the game.

"Kunitz asked me, 'What expression do you use when you get excited?' Ever since I was a kid, I would say, 'Holy Cow!' or 'you huckleberry!' So that's what I'd say, and it was great advice. I never got thrown out."

But where in the world did Scooter ever find the word huckleberry and how did he come to use it? And what is a huckleberry? No biography or article or interview of Rizzuto gave the history of his deciding on the word huckleberry or from whence it came. It is one of those locks biographers fret over for decades.

A huckleberry is a small, dark berry, in the same family as a blueberry. The huckleberry is the state fruit of Idaho.

"[I]n the early part of the 19th century the word became a synonym for something humble or minor, or a tiny amount," wrote Michael Quinion, a British etymologist. "Later on it came to mean somebody inconsequential. Mark Twain borrowed some aspects of these ideas to name his famous character, Huckleberry Finn. His idea, as he told an interviewer in 1895, was to establish that he was a boy 'of lower extraction or degree' than Tom Sawyer."

Huckleberry was also used in several 19th century phrases. "I'm your huckleberry," was meant to mean that one was the right person for the job. The phrase "a huckleberry over my persimmon" was used to mean "a bit beyond my abilities." One of the meanings for the word given in *The Random House Historical Dictionary of American Slang* is "a foolish, inept, or inconsequential fellow."

It is possible a teacher taught, without intention, the word to Rizzuto, since he insisted even into his last years that he started using it in high school. Maybe he overheard it? On the radio? In conversation?

There is no doubt huckleberry was his derisive chortle, whether said kindly or not. When a player made a gaffe, he would shout it. When an announcing partner would make a mistake or expose one of his idiosyncrasies, he would call them a huckleberry. It was an interchangeable word applied to each situation in Phil's own way. But the origin, if there ever was one, is lost to time.

When the 1934 campaign concluded, closing out Phil Rizzuto's second season on the baseball team, he emerged as its new star. In his second year, he led the team in hitting with a .354 average and was elected team captain. He also received an All-Scholastic rating. *The Long Island Press*, printed in Queens, named Rizzuto the city's best high school third baseman.

Still, Rizzuto held no notions of becoming a big league player. It was Kunitz who saw the boy's love of the game and prodded him.

"Kunitz kept asking scouts to watch me, but I had no professional notions," Rizzuto said. "He gave me the idea I could become a professional ball player, and that gave me quite a kick."

"Sure, you are small. But you will fill out. You are fast, a great fielder, you have an acute baseball sense," Kunitz told the young infielder. Rizzuto shook his head and laughed at his coach's encouragements. Eventually, Phil heard what Kunitz was saying and started listening to his advice. Phil needed more experience, more seasoning. He needed to mature. Kunitz told him to get as much playing time as possible to continue to hone his skills. On the weekends in the summer of his first two years of high school, Phil played in the Queens Alliance League for the Glendale Browns. And in 1934 he played out on Long Island, in Nassau County, for a semi-pro team in Floral Park.

"That was the first team [that] paid me any money, but not very much of it," Rizzuto remembered years later. "We charged admission but there were expenses and we had to pay guarantees to the teams we met. We didn't get a salary but it was arranged that we'd split up the profits at the end of the season. We did and I got $120 for playing in 80 games."

Since Phil was both underage and technically still an amateur, he adopted an alias, which was Reilly. Newspaper box scores of the day still carry that surname playing shortstop in those years.

The next spring, Phil had another great season for Richmond Hill High School in 1935. He was again picked by the *Press* as an All-Scholastic.

Meanwhile Kunitz, who knew quite a few people, had convinced a scout from the St. Louis Cardinals to come take a look at the young sensation. The Hilltoppers were playing John Adams (another Queens high school). The game was played at Dexter Park, home of the well-loved semi-pro Bushwicks.

"In those days, many a Dodger fan was saying that the Bushwicks could beat the Brooks and there was good chance they were right," *Daily News* sports scribe Joe Trimble wrote.

Phil shone brightly that day. He had three hits and turned in an acrobatic play—he made a diving stop and threw out the base runner while sitting up from the grab. Phil knew he had played well and was convinced the Cardinals scout would ask him to meet other Cardinals brass, the most important one being the famed Branch Rickey.

"I played a whale of a game in the field. That was June 1935. I weighed 135 pounds," Rizzuto remembered.

"You had a pretty good day, but to tell you the truth, kid, you're not built to be a ball player. You're too small."

The disappointed teenager was devastated.

"Don't worry, Phil," Kunitz tried to comfort the boy. "There'll be others." Kunitz's words would prove to be prophetic.

The scout from the Boston Red Sox that came to watch the young, diminutive Rizzuto was named Egan. He came to Phil's PSAL games as well as his Floral Park games. Eventually Egan approached Rizzuto and offered him a $250 signing bonus. That was a lot of money at the height of the Depression, especially to a boy whose family had experienced the worst of the economic hard times.

Still, Rizzuto was a minor and needed to talk over the idea with his parents. He shook hands with the scout and went home to discuss the matter. His parents were as enthusiastic as he was and encouraged him to take the money. The young Rizzuto hardly slept a wink that night, sure he was on his way to baseball glory with the Boston club.

The next morning, Phil waited for Egan at the appointed place and time. He waited for two hours before finally giving up and going home. "I never heard of Egan again," Phil said. "At the time I was sore, and I told myself that he probably forgot all about me and went to a bar. But I guess he just decided I wasn't good enough to waste that kind of dough on."

Of course, Kunitz had been pressing the Yankees, as well. Rizzuto claimed in an early biography that the first Yankees scout to come and take a look at him was George Mack. However, Mack was a well-known New York Giants baseball scout who, by all accounts, was working for them around this time (approximately mid to late 1930s). Regardless of whom the actual scout was, Kunitz was encouraged. And his efforts ultimately led to some inspections by Paul Krichell, who was the head of the scouting department for the Yankees. Nothing came of these early visits, and Phil did not learn about them until some time later in his career.

Never discouraged, Kunitz thought another way into the majors was by playing college baseball. This was a fertile ground for finding talent in those days, with famous players like Lou Gehrig of Columbia and Frankie Frisch of the Fordham Flash, to name a few. This was a stretch by Kunitz, who was keen to get his man into the majors. But asking Rizzuto to qualify and then attend college was a tall order. Phil was bright, quick, street smart, but he was no student—especially not of Columbia or Fordham caliber.

In 1935, Richmond Hill had a game scheduled at Baker Field to play the freshmen of Columbia University. It was a cold, windy day, and the game was a high scoring affair. Rizzuto's teammate Benzenberg was the star that day.

George Vecsey, who was then the editor of the *Long Island Press* and who later went on to work for the Associated Press, covered the game. Vecsey's two sons, George and Peter, both went on to become sports columnists. Vecsey went over to Ralph Furey to chat, thinking that Benzenberg looked like a candidate for Columbia.

"I'll take the little runt at third base," Furey shot back. "He's got the makings of a good player. He can hit, he's fast, and he's got what it takes to make a fine shortstop." Furey did pursue Rizzuto and considered offering him a scholarship, but Rizzuto's grades were not up to snuff.

Rizzuto also made a tryout for Fordham University. Kunitz arranged a workout up at the Rose Hill Campus for the famed baseball coach and university athletic director Jack Coffey. Born in 1887 in New York City, Coffey was an infielder for the Boston Doves in 1909 and did not play again until he was picked up by the Detroit Tigers in 1918 before being sold to the Boston Red Sox for the remainder of the season. He was the only man in baseball who had been a teammate of both Ty Cobb and Babe Ruth in the same season. He went on to coach Fordham baseball from 1922–55, and the current campus baseball stadium bears his name.

"Fordham had a great team then," Phil said later. "Babe Young, who later played with the Giants, was on first base, and Tony DePhillips, who was signed by the Yanks, was the catcher. I worked out at short and took batting practice, and when it was over, Coffey offered me a scholarship. He insisted I would have to come out for football, too."

Coffey figured Rizzuto's speed would be a tremendous asset in the Ram football backfield. In those days, Fordham was a powerhouse of college football, coached by the famed Jim Crowley. Coffey thought that Rizzuto would make for a good scat back, someone who could easily elude or run away from much bigger but slower men.

"Somebody must be nuts," Rizzuto said then. "I can't play football. I'll get killed with all those big guys in there."

His grades and his lack of interest in both studying and in college football all conspired against the young Rizzuto. He was despondent. It was clear he was not going to college. Not without a scholarship, and certainly not without the grades. The young Phil entertained the notion of quitting baseball altogether.

By 1936, Rizzuto began to fall behind his classmates academically. He had played hookey once too often, and he could not make up the lost ground. By the spring of 1936, Rizzuto, much to the disappointment of his parents, quit high school. To him, being in school was a waste of time. He was not interested in applying himself. Rizzuto was depressed and without prospects.

Despite the defection of his star player, Kunitz and Rizzuto never lost touch, and Kunitz would not give up on the diminutive athlete. A bond had formed between the two tough, resilient men. In the meantime, Rizzuto found work at S. Gumpert & Co., manufacturers of food stuffs for hotels. He had gotten the job by his reputation playing baseball. The company had a team in the Brooklyn Industrial League, which played games around twilight at Prospect Park Parade Grounds in Brooklyn. The team needed a shortstop, and Rizzuto needed employment. At this job, Rizzuto learned how to make large batches of pudding. Assisting another man, they would lift heavy drums of syrup and 100-pound sacks of sugar into large mixing bowls to make butterscotch pudding. Rizzuto, though small, was strong for his size, and the work helped him build valuable muscle strength.

Despite his lack of success in impressing major league scouts, Rizzuto still held firm in his belief he was major league material. Kunitz had not lost faith in Rizzuto, either.

"I had a good summer. I hit against Satchel Paige and other good pitchers," Rizzuto said later. Kunitz was finally successful in the summer of 1936 in getting Phil a tryout with his beloved Brooklyn Dodgers.

This was the thrill of a lifetime for the young Rizzuto, the avid Dodgers fan. His uncle took him to the tryout. They went in "Uncle Mike's car—one of those old cars, with the balloon tires." As he approached Ebbets Field, the excitement got to him. But his euphoria soon dissipated when he got down to the field. There were hundreds of potential Dodgers on the field. It was a mass tryout.

As Phil told it many times, when he approached, Casey Stengel, then the Dodgers' manager, uttered the famous line, "Go and get your shoeshine box," as he dismissed Rizzuto before the tryout even began.

"He took one look at me, and I will never forget this—I would never let him forget this, either—he said, 'Listen, kid, you better go and get yourself a shoeshine box. That is the only way you'll make a living,'" said Rizzuto in an interview in 2000 for the Hall of Fame. "I was crushed."

Rizzuto loved telling the story before he started playing for Stengel. During his days playing under Stengel, however, Rizzuto sometimes denied the story. He tried pawning off the story on others. "The story is that Casey chased me out of the park. It is not true. Casey never saw me," Rizzuto said. Whenever he recounted it while playing for Stengel, Stengel thought Rizzuto was showing him up, and it further infused the bad blood between the two with more poison. But after his days of serving under Stengel were over, he resumed telling the story. It was a wound—no matter the honors and accolades—that would never heal for Rizzuto. "That stayed with me, made me work harder," he said.

Dodger coaches Otto Miller and Zack Taylor supervised the event. There were anywhere from 150 to 300 young men between the ages of 16 and 18 at any one of the numerous events.

"It wasn't much of a tryout. They'd line up about 100 of us on the left field foul line and run us to the right field wall. The slowest guys were dropped out. I got there in time, but nobody gave me a second look," Rizzuto said. "Yes, I was the smallest man there, too. Everyone wonders about my size. I've had a great deal of trouble convincing people I am a ballplayer—even some managers."

Dan Hirshberg, another Rizzuto biographer, pointed out that Rizzuto had contradicted his own interview, saying, "The first 50 to finish [the race across the field] were told to stay, [and] the rest were invited to go home. A simple system, it struck me. I was one of the early finishers, so I stayed."

Rizzuto was eventually invited to try his luck in the batter's box.

"A big right-handed kid was pitching. I had been a good hitter in high school at Richmond Hill and even managed to get my base hits in semi-pro competition on Long Island," Rizzuto said later. "I felt nervous, but I felt sure I would at least hit the ball. But I never did get much of a chance to. The first pitch hit me squarely in the middle of the back and knocked me down. It hurt like the devil, and the wind was knocked out of me. I probably should have gotten out of the batter's box and rested until the pain left. But I didn't want them to think I was afraid. So I stepped right in again. Then I could hardly swing and, after missing a couple of pitches, heard Miller say, 'Okay, sonny. That's all. I don't think you'll do, little fellow. Good thing you didn't get hurt by that big guy.'"

"One of the Brooklyn coaches told me I was too small. He told me to try something else and forget baseball," Rizzuto said in another interview years later.

Dominick Angotti, Phil's uncle from his mother's side, tried to console Rizzuto as tears welled up in the young man's eyes.

"Don't feel too bad about it. It wasn't much of a tryout and you really didn't fail," the thoughtful uncle said. "No wonder the Dodgers are in seventh place—they don't even know how to hold a tryout!"

New York Daily News sportswriter Joe Trimble told a great story connected to this incident. Once, during a television interview with Brooklyn outfielder Gene Hermanski during the 1949 World Series, Rizzuto was asked to recount the troubles he had breaking into the major leagues. He recounted the Dodgers tryout in short. Then Hermanski goaded him, saying on air, "Tell them who was managing he Dodgers when they tossed you out because you were too small."

Rizzuto admitted it was Stengel, and the crowd roared. Casey, never to be outdone, approached Rizzuto at his locker the next morning, waddling up he said, "You think you're big enough for the big leagues now?"

The story persisted. Even the next year, *Time* magazine ran this line after Rizzuto had walked home with American League MVP honors for the 1950 season: "Fifteen years ago Casey Stengel, then manager of the Brooklyn Dodgers, took a quick look at a skinny little kid who claimed to be a shortstop. Casey gave the youngster a blunt piece of advice: 'Go peddle your papers, Shorty, you're too small ever to become a major leaguer.'"

Rizzuto himself recounted this story for the Hall of Fame Legend Series in 2000, saying, "I just got out of high school, and Casey Stengel was managing the Dodgers. He took one look at me, and I will never forget this—I would never let him forget this, either—he said, 'Listen, kid, you better go and get yourself a shoeshine box. That is the only way you'll make a living.'"

No one has ever confirmed Rizzuto's version of events. It would become clear later on in life that Stengel was not among Rizzuto's favorite people. While Casey openly favored Yogi Berra in later years, he was ruthless with his other stars, and even Berra was not immune to a tirade here and there. Did Rizzuto change his story to make peace with his manager? Did he change his story from time to time to avoid conflict? Possibly. It was his way. Rizzuto disliked conflict. Avoidance was a coping skill. Certainly during Casey's lifetime, Rizzuto demurred, insisting Casey was not present. But he sometimes backtracked and told the story repeatedly especially after Casey's death.

Only a couple of weeks after his disastrous tryout at Ebbets Field, Phil got an offer from the New York Giants for a tryout at the Polo Grounds. His uncle Dominick drove him up to the large stadium. It was much bigger than Ebbets Field.

"My experience with the Giants was even briefer," Rizzuto joked later in life.

Bill Terry was then the manager of the New York Giants. Bill Terry was one of the greatest players ever to play the game, and he was eventually enshrined into the Baseball Hall of Fame. Terry played for John McGraw from 1923–32. A big gruff first baseman, he had a lifetime .341 batting average. He was a three-time All-Star and a World Series champion. And he had assumed the mantle of manager when McGraw was removed and managed the Giants from 1932–41. When the team won the 1933 World Series, he was a player-manager. Terry was bigger than life, especially to Rizzuto. But Terry was not there. He was elsewhere the day they held this tryout.

One of the coaches running the tryout was Frank "Pancho" Snyder. Snyder was also a big gruff man, "a huge man with the build of a wrestler," Trimble wrote. He had been a catcher in the National League for 16 years and was battle-scarred and tested. "A hard-boiled character," he marched toward the approaching Rizzuto, shooing the boy away.

"A scout for the club asked me to come to the Polo Grounds. Pancho Snyder took one look at me and refused me a uniform and a tryout," Rizzuto remembered later.

"Kid, you are too frail for baseball. Stay and watch the Giants play the Reds, if you like, but we can't use you," Snyder told the small infielder. Rizzuto persisted.

"You're too small, kid. You'll never do."

Rizzuto was devastated and embarrassed.

It was only after all these failures that Paul Krichell rose above the horizon in Rizzuto's vision. Indeed, he had heard about Rizzuto's play and had seen the young man for himself. Krichell was concerned about Phil's size, but his drive, his desire, and his love of the game were branded in the chief scout's mind.

Paul Bernard Krichell had played for the St. Louis Browns as a catcher for two seasons in 1911 and 1912. In Rizzuto's favor was the fact that Krichell was also small in stature yet had played at the major-league level. Krichell was once described as "a smallish, cruller-legged guy." In two seasons, he made only 87 appearances and ground out a paltry .222 batting average. On the other hand, Krichell had a love of the game, and had excelled as a scout. After coaching for the Red Sox in 1919, he followed Boston's head baseball executive Ed Barrow to the New York Yankees in 1920. And his first big signing was none other than Lou Gehrig. In his early career, Krichell discovered all but one of the infielders from the Murderer's Row team of 1927—he had also discovered Tony Lazzeri and Mark Koenig. He would go on to discover Rizzuto, Charlie Keller, Vic Raschi, and Whitey Ford, among many others. Krichell was the chief scout of the New York Yankees for 37 years, his employment ending with his death in 1957. He was the longest tenured employee in the history of the organization at that time. In 1947, he was given an honorary World Series ring. He is generally considered one of the greatest scouts in the history of the game.

Joe Trimble once described Krichell as "the finest judge of baseball talent there is in the world…more than any other man, [he] is responsible for the unceasing flood of talent which has been funneled into Yankee Stadium."

Krichell didn't believe in mass tryouts. He told Trimble, "If you try to look at too many kids, you really don't see any of them. Give a good look to a few at a time, and you are more apt to come up with the good ones. At least, you won't miss a kid because you didn't happen to pick him out from among a hundred others."

In August 1936, Phil received a letter from Krichell inviting him to try out at Yankee Stadium. Phil was excited but wary. If it was another mass tryout, it might not be worth the pain.

"By this time I was fed up with the 'too small, too frail' routine. But I went to the stadium, and there I met Paul Krichell, the first man from a major league club who gave me any encouragement," Rizzuto recalled later.

Phil was delighted when he found out that this was not a mass tryout—only around 25 young men had been invited to Yankee Stadium. It was the largest ballpark of all three city stadiums, and yet this was the smallest gathering of talent he had witnessed. He felt good about this. Rizzuto felt during warm ups that things might go differently this time. And he was right. Like Kunitz, Krichell had warmed to the idea of Rizzuto. And this tryout was like no other. For Rizzuto, it would last an entire week.

"We were divided into two teams. We played a regular game—three innings—every day for five days. The Yankees were home at the time, and we worked out before they came on the field at noon. I played second base the first day and shortstop on the other four," Rizzuto remembered.

Yankees coach Art Fletcher, Joe McCarthy's assistant manager, batted infield practice. Krichell supervised the games.

"It was wonderful. We saw Gehrig and Dickey and the other great Yankees. And Tony Lazzeri actually spoke to me. I guess I'd have gone home happy after it was over just for the fact that I'd been so close to the guys," Rizzuto said.

The group was filled with major league talent. Among the young men were Tommy Holmes and Jim Prendergast, who both eventually played for the Braves.

"It was a good thing I knew how to bunt and steal, although I did hit one in the seats. I hit a home run down the left field line, it hit the foul pole," Rizzuto recalled in 2000.

Krichell approached Fletcher, a man of medium height but well muscled, was also an accomplished baseball man. He had played most of his career at shortstop for the famed John McGraw of the New York Giants, where he played in four World Series. He had managed the Phillies for four years from 1923–26, then came to the Yankees where he coached from 1927–45—meaning he would be a coach on ten pennant-winning teams. Fletcher knew wining baseball, and he knew talent. His opinion was very important in Krichell's eyes.

Asked if he saw anyone he liked, Fletcher responded, "I'll take the little one out there at short. He handles himself like a major leaguer right now."

After the fifth and final workout, Fletcher approached Rizzuto. "How would you like to go away, kid?"

Phil couldn't believe his ears. "Yes!" He raced to the locker room, put on his street clothes and dashed from the House That Ruth Built to the nearest pay phone. He made two calls. He called his mother at home. Then he called Kunitz.

In those days, a sandlot player could not be signed by a major-league club. The offer had to come from a minor league team. Then the major-league club would "buy" the player's contract when they brought him up the majors. But Rizzuto wasn't ready for the majors anyway. Krichell had originally intended to send Rizzuto to the Class D team in Butler, Pennsylvania, which was part of the Pennsylvania State League. But that plan was eventually scrapped, and Rizzuto received an official contract from the Yankees Class D affiliate in Bassett, Virginia. The reason? The Virginia season, due to weather conditions, started a full month earlier, and it was an extra $75—a month's pay according to his new contract.

"I thought it was pretty good money," Rizzuto said. "The kids around home who had jobs were making about $12 a week then."

• • •

Later in life, Rizzuto told *Yankees* magazine a slightly different version of the story. Instead of talks with Fletcher and Krichell, he had a discussion with chief executive Ed Barrow. But it would seem unlikely that Barrow would have bothered himself with such a young, raw recruit who was still a long shot to make the major-league club. This kind of revisionist history was not uncommon amongst players of the era, who were not especially given to fact checking for countless interviews set up by the publicity department during a summer's campaign.

However, Rizzuto would certainly spend more time with Barrow in the future. In later years, Barrow would boast, "Rizzuto cost me fifteen cents, ten for postage, and five for a cup of coffee we gave him the last day he worked out at the stadium."

The final act of this drama was played out at Yankee Stadium. Since Rizzuto was still a minor, one of his parents had to sign the contract for him. Mama Rizzuto signed the document, but not before going to Yankee Stadium herself and asking a few questions.

"I went to New York to see Mr. Krichell. I wanted to know more about it. Phil was only seventeen and had never been away from home. I didn't know anything about baseball or its ways," she said later. "Mr. Krichell assured me that Phil would be all right. He said that he would see to it that he was placed in a good, clean place to live and that he would be safe in Bassett as he would be at home. I signed the contract after he promised me nothing would happen to my boy."

While Mama Rizzuto's concern may have been real, the rest was all an act. Rizzuto had lied to Yankees management about his age. Other players had convinced him to tell them he was younger than he really was.

According to Jack O'Donnell of MajorLeagueBaseball.com, "Rizzuto once told *New York Daily News* baseball columnist Bill Madden that he had lied about his age by a year after some players told him it would add a year to his career."

Murray Chass of the *New York Times* told a similar story about Rizzuto and this common practice amongst major leaguers, which continues to this day. "In the late 1970s, Phil Rizzuto was hit by a ball while coaching at spring training and had to be taken to a doctor. When a nurse asked his age, Rizzuto gave Sept. 25, 1916. On the ride back to the stadium, Rizzuto leaned over to the driver and said, 'Now don't you tell anyone.' Rizzuto's listed birth date was Sept. 25, 1917."

"A couple of the old ballplayers said when they ask you how old you are, make it lower than your regular age," Rizzuto told Chass. "There was something about when you got into your 30s they wanted to get rid of you. Tommy Henrich cheated by four years."

John Fogg of the *Washington Times* wrote, "Many of the prevaricators of that era came clean at the end of their careers," Don Zimmer told Chass. "When we left Brooklyn and went to Los Angeles Pee Wee [Reese] said he was 38 or 39 years old," Zimmer recalled. "Our first year there, 1958, was Pee Wee's last year, and all of a sudden he became 41 or 42 in a hurry because it had to do with his pension. I heard a lot of guys say they were 38 and became 43 overnight after they quit."

Questions of age aside, Phil Rizzuto was going to get his chance at being a big leaguer. But the prejudices against his size would not diminish.

3

TALES FROM THE SOUTH

Phil was excited. At 19 years of age, he was going to a faraway place, and once there, he would play baseball for more money than he had ever made before. His mother was not so sure. She had confidence her young son could get along in the world, but she still clutched her heart with her mother's concern.

"I wasn't sure it was the best thing. He was so small and he didn't look very much like a ballplayer. Even though Mr. Krichell had assured me he would be all right, I was not very happy," Phil's mother said years later. "His Dad and I both felt that the Yankees were too big a team and that he was too little to ever make the major leagues. This going to Bassett, a place we had never heard of, didn't seem like the best thing for him. I wished it had been somewhere closer to home."

Phil got a going-away party. His mother always threw a going-away and a coming-home party whenever one of her children left home for any length of time. "It was always much better when they came back from some place. Then I could enjoy myself," Mrs. Rizzuto said. "But I don't like the 'going-away' parties, because those always meant that I'd be without one of my children for a while."

Before Phil got on the southbound train to Bassett, Virginia, Phil Rizzuto Sr. pinned $20 to Phil's undershirt. He did this in case thieves aboard the train might fleece his young, naive son of everything else. It was a spring day in 1937. His father was not convinced of his son's career goals.

"I'll let you try this. But if you don't make it right away, then you have to go out and find work," the senior Rizzuto told his son.

The train took the younger Rizzuto down to the southern part of Virginia. Bassett, not far from the North Carolina border, was a company town. It was named after John David Bassett and C.C. Bassett, who founded a large furniture manufacturer. John David Bassett was a delegate to the Republican National Convention from Virginia in 1924 and 1928. Bassett Furniture's headquarters have remained in Bassett, Virginia, since the company began in 1902. Its factories and business employed northward of 3,500 people at one point. Bassett was one of eight small communities that made up the Bi-State League.

Rizzuto was a long way from home for the first time in his life. There was no Italian food to be found, and for the first time he encountered foods like grits and other southern culinary delights. He also encountered severe Jim Crow laws, which affected more than 1,000 African American residents of the town. However stark, it should be noted that even into the 1940s in New York City, famous black athletes had to be escorted through the kitchens of the Waldorf Astoria to attend functions there, as the hotel did not allow people of color to enter through the public lobbies. Still, the laws in the south were much more severe. Restrooms, water fountains, even restaurants were all segregated.

"It was a beautiful trip. We went through Washington, D.C., and stopped in Richmond, Virginia. First taste of southern-fried chicken—I'll tell you it was delicious. But they gave me, what's that stuff that looks like oatmeal? Grits. They gave me these grits. I didn't know what to do with them so I put them in my pocket," Rizzuto remembered in 1994.

"There was just a mountain and a drug store and a diner and a little bitty hotel and a movie. That's all they had in the whole town," Phil said in a radio interview years later. One of the things that made an impression on Rizzuto was the loud thunder and bright flashes of lightning in the mountains, which only fed his fear of them. It was rumored that a player in the Piedmont league died that year after being hit by lightning. This was something he would recall the rest of his life.

Phil reported to Ray White, a former Columbia University pitcher. White, a big, imposing right-handed pitcher, was remembered by baseball historians for hitting Lou Gehrig in the head with a ball during a June 29, 1934, exhibition game with the New York Yankees. Each shared a mutual dislike for the other, despite the fact that both were Columbia grads.

"They didn't like each other," said Bud Mehany, a longtime friend of White's. White had been a dominating pitcher in the Ivy Leagues, with long arms and a wicked fastball. But Gehrig, after previously being introduced to the young pitcher, snubbed him on a later occasion.

In the famed exhibition at Norfolk, White wanted to prove to the Yankees' brass that he was major league stuff, but he was tattooed for three runs in the top of the first inning by three Yankees, including Ruth and Gehrig. When Gehrig came up the second time, White threw high, tight, and inside. Gehrig, astonished, failed to move fast enough, the ball hitting him just above the right eye. According to some accounts, Gehrig crumpled like a rag doll. The ball struck him with such force it popped foul into the stands.

"I swear to God, you would have thought he was dead," said Tars shortstop Robert Stevens.

Gehrig recovered by the next game, but White's major-league hopes were dashed. White had gone 17–6 in 1934, with a 2.77 ERA but never made it to the majors. He made no apologies for the pitch and earned the enmity of the Yankees higher-ups.

Ray White was the manager of the Bassett team in 1937, and he would lead the Norfolk Tars to the Piedmont League pennant in 1938. The team was known as the Bassett Furnituremakers and had been founded in 1935. The team excelled for the short period of time they were in existence. The team played six seasons from 1935 to 1940 and won three league championships. In that same period, the team changed its affiliate associations three times (New York Yankees 1936–37; Cincinnati Reds 1939; Brooklyn Dodgers 1940).

"Each town or each city was within a radius of 75 miles, and the entire schedule was played in one-day or one-night stands," Trimble wrote.

"We never stayed overnight in another town—it was back on the bus to Bassett after every game," Phil recalled. "We never saw a hotel at all. Each of us got thirty-five cents a day meal money. The League rules set a limit of fifteen players on each squad. We had two catchers, six pitchers, and seven other players. If anyone was hurt or a pinch-hitter was needed, a pitcher had to go into the game in some other position, as an outfielder or an infielder."

Despite an advance word from Krichell, Ray White was not impressed initially with his new charge. Reportedly he said to his coaching staff, "One thing, anyway, if this peanut is the fragile kind, this is the right league in which to find it out."

This sentiment was true. This was no fancy league. As Milton Shapiro wrote at the time, "The games were often played on inferior fields, little better than sandlots—studded with pebbles, rock outcroppings, and baked hard from the Southern sun." He went on to point out that teams traveled "in a creaking, springless bus." There were no days off. There were no days between games and no one to spell you for a day. It would be a hard, grinding season.

One can only imagine a young, small, New York City 19-year-old alone in a boarding house for the first time. The room was probably comfortable at best—certainly not first-class accommodations. For a kid a long way from home in a world so different, the pressure Rizzuto must have felt, just like any kid in the same situation, must have been incredible. One can only imagine violent and wild swings of thought ranging from a defeatist moment of self-doubt to flights of fancy imagining this was just the first stepping stone on the way to playing at that magnificent Yankee Stadium. Now he would need to prove himself all over again to a new group of men who were just as convinced as the previous group that he did not belong.

The first two weeks went beautifully. Rizzuto found a groove both at bat and playing on the infield. He was starting to play his aggressive game, and White and the coaches were beginning to take notice.

Bassett was in first place on top of the standings. Rizzuto was fast becoming a popular player—both with teammates and with the crowds. White started filing promising reports about the small kid from Queens, New York.

• • •

There are two versions of what happened next. While it has been impossible to suss out the truth, the versions still lead to the same end. Rizzuto told Trimble in 1951 that he became hurt pivoting while turning a double-play. As he pivoted to throw, he became the target of the base runner, as base runners are instructed to do especially against smallish infielders, hoping to dislodge or help misdirect the throw. Rizzuto had encountered this many times before. He got up hurt with a charley-horse, a term otherwise known as a sore muscle. Every baseball player has gotten a charley-horse at one time or another. It is an injury that with a little rest usually goes away. It rarely seems serious, especially in the machismo of professional sports.

Later Rizzuto told a different version. He told *Yankees* magazine, "I was running to first base one day and stepped into a gopher hole. I heard something pop [in my left leg] and it really hurt."

Maybe a combination of these two things is true. Maybe he hurt it running the base paths and aggravated it turning a double-play, or vice versa. But the end result remained—he had aggravated a pulled muscle, or worse. The real problem for Rizzuto was there was no chance for rest, and there was limited medical care. Rizzuto was determined to prove his worth on the field and value to the organization. And he wanted to prove that despite his size, he could make it in the big man's game.

"We had no trainers or anything in D ball in those days," Rizzuto said. White, he said, "was the manager and also the trainer, the bus driver, and road secretary."

So Phil played on, and White dealt with his injured star as best he could. "Every night he would rub my leg, but it kept getting worse," Rizzuto said. The leg got worse, and it became increasingly hard to make the pivot for the double-play or to get power out of the leg to drive the ball. White continued to treat the leg himself.

"He wound a big wad of adhesive tape around the handle of a broken bat and kneaded the sore muscle in a fashion of a massage," Trimble wrote. "Then the manager would tape it tightly" so Rizzuto could play with a minimum amount of pain.

This amateurish attempt did allow Rizzuto to play longer. And it gained for Rizzuto a certain amount of respect for his grit from White. However, by delaying proper medical attention, they were actually putting Rizzuto's life in serious danger.

In mid-May, a local umpire officiating a game pulled Rizzuto aside. "An old umpire took me aside one day and said, 'Look kid, you are badly hurt, and the sooner you get to a hospital, the better.'"

Rizzuto and White waited a little longer until they finally went to see Dr. Johnson in Bassett, who was a practicing physician with his own private practice and was also doctor for the local railroad. He examined the wound closely.

"What has happened is that the muscle in your leg has pulled apart. It's something that happens maybe once in a million cases of strain," Johnson said. While this news didn't seem so bad, the next news was devastating. The wound, having not seen medical treatment for so long, was now gangrenous. An operation was needed immediately. Any further delay might prove debilitating, even life threatening.

"If this had continued for a few more days, we would have had to take the leg off," the doctor said.

There was no time to wait for formal permission from the Rizzuto family for the operation to proceed. Shaken by the news, White accepted responsibility for the operation, and Phil went into surgery. In the meantime, Rose and uncles Dominick and Alfred made their way down to Roanoke to see the convalescing young man.

"When I woke up 17 hours later, my mother, my uncle, and brother were around my bed, and the doctor told me I would never play again," Rizzuto said later. He had 37 stitches. "The doctor cut six inches off the muscle and tied the ends off to the other muscles. I have a big hole in my leg, and it extends from my knee to my thigh."

Rose had thought she might see her son play professionally, now she was sitting by his bed in the hospital. "I never thought he'd play ball again after that. Dominick and I drove home with the feeling that Phil would be back with us after they let him out of the hospital and that the Yankees would no longer be interested in him. Baseball, of course, was not as important as his health and I was worried that he might be lame."

"Will I play again?" Rizzuto repeatedly asked the doctor.

"I don't know yet, son, I don't yet," the doctor answered time and again.

"I was out of action for three months," Rizzuto told *The Sporting News.*

Sometime in early August, Rizzuto visited the doctor. The doctor examined and probed the pink and bright red scar running down Rizzuto's thigh. He asked Rizzuto to do a series of simple exercises to see the muscle's reaction and to read the level of stress on Rizzuto's face. Once Rizzuto completed the movements with ease, the doctor told him to get dressed. Rizzuto asked if he was ready.

"The incision has healed nicely. You'll have a mean scar there, but it's okay. The muscle seems to have come back into shape. There's certainly no trace of complications or residual infection. As for baseball," the doctor hesitated, "there's only one way to find out. Tomorrow, I want you to go out on the field and run just as hard as you can. Don't favor the leg. Try to run naturally. If it doesn't hold up now…it never will." Rizzuto walked for a week and continued his exercises, as the doctor ordered. Then came the day of reckoning.

"When I came back I was afraid my career had ended. I had been quite a runner. In high school I used to steal second and third," Rizzuto said. "I cut loose, and the muscle held."

White was unsure, even though Rizzuto felt fine. He let Phil play three innings the first few games and slowly increased the amount of playing time until Phil was fully back in the lineup.

Phil came back to playing with a vengeance. He played in 67 games overall that season. He batted .310 with 53 runs scored and 32 RBIs. And his bat had been hot with something extra on it, smacking 17 doubles, five triples, five homeruns, topped of by six stolen bases. Along with his help in the field—a .933 fielding percentage—the team won the Bi-State League pennant.

According to sportswriter Milton Shapiro, the pennant-clinching game was classic Rizzuto demonstrating his abilities as well as his value to the team. With the score in favor of Martinsville, 2–1, Rizzuto came up to bat. Making a big show of it, he rubbed dirt in his palms from the batters box and surveyed the outfield dramatically. When the pitcher let loose with the ball, only then did Rizzuto flash the bat across the batter's box and reveal he was bunting. Rizzuto had touched first before the startled third baseman even reached the ball. Once on base, Rizzuto stole second, and then on a bloop single he scored in dramatic fashion to tie the score, sliding around the catcher who was blocking the plate.

In the sixth inning, Rizzuto dove into the hole and stopped a sure-fire line-drive single by backhanding the ball, firing his own bullet to home plate, and nailing the runner from third. Now with two men out, the next batter went to a full count before popping up a Texas leaguer, a ball known for embarrassing infielders and outfielders for more than a century. Rizzuto was among those who raced after it—he called off the other players and made a spectacular over-the-shoulder catch.

On his next at bat and with one man on, Rizzuto showed bunt on the first pitch, and the infield crept in, playing the bunt. Rizzuto awaited the pitch, pretending he might bunt, but at the last second he reset himself and walloped a single that whistled past the third baseman's head. The ball shot into left field, and Rizzuto got a stand-up double. Slightly after Rizzuto arrived at second base, the runner scored, and the Furnituremakers made it stick, 3–2, for the win. Rizzuto could make things happen, and the Yankees brass was beginning to take notice.

Because of his shortened season, Rizzuto fully expected to return to Bassett the following spring, but the gears of the Yankees machine were grinding forward—to his advantage. The Yankees were dissolving their affiliation with the Bassett Furnituremakers, and Georg Weiss, the head of the farm system for the Yankees organization, decided to move Ray White up to Norfolk, Virginia. There he would manage the Norfolk Tars in the Class B Piedmont League. White wanted Rizzuto to make the jump to Norfolk with him.

Norfolk would be a big move for Rizzuto. The Piedmont League was a real proving ground for Yankees talent. And the level of competition would be far superior to what he had seen in the Bi-State League.

The Piedmont League operated between 1920 and 1955. Though many teams came and went, the cities were notable large towns and small cities, such as Durham, High Point, Winston-Salem, Asheville, Portsmouth, and Rocky Mount.

White felt Rizzuto could hold his own there. However, White had one problem—Norfolk already had a star shortstop. His name was Claude Elliott

Corbitt. Corbitt was seen as something of a local product from Sunbury, North Carolina. To make matters worse, he had played baseball at Duke University in Durham. The tall and thin Corbitt, who was two years older than Rizzuto, was a crowd favorite. And he was well-liked by Weiss and the other Yankees staff. Never one to stand on ceremony, White did not let the inconvenience of Corbitt's existence stand in his way.

Weiss originally did not approve the move of Rizzuto to Norfolk, but White's insistence paid off, and Rizzuto became a Tar. He also doubled his salary to $150 per month.

It was a difficult spot for both men. They were pitted against each other for the same job almost immediately. The incumbent Corbitt started off on a tear, hitting .321 to lead the club. And the fans cheered on their local boy. Rizzuto was discouraged. He was sitting the bench, watching Corbitt pound the ball, and felt he was probably headed to a demotion to Class C ball. But Rizzuto's luck was about to change.

In the late spring of 1938, the organization sent word down to White that he had to give up one of his star shortstops. Weiss didn't see the point in having one of his hot young prospects watching the other one play, especially when their Class A Augusta, Georgia, team, in the South Atlantic League (also known as the Sally League), needed a shortstop.

The move worked well for White. White gave up Corbitt, who deserved the promotion to Class A ball one step closer to becoming a Yankee, and gave Phil a chance to play. It was not an easy decision for White. He had his convictions. White was convinced he had sent the more mature player up, and he also thought Rizzuto, whose intangibles did not show up on a stat sheet, might in the end make the difference between a good season and a championship. In the short term, White took a beating from the fans, who were sore White had shipped their local man out of town to bring in this short boy from New York. There were howls for his scalp from fans and the press.

Corbitt would go on to knock around the minor leagues until 1941. He then served four years during the war before returning home to baseball. He finally caught on in 1945 with the Brooklyn Dodgers. By then he was 30 years old with some of his best years already behind him. He played three more years, all with the Cincinnati Reds, accumulating a .243 batting average, in a grand total of 215 games in four seasons. While Corbitt could field well, he had trouble hitting better pitching.

The Tar team did not suffer because it was loaded with talent. Phil's other teammates included Billy Johnson, Aaron Robinson, and Gerry Priddy, all of whom eventually made it to the major leagues.

Rizzuto responded to his opportunity just the way White had hoped. He hit .336 the rest of the season, scoring 97 runs, and hitting 24 doubles, 10 triples, and 9 homers, with 58 RBIs and 26 stolen bases. While the Tar fans had liked Corbitt, they warmed to Rizzuto's fiery play. He eventually became a crowd favorite, and the local newspapers took to calling him "The Flea," due to his diminutive size and his blazing speed.

During one game against Portsmouth, the opposing second baseman was robbed of two base hits by Rizzuto (who fielded a beautiful soft bunt bare-handed and threw the runner out and took an over-the-shoulder catch of a pop fly into the short-left outfield) and was put out while Rizzuto was turning a double play. The player rolled into Rizzuto, trying to break up the double play. He was not successful. When the two got up, Eddie Stanky dusted himself off and said to Rizzuto, "Next time, get out of the way. A little kid like you could get hurt."

"I made the play, though, didn't I Eddie?" Rizzuto retorted.

"Yeah," Stanky admitted, "but I'll get you next time." It would not be the last time the two of them would collide in baseball that year, as the teams played each other often. The two would be linked inextricably in one of the most debated moments in World Series history.

Rizzuto came one vote shy of winning the Piedmont League MVP honors, falling to Cuban-born Roberto Estalella of the Charlotte team.

The other positive thing that 1938 brought was a partnership with second baseman Gerry Priddy. At one point early in the season, when Corbitt was still there, Rizzuto had played third several times, and Priddy had played shortstop. While Rizzuto performed passably, Priddy was apparently dreadful. With the exit of Corbitt, and after some experimenting by White, the two found their natural positions. The two developed into one of the best double-play combos in the minor leagues in 1938. They had been the talk of the minor league world, and newspapers were paying attention.

Gerald Edward Priddy was born in Los Angeles, California. Priddy was signed by the New York Yankees Southern California scouting chief Bill Essick. Priddy had been a well-known Los Angeles sandlotter. Signed to a Class D team, like Rizzuto, he played with a small team in Rogers, Arkansas, of the Arkansas-Missouri League.

"Priddy, a moon-faced, deep-chested youth, was just a year younger than the little shortstop. He hit .336 at Rogers and so was promoted to Norfolk," Joe Trimble wrote.

Rizzuto recalled Priddy this way: "Priddy. That huckleberry. He was something else. We were close even though we were opposites in a lot of ways. He was cocky…oh he was sure of himself. Me, on the other hand, I was shy and always worried. He took me under his wing, but he loved playing tricks on me, too…like nailing my shoes to the floor, ripping up all my fan letters, all those things."

"There they began an association which was to make them the most talked-of second-short combination in the minor leagues for the next three years and ultimately bring them to Yankee Stadium together," Joe Trimble wrote.

"Every writer I know has a list of several hundred books he would like to write, but knows he never will," wrote baseball historian Bill James. "On my list is a joint biography of Phil Rizzuto and Jerry Priddy. They were magic together; everyone who saw them wrote it. They were Astaire and Rogers, Rodgers and Hammerstein, Laurel and Hardy, Tinker and Evers, Trammell and Whitaker."

Trimble continued, "Phil and Jerry became a Damon-and-Pythias duo, inseparable on the field and off. Seldom, too, was one of them spoken of without the other—they just seemed to be twins. Around second base they seemed to be fused into one super-human. Baseball men all over the country—scouts, owners, and newspapermen—passed the word that the Yankees had come up with the greatest second-base pair in minor league history."

One of their signature defense plays was to rob batters of hits if they hit the ball back at the pitcher. Normally a sure hit that would race past second base, Rizzuto and Priddy came up with a new ballet of sorts. Both would converge. Rizzuto would dive for the ball, and Priddy would set his feet. Rizzuto, from the ground, would shovel the ball to the waiting Priddy, who would then fire to first base.

"I was eight years old and saw at least 20 games that season, thanks to my Dad and two women who were neighbors, who rarely missed a game. The cry 'Rizzuto to Priddy to?' was common," wrote Tars fan Bill Prince in a comment to a story in the *New York Times*. "I met Phil sometime during World War II when he was stationed at the naval base in Norfolk. I met him through several of my Italian friends. I was a Yankee/Rizzuto fan hereafter."

"It was a spectacular play in execution, and even on those few occasions when it didn't work it drew cheers of approval from the grandstand," wrote Milton Shapiro, a well-published sports journalist and Rizzuto biographer.

On the field, Priddy became Rizzuto's de facto protector, though Rizzuto never shrank from confrontation on the field. Once or twice opposing players came in spikes high at Rizzuto, a dirty play in baseball with the intent of scaring off or injuring a second baseman or shortstop covering the bag at second base. Priddy finished such fireworks with fisticuffs, and word soon got around the league that if you tried to injure "The Flea," you'd have to go through Priddy. Any such attempts diminished substantially. Meanwhile, Priddy was also pretty handy with a bat in his hand. Priddy played in 132 games, hit .323, and led the league with 36 doubles. He also had six triples, nine home runs, and 73 RBIs.

The Tars were headed to take the league pennant when Portsmouth rallied late in the summer and came into Norfolk for a three game series only a half-game behind. The first game was a scoreless affair for the first five innings. In the sixth inning, Eddie Stanky singled, and a sacrifice pushed him to second. The next batter hit a high line drive over the shortstop's head with Stanky on his way to third. But Rizzuto leapt just high enough, knocked down the ball, turned and rifled the ball to third, just beating Stanky. A fly out and the threat was blunted.

In the Norfolk sixth, Rizzuto walloped a double, and Phil promptly stole third on a hit and run in which Billy Johnson missed the ball. Then, with Rizzuto on third, Johnson hit a long sacrifice, and the Tars went up 1–0.

That score held up for a little while, but Portsmouth was a good team and broke back for two runs, and they still had loaded bases with no one out. A line drive landed at Rizzuto's feet in a cloud of dust. The crowd got up on its feet. Playing the possible wild-hop ball, Rizzuto dove into the cloud of dust, smothered the ball, and fired a throw to the plate, snuffing out the possible run. The catcher then pivoted and gunned down the base runner for the second out. With men still on second and third, the next batter was out on a pop-up in foul territory, and Norfolk avoided absolute disaster.

In the bottom of the ninth, there was one out with Aaron Robinson standing on third and they were still down 2–1. Rizzuto took the first pitch—a ball. He swung and missed the second pitch, then took the third pitch for another ball, making the count 2–1. On the next pitch, he squared away, and bunted perfectly down the third-base line. Rizzuto raced to first and was safe. And so was Robinson, who had crossed home plate before the catcher could apply the tag. The score was tied. Now Rizzuto was on first with only one out, and Johnson was up again. The Portsmouth pitcher threw twice to first, hoping to put the breaks on "The Flea" lest he break for second.

As Johnson stepped into the batter's box, Ray White flashed the sign for hit-and-run. On the pitch, Rizzuto took off like a jack rabbit, and Johnson responded with a line drive deep into the outfield between two defenders. Rounding second, Rizzuto could see one of the fielders bobbling the ball and knew he would turn at third, as well. Ray White waved him in. As he zeroed in on home plate, he saw the catcher squat to block the plate, and he could hear the crowd roar. He knew the ball was catching up to him in a fast way. As he came closer he broke into a slide and felt the catcher stab at him. But it did not matter because his foot had already touched the plate.

"Safe!" The Tars fans went wild in the stands. The Tars swept the next two games and were crowned Piedmont League champs.

Phil went home to his parent's house that fall very proud of what he had accomplished. And he had also allayed the fears and worries of his parents.

"They moved him to Kansas City the following season," Phil's mother recalled. "And that impressed both his father and myself. He still wasn't making much money—he never really did in baseball until after the war—but he was getting ahead."

4

Go West Young Man

"In 1939, I was promoted all the way to Kansas City," Rizzuto told *The Sporting News*. "I will never forget that spring training season. The older players made life miserable for me. They played every conceivable trick on me. Buzz Boyle's idea of comedy was to get a hold of a letter from your family, tear it to bits, and lay them neatly on the bench near you."

"When Rizzuto arrived at the Blues spring training base in Haines City, Florida, last March, the experts gave him the once over a couple of times and then decided that while he might have some natural talents he was too small to do much good in the American Association with its speedy style of play," one American Association League press release stated. "Training season wasn't many days old before he was one of the sensations of the camp."

In 1939, Priddy and Rizzuto started spring training early, working out with the Class AA affiliate Kansas City Blues, one of the top farm teams of the Yankees organization. While the Yankees brass had tentatively targeted the pair for Class A, there was some worry that they might be advancing the dynamic duo a little too fast. However, there had been real excitement about the rumor that the Yankees had been offered $500,000 for the pair but the Yankees weren't selling. Just to work out with the Blues was a tremendous compliment to both young men, and they knew it was the opportunity of a lifetime. At the end of 1939, the Yankees were actually offered $250,000 for the pair or $150,000 for Rizzuto alone, but Yankees General Manager Ed Barrow turned the offers down despite the fact that there was no room for either player at the top of their organization.

Both responded. "They made such a hit in spring training that Billy Meyer, manager of the Blues, asked for their transfer to Kansas City," Milton Shapiro wrote.

Meyer broke into the majors with the 1913 Chicago White Sox, but he played only one game. Three years later, he returned to the American League with the Philadelphia Athletics. He appeared in 50 games for a squad that won only 36 games and lost 117. A generation-and-a-half later, Meyer piloted the worst team in Pittsburgh Pirates history, a Bucs team that won only 42 of 155 games in 1952. With these two teams, Meyer accomplished a dubious distinction—that of having played for and managed two of the worst teams in the history of Major League Baseball.

In spite of these two milestones, Meyer was a highly respected figure in baseball. From 1936–47, he ran a series of top farm clubs for the New York Yankees, including Oakland of the Pacific Coast League, Kansas City of the American Association, and Newark of the International League. He won four league championships. Meyer had the unfortunate luck, however, to be one of the best managers in the minor leagues at a time when the legendary Joe McCarthy (ironically, a close friend of Meyer's) helmed the Yankees. Thus, Meyer was never called up to manage the Bombers and made a 20-year career managing in the minors.

In a further cruel twist of fate, Meyer was passed over three times by the Yankees to be McCarthy's successor between 1946 and 1947 (Bill Dickey, Johnny Neun, and Bucky Harris got the nods instead, in that order). In 1948, Meyer went to the last-place Pittsburgh Pirates and brought them up to fourth place by the end of that year's campaign. He was named Major League Manager of the Year. At the end of 1948, newly appointed Yankees general manager George Weiss fired Harris. He knew and respected Meyer from their long association in the Yanks' farm system, so he asked Pittsburgh for permission to talk with Meyer. But the Yankees overtures were rebuffed, and Weiss was forced to hire his second choice, Casey Stengel. Stengel would win ten pennants in 12 years in the Bronx on his way to the Baseball Hall of Fame.

"Then 45 years of age, Billy had been in baseball for 28 of them as a player in the minors [he was a catcher] and manager," Joe Trimble wrote.

Trimble pointed out that then-Yankees farm manager George Weiss "always picked his minor league pilots just as carefully as most men do their wives. He had many good young prospects scattered throughout the fertile nurseries and wasn't of a mind to have any of them retarded by poor handling."

According to veteran sports scribe Milton Shapiro, "What little polish [Rizzuto and Priddy] needed manager Meyer applied liberally. A veteran minor league manager, he was considered one of the best in the minor league chain. He knew how to work with young players, to smooth rough edges, to add the fine points of baseball technique and strategy that often meant the difference between an adequate player and a star."

At Kansas City, Priddy's place was pretty well set, but for Phil, as had been the case in Norfolk, there was an incumbent he had to unseat. Meyer's decision was tough. Billy Hitchcock was the player—coming off a knee injury from the year before, he started off in spring training like a rocket, batting and fielding well. Complicating the matter was that Rizzuto was making $300 a month, and if there was no spot for him, it was a big salary to ride the pine.

"Born William Clyde Hitchcock on July 31, 1918, in Inverness, Alabama, he was the son of James Franklin Hitchcock, clerk of the circuit court of Bullock County, Alabama, and Sallie Louise Davis," wrote William Akin, a baseball historian. Hitchcock had four brothers and two sisters. "Billy starred in two sports at Alabama Polytechnic Institute (now Auburn University). The 6'1" 185-pound All-Southern Conference tailback led Auburn to its first bowl game, the Bacardi Bowl in Havana, where he scored Auburn's only TD, a 40-yard run, in a 7–7 tie against Villanova. As captain and shortstop on the baseball team, he led the Tigers to their first conference baseball title."

Later in life, Hitchcock would go on to become a respected manager and baseball executive. Early in the 1970 season, Hitchcock was asked to become head of the Southern League, which had been reconstituted in 1964. "He acted to reorganize the league…brought in additional teams, set up a divisional format with a postseason playoff, and in 1976 the league introduced a split season. The addition of Nashville in 1978 pushed league attendance over 1,000,000 for the first time, up from 333,500 when Hitchcock took office, and rose to 1,761,192 when he stepped down in 1980," Akin wrote.

In 1939, Jack Saltzgaver was at third base, Rizzuto or Hitchcock would wind up at short, and Priddy was at second.

"I had played shortstop in college," Hitchcock recalled. "I reported to Kansas City in the spring of 1939. I don't think they expected me to play at Kansas City because that was my first year…Phil and Jerry of course had been playing at Norfolk, and they figured that would be the combination. I don't know, I just had a good spring and things went well for me down there. Bill Meyer decided to take me north as a utility infielder and, as it turned out, Saltzgaver couldn't play every day, and I started to play a lot of third base that year."

Meyer then went to work molding the popular duo even further. He especially worked with Rizzuto on his techniques. If there was one knock about Rizzuto, and he was first to admit it, he was getting knocked down too often on double-plays. Given his light stature, Meyer was concerned for his young star's health.

"One of the most important—and toughest—things on a double play is getting rid of the ball after you've touched second," Meyer said to Rizzuto. "You got to glide across that bag and get in a spot to throw to first. If you're going to stick around the bag, the runner's gonna slide in there and knock you down every time."

"Oh, man, I remember a lot of things about little Phil," Hitchcock recalled years later. "He's just a great guy, a wonderful little fella. We always teased him. He's very naive, you know, and he was always the butt of all the jokes fellas would pull on him. He'd go along with them and I always said, that Rizzuto, he's dumb like a fox. He knew what was going on all the time, but he allowed everybody to have a good time and get a lot of fun out of it. He'd just go along with it. He was a grand fella, very good hearted, very personable, very likeable. He was just a youngster then, of course, but he was a fine fella and what a ball player."

It was in Kansas City that Phil earned his famous nickname "Scooter." The moniker was hung on him by Billy Hitchcock and Ralph "Buzz" Boyle.

Hitchcock looked at Phil's short legs during one game and told him, "You ain't runnin,' you're scootin.'" And it was Boyle that made it stick, referring to Rizzuto as Scooter.

"Anybody'd ask why, well, one of the most greatest and exciting things is to watch Rizzuto hit a triple. He's a short little fella, you know, and he'd take these short little strides, but he could run and he'd hit a triple," Hitchcock said. "When he'd round first base and go into second base, it always seemed as he rounded second that he'd lose his cap.... I'd say he looked like a scooter running around that infield.... This is my thought on the thing, and I think I'm the one who put 'Scooter' on him."

"For many years, Rizzuto himself attributed the 'name caller' as Hitchcock," wrote Rizzuto biographer Dan Hirshberg, "Others—including [Sid] Bordman—say it was the veteran...Boyle."

Regardless, Priddy and Rizzuto had an excellent year in 1939. Both did well at the plate. Phil hit .316, and the taller and heavier Priddy topped him with .333. Rizzuto said in later years that it was the time he "first saw *pitching*."

The young infielders were not just playing well but incessantly talking strategy. How to anticipate both the hitter and the opposing manager. How pitch counts changed strategies. They questioned each other about situations and how to read and react. It was an incredible learning experience. They analyzed the game constantly.

"There's always something new to learn in baseball," Rizzuto said years later. "Always new men coming into the league, and you have to learn all you can about them to play them right."

Phil proved to be a popular player, and the organization was happy to play off his popularity. It made for good press. The public relations people often issued press releases featuring the scrappy little shortstop, or offering tidbits about him.

"Good things, it is said, come in small packages," began a missive from the American Association in a piece titled, "Newcomers Worth Watching in the American Association." The press release was all about Rizzuto, "a young man who has been playing a lot of baseball for the Blues around shortfield ever since the season opened."

The same press release referred to Rizzuto as "one of the 'runts' of the American Association...but he packs plenty of wallop in the Louisville Slugger that he totes with him several times daily to the plate."

"I watched Phil Rizzuto play for the Kansas City Blues in 1939 and 1940. He and Jerry Priddy, who played second base for the Blues, were absolutely the best shortstop/second base combo ever," wrote Robert Long, a lifelong Yankees fan, many years later.

"The Bainbridge Apartment also counted among its guests several ballplayers from the New York Yankees American Association farm club, the Kansas City Blues. Downstairs from me lived Gerald Priddy and Phil Rizzuto, on the way up to greatness," remembered broadcast legend Walter Cronkite, who was a fledgling journalist at the time.

Scooter was well liked by his teammates, and about the only thing Priddy wouldn't run interference on for Phil was when one of the guys was trying to put a gag over on him. Phil was the mark on many a clubhouse hijinx.

"I think [pitcher] Johnny Lindell was the No. 1 prankster," Sid Bordman, a batboy who joined the Blues in 1940. "[Lindell] picked on him a lot. He was the ringleader. They used to nail his shorts to a locker and do all sorts of stuff like that. They picked on him a lot in Kansas City."

Another story that was emblematic of Rizzuto's resilience was a gag that was played on him by teammate Buzz Boyle. Boyle, a natural practical joker, had previously been in the Dodgers organization (usually a much looser organization that tolerated many more characters). Boyle convinced Rizzuto that a new machine was about to be marketed that could increase one's height. Through a combination of "treatments" both physical and medical, one could increase one's size 3 to 4 inches. Rizzuto, at first skeptical, eventually fell for Boyle's clever ruse. Boyle explained that the machine was not yet on the market, as its inventor was still clearing patents and financing though he claimed that the doctor had treated a friend of his with great results. Boyle was so convincing, Rizzuto eventually told others that he would soon be signing up for the product. Only after a local writer picked up on the story and wrote a piece about it did Rizzuto finally wise up to the truth.

Later, when Boyle got into a batting slump, Rizzuto walked into the clubhouse with a giant box, tall and thin, and placed it at Boyle's locker.

"Here Buzz, a present from me to you," Rizzuto said setting down the box. "What's in it?"

"A stretching machine. For your batting average."

That year Rizzuto hit .316 and scored 99 runs. He hit 21 doubles, 6 triples, 5 home runs, and notched 64 RBIs. He also led the league in most sacrifice hits with 23. The Yankees were very pleased.

• • •

By all accounts, Phil Rizzuto had never been what some might refer to as a ladies' man. Not that he didn't fancy girls or women, but because he was so focused on his goals, he would let few things interfere. While other high school boys were courting young ladies, sitting in soda shops, sharing an egg cream, and listening to the radio, Phil somehow always found his way onto a ball field.

"I guess there wasn't anything in his life but baseball as long as I can remember," Rizzuto's mother recalled. "There always were lots of girls around, friends of our own daughters and others, but Phil never gave any of them a second look. He was very shy, of course. He wasn't interested in parties or dates while he was in high school and never thought about anything except the next ball game. We had a hard time getting him to dress up in his Sunday suit even at Easter. I can't remember him ever having a date before he left home to go to Bassett."

Phil was a little over nineteen when he first left home on the train, with the money safety pinned to his clothes in the spring of 1937. Whether or not a young girl in his early playing days had caught his fancy is not known. But it wasn't until Phil got to Kansas City in 1939 that he actually began to date.

There in Kansas City, Phil had met the brown-haired Betty Dresser. The two were smitten with each other and began going steady. Betty attended many games at Blues Stadium, and they shared a coke and an occasional auto ride. Phil was only 21 years old, and Betty two years younger than he, so marriage at the time did not seem an option. They were teenage sweethearts.

"Betty's family was crazy about Phil," Trimble wrote. "Her folks hoped that, in time, something might come of the association. But tragedy struck their pretty daughter. She underwent what seemed to be a simple tonsillectomy in 1940 and died from a throat infection. Mrs. Dresser, heartbroken, buried her and erected a tombstone which she knew would have pleased her little girl. On it was carved a facsimile of a ball player, which looks a great deal like

Phil himself. Rizzuto visited the grave in Kansas City when the Yanks played an exhibition there in 1941."

Baseball provided both solace and success. The Blues won 107 games, and Billy Meyer was named Manager of the Year by *The Sporting News*. Gerald Priddy was the only player in the league to play all 155 games—he finished third for the batting title and led the league in doubles. Teammate Vince DiMaggio (who was eventually sold to Cincinnati) slammed a league-leading 46 homers. Unfortunately for Priddy and Rizzuto, Frank Crosetti and Joe Gordon both played very well in 1939, and the Yankees won their fourth straight World Series. Both Priddy and Rizzuto were headed back to Kansas City.

That year also saw the emergence of Harold "Pee Wee" Reese in Louisville, who led the league with 18 triples and 35 stolen bases. The two would see more and more of each other over the next fifteen years and be compared constantly.

Back home in Glendale, Phil worked as a baker in the off-season, and he was an avid bowler. Rizzuto was a lifelong movie fan, and his favorite stars were Mickey Rooney and Lana Turner, while his favorite feature film was *Gone With the Wind*. His favorite radio personalities were Bob Hope and Judy Garland, and he also enjoyed the Kay Kyser and Jack Benny shows.

The 1940 edition of the Kansas City Blues repeated, even without Vince DiMaggio's sledgehammer bat. With the infield intact, the team played incredible defense and took the pennant.

Regarding the 1939 and 1940 Blues teams, former batboy Sid Bordman told Dan Hirshberg, "Those two teams were great teams. That infield was intact for two years, probably the greatest minor league infield of all time. Probably better than a lot of major league infields."

Rizzuto shone in a game against the New York Yankees when the big club was barnstorming, as it usually did in those days, before the season started. On March 28, 1940, *New York Times* veteran baseball man John Drebinger wrote, "The farm hands did quite a piece of snappy fielding, too. In the fourth, Phil Rizzuto, the pint-sized shortstop from Ridgewood, who some day may replace Crosetti, dashed over the ground like a rabbit to snare DiMaggio's short fly in left." Drebinger also referred to Rizzuto as "the midget" later in the article.

His play was exemplified by this small tidbit from a game against Minneapolis. Hub Walker, a former major league outfielder, had a special batting stance when an important at-bat was afforded him. He would get in a stance showing bunt, and after the infield had adjusted (the first baseman charging toward the plate, the second baseman sliding over to first to cover the bag), he would change his grip when the pitcher threw the ball. With a small choppy swing, he would invariably attempt to hit into the hole vacated by the second baseman. Fast and agile, he could almost always beat the throw to first.

Tom Sheehan, the manager of the Minneapolis team said, "It never failed so long as Hub was able to make connections with the ball, which he did most of the time. It was the perfect play—there was no defense for it. At least, we thought there wasn't any when the bunt was executed properly.... We pulled it a few times against Kansas City, as well as every other club in the league."

Phil was waiting. "The split second he saw Walker shift his grip on the bat, [Rizzuto] raced across the infield toward second," Milton Shapiro wrote. "Walker pushed the ball toward the usual spot, and [Rizzuto], a fast runner himself, stabbed the ground ball on the first-base side of second and nipped Walker at first by a step."

Walker stood in disbelief after the amazing play, appealing to the umpire. The crowd roared. There stood Priddy with the ball that Rizzuto had thrown.

"Rizzuto outfoxed us. He saw what was coming," Sheehan later remarked. "It was a great play for Rizzuto to field the ball, let alone throw out the runner, because Hub gets a tremendous jump from the plate on that particular play."

In a game against Toledo, Phil bunted to get to first. He stole second, stole third, and raced home for the score on a slow roller to the second baseman. He tripled in the fifth inning with the bases loaded, giving his team a 6–4 lead. He ended the game on defense with the bases loaded by starting a double play that went short-to-third-to-first.

Rizzuto's base-running hijinx were also well documented. He would gyrate once on base, jumping around, trying to distract the pitcher and any other player he could. Johnny VanderMeer once threatened to bean Rizzuto because he was convinced the puckish base runner was stealing signs, when all he was really trying to do was distract him. It worked.

As a player and as a personality, Rizzuto became more and more popular. And the American Association was happy to promote him. One press sheet from April 30, 1940, noted that the young "$100,000 shortstop" (a reference to the rumored offers made for Rizzuto's dazzling talent by other clubs) had acquired a new hobby—snipe hunting.

This was a tongue-in-cheek reference that showed how popular Rizzuto was, yet how much the team continued to play jokes on its diminutive New York–native shortstop. Snipe hunting was a popular gag played by southern boys on their northern counterparts. Most southerners knew what a snipe hunt was. So the press release was a well-placed but well-meaning jab.

In 1939, the unsuspecting Phil was asked if he would like to go snipe hunting. Everyone was going, he was told. They cajoled him into attending. The "hunt" took place deep inside an orange grove about six miles outside of spring training camp.

Phil was told to hold a flashlight and stand in the middle of the grove. He was told that he would be the one to catch the little bird with a bag and a loaf of bread.

"How?" asked the gullible Rizzuto. It was explained that the other players would go into the grove, form a line, scream and shout, and drive a bird across the orchard, and it would come running right at him.

"The snipe will be running right at you. Just flash the light in the bag and throw in a piece of bread. The snipe'll run right into the bag," it was explained.

Phil was left in the dark, and the serious-looking hunters wandered off into the dark. Minutes passed like hours for the small man, standing deep in the orange grove. Eventually, he heard noises and noticed movements in the dark of the woods—suddenly his teammates came screaming and yelling at the top of their lungs. The startled Rizzuto flashed the light into the bag and threw in a piece of bead and repeated the process. When he remarked that he had not seen the bird, the team cracked up laughing.

Finally, he understood that he had been had.

In 1940, his second year, the team decided to try the same thing to a rookie. Supposedly, Rizzuto himself would be in on the prank, being one of the leaders. When the team dispersed into the woods, however, everyone, including the rookie, disappeared, leaving Rizzuto alone in the dark orange grove.

Minutes later, the local sheriff appeared and brought Rizzuto, under suspicion of prowling, down to the local county lock-up for holding. Rizzuto was placed in a cell for several hours. He was sick with worry. Hours later, the entire team showed up, and it became obvious that Rizzuto was the butt of the joke once again.

It is a testament to his popularity that the league press release in 1940 then listed his hobby as snipe hunting, reporting, "Philip is developing into a snipe hunter of the first order. It seems he has already made several extended journeys in quest of the elusive snipe but reports as to the success of his ventures vary. In any event, Rizzuto has never yet turned down an invitation for such a foray.... Questioned as to the number of snipes he has 'bagged' in his numerous expeditions, Rizzuto merely grinned and replied somewhat phlegmatically, 'I ain't a sayin'.'"

Rizzuto's even temperament and easily startled demeanor made him the perfect butt of all jokes. And he went along with many a gag. Some believed he let people think he had not yet caught on long after he was aware what the situation was. But there were few who didn't take him seriously on the baseball diamond.

In 1940, Rizzuto had his best year ever in minor league baseball. He stole 35 bases. He hit a career high .347 with 127 runs scored. He hit 28 doubles, 10 triples, and 73 RBIs.

Priddy batted .306 that season, a notch down from his previous year's gaudy numbers. But still, he powered 112 RBIs.

"The way things stand now the Yankees aren't going to be able to make room for both boys. How could Priddy, good as they say he is, ever hope to get Joe Gordon off second base, for example? Rizzuto, it would seem, has a better chance to make the team, because Frank Crosetti, the shortstop, is getting along. One of these days he will have to be replaced," opined veteran sportswriter Joe Williams. The sporting world remained enamored of the baseball duo, however, and Williams' opinions were salient. Gordon was 26 years old and still very competent. Williams did pay the pair their due, writing, "After this season, the greatest double play combination the minors ever saw seems definitely fated to be broken up."

With the season behind him, Rizzuto's accolades poured in. He was voted most popular player by the Kansas City fans and the American Association's Most Valuable Player of the Year. And a panel of sports scribes from *The Sporting News* voted Rizzuto the most promising younger player of the minor leagues that year. It was also noted at the time that Phil's brother, Fred, had received a tryout with the Yankees' Butler, Pennsylvania, farm team in 1940 but was not successful.

With all these accomplishments, baseball writers and executives, as well as Yankees brass, were assured that Priddy and Rizzuto would be the keystones of the defense for the next generation—1940 had been a very good year.

II

AT PLAY
IN
RUTH'S HOUSE

5

LITTLE DAGO

Spring 1941—there were 132,122,000 people living in the United States. A Nash automobile cost the average consumer $780. A Packard of the same size cost roughly $907. A three-room apartment in New York City cost $82 in rent per month. A maple bedroom set to furnish your rooms would set you back another $49.98. Milk was 13 cents a quart, and a loaf of bread cost eight cents a loaf. The average national salary was $1,299 per year.

In 1940, Hoboken, New Jersey, native Frank Sinatra made a name for himself as the young troubadour for the Harry James Band, and a swinging clarinetist, Benny Goodman, started his own band to solid success. Most popular of the era was Alton Glenn Miller, an American jazz musician, arranger, composer, and band leader. From 1939 to 1942, Glenn Miller was one of the best-selling big-band recording artists in the world. His band's popular hits included "In the Mood," "Tuxedo Junction," "Chattanooga Choo Choo," "Moonlight Serenade," "Little Brown Jug," and "Pennsylvania 6-5000."

Other popular songs of the time included tunes like "You Are My Sunshine," "When You Wish Upon a Star," "All or Nothing at All," "You Made Me Love You," and "This Love of Mine." On the big screens across the country, movies such as *The Philadelphia Story, Fantasia, Rebecca, The Grapes of Wrath, How Green Was My Valley, Citizen Kane,* and *The Maltese Falcon* thrilled audiences.

However, one topic was more dominant than any of these in the eyes of a nervous nation—war.

In September 1939, Hitler had unleashed his Blitzkrieg on Poland. At the end of November 1939, the Soviet Union attacked Finland. By May 1940, the Nazis had invaded Denmark, Norway, France, Belgium, Luxembourg, and the Netherlands. On June 14, 1940, the Germans entered Paris. And in the same month, the Soviets had invaded the Baltic states. In October 1940, the German entered Romania, and Italy invaded Greece.

Since September, Americans had been seeing newsreels of the bombing of London by the German Luftwaffe. The city lay in ruins, but the newly elected British Prime Minister was stirring Britons on to fight a never-ending battle against their German counterparts, encouraging them to "never give up."

By the spring of 1941, the war in North Africa between the Germans and the British was about to escalate, bringing home the names of exotic cities and towns most people only heard about in their churches and temples. Meanwhile, President Roosevelt had signed the Lend Lease Act, exchanging aging U.S. warships for the lease of British possessions around the world for 99 years.

By late May 1941, two of the largest and most impregnable warships ever created, the British warship *Hood* and the giant German destroyer *Bismarck*, had both been sunk, thus signifying a crucial turning point in the balance of power between naval and air power and an exchange of queens in the chess match that was the naval war around the world.

These were the headlines across the newspapers every day in America, as the peace-time army was only in the infancy of turning from a professional army to a citizen's army as the war's boundaries continued to expand. The shadow of this world war loomed over all of 1941.

"You read the sports section a lot," Rizzuto said, "because you were afraid of what you'd see in the other parts of the paper."

In several interviews during his minor league days, and even well into his professional life, Rizzuto always held on to two immutable facts:

1. Babe Ruth had been his childhood idol despite a love of the Dodgers.

2. Joe DiMaggio was his favorite professional ballplayer and the best player he ever saw in his life.

He would now get a chance to meet both.

Phil Rizzuto had been to Florida in the springtime before with Kansas City. But 1941 was a different year. He was now in St. Petersburg, Florida, and he was playing on Miller Huggins Field. Even then, the Yankees organization had an awe-inspiring history. Gehrig. Ruth. Huggins. Lazzeri. Dickey. The list went on and on.

Miller James Huggins was born on March 27, 1879. He was nicknamed "Mighty Mite," as he stood no taller than Rizzuto at 5'6" tall. Huggins proved very adept at getting on base. During a 13-year career from 1904 to 1916 with the Cincinnati Reds and St. Louis Cardinals, he led the league in walks four times and regularly posted an on-base percentage near .400. He scored 100 or more runs three times and regularly stole 30 or more bases. He finished his career with 324 swipes.

But it was as a manager that Huggins shone. From 1913 to 1917, he managed the St. Louis Cardinals with no great distinction. But then went to the burgeoning Yankees. Huggins presided over six American League championships (1921–23, 1926–28) and three World Series championships (1923, 1927, and 1928). He finished his managerial career with a 1,413–1,134 record. His 1,413 wins as a manager ranks 21st all time.

Huggins managed the team until his death at the age of 50 on September 25, 1929, of erysipelas, which was visible under his right eye. Out of respect, the league canceled its games for the following day. Thousands of fans attended a farewell in his honor to view Huggins' casket at Yankee Stadium.

The field inside Yankee Stadium itself was nothing to shock anyone. Rizzuto had already played in bigger and better ballparks as a minor leaguer. But this was no ordinary stadium. Many a minor-league sensation had flopped on this field. A budding star was nothing here until he blossomed— if that happened. This would be the toughest proving ground of his young professional life.

The first test came that February when he tried to enter the clubhouse. Fred Logan was the Yankees clubhouse man at the time. His assistant was Pete Sheehy.

"In 1926 Fred Logan spotted a 16-year-old kid trying to sneak into the stadium and asked him to help carry some equipment trunks in exchange for free admission. That was one of the best trades the Yankees ever made, because the kid, Michael Joseph Sheehy, stayed on the job for the next 59 years," Moss Klein wrote in *Sports Illustrated*. "Logan called him Silent Pete, because he was so quiet, and eventually the name became simply Pete."

"The Yankees clubhouse man, Fred Logan, sold the players their hose, kangaroo-leather baseball shoes and undershirts, all at prices well beyond their original cost," wrote baseball historian Paul Voltano.

"Beat it, Sonny," he growled, shaking his close-shaved head vigorously and waving a gnarled hand in the direction of the small bleacher stand adjoining the field. He then added, in a tired voice full of exhaustion usually reserved for pesky fans, "You can see the players when they come out on the field and get autographs signed, too. Outside, now!"

Rizzuto objected, trying to explain to Logan that he did indeed belong. But Logan wasn't buying it, and was about to give the small, persistent Rizzuto the bum's rush, when he was suddenly defended by Lefty Gomez, star pitcher of the Yankees.

"Aw, let him in, Fred," Lefty said. "He belongs here." Then, to Rizzuto, he said, "Come on in here, you cockroach, before one of these Florida grass-hoppers steps on you!"

Gomez was amongst the most colorful players in baseball ever to don Yankees pinstripes. Vernon Louis "Lefty" Gomez was born on November 26, 1908, in Rodeo, California, near Oakland. He was a Portuguese-American left-handed pitcher who played for the New York Yankees between 1930 and 1942. In both 1934 and 1937, he won pitching's Triple Crown by leading the league in wins, ERA, and strikeouts. His .649 career winning percentage ranks 15th in major-league history among pitchers with 200 or more decisions.

Gomez was known for his quick wit and great quips. In a game against the Cleveland Indians, he came up to bat when it was slightly foggy. Bob Feller was on the mound. Gomez struck a match before stepping into the batter's box.

"What's the big idea?" griped the umpire. "Do you think that match will help you see Feller's fast one?"

"No, I'm not concerned about that," Lefty said. "I just want to make sure he can see me!"

The perfect story that illustrated Gomez's unique sense of humor happened in a game in 1937. Tony Lazzeri and Joe McCarthy had both been lauded as heads-up baseball people. Gomez decided to have some fun. While on the mound, a slow roller was hit back to Gomez. He should have thrown to Frank Crosetti at shortstop, starting a double play. Instead, he threw to second baseman Lazzeri. Tony caught the ball in self defense.

Shocked, Lazzeri asked, "Why the hell did you throw the ball to me?"

"Tony, all I've been hearing is what a smart player you are. I just wanted to see what you would do with the ball if you got it when you didn't expect it," Gomez quipped.

Then Yankees manager Joe McCarthy angrily huffed to the mound. "What's the big idea of throwing to Lazzeri?"

"I forgot which Italian to throw to. With Crosetti at short and Lazzeri at second, I couldn't think of which Italian to throw to."

"It's lucky you didn't see Joe DiMaggio!" McCarthy shouted, while pointing to centerfield.

Phil went into the clubhouse and found his locker right between those of Bill Dickey and Red Ruffing, both of whom were large men.

"To tell you the truth," Phil said years later, "when I first saw those big guys down there at spring training, I didn't think I'd make it. They were so darned big—DiMaggio, Henrich and Keller, Ruffing, Dickey, Lindell, all of them. I was really discouraged for quite a while."

He may have been discouraged, but few rookies shouldered such high expectations. Sports scribe Joe Trimble explained, "Rizzuto received most of the publicity, not because he outshone Priddy by such a wide margin, but because there was a shortstop's job waiting on the Yankees. Frankie Crosetti, after nine years as a star player, had gone into eclipse the previous year. He was slowing up a field and had practically forgotten how to hit. In 1940 he had the lowest batting average of any regular player in the major leagues, exactly .194. In 546 times at bat, he had made only 106 hits and had driven in the anemic total of 31 runs."

To be sure, Rizzuto was no wilting flower in the face of a challenge, but the press had started to follow him more closely.

In September, the Yankees bought the contracts of nine players, including Priddy's and Rizzuto's. "Among those obtained from Kansas City are shortstop Phil Rizzuto, who hails from Glendale, Long Island, and second baseman Gerald 'Jerry' Priddy, Rizzuto's partner in Kansas City's crack double-play combination."

When the Federal Government began the draft in October 1940, Rizzuto's name made the *New York Times* yet again.

"Although baseball's bigwigs apparently intend to let the wheels of the nation's military machinery take their course and will make no concerted effort to have their players receive deferred draft classification, the local clubs are keeping a close check on current developments," Drebinger wrote. "The Yankees' chief concern lies with…Tommy Henrich and their prize Kansas City infield recruit, Phil Rizzuto."

Several months later, John Kieran, in the "Sports of the Times" column, quipped, "It appears that the Yankees will have a sprightly infield this year unless Phil Rizzuto, their new shortstop, gets a sore arm saluting second lieutenants in some Army training camp."

By Christmastime, the publicity for the duo started to rage like a fire throughout New York City. Drebinger wrote a huge article devoted solely to Rizzuto and Priddy.

The article went on to say that the Yankees were solid contenders to take a pennant and that their fortunes were closely tied to a pair of Yankees farm hands.

"I think Rizzuto and Priddy will add plenty of pep to the team and give us one of the best second-base combinations in the business," Joe McCarthy, puffing on a big cigar, told Drebinger. "In my opinion, these two boys were the outstanding second-base combination in the minor leagues for the past two years."

While Drebinger pressed to see if Gordon and Crosetti were really through, McCarthy demurred, saying he would not make any changes to the lineup "until after spring training."

But Ed Barrow was more bullish, telling the newspapers two days later, "I know of no reason why we shouldn't come right back and finish on top again."

"If Rizzuto and Priddy, the highly touted Kansas City recruits, come through, it is thought likely that the veterans Red Rolfe and Frankie Crosetti will be placed on the market." Three days later *The Sporting News* announced their No. 1 awards for baseball in 1940. Rizzuto was voted No. 1 player in the minor leagues.

Around the same time, *The Saturday Evening Post* ran a large article about Phil, anointing him "Rookie Number-one."

And in the *New York Times*, Kansas City trainer Eddie Froelich said of Rizzuto, "He's just born to be a great player. Let's take him apart and judge him on his merits. First, his arm. What an arm! He can get the ball away as fast as Durocher ever did, and you know Durocher could do that better than any shortstop that ever lived.... As for running, he is in some respects a better runner than Pee Wee Reese. He is a good slider. He breaks fast. He has split-second thinking, runs on his intuition, and takes advantage of every opportunity. I've seen him tear around those bases in the best Cobb manner and score all the way from first on a single more than once on hit-and-run plays."

Froelich went on to talk abut Rizzuto as a hitter. He pegged Rizzuto as a slap hitter who could occasionally slam one out of the park. "But he really is a sharp hitter. He hits to all fields, down the foul lines, between the fielder, and nobody knows how to pitch him."

"The first people to become alarmed over the winter-long tub-thumping were the Yankees themselves, President Ed Barrow and George Weiss, head of the farm system. Phil received word from headquarters that he was getting too much publicity," Trimble explained. "Phil had not signed his contract at the time and, in urging him to soft-pedal the hurrahs, Barrow may have been motivated by motives of finance rather than psychology."

Rizzuto was not the front office's major concern, as Rizzuto readily signed his $5,000 contract. And the celebrating began. One of the most memorable moments that winter season, aside from all the accolades in print, was a large party thrown in his honor in February, just before he was to report for spring training.

"Friends and admirers of Phil Rizzuto, Glendale youth, who is expected to be in the Yankees' infield when the American League baseball season opens, will give him a testimonial dinner tonight at the Rhineland Garden in the Ridgewood section of Brooklyn. Among the invited guests will be Marius Russo, Yankee pitcher, who lives in Ozone Park." The Rizzuto clan showed up in force, as well as old friend Al Kunitz.

However, some time just after this party, Phil was struck with a flu. According to newspaper reports of the time, Rizzuto "was advised by President Ed Barrow to leave without delay for St. Petersburg, Florida, where the club will open its training camp February 23." Rizzuto accordingly arranged to leave on February 16, a week in advance of his original schedule.

Camp opened on February 23 to one of the largest crowds ever to show up in St. Petersburg to see the Yanks in Florida. It was hot, sticky, and the excited crowd sat and watched a two-hour drill in the rain. The Yankees had brought down the rookies first, and they were looking to experiment with freshmen everywhere in order to shore up whatever positions they could. Rizzuto was at short, Priddy at second, Johnny Sturm at first base, and Buddy Blair at third.

"Coach Art Fletcher put the rookie stars through a drill that brought frequent bursts of applause. All four, especially Priddy and Rizzuto, made spectacular stops, catches, and plays," wrote sports scribe James P. Dawson.

By February 26, the newspapers had already conceded that the accomplished Crosetti could not compete with the youthful Rizzuto. "Crosetti is faced with a stern battle to win the shortstop position from Rizzuto," Dawson opined. Also featured prominently in the article was a picture of Rizzuto and Priddy in the throes of turning a double-play.

"I have played alongside Jerry Priddy for three years, and it would be great to continue with him on the Yankees," Rizzuto told famous sports journalist Dan Daniel of *The World-Telegram*. "He is the best second sacker I have seen. He can get rid of the ball from any position."

Daniels wrote in another article, "Rizzuto may poke an occasional homer. But he is not a four-base hitter. Priddy is. He likes the ball rather high. As a second-sacker, Jerry makes the perfect team with Rizzuto. Both get the ball away with remarkable speed. In fact, they may have to slow down just to put a trifle more on the ball."

"Believe me, it was not easy for Jerry Priddy and me in the Yankee camp," Rizzuto said years later. "For more than a week, the atmosphere was cold. I was after Frank Crosetti's job; Priddy was aiming at Joe Gordon's."

By the first week in March, Priddy and Rizzuto had secured, it seemed, starting jobs, which McCarthy himself had announced. Also announced was the sale of Babe Dalhgren from first base, which opened it up for the veteran Joe Gordon. McCarthy was pleased.

"Priddy and Rizzuto measure up as a highly satisfactory second-base combination. Like the rest of the infield, they are great throwers. Rizzuto is small to be sure, but he'll get many a ground ball a bigger fellow wouldn't get. I think too he'll leap high enough to spear line drives. And he'll get many a base on balls at the plate," McCarthy told the press.

In the first intra-squad game, Rizzuto was spiked by Mike Chartak, a rookie outfielder. And Priddy aggravated a bone bruise in his glove hand, but both were fine. Rizzuto was cut, but he was bandaged in between innings and continued to play, prompting a writer to describe his play as "snappy." Rizzuto was already so popular, the *New York Times* blared the headline, "Rizzuto Spiked in Yankees' Game" the following day.

It was around the end of the first week of March when Frank Crosetti arrived in camp.

Frank Peter Joseph Crosetti was born Oct. 4, 1910, in San Francisco. He grew up in North Beach and played sandlot baseball there and in nearby Oakland. Crosetti was second in a solid line of Italian-American, San Francisco–area born Yankees. Tony Lazzeri made it to the Yankees first. Crosetti followed him. Joe DiMaggio would follow Crosetti four years later.

Nicknamed "The Crow," Crosetti batted and threw right-handed. He helped the Yankees win the World Series in 1932, 1936–39, 1941, and 1943. In his career, he played in 1,683 games and had 1,006 runs and 1,541 hits.

ESPN.com reported at Crow's death that he "was known for old-school tactics such as stealing the opposing team's signs from the dugout, hiding a baseball to tag out a base runner, and getting on base by purposely getting hit by pitches."

"Crosetti, particularly, taught him to take advantage of his size to make his minute stature a favorable factor, rather than a detriment," Trimble once wrote. "The outstanding feature of Phil's shortstop technique is that he actually does stop the ball short. He plays a very shallow position, compared to most other shortstops, and there is no man in baseball who can play a ball as low as Rizzuto."

"If I played too deep, I'd be letting the ball play me," Scooter said. "I prefer to rush the ball and play it low. For one thing, that makes the throw to first shorter for me. I don't have the 'gun' that some others have and, by playing close, I save time. When you figure out how many runners are beaten at first by half a step, that split second I save becomes important."

"There probably wasn't a single phase of baseball that Crosetti didn't touch in his education of Phil that spring—hitting, fielding, base-running, sliding, playing the other hitters, and even the art of getting hit with a pitched ball without being damaged, a faculty for which the Crow was famous," Trimble continued.

"Crow was a great teacher and a real company man," Yogi Berra once said. "What I'll remember most about him was that high-pitched voice and how he guarded those baseballs like they were his own…. And when he threw batting practice, if you tried to hit the ball out of the park on him, he'd walk off the mound. He wanted you to work on things."

"Rizzuto obviously occupied a special place in Crosetti's heart. Not only was Phil a great defensive player, he gave his complete support to Frank by encouraging the younger players to do it 'Crow's way,'" pointed out Joe Carrieri, who was the batboy for the New York Yankees in the 1950s. Carrieri noted that Rizzuto also held a special place for Crow because he continued the tradition of great Italian infielders, dating back from Lazzeri, who played with Ruth and Gehrig, to Crosetti himself, and then Rizzuto in the late 1940s and early 1950s.

"Crow was just great to me," Rizzuto said many years later. "He taught me so much about the position, how to play the hitters, etc., and here I was taking his job. He was just a wonderful guy, and I had such admiration for him."

However, it was Joe DiMaggio who finally arrived in camp after holding out for some time, who finally broke the ice in the clubhouse for Rizzuto.

"I was coming to take Crosetti's job. He was a big favorite," Rizzuto said. "I wasn't exactly ostracized, but I wasn't accepted. I was having trouble getting into the batter's cage. After four or five days, DiMaggio came over."

"Look, let the kid in there to take his turn," DiMaggio said to the others. A quiet man, what little he said spoke volumes.

"That really broke the ice. Joe took me under his wing," Rizzuto said.

"Rizzuto, I saw what was happening out there. I could have stopped it anytime I wanted. But I wanted to see what kind of stuff you were made of," McCarthy said to Phil many months later. "The truth is, you should have been more aggressive. How are you going to deal with these other teams if you can't deal with your own teammates?"

Joe DiMaggio was actually born Giuseppe Paolo DiMaggio in Martinez, California, on November 25, 1914. He was the fourth son and the eighth child born to Giuseppe and Rosalie DiMaggio, Italian immigrants who had reached this country's shores in 1898. They moved to North Beach, a heavily Italian neighborhood in San Francisco when Joe was a year old.

Joe's father was a fisherman, a family occupation dating back generations. Giuseppe's two oldest sons, Tom and Michael, joined the family business. Joe later recalled an absolute dread of his father's work, the smell of dead fish made him sick to his stomach. In anger, Giuseppe deplored his son as "lazy" and "good for nothing."

Vince, Joe, and Dom all played sandlot baseball. It was only after Joe became the sensation of the Pacific Coast League that his father was finally won over to baseball as a passable living. There are scores of stories like this for players of Italian descent.

Tony Lazzeri had been the first great baseball star of Italian American heritage, and he had played for the Yankees. He had come from the San Francisco, California, area, too. He and Babe Ruth had been close friends and were constant companions. Ruth often called Lazzeri not by his name but by the monikers "Dago" or "Wop."

Crosetti had become the other Italian-American star of the team. The Yankees in those years found numerous Italian players to appeal to the large Italian populations in the New York metropolitan region. Tony Lazzeri made it to the Yankees first, followed by Crosetti and five years later by DiMaggio.

According to ESPN.com, "Their personalities became clear soon after the Yankees acquired DiMaggio and Lazzeri offered to drive Crosetti and the rookie from San Francisco to Florida for spring training."

"Tony didn't talk much, and DiMag didn't say a word. He just sat in the back seat and looked out the window," Crosetti recalled. "We would go two or three hours and then look at the other guy and say, 'Wanna drive?' and then we'd shift places," Crosetti said. Sometimes that was all the conversation in the car.

"Finally, on about the third day, I said to Tony, 'Let's let the kid drive.' So he turned to him in the back seat and said, 'Wanna drive, kid?'"

"I don't know how," said DiMaggio, who then went back to staring out the window.

"I don't know if he was pulling our legs or not," Crosetti said.

Frederick G. Lieb, president of the Baseball Writers Association, wrote in 1923, "Next to the little red school house, there has been no greater agency in bringing our different races together than our national game, baseball. Baseball is our melting pot." Lieb had no idea how truly prophetic his words would be when Jackie Robinson later broke the color barrier and what it would mean to the nation.

"Imagine opening your latest issue of your favorite sports magazine and seeing a story entitled, 'Watch Those Walloping Wops.' Such language is inconceivable today, yet that story, by noted baseball writer Dan Daniel, appeared in 1938, at a time when terms such as 'wop' and 'dago' routinely appeared in coverage of Italian American ballplayers, even in such distinguished publications as *The Sporting News* and the *New York Times*," wrote journalist Lawrence Baldassarro in *Nine: A Journal of Baseball History and Culture*. "The use of such ethnic epithets was only the most obvious indication of the ambivalent media treatment in the twenties and thirties of Italian American ballplayers, who were then entering the major leagues in unprecedented numbers. Stories that claimed to celebrate the sudden surge of

Italian players were sometimes written in a style that was at once patronizing and slightly derogatory. In other words, praise mingled easily with a barely masked smirk that was betrayed frequently by stereotypical depictions that suggested that these athletes, talented though they may be, were not yet fully assimilated Americans."

But to be sure, while the writers were guilty of this kind of use of language, the players themselves, including the Italian players, used the same terminology.

"The Yankees called Tony Lazzeri 'Big Dago,' Frank Crosetti 'Little Dago,' and Joe DiMaggio just 'Dago,'" wrote Joseph Dorinson in his biography of Jackie Robinson. Later, DiMaggio was sometimes referred to as the 'Big Dago.' At 6'2", DiMaggio towered over many of his Italian American teammates like Rizzuto and later Yogi Berra.

Life magazine, in a 1939 article intending to compliment DiMaggio, said, "Although he learned Italian first, Joe, now 24, speaks English without an accent, and is otherwise well adapted to most U.S. mores. Instead of olive oil or smelly bear grease he keeps his hair slick with water. He never reeks of garlic and prefers chicken chow mien to spaghetti."

Baseball reporter Jack O'Connell wrote, "Another nickname Rizzuto had in the politically incorrect past was 'Little Dago,' a derogatory term for men of Italian descent, but in a way it, too, was a compliment, since it was a play on 'Big Dago,' which was what many opponents called Hall of Famer Joe DiMaggio." And Phil proved to be proud of that moniker.

Rizzuto often said in later years that, knowing DiMaggio was backing him up in center field, he felt he could take extra chances chasing a grounder at short.

"I heard…Phil Rizzuto tell a story to a group of people at a dinner, and it's always described to me what special athletic leadership is all about, like a Bill Russell or maybe some of the other sports legends," former Mayor of New York City Rudolph Giuliani wrote. "Phil said that even when the Yankees were losing by eight runs in the eighth inning, when he ran out to shortstop in the bottom of the ninth inning, and he looked to center field and saw DiMaggio standing there, he said to himself—*we're going to win*. It was the special ability to lead by example."

Ted Williams spoke for many when he said, "Joe was simply the greatest player I ever saw, as well as the most graceful."

According to Rizzuto, "There was an aura about him. He walked like no one else walked. He did things so easily. He was immaculate in everything he did. Kings of State wanted to meet him and be with him. He carried himself so well. He could fit in any place in the world."

After DiMaggio had intervened on Rizzuto's behalf, the two became friendly. "After that we had a great relationship. I guess it was because I knew when to be quiet. Joe was an introvert, he spoke very little. He loved movies and he'd ask me to go with him. Here I was a rookie. I was in such awe of him," Rizzuto said.

Size continued to be a major concern among baseball people and sportswriters in particular. While the Yankees had publicly anointed him starter, there were worries he might not hold up under the strain of a whole season in the major leagues. Indeed, Crow remained with the Yankees as a utility infielder until 1948.

His new teammates were just as quick to help him with tips on everything from game play to off-field matters, but took great delight in good naturedly kidding him about his size. One day, while showering, Lefty Gomez raced through the locker room with a stool, and ran into the showers.

"Hey, kid, you better stand on this," said Gomez with a serious face. "You're so small, I'll bet the water is ice cold by the time it gets down to you."

"Everyone wonders about my size," he told Arthur E. Patterson. "I've had a great deal of trouble convincing people I am a ballplayer—even some managers."

"Phil will look mighty small to the Yankee fans the first day they see him," Froelich warned. "He looked awfully small to me. After he hit a 370-foot triple to right field, I changed my mind. He got big overnight."

His fielding always impressed, but his bat spoke volumes. By mid-March, Rizzuto had made a lasting impression. Headlines in New York papers read, "Rizzuto Sets Pace as Yanks Win 8–2." In one game, he singled, tripled, stole a base, and turned several spectacular plays in the field. However, this performance was overshadowed by Rizzuto's need to appear in front of a draft board because his number had come up. "Inspired, no doubt, by receipt of another message from his fans in the Selective Service Administration, the Scooter, Phil Rizzuto, projected himself copiously in another Yankee victory…. It was a memorable day for one Phil Rizzuto," lauded sports writer James P. Dawson, who noted Rizzuto's "slugging and sparkling defensive play" yet again.

Apparently, Scooter had received a letter before leaving St. Petersburg for a road trip that his presence had been requested by the Federal Government. "The letter, though it came as no surprise, caused indescribable confusion in the ranks of the Yanks."

Such was the confusion that Joe McCarthy himself called the local St. Petersburg board to find out exactly what was going on. The board assured McCarthy that the visit would be a routine one, expressing that Rizzuto needed to have a physical examination and to formally register with them.

The United States had not yet entered the war, and draft boards of the time were "lenient with deferments," noted sports scribe Milton Shapiro.

"Both my father and brother were out of work for quite a while," Phil said, "and Pop got a part-time job as a night watchman on the docks just recently. He makes only twenty bucks a week."

Thus, the case was made, as it was in those days, that Phil was practically the sole supporter of his family. He was given a 3-A classification. However, official word would not come from Queens, New York, until the end of March. Nonetheless, the press followed the entire saga as major news, with one headline actually reading in all cap letters, "RIZZUTO IS EXAMINED."

"One of the important question marks placed after the Yankees' chances in the coming American League pennant race was removed yesterday when it was learned that Phil Rizzuto, crack rookie shortstop, had been placed in a deferred class by his local draft board," reported the *New York Times*. "Rizzuto, who has been burning up the grapefruit league with timely and consistent hitting, has been placed in Class 3A because of dependents."

While Rizzuto was dazzling everyone who came to watch him, Priddy was not faring as well. "Priddy, suffering by comparison in the minds of the players and writers who recalled Gordon's amazing second-base play, wasn't as big a hit a his partner," Trimble remarked. There was nowhere but up from Crosetti's overall play for Phil, as Crosetti was too old to play effectively over an entire season. Old Marse Joe, as McCarthy was sometimes called, felt Crosetti could still be counted on as a role player, who could spell Rizzuto when he experienced an injury or a slump, and still deliver timely hitting and fielding. He just couldn't do it over the course of a long season. Gordon, on the other hand, was still a solid player, young enough to withstand a full campaign. The bad news for Priddy, though, was that Gordon was marginal at first base.

Sid Bordman, former Kansas City batboy, and then *Kansas City Star* sportswriter, once said, "Rizzuto and Priddy were good friends and a great double-play combination, but really, they were different type people. Priddy was a sort of hot dog in a way. Thought he was pretty darn good, and he was. But Rizzuto was never like that. He never had a big head."

Around April 3, Rizzuto had a bad charley horse. Remembering his ailment when he had not nursed it in the minors, special care was taken of Phil, and he was not inserted into the lineup again until April 10. This gave Crosetti a chance to prove his mettle, and he responded, thus keeping a job with the Yankees for years to come.

Rizzuto first played in front of a metropolitan crowd when the Yankees went to Ebbets Field to play the cross-town rival Dodgers in the first of three exhibition games there. The first game was on April 11, 1941. By this time, Priddy was out with a bum ankle and would miss the opening weeks of the season. Rizzuto was understandably nervous as his family and friends formed a large contingent in the stands, including 300 students and teachers from Richmond Hill High School. Though he went 0-for-4 at the plate, he walked and scored a run, and he had four putouts and three assists. He also muffed three plays. Charlie Keller knocked out a pair of homers, and the Yankees won 7–6 in the ninth.

The Yankees won again the next day despite his 0-for-5 performance at the plate. This time there were no muffs, as he handled three chances without a hiccup.

In the second inning, Joe Medwick and Cookie Lavagetto both singled to start off the inning with no outs. The Brooklyn fans began to stomp their feet in the stands and erupt with cheers and jeers. Lefty Gomez was the pitcher. He saw Rizzuto was visibly nervous. Gomez asked for time and called the stunned Rizzuto to the mound. Gomez put his arm around the young, small shortstop.

"What's new, kid?"

"Whaddaya mean, 'What's new?' Is that what you called me over for?" asked the shocked young man.

"Naw. But I hear your folks are in the stands. I want to make them proud of you. Can't you see your mother saying her to friends now, 'See! When the great Lefty Gomez is in trouble, he turns to my boy Phil for advice,'" said Gomez with a smile.

Rizzuto chuckled and finally relaxed.

The Yankees took the final game in the series, 3–0, back at Ebbets Field. Rizzuto finally broke out of his slump, going 2-for-4 and participating in two of the Yankees seven double plays that day. He also had five assists.

Then it was down to Washington for opening day. The Yankees played the Washington Senators. In those days, the Senators were the first game of the season, as the President traditionally threw out the first pitch to start the season.

"The whole season was like a fairytale," Rizzuto once said. "On Opening Day, in Washington, President Roosevelt threw out the first ball. I stood ten feet away. I couldn't believe it. Everything about my rookie year made a deep impression on me. I can remember it all: my first hit, my fist error, my first everything."

"After an interminable number of feints for the benefit of news photographers, Mr. Roosevelt finally sent the ball flying into the scrambling mass of ballplayers. This contest, at least, went to the Senators," chided John Drebinger of the *New York Times*. And thus the season began.

But not before Rizzuto and Priddy were feted by loyal Norfolk fans.

"Events leading up to the inaugural ceremonies began shortly before 2:30 when, by way of letting the sweltering crowd know something was about to happen, a huge floral horseshoe was wheeled out to the center of the diamond. It was a gift to Gerald Priddy and Phil Rizzuto, the Yanks' newly welded second-base combination," Drebinger reported.

Two young girls pushed strollers loaded with wrapped gifts down toward home plate. Each carriage was filled with wrapped boxes. Inside were dress shirts, socks, ties, slippers, pajamas, and all manner of gifts. The two were very happy. Rizzuto went 0-for-4 batting lead-off. But his picture appeared in the press the next day, as he was photographed taking the first pitch of the season. Marius Russo, one of Al Kunitz's finds, pitched a three-hitter for the Yankees, and they won 3–0.

"I remember going to New York early that year [1941], and why they didn't pull the shift on me that day I'll never know. Marius Russo was pitching, a left-hander with a sidearm fastball that sank. He was good in the Stadium because right-handers couldn't get the ball in the air off him," Ted Williams said.

That year, Williams hit .401. After he had hit a double during a game against the Yankees, he stood on second base and said to Rizzuto, "You play hard. I love this game, and you better love it, too." The two became lifelong friends. Rizzuto was also lifelong friends with both Joe and Dom DiMaggio, and Dom was one of Williams' two or three best friends for the rest of his life.

"If they seemed an odd couple, it was a genuine warmth they shared," wrote sportswriter Mike Vaccaro. Rizzuto's respect for Williams grew. When manager Joe McCarthy later insisted that Rizzuto jump up and down on the field during Williams' at-bats to distract him, the young Scooter refused.

"I felt funny doing that."

"With Priddy still nursing a lame ankle, Gordon was back at second base instead of first, while Johnny Sturm held down the latter post," continued Drebinger. McCarthy had placed Rolfe at third and, according to Drebinger, "the diminutive Rizzuto was making his major-league debut at short, and the combination clicked for three snappy double plays that made the going for Russo easier."

The following day the boys were treated to an opening day at Yankee Stadium. Again, Rizzuto did not hit but fielded well. His hometown debut went well enough, except for an incident off the field.

"I had driven my 10-year-old Ford up to the stadium from Long Island that morning," Rizzuto remembered. "It was a real jalopy—what the kids today call 'hot rods.' It was a convertible at one time but was strictly an open-air chariot by the time I got it. There was no windshield, the canvas top was in ribbons, I had pinup pictures of Hollywood babes pasted on the dashboard and even had fur tails flying from the hood.

"There was only one parking place left when I arrived, right between two big, beautiful cars. One was Ruffing's Cadillac and the other was Gomez's La Salle. I guess someone told [Ed] Barrow about it, because I got the devil from him.

"'That thing looks terrible out there. Get it out of there after today and never let me see it again. Don't you realize you are with the Yankees, young man?'"

Years later, Rizzuto wisecracked, "I should have asked him for the money to buy a better car, but I was too dumb. I'd know better now."

The Yankees lost their home opener to the Philadelphia Athletics, 3–1, on April 15, 1941.

"I got the chills the first time I saw it," said Rizzuto about Yankee Stadium's distinctive façade. "And I still get chills."

Rizzuto continued to play well in the field, but he was sometimes still tight at the plate. Eventually Priddy returned to the diamond, and the two played together.

It took awhile for Phil to get his first hit.

"I'll never forget how hard I had to work for that one. We opened in Washington that year. Dutch Leonard shut me out in the first game, and Sid Hudson did it the next day. We came home to the Stadium and played the A's. I was horse-collared again in the opener of that series, but I don't remember who pitched for them. [Editor's note: It was Chubby Dean.] Then, in the second game, Jack Knott was their pitcher. Pete Suder, my old Kansas City buddy, was playing third for them, and my first two times up he made a couple of fancy stops to rob me of hits. Then, in the seventh inning, I laced one to left field on a line, and I had my first major league hit," Rizzuto recalled.

Tommy Henrich remembered a game early in the season. Phil was playing well. But Priddy was not. He had made an error in the field and was hearing it from a local boo bird in the seats. After the inning ended, the two came into the dugout and sat near each other, as they often did. Marse Joe was seated alone on the other end of the dugout, as usual.

"Some guy is heckling him. And he comes into the bench and he's mad," Henrich described Priddy's state.

"Doggone that son of a gun up in the stands," Priddy said to Rizzuto, with Marse Joe listening. "I'd like to get my hands on him."

"What's he like, Gerry? Has he got black hair?" Scooter asked.

"Yeah, he's got black hair."

"Kind of curly?"

"Yeah, it's curly."

"Has he got a black mustache?"

"Yeah."

"That's my dad," Rizzuto said.

"That little dago's got it," pronounced Old Marse Joe loudly about Rizzuto's father.

"Phil Rizzuto lost his cap yesterday, and he didn't mind it a bit. He was pounded and pummeled, but he enjoyed it. For the little Yankee freshman had just hit his first major league home run at the Stadium," Arthur Daley wrote on April 24, 1941, in the *New York Times*. "He could not have chosen a more auspicious moment because his 400-foot shot came in the eleventh inning and gave the Yanks a 4–2 victory over the Red Sox."

• • •

Ernest Furone, a second cousin, noted that his first real meeting with Phil Rizzuto occurred "sometime in the late thirties," before Phil took up with the Yankees.

"The occasion was a wedding reception for Phil's sister, Rose, in the basement of the Rizzuto family's Liberty Park home at 64th Street and 78th Avenue, just south of Cooper Avenue," wrote Bill Mitchell in the *Times Newsweekly*, the Ridgewod newspaper. "Furone credited another relative, the late Joe Pascuzzo, with taking him to see his first major league game.... Pascuzzo and Rizzuto, who were about the same age, enjoyed a closer relationship as first cousins. In addition, Pascuzzo's mother, Rose, was Phil's godmother."

There were many photos of Phil Rizzuto that Ernest Furone kept through the years. One of his personal favorites was a group photo taken outside the

Rizzuto house in 1941. Phil brought home fellow rookie Charley Stanceu to Glendale after some of the boys from the neighborhood had gone to see Phil play at Yankee Stadium.

One of the things Ferone always talked about was the fact that Rizzuto would show up, even after Yankees games, to play softball in the schoolyard of P.S. 77 (now I.S. 77). Rizzuto was a P.S. 68 graduate. Furone remembered one game in particular.

"We had a pitcher, George McArdle, who went to P.S. 77," Furone recalled. "He was in the seventh or eighth grade, and he struck Phil out. That's all that people talked about for days and days—he struck out Phil Rizzuto."

But that didn't stop Furone from being a lifelong Rizzuto rooter. Rizzuto continued to be a local favorite and was always happy to stop and talk to almost anyone—which was one of the traits that made him such an endearing character.

"After a particularly great game in the 1941 season, a cheeky and adoring teenager—knowing that Phil Rizzuto lived in Queens—looked up his number in the telephone book," Dr. Robert Marchisotto, now of Princeton Junction, New Jersey, recounted. "Astounded when he heard a voice on the other end verifying that he was indeed Phil Rizzuto, and duly recovered from the shock, the teenager proceeded to congratulate him and talk baseball with him until his change ran out. Gracious to the last nickel! Think anything like that can happen today?"

Rizzuto's debut with the Yankees continued to draw attention. John Kieran wrote in "The Sports of the Times" column, "The rise of Rizzuto with the Yankees has added to the chatter about shortstops. There are some good ones around." Kieran extolled several shortstops, old and young around the league, but also added, "Yankee Stadium fans sold themselves in a hurry on Scooter Rizzuto, the kid from Kansas City. He can go to his right and kill off his men with a rifle peg to first base. There's a fellow named Frankie Crosetti with the Yankees who wouldn't go to waste if the Yankees unchained him from their bench. He can play shortstop with a smooth style."

"It will take some time to decide how the honors are to be divided among Pee Wee Reese, Eddie Miller, Scooter Rizzuto, and Lou Boudreau," Kieran continued. "Just now it's a matter of local option. There may be added starters in that race, too. They come up fast. Witness Rizzuto."

"How good is he?" asked sportswriter Herbert Goren in his column for the *New York Sun*. Goren was affectionately known as the Old Scout. "Can he run and throw with Reese? Can he hit with Miller? What does he do best?" Miller was a reference to Eddie Miller of the Boston Braves. "The answers as yet are incomplete. Rizzuto has shown aptitudes in all directions. He is an exciting performer and a real competitor, with the spirit of a sandlotter. He is eager to meet up with the best that others can throw against him."

"Phil has functioned best on double plays, either in starting them or in pivoting; and has yet to make a bad throw to second base. He has speeded up the team double-play production tremendously."

Mel Allen told Rizzuto biographer Dan Hirshberg of his impression of those first few weeks. "Nobody had a real perception of him until he took over for Crosetti. He did an excellent job of leading off. He was short to begin with, and most people's reaction to a smaller guy is greater, especially at the outset. He could bunt, he could steal a base. He could range well at shortstop. He got rid of the ball quickly, although he didn't have a strong arm. But he made the double play."

While Phil's fielding was impressive, his overall hitting was not. Despite a few heroics, his batting average for the season was an unimpressive .200.

By the night of May 15, the New York Yankees were 14–15 and had run up against a buzz saw of American League opponents who had clobbered the once-proud club. The Indians and the Red Sox had pummeled the Yankees, who were neither hitting nor fielding particularly well. McCarthy had been a victim of a slow start in 1940 and was fearful another slow start would thwart his chances of another pennant.

Things were so bad, Arthur Daley wrote, "The Yankees continued to move with great rapidity at the Stadium yesterday but, unfortunately, they still were in reverse gear. The most crushing defeat of a losing streak that now has reached five games saw the New Yorkers toppled by the White Sox."

"My throwing became worse, and I started pressing more and more," admitted Rizzuto in the *Saturday Evening News* years later. "Until I lost my confidence to throw out any runner."

McCarthy met with Barrow on the morning of May 16 in the Harry M. Stevens, Inc., office at the Stadium. In those days, the Stevens family handled the concessions for all three New York City ballparks.

"It's no good, Ed. Gordon's not going to make it at first base, and the kids are jittery. The others haven't got enough confidence in the youngsters yet. We are good enough to win the pennant, but we better get started. I'm going to bench Priddy and Rizzuto, put Gordon back on second and Crosetti at short, and try Johnny Sturm on first," Old Marse Joe told Barrow.

Barrow had never interfered with McCarthy's baseball decisions, and he assented.

When Phil arrived on the field at 11:30 AM to workout on the morning of the 17th, he saw Art Fletcher send Priddy up to McCarthy's office. Priddy came back minutes later, depressed. McCarthy had delivered the grim news to the youngster. Rizzuto tried to console his friend.

"I really didn't think I was due for the same medicine. I knew the team wasn't doing good, but I felt that I was just hitting my stride. And that we would soon get off on a three- or four-game winning streak, which would cure all our troubles," Rizzuto confessed. But minutes later Fletcher saw Rizzuto and told Phil that he too was ordered up to McCarthy's office.

"McCarthy asked me to sit down when I entered his office," Rizzuto recalled.

"I'm going to give you a rest for a while, Phil," McCarthy said.

"It was the first time I had ever been benched, and I had a sinking feeling in my stomach. I pleaded with him to let me stay in the lineup."

"It will do you a lot of good to sit down for a while," the manger said.

Rizzuto admitted later that he was in a fearful dread that he would be a flop in the majors after that meeting and that he would be sent down to the minors again. He was terrified.

"You'll get a different view of the game when you're sitting with the other fellows," McCarthy said, trying to soothe his young charge. "Sit near me when the game starts. There'll be situations on the field I'll want to point out to you. Just remember what you are told."

To Phil's credit, he made no excuses to the press before the game when the lineup was announced. "I don't blame my bum start on publicity," he told the press. "Sure, I saw all the nice things that were written about me. But they didn't hurt. I was pressing too much, that was all."

"Joe McCarthy had shaken up his lineup almost to the point where it couldn't be recognized. Rookies Phil Rizzuto and Jerry Priddy had been benched, Frank Crosetti was back at short, Gordon at second, and Johnny Sturm at first," reported sportswriter Louis Effrat. "McCarthy feels that Rizzuto and Priddy will learn a great deal just by looking on from the bench."

McCarthy took no chances with his young charge. He benched Rizzuto on numerous occasions. These were not punitive actions. He spelled Rizzuto when he needed rest. Crosetti played at shortstop in 32 games that year.

"Joe McCarthy was my favorite," Rizzuto recalled. "He had great power. He could do things then that you couldn't do now.... I loved him because he was a smart manager who would never embarrass you, like other managers. If he had something to say to you, he would say it in his office. He was a percentage manager who didn't platoon. You knew you were in the lineup every day, unless you were hurt. But you had to eat, drink, and sleep baseball, twenty-four hours a day. There was no messing around."

"McCarthy says I'll be benched for a week or so. He didn't say exactly. But I'm not worrying. All the fellows have told me not to let it get me down," Rizzuto told the press. "Joe Gordon told me that when he first came up, he got off to a bad start and they took him out of the lineup for a while. When he got back in, he went on like a house on fire and has ever since.... They tell me to just keep my eyes and ears open and my chin up, and I will return."

In truth, neither Priddy nor Rizzuto were the cause of the Yankees slump. The pitchers and the big hitters were sputtering, and the team was not operating to its fullest potential. The shake-up was as much for the veterans as it was for the rookies. It was a wake-up call for the team, and the team got the message.

McCarthy gave both men a chance to play in an exhibition game in late May against the Norfolk Tars. Priddy and Rizzuto both acquitted themselves well. Rizzuto hit the game-winning double to seal the 7–4 victory in the seventh inning. Once again, adoring Norfolk fans showered the two with presents before they departed for Washington for their next game.

"[McCarthy] would point things out that Crosetti was doing," Mel Allen said. "Joe McCarthy was smart in spoon-feeding Phil, letting him adjust to the major leagues."

Rizzuto sat on the bench for about a month, and in that time the Yankees came back to life. By mid-June they were 33–22 and had just come off an eight-game winning streak. In that short period, Crosetti played well. He fielded well and he hit well, batting around .300, and there was a concern on Phil's part that he would not get back to playing full time. Then Crosetti collided with a sliding base runner, which left a bad spike wound in his left hand. He was sidelined.

Rizzuto was put back in the lineup. There was no pressure now. He played alongside Gordon, who was still holding down second base with a solid batting average and was showing some decent power numbers. Priddy would be relegated to playing in only 56 games the whole year. Phil felt no need to press, as the team was now moving under its own power. If he suffered mistakes, the team was playing well enough to overcome them.

"Although Rizzuto was benched for a while," Tommy Henrich remembered, "he eventually played up to his potential and didn't allow the big-league jitters to get to him at all. But Priddy did. It wasn't surprising to me because Phil was a pretty cute and calculating guy at a young age. He knew his way around. Let's put it that way."

Together with Gordon, Rizzuto was now part of another dynamic field pair. They became well-tuned to each other.

Scooter was always popular, even with opposing players. Ted Williams stopped the kid during warm-ups just after Rizzuto got back into the lineup, saying, "It's not really as tough as it seems, kid. To tell you the truth, I was plenty scared when I first came up. But once or twice around the league—and I knew I had these pitchers licked. You'll see, it'll be the same way with you."

Phil's bat started working. He clouted a home run in a loss to the Detroit Tigers on June 21, keeping alive a streak of 17 games in which the Yanks knocked at least one ball out of the park, tying a major league record. On the next day, DiMaggio smashed another one, and the Yankees broke the record for consecutive games with at least one home run.

But more important that year was DiMaggio's record 56-game hitting streak.

"The Yankee Clipper started the 1941 season slumping. He managed a single in four at-bats on May 15 against Edgar Smith in a game the Yankees lost to the White Sox, 3–1," wrote baseball historian Harvey Frommer. "Hits in both games of a doubleheader on June 1 against the Indians moved the streak to 18. It was at 19 the next day, the day Lou Gehrig died."

"That's when I became conscious of the streak," DiMaggio said. "But at that stage I didn't think too much about it."

"Newspaper and radio began to dramatize what Joe DiMaggio was doing. Most games then were played in the afternoon, and radio announcers would routinely interrupt programs with the news of the Yankee Clipper's progress. Day and night, [the] Les Brown band's recording [Les Brown and His Orchestra recorded "Joltin' Joe DiMaggio" in 1941] was played by radio disc jockeys," Frommer continued.

"Joe never showed any emotion," Phil said of DiMaggio's streak. "But one time during the streak, he got mad. Johnny Babich of the Athletics came out in the papers and said he was going to walk Joe every time up. Joe got very upset when he read Babich's comments in the paper. And Babich meant it. He wouldn't throw Joe a strike. Joe had to reach out and swing at a bad pitch to get a hit."

While George Sisler's American League record for hitting in consecutive games was 41, Willie Keeler's mark of 44 was the major-league record.

"On June 29, DiMaggio singled off Washington knuckleballer Dutch Leonard in the first game of a doubleheader. A seventh-inning single off Walt Masterson in the second game set a new record...42. The taciturn DiMaggio became America's most famous athlete, pestered by the media, ogled by fans, adored by his Yankee teammates," Frommer wrote. "Before 52,832 at Yankee Stadium on July 1, DiMag paced a doubleheader sweep of Boston. The Yankee Clipper rapped out two hits in the first game. The nightcap was called after five innings, but DiMaggio got a hit and tied the 43-year-old major-league record of 44 set by Willie Keeler."

"Then someone stole his bat after he broke Sisler's mark," Phil remembered. "Broadcasters pleaded over the radio for the guy to return the bat. He did the next day."

In Cleveland, on July 17, 1941, DiMaggio and Lefty Gomez were in a cab headed to the ballpark. "I've got a feeling that if you don't get a hit your first time up tonight," the cabbie told him, "they're going to stop you."

"Who the hell are you?" Gomez snapped at the cabbie. "What are you trying to do, jinx him?"

"Before 67,468—40,000 of whom had purchased their tickets some time in advance—veteran left-hander Al Smith took the mound for Cleveland. It was not the Indians the throng came out to see. It was Joltin' Joe DiMaggio," Frommer wrote.

"I remember the night the streak ended. Kenny Keltner was playing so deep at third base that Joe could have bunted and *walked* to first base before the throw. But Joe wouldn't do that," Rizzuto continued. "And Keltner made two sensational stops to break the streak."

"I can't say I'm glad it's over," DiMaggio said after the game. "Of course, I wanted it to go on as long as I could." Frommer calculated the accomplishment: During the streak Joe DiMaggio had 91 hits, 22 multi-hit games, five three-hit games, four four-hit games, plus a .408 batting average that included 15 home runs and 55 runs batted in.

"Joe and I were the last players in the clubhouse after the game. Then we walked to the hotel up the street. There was a bar between the hotel and the park," Rizzuto remembered.

"I'm going to stop," DiMaggio said.

"I'll go with you," Phil said.

"No, you go back," Joe answered.

"He wanted to be alone. He went in but he came right back out. He had left his wallet in the clubhouse safe. He knew that the clubhouse was closed, so he asked me to loan him some money. I had $18 for the whole road trip, but I gave it to him anyway. I was just a rookie making $5,000 a year. I never got the money back. He never returned it. But I wouldn't accept it if he did."

Rizzuto would tell the story in almost exactly the same way to anyone who would listen how he, the young rookie, had lent the great DiMaggio money. He would tell it over and over again the rest of his life. It was always a hit at the banquet dinners.

"Finally, after sitting in the audience one evening at a banquet and hearing the story one more time, Joe, by then in his seventies, approached Rizzuto," wrote *Kansas City Star* reporter Jonathan Rand.

"I'm tired of you always telling that," DiMaggio said, waving money at Phil, getting a laugh from the audience. "Here's the damn $18!"

"I can't take it. It would ruin the story!" Scooter replied.

Coincidentally, Rizzuto's longest personal batting streak happened about the same time as DiMaggio's. "Same time as Joe did. I had a 16-game hitting streak. But nobody knew it but me and my mother. I was living at home then. Nobody paid attention to it. Including me."

The year turned out fine for Rizzuto—he had several game-winning hits, including a line-drive single against the Browns in the eighth inning, helping to win the game, 7–5, on June 25, when DiMaggio's streak was still at 37. And by July 13, John Kieran noted in his column, "By the way, those who laughed when little Scooter Rizzuto of the Yankees bogged down at the plate in the early going should take another look. The little fellow has edged into the .300 class."

On August 5, "Keller, Rizzuto, DiMaggio, and Rosar Deliver Long Hits to Rout Chase of the Senators," shouted the headlines in the sports section of the *New York Times*. But more importantly, noted John Drebinger, "When Rizzuto cut loose with his man-sized triple in the fifth, the half-pint shortstop had the distinction of becoming the fifth Yankee to reach the 100-hit total for the season. The other four who beat him were DiMaggio, Red Rolfe, Keller, and Gordon." That was pretty heady company for the rookie.

Priddy was put back into action on August 24 when McCarthy, fed up with a losing streak in the absence of an injured DiMaggio, activated the rookie. Playing at first with a revamped infield, which still also included Rizzuto and Crosetti at third base, Priddy whacked in two RBIs and helped win the game.

The Yankees took the American League pennant that year in record time, clinching on September 4. It was McCarthy's sixth pennant with the Yankees.

On September 28, Rizzuto was part of another record. In a 5–0 loss to the Washington Senators, the Yankees tied a league record for double plays in a season.

"In the third inning, the McCarthymen executed a neat double-play, their 194th of the season, which brought them into a tie for the all-time major-league record created by the Reds in 1928 and equaled in 1931 by the same outfit," wrote sportswriter Louis Effrat. "If Phil had had his way, he would have touched everyone in sight, including Gordon."

Another thing Old Marse Joe did for Rizzuto was change his roommate. Halfway through the season, Rizzuto found himself rooming with Lefty Gomez. McCarthy wanted Rizzuto to become a proper Yankee. The affable Gomez was happy to oblige.

One morning, Rizzuto was getting dressed. Gomez asked him where he was going so early.

"Breakfast. Aren't you coming down to the dinning room?" asked the rookie. Gomez picked up the hotel room phone.

"Room service," Gomez requested. "Send up a couple of breakfasts, will you? Juice, bacon and eggs, soft rolls and a pot of coffee And don't forget some marmalade." He then hung up the phone and turned to Rizzuto. "That's how you eat breakfast when you're a Yankee."

Several days later, Gomez eyed Rizzuto as they were dressing in the clubhouse. "What's the matter?" queried the rookie.

"That suit you're wearing, where'd you get it?"

"Nice isn't it? I bought it in Kansas City. First new suit I've had since I left high school."

"Yeah? Well, maybe you wowed 'em in K.C. with that thing, but you're a Yankee now. From now on use my tailor," Gomez growled. A little while later, Gomez saw Rizzuto in his jalopy, and Gomez got out of his car to walk over to him. Before he could say anything, Rizzuto replied, "I know, I'm a Yankee now." And Rizzuto promptly bought a better automobile.

By the end of the season, Rizzuto had a shiny, brand new .307 batting average to park alongside his new car. He had hit 20 doubles, nine triples, and three home runs, scored 65 runs, knocked in 46 RBIs, and stolen 14 bases.

The 1941 World Series pitted the New York Yankees against the Brooklyn Dodgers. This was the first in a series of what became known as the Subway Series World Series between the two clubs, who would face each other seven times between 1941 and 1956, though the Yankees had previously faced the New York Giants five times in the fall classic.

The Dodgers were managed by Leo Durocher. He was also known as "Leo the Lip" and "Lippy." Leo Ernest Durocher was born on July 27, 1905, in West Springfield, Massachusetts. Leo had come up as a shortstop with the Yankees in the late 1920s, and after a stint with the Cincinnati Reds, he moved on to the St. Louis Cardinals, who were nicknamed the Gas House Gang for their style of play. They were loud, brash, and played a tough, rough version of baseball. They came in spikes-up at second base, as a rule. They often did not shave and wore dirty uniforms that were seen as a sign of disrespect to other teams.

"Why, they wouldn't even let us in that league over there," Durocher said of the American League when he was with the Gang. "They think we're just a bunch of gashousers." The phrase *gas house* referred to manufacturing plants that used coal to produce gas for lighting and cooking. These factories were common fixtures in U.S. cities before the use of natural gas became more popular. These factories were known for the foul odors they emitted and were normally located near the poorest neighborhoods of American cities. Gashousers generally stank, as the smell of the factories typically permeated their homes, clothes, etc.

The Gas House Gang had numerous stars that were well trained, played hard, and won. He molded his Dodgers in the image of those rough-and-tumble teams. Durocher had become known for the phrase, "Nice guys finish last," but he never actually uttered the words. He had said one thing, and the press had turned the phrase for him. Durocher accepted the gesture.

He was always colorful from his youth to his mature years. He especially disliked the Yankees. He had played for them in his youth, and his outspokenness alienated him from Yankees ownership. It was not the Yankee way. His penchant for passing bad checks to finance his expensive tastes in clothes and nightlife sent Yankees general manager Ed Barrow to wit's end. Durocher was waived.

Leo loved opining for the press and would do so at the drop of a hat. Where McCarthy was seen as an older, quieter field general, Durocher was more of a chain-gang enforcer. He was loud, crude, and pushy. But all this bluster belied a very smart baseball mind, shrewd and calculating. To this day he remains one of the winningest managers in the history of the major leagues.

While Rizzuto would only play a minor part in this series, his defense would be of incalculable importance. And of course, this would be the first time he would be compared head-to-head with Dodger shortstop Pee Wee Reese since their minor league days.

If Durocher was loud and brash, Pee Wee Reese was known as the Little Colonel. He was considered the field manager of the Dodgers. During his career, it was Reese who would eventually give the lineup card to the umpire, a privilege usually reserved for the manager. Reese was tough, but he was nothing like Durocher.

Harold Henry Reese was born July 23, 1918, in Ekron, Kentucky. He earned the name Pee Wee early on in life, it was given to him as a young champion marble shooter. While playing for the Louisville Colonels, his teammates often called him The Little Colonel, and that name followed him, too. Eventually, after years with the Dodgers, he was simply referred to as The Captain.

Reese was born and raised near racially segregated Louisville, Kentucky. Reese signed with the American Association's Louisville Colonels at the age of 18. By 1938, he was one of the top prospects in the minors. Boston Red Sox farm director Billy Evans recommended the Red Sox buy the team. Reese was seen by Red Sox management as the new replacement for longtime shortstop Joe Cronin, who didn't have many playing years left.

As a player/manager, Cronin was not interested in retiring himself from the diamond. Reese became expendable, and so the Red Sox worked to get rid of him. Many in the league assumed he must be damaged goods if the Red Sox were getting rid of him. However, on July 18, 1939, Reese was sent to Brooklyn for $35,000 and four players to be named later.

Reese was called up to Brooklyn in time for the 1940 season. In this case, player/manager Durocher was happy to retire as a player, and Reese got his chance. Reese was an excellent fielder and hitter. He could run, throw, and catch and like Rizzuto, he was diminutive in size. Both Reese and Rizzuto were play-makers who helped their teams. Where Rizzuto was a beloved, crowd favorite, Reese was the respected, thinking man's shortstop. The two were compared constantly throughout their careers and post playing days.

Rizzuto became even more loved in the metropolitan region as a broadcaster. Reese achieved fame and respect as the captain of his team and as a staunch and stalwart supporter, companion, and defender of Jackie Robinson, especially in the challenging days when Robinson broke baseball's color barrier in 1947.

"Pee Wee helped make my boyhood dream come true to play in the majors, the World Series," said Joe Black, another of Major League Baseball's black pioneers. "When Pee Wee reached out to Jackie, all of us in the Negro League smiled and said it was the first time that a white guy had accepted us. When I finally got up to Brooklyn, I went to Pee Wee and said, 'Black people love you. When you touched Jackie, you touched all of us.' With Pee Wee, it was No. 1 on his uniform and No. 1 in our hearts."

"Our careers kind of paralleled," Reese said of Rizzuto. "I played against Phil in the Association. He played with Kansas City, and I was with the Louisville Colonels. I played against him in 1939. They had a great ball club. They had quite a few people who went up and played with the Yankees."

"Later we played in the service together overseas in a series between the army and the navy. And of course we played against each other in the World Series. I know I didn't make a big deal of who was better, and I don't think Phil did either. That made good copy for the press. The only thing I wanted to do all those years was to beat the Yankees. I wasn't concerned whether I was outplaying Phil."

The Dodgers' lineup was a formidable one.

The Series opened in Yankee Stadium, and the Bronx Bombers grabbed a 3–2 victory behind Red Ruffing's complete-game pitching and second baseman Joe Gordon's solo homer and RBI single. But it was during the Dodgers' seventh that Rizzuto had his most trying moment.

Dodger Cookie Lavagetto hit a slow roller to Rizzuto, who grabbed it and threw wildly over Sturm's head. It was a case of World Series jitters. It looked like the mistake would cost the Yankees when Reese and Lew Riggs both singled, scoring Lavagetto. Rizzuto kicked the dirt, angry at himself for allowing Brooklyn a chance to get back into the game in a tight affair.

Jimmy Wasdell then pinch hit. He got a piece of a pitch that popped up for a high foul ball. Rolfe tripped while making the routine catch for the out. With Rolfe falling, Reese jumped at the chance to race to third from second. Rizzuto, seeing the opportunistic Reese jump for third, raced his counterpart to third, sticking his glove out. Off balance, Rolfe got Phil the ball, and the shortstops slid into the base in a cloud of dust.

The umpire shouted "OUT!" Rizzuto's heads-up play had lead to a double-play that broke the back of the Dodgers' rally. The Yankees held on 3–2. Despite his poor performance at the plate, he was glad he had righted his wrong.

The Dodgers reversed the score the next day, taking Game 2, 3–2. In the game, Mickey Owen came in hard to second base, trying to take out the shortstop. It was clean but dramatic.

"Phil Rizzuto exhibited a discolored nail on the big toe of his left foot," James P. Dawson reported. Rizzuto had been seen exchanging words at the plate with Owen in the fifth inning.

"Well, you'd argue with a fellow too, if he banged into you the way he did to me and without reason," Rizzuto responded.

"We missed a couple of double plays, one in the inning when they tied it up with two runs," McCarthy told the press.

Then Richmond High alumnus and Al Kunitz protégé, Marius Russo, took Game 3 by a count of 2–1 at Ebbets Field.

While Phil did not feature prominently in Game 4, he was an odd footnote. In the fourth inning, Larry French came in to pitch. He threw just once. It counted as neither a strike nor a ball. It was a wild pitch, and with it French created a record that was "never equaled or approached," said the *New York Times*.

French replaced Kirby Higbe, who had started the game and thrown 3⅔ innings before being chased out. "French's pitch was almost a wild one. Mickey Owen blocked the ball far to his left and, finding Johnny Sturm halfway to second base and Phil Rizzuto off at second, fired the ball to Dolph

Camilli. Dolph relayed it to Lew Riggs, who threw to Pee Wee Reese, and the latter chased down Rizzuto and tagged him out." French recorded the out without throwing an official pitch, according to the scorers.

The Dodgers went into the ninth inning leading 4–3. With two outs on them and two strikes on Tommy Henrich, the Yankees were down to their last pitch.

"Rumor had it that [Hugh] Casey had thrown a spitter; Leo Durocher said no, Pee Wee Reese called it 'a little wet slider,' and Billy Herman thought that Owen might have 'nonchalanted' it. Ironically that season, Owen had set the National League catchers' record of 476 consecutive errorless chances accepted while setting a Dodger season record by fielding .995," wrote baseball historian Tom Gallagher.

Instead, the pitch got by Owen magically, on what should have been the final strike. Henrich, realizing what happened, raced for first, and was safe. The Yankees went on to to score four runs and then closed out the Dodgers, taking the game, 7–4.

"I was just as popeyed and excited as anyone—I didn't even see Owen miss the ball," Rizzuto recalled. "I had my glove and Keller's and DiMag's in my hand. I stood at the end of the dugout, ready to rush down to the clubhouse under the stands. I thought the game was over when the big shout went up because I had seen Tommy miss his swing. I was halfway down the dugout steps toward the alley leading to the locker room when I heard them shouting from our bench and turned around to find people running all over the field and Henrich on first base."

"The condemned jumped out of the chair and electrocuted the warden," one sportswriter described the Yankees' ninth-inning comeback.

"Had Owen held onto Hugh Casey's pitch, the Dodgers would have won, 4–3. Instead, the Yankees rallied to win, 7–4, and became World Champions the next day. A scrapper who batted as high as second in the order, Owen was blackballed after leaving the Dodgers in 1946 to be a player-manager in the Mexican League. He returned in 1949 with the Cubs, coached, scouted, ran a baseball camp, and was still playing in old timers' games in his seventies," Gallagher wrote.

"It couldn't, perhaps, have happened anywhere else on earth. But it did happen yesterday in Brooklyn," Drebinger famously wrote in the *New York Times*, "where in the short space of twenty-one minutes, a dazed gathering of 33,813 at Ebbets Field saw a World Series game miraculously flash two finishes before its eyes."

"Ernie 'Tiny' Bonham then put the Dodgers out of their misery, tossing a four-hitter in Game 5. Henrich homered in the Yankees' Series-clinching 3–1 triumph," *The Sporting News* reported. "The power-laden Yanks, who had scored another of their patented pennant runaways in 1941 [winning by 17 games], hit just two home runs and batted only .247 in the World Series. Still, they managed to blot out the Dodgers, who got even less offensive production [one homer and a .182 average] and a couple of tough breaks to boot."

Rizzuto was happy. He received close to $6,000 from his World Series winner's share, and in his rookie season he had played well, established himself, and won a World Series, all in his hometown, New York City. The accolades followed. The final tally of the year revealed that the Yankees had turned 196 double plays, thus breaking the old major league mark of 194—and Rizzuto was feted for that.

It was clear Rizzuto was both a crowd favorite and a hit as a ballplayer. But Phil Rizzuto was about to be knocked out flat, and he didn't even see it coming.

6

Scooter in Love and War

The hoots and hollers of the clubhouse were still in progress. The yelling by players, coaches, and executives was still ringing throughout the building, when DiMaggio approached Rizzuto in the clubhouse. He asked Phil if he was driving home after the party.

"I sure am," replied the jubilant Rizzuto. "I can hardly wait to tell my folks the surprise I figured out for them. I'm going to take my World Series check and pay off the mortgage on the house."

DiMaggio nodded with a smirk. "Just about. Well, anyway, why I asked you about your driving home, could you do me a favor and drive me to LaGuardia Airport? I'm catching a plane for San Francisco tonight."

"Sure, Joe."

"And listen, if you could do me one more favor," DiMaggio said. "I had an appointment to speak at a firemen's meeting in Newark tonight, but this thing in Frisco came up suddenly and I can't make it. Will you call Chief Emil Esselborn for me? Tell him what happened and that you'll come in my place."

"Oh, no," Phil laughed. "I'll call this chief what's-his-name for you, but I'm not making any speeches."

Phil dropped DiMaggio off at LaGuardia and went home. He called Chief Esselborn as DiMaggio requested. He apologized for Joe, but did not volunteer to speak. Instead, Esselborn prevailed upon him to come to the firemen's banquet and say a few words. Rizzuto politely refused, but Esselborn could not be dissuaded, and Rizzuto relented.

95

As his friends were gathering at the Hotel Commodore for the big party the night after, as was the Yankees' organization tradition in those days, Rizzuto found himself bewildered and alone on his way to Newark, New Jersey.

"I imagined how disappointed the men at the affair would be when a little squirt like me showed up instead of DiMaggio," he recalled. "But I didn't have anything to do, and Esselborn was sort of in a hole, so I went."

Emil Esselborn was born in Essex County, New Jersey, in 1884. The Esselborn family was a tightly connected family in northern New Jersey. Emil Esselborn was the fire chief of Newark. He and his wife, Margaret, and their children, two daughters, Cora and Florence, and one son, Walter, lived at 15 Schley Street.

"Joe had a family illness, but they were still expecting him. So I get booed," Rizzuto remembered years later. But, always a fan favorite, Phil hung around, told a few stories, and the crowd warmed up. He signed autographs, and the event ran long.

The grateful Chief Esselborn invited Phil over to the house for a cup of coffee after the affair was over. Phil accepted the invitation. It was one of the most important decisions of his life. He had taken only a step or two into the Chief's house when he saw Cora, the younger of the Esselborn sisters.

"Those legs, her red sweater, those blue eyes," recounted Phil breathlessly, even years later.

"I saw The Kid," Phil recounted, with the glow still upon him, "and I guess my eyes must have popped. I knew this was it. I went there for a cup of coffee, and I was in love before I even got into the dining room. That was all. I didn't go home for a month!"

A beautiful blonde girl with a slim, fashionable figure, Cora was easy on the eyes. Cora Anne Esselborn was born in 1920 in Essex County, New Jersey. The "Dutch-Irish beauty, then nineteen, was a knockout." And for many years after, despite the birth of four children, Cora retained her trim figure. In 1951, Trimble wrote that Cora "is the most beautiful of the ball players' wives." Ironically, it was Rizzuto and Berra, among all the Yankees, who had the most stunning wives, both of whom retained their looks well beyond their years.

According to Trimble, "Phil was bowled over and showed it. Cora, with the reserve of a correctly-reared young lady, didn't reciprocate with a spontaneous demonstration. She had heard of Phil Rizzuto, of course. Jim Ceres, an avid Yankees fan who accompanies the team to spring training each year, was dating her sister Helen. Jim and Chief Esselborn talked about the Yankees continually. Pop listened to the games whenever he could, too. Cora, however, was not really a fan...Rizzuto began a whirlwind courtship that night—it was literally true that he didn't go home for a month."

"I was not so interested in sports," Cora said years later. Cora herself was more interested in art. She had studied art in a Newark art school and was thinking of becoming an illustrator for books and magazines. "I knew there had been a World Series. You couldn't help knowing that in our house. My father ate up baseball. But the only baseball name I knew was Joe DiMaggio. I had never heard of Phil Rizzuto."

"I was walking on air when I left her at midnight," he said. "I wanted to be with her all the time. I drove over to the Douglas Hotel in Newark and took a room. For thirty days straight we had dates. And after I took her home each night, I rushed back to the hotel and called her up. Then we'd talk for three hours more!"

This was a version of the story Rizzuto told many times over, but he also told alternate versions as well, relocating the event to a communion breakfast and a pancake breakfast. Regardless of location and time, the basic story never changed, despite the storyteller's slight embellishments and changes of venue.

By early November, Phil was so in love with Cora that he asked her to marry him. Cora wisely refused. It wasn't that she didn't love Scooter, but that it had all happened so fast and they were both so young.

"I just wanted time to think about it," Cora said later. "Every girl does, I guess. I was still pretty young, and there didn't seem to be any need of hurrying. I enjoyed living at home, helping my mother. I wasn't working at a job, and it's a good thing I didn't have one. I would never have been able to keep it because I would have fallen asleep every day after those nightly phone calls."

For Phil, her initial rejection was devastating. The two were spending up to 14 hours a day with each other. He had convinced himself that Cora was the only woman for him, and he was equally convinced that he was the only man for Cora. Dejected and blue, Rizzuto packed up and went home to Glendale. But the idea of spending more time at Glendale seemed depressing to him. So he packed up his bags and drove to Norfolk. There he spent time with friends and licked his wounds.

"December 6, 1941: [The] lead domestic American news stories that day are a car crash in Baltimore, a train wreck in Kentucky, the death of a Civil War veteran, and the murder of a 12-year-old girl at a 'petting party.' In Seattle, a gun-toting burglar breaks into a local doctor's home at 4:30 AM and makes off with a purse's entire contents: 15 cents. As there are only 16 shopping days 'til Christmas, newspapers are packed with ads, which link consumer goods to the defense push ['This Christmas...Give the 8 Freedoms of (Glover) Pajamas That Really Fit!']," wrote David Lippman for the *New York Daily News* in 2007.

The *New York Times* headlined its story: "Japan rattles sword but echo is pianissimo."

Life magazine said, "Japan is desperate and getting weaker every day."

On December 7, 1941, less than a month since he had last seen Cora, Phil Rizzuto heard the news with the rest of America. The Japanese had bombed Pearl Harbor, the Pacific Fleet's largest naval base in the Hawaiian Islands.

The air portion of the attack on Pearl Harbor began at 7:48 AM. Ninety minutes after it began, the attack was over, 2,386 Americans died (55 were civilians, most killed by unexploded American anti-aircraft shells landing in civilian areas), a further 1,139 were wounded. Eighteen ships were sunk, including five battleships.

On the evening of Pearl Harbor, Lefty Gomez, ever the prankster, called Rizzuto at home.

"Phillip is in Norfolk," replied Phil's mother.

"In Norfolk!" gasped Gomez in mock horror. "Call him and tell him to take the next train for New York. We need every man we can get to help defend Yankee Stadium!"

Rattled by the news, Mrs. Rizzuto did not stop to consider the source, but instead called Cora, who was the only person Phil would listen to. It seemed Cora, who knew better about Gomez, nevertheless called Phil, glad to resume their relationship.

"I'm coming right home," Phil said. "And this time, no nonsense about us getting too serious."

Phil and Cora dated throughout the winter, until she saw him off for spring training. Once Phil returned for the 1942 season, he and Cora resumed their dating, seeing each other once or twice a week that summer. "I didn't see her nearly as much as I wanted to," he recalled. "It just wasn't possible. The team was on the road half the time, and when we were home, I had to be home early and stay in shape." That summer, Cora assented to marriage, but no date was established.

Meanwhile, Joe McCarthy, and every other manager in Major League Baseball, was concerned how their rosters would be affected. Roosevelt had publicly stated that he wanted baseball to continue for the morale of the country. But that didn't stop some men from signing up with Uncle Sam and others from being drafted.

"Joe McCarthy is confident that despite war conditions his world champion New York Yankees 'are going to be tough again,'" reported the Associated Press from Florida.

McCarthy said he thought his infield would include Rizzuto and Gordon in their previous roles, and Priddy would get more playing time. "Priddy is a much better hitter than last year indicates, and he should be a real asset to the team this year."

Rizzuto and the Yankees came to terms on February 10, 1942. "Rizzuto brought his contract to President Barrow—unsigned. After a few minutes of conversation, however, he was in the fold with permission to St. Petersburg, Florida. A week or more ahead of schedule," James P. Dawson reported. The subtext here was that Rizzuto, "the mite shortstop," had brought in his contract for negotiation. But the blustery Barrow reamed the upstart infielder, demanding he sign the contract and report to camp early, to boot. "It is presumed that Rizzuto received a substantial increase. Handicapped by colds and a sprained ankle during the off-season, he received permission to work out with the battery squad."

The reason for Rizzuto's early reporting to camp was that McCarthy thought that Rizzuto needed more sharpening. "A new style of play, which will enable him to cover more ground at shortstop, is being perfected by Phil Rizzuto at the Yankee proving grounds," Dawson continued. "Boiled down, the Rizzuto instruction is calculated to make the Scooter even faster in execution of double plays and at the same time to equip the midget shortstop with the speed to spoil drives that have been going for singles over second base."

"Rizzuto is going around drives instead of charging. Whereas Scooter used to dive with both hands, McCarthy is now training him to reach with his gloved hand on the run and, without loss of motion, to flip first. As he demonstrated today, even when he juggles a hard drive, Rizzuto still has time to recover and step on second to force a runner," Dawson wrote.

"It is something I should have known myself, but it took Mr. McCarthy to point it out to me," Scooter said. That said, he had earned $6,000 his first year as a Yankee and received $7,500 for his second season.

Scooter improved through spring training, and the Yankees opened the season at the Stadium in grand fashion. Judge Kenesaw Mountain Landis, the commissioner of baseball, handed out the World Series rings to the team, and Mayor Fiorello LaGuardia, along with McCarthy and Red Sox manager Joe Cronin, tugged on the halyards to hoist up Old Glory.

"Mayor LaGuardia, wearing the cap of Scooter Phil Rizzuto, tossed a high, hard 'first pitch' over the heads of assembled photographers to the waiting Bill Dickey." The Yankees won their opener 1–0 on Charlie Keller's fourth-inning RBI single. Rizzuto went 0-for-3 but had three put-outs and five assists in front of 30,000-plus fans, with a large contingent of uniformed men in the stands.

The Yankees cruised all season long, and Rizzuto played well. His fielding and hitting were up to the task. He had been picked for the All-Star Game yet again and had firmly established himself in the league. So much so that he drew numerous comments from Red Sox manager Joe Cronin in a lengthy interview with John Kieran in *Sports of the Times*. "It's funny how there are good shortstops all around the league and other times you couldn't find one with the help of the FBI," Cronin said.

Referring to Lou Boudreau, Johnny Pesky of the Red Sox, and Vernon Stephens of the Browns, Cronin said, "Rizzuto isn't as good a hitter as those fellows, but he's a whiz in the field.... This Rizzuto is something special. One day against us he made all of the five test plays against us. He went away, over toward third base, for a grounder and got his man. He came in fast on a slow roller. He went behind second for a high hopper and threw the runner out. He ran back and made a good catch on a pop fly. He was lightning fast as a middleman on a double play. There you are! Those are the things you want to know about a shortstop. And he did all of 'em in one game against us. The kid's a marvel!"

Cronin sang the praises of his own infielder, Pesky, whom he highly touted, but he was nonetheless enamored of Rizzuto. McCarthy's faith and hard work was rewarded by the Yankees defense in early August.

"Putting on a show of versatility that fairly dazzled a gathering of 17,956 onlookers, the Yankees tonight battered the [Philadelphia] Athletics, 11 to 2, exploded fifteen hits and, notwithstanding all this taxing effort, found the time to set an all-time major-league record for double plays," John Drebinger wrote on August 15. Of the record setting seven double plays, "Three were turned in by that scintillating keystone combination of Phil Rizzuto and Joe Gordon who at times moved so swiftly it was difficult for the eye to follow their lightning gyrations." Drebinger also noted that, "Little Phil and Joe-the-Flash moved so fast, [Billy] Knickerbocker was retired for the second out before he had come within ten feet of first base."

On August 28, Rizzuto undoubtedly had his finest game of the season against Cleveland at the Stadium. Leading off, he went 3-for-4 with two doubles and scored three runs. But more importantly, his play in the field was shut-down quality. He had two put-outs and five assists.

"Little Phil Rizzuto, the half-pint shortstop of the Yankees, moved like two streaks of lightning at the Stadium yesterday, and this singular performance...was enough to sink Lou Boudreau's Indians 3–0," went the praises of John Drebinger. "It was Little Philip, the mighty mite of the world champions, who drew major shrieks of delight from the ladies day crowd of 16,725.... And not wholly satisfied with this, Little Phil saved the shutout for [Spud] Chandler in the ninth by coming up with a dazzling stop behind second base and nailing Dean at first for the final out."

Eleven days later, Rizzuto received his induction notice. "Shortstop Phil Rizzuto of the New York Yankees has been ordered to report at the Norfolk Training Station October 10 for recruit training," the Associated Press reported on September 11. "Rizzuto was sworn in as a seaman first class earlier this week at the naval recruiting station here. After completing his recruit training, Rizzuto will report to the commanding officer of the Norfolk Station for 'such duty as the commandant of the Fifth Naval District may assign,'" the Fifth Naval District public relations office announced.

In another odd twist, Rizzuto found himself in the middle of a feature article—not in the sports section, but in the book review section of the *New York Times* that same week.

In a review of a book titled *What's Your Name?* by Louis Adamic, Rizzuto was used as an example. Adamic's book was about the Americanization of foreign names, as was practiced by many immigrants as an attempt to assimilate into the fabric of American society. Adamic's name, according to the treatise, would be Adams. The reviewer and the author's main point is that a person might go by another name, but it is that person's self-confidence that really counts, no matter the name. The reviewer pointed out that the book was more entertaining than important. "One might assume from this then, that Anglicizing 'foreign' names produces the confidence that wins pennants," wrote John Chamberlain in Books of the Times. "Unfortunately for any such theory, however, the pennant-winning New York Yankees have specialized in hiring athletes who refuse to Anglicize. The Yankees Joseph McCarthy is not known to the public as 'Joe Mack.' Nor do Phil Rizzuto and Frank Crosetti appear in the box score as 'Rice' and 'Cross.'"

Phil batted .284 that year, notching 68 RBIs and scoring 79 runs. He hit 24 doubles, seven triples, and four homeruns. He had compiled a career-high 22 stolen bases and finished 19th in MVP voting for the season that year. Phil was considered the best defensive shortstop in baseball, and he led the league with 324 putouts and 114 double plays.

The Yankees went on to the World Series that year, and they faced the St. Louis Cardinals. Rizzuto batted a lusty .381, with a slugging percentage of .524. The Cardinals were no joke, having won 106 games that year. The Yankees took the first game in Sportsman Park.

Due to report on October 7, Rizzuto said later, "I would have missed the sixth and seventh games of the Series, if it had gone further. The only ones who knew that were Cora, McCarthy, and myself."

Despite heroics by Rizzuto that year, poking his first postseason home run, the Yankees lost four games in a row after winning the Series opener, and the championship went to St. Louis. It was the first time the Yankees had lost in the World Series since 1926. But from there, Phil and Cora had dinner at Joe DiMaggio's apartment, and then flew to Norfolk to stay with Uncle Sam.

"Fred Hutchinson, the Detroit pitcher, suggested to Scooter that, if he applied in time, he could be stationed at the U.S. Navy Training Station in Norfolk, Virginia," wrote sports biographer Gene Schoor. "The idea appealed to Scooter. Bob Feller, the all-time great pitcher, and Hutchinson, as well as a number of other good ballplayers, were already stationed there. Phil didn't like the possibility of his being drafted into the Army, and the Air Force didn't appeal to him much—Phil had a fear of flying."

"It got pretty lonely during those couple of months in boot camp," Phil said. "I called up Cora and said it would be a wonderful idea if we could be married in January." However Cora had already made up her mind—she would be a June bride. In the meantime, Phil withstood eight weeks of basic training.

On January 29, Rizzuto received a real shock. Jerry Priddy had been traded. Attempting to bring in William Zuber, a big right-handed pitcher from the Washington Senators, the Senators traded Zuber and some cash for Priddy and Yankees pitching prospect Milo Candini.

"The transfer breaks up the pony keystone combination of Phil Rizzuto and Priddy, which the Yankees brought up from their farming system in 1941…but the pair were partially dissolved when Priddy could not displace the brilliant Joe Gordon at second base," John Drebinger reported. "Priddy proved a handy utility man, frequently filling in at first and third. Now he is with the Senators, and Rizzuto is in the navy."

Priddy only batted four points below Gordon in 1942, but his slugging percentage in 1942 was .381, while Gordon's was .491. However, Gordon had played in 147 games, and Priddy had only played in 59. And Gordon had finished 16th in MVP voting for 1942.

"An outspoken infielder who gained a reputation as a clubhouse lawyer, Priddy...couldn't oust Joe Gordon once he reached the majors. After criticizing Yankee manager Joe McCarthy for not playing him, he was traded to the Senators," wrote baseball historian Norman L. Macht, shedding some light on the reasons why the Yankees' brain trust let Priddy go.

In all, Priddy played 11 seasons in the majors. He had a career batting average of .265 and a slugging percentage of .373. In 1948 and 1949, Priddy came close to fulfilling his potential with the St. Louis Browns, batting in the .290s those years, and driving in 142 runs for those combined years. Four times he accumulated votes in the league MVP voting, never finishing better than 15th (1948).

Despite their subsequent separation by league standards, Priddy and Rizzuto were photographed palling around in Norfolk, for an exhibition game for enlisted men. Rizzuto was seen sitting down in a rowing tuck, holding baseball bats like oars, with Priddy laughing.

In March 1943, Rizzuto's name appeared in numerous headlines, but it was not for anything he did. His planned replacement at short, George Stirnweiss, was called up by the draft board for induction. The war was marching on.

First class seaman Rizzuto's duties in the summer of 1943 consisted largely of playing ball with the Norfolk Naval Training Station team. "They played five or six games a week, including an occasional double-header. Gary Bodie, the coach, was a Chief Boatswain in the regular navy—a hard-bitten salt who never let personal preferences [his or anyone else's] interfere with the operations of the navy," Joe Trimble wrote.

• • •

Phil Rizzuto finally married Cora Anne Esselborn. However, according to Trimble, "The Rizzuto-Esselborn nuptials...were surrounded by zany events which might have been born in the fertile minds of the Marx Brothers."

With Gary Bodie's permission, Rizzuto had set the date as the 23rd of June at Cora's behest. Bodie agreed, fully intending to honor the request. However, several weeks later the NTS (Naval Training School) put forth a lack-luster effort in a loss to the Norfolk Naval Air Station nine. Flabbergasted, Bodie immediately scheduled a doubleheader with the Air Station team for the next day.

The diminutive Rizzuto reminded Bodie that the day had purposely been left open because of his impending nuptials. All the ballplayers were intending to use their liberty to attend the wedding. Bodie rebuffed the shortstop, refusing to listen to reason.

"There's a doubleheader tomorrow," Bodie thundered, "and every one of you guys better be here to play it. That's final."

Phil was flustered. Cora, and all the Rizzutos and Esselborns were already en route to Norfolk from the New York metropolitan area. The church was reserved; the priest was scheduled. To top it off, a banquet room had been booked at the Monticello Hotel in Norfolk for the reception, and a honeymoon suite awaited at a Virginia Beach hotel.

According to Trimble, "The raw deal was too much for Phil's best friend on the team, Dominick DiMaggio, to take, however. Joe DiMaggio's younger brother, outfielder for the Boston Red Sox, quickly made a bold move."

"Coach, if Rizzuto doesn't get tomorrow off for his wedding, there won't be any game. I won't play and neither will anyone else. We strike if you try to make him show up here tomorrow," DiMaggio told Bodie.

Bodie, furious, threatened DiMaggio and others with sea duty or worse.

"Do anything you like! There's nothing in the regulations which says that we have to play baseball. Send me to sea if you want to. I was happy back in San Francisco with the small-boat detail I had. That was sea duty, of a sort. The navy brought me across the country to play baseball, [and] I didn't ask for it! Same goes for the rest of us. Show us one rule which says we have to take orders to play baseball!"

Bodie knew a complaint against the men wouldn't hold, so he backed down and the doubleheader was rescheduled and the wedding proceeded. Or so Cora and Phil thought. Now that the loving couple had cleared Uncle Sam, they had to make it past their family and especially their friends.

Before the reception at the Monticello, Cora and Phil were married in a small Catholic church just off the base. Many of the players and other enlisted men attended. Many newspapers carried the news, with the added addendum, "Rizzuto is currently leading the Norfolk naval training station baseball team in hitting."

According to Trimble, "Before the party was over and before the bride and groom were permitted to depart, three of the players and another sailor quietly sneaked off. Dom DiMaggio decided to fix up his best friend but good, and he took along Don Padgett, ex-Dodgers catcher-outfielder; Benny McCoy, who had played second base for the Philadelphia Athletics; and Morris Siegel, a sportswriter who was serving his country as publicity man for the team."

Once at Virginia Beach, DiMaggio posed as Rizzuto and was given the keys to the bridal suite. Together with the others, they went up to the Rizzutos' hotel room and started playing cards. In the meantime, Rizzuto had been pulled over by a highway patrolman.

"This is an air-raid drill, ordered by the army," he stated amiably. "All traffic must stop until we hear the all clear. Hope you don't mind if I sit here with you." It wasn't a joke. This was a real air-raid drill, with the sirens howling and an overwrought Cora crying in the front seat.

Finally, when Phil and Cora got to their room, they were shocked to find a card game going on in their suite. Rizzuto pleaded with the guys, but they scoffed and told him they would only be a few minutes longer. Eventually the men suggested they order room service, as they all needed coffee. The game continued for an hour until the gag was finally over, and they all politely thanked the bride for the use of the room, and left.

Phil bought a 1929 Ford Model A, and he and Cora lived off base in a small apartment. He bought the car from soldiers who had shipped out. It wasn't much of a car, but it allowed them the mobility they needed. The players loved to make fun of the car and often played jokes on Rizzuto, taking the car and parking it in odd places like the bullpen or tipping it upside down and walking away. One time they parked it between two trees so tightly, Phil couldn't move it.

"We had very little else to do besides play baseball," Phil recalled. "We'd report for muster in the morning, then go out and practice. If it was too hot to practice or we were too lazy, we'd go under the stands and drink beer or play cards. In the afternoon most days, we'd play a ball game."

Men bored with nothing else to do but drill, play ball, and fight the long, interminable droughts of quiet often found relief in pulling pranks, as soldiers have been wont to do for centuries.

"Hutchinson, a broad-shouldered mountain of muscle, and Vinnie Smith, of equally strong physique, used to delight in playing tricks with the car," Trimble wrote. "Every now and then one of the pair would swipe the keys from Phil's sailor pants in the locker room while the shortstop was out on the field, practicing or playing in a game. They'd drive the car right into the dugout, scattering the rest of the team, or else spin right out on the diamond with it and delight all onlookers by chasing Phil all around the field in a wild attempt to run over him."

"Lots of times I had to climb the backstop screen or dive off into a hole under the bleachers to get away from those maniacs!" Rizzuto remembered.

Once, when one of the teams was visiting, the players experienced a rain delay. They sat around in the clubhouse, recalling the "old days," when suddenly Ted Williams (among the visiting players), gave a nod to a number of others in the room. They grabbed little Phil, tore off his clothes, and stripped him down to nothing.

"While three or four held him down and kept his struggling to a minimum, Williams took a bottle of indelible red mercury solution which was used to paint parts of the body before adhesive tape wrappings were applied," Trimble wrote. "Ted then painted many kinds of messages and remarks on Phil's hide, some of them slightly obscene, and the others held him down until the red dye dried thoroughly. It was impossible to get it off with any available solution and it just had to wear off, a process which took a few days." Phil had to go home to his bride, and she saw their handiwork.

In early September, an All-Star navy baseball World Series got lots of press, pitting the training station men against the navy airmen. It was staged as a seven-game series. Pee Wee Reese was among the airmen.

In late September, the Yankees team voted small shares to those who had been drafted and could not be with them. Rizzuto, Ruffing, DiMaggio, Henrich, and others were rewarded with $500 each. The Yankees played the

Cardinals again in the fall classic, and the American League and McCarthy took their revenge in five games.

"The Rizzutos lived happily together in Norfolk for barely six months. At the end of 1943, the ball players were shipped out, in response in part to complaints from government officials about what was perceived as preferential treatment," Dan Hirshberg wrote.

Speaking honestly, Rizzuto said later of his year in Norfolk in 1943, "That was like a picnic. We had great teams. But the parents protested—they said the athletes were coddled. I couldn't blame them. Their sons were in the middle of the fighting. So all of us athletes were shipped overseas. But we weren't trained for fighting; we were trained to raise money for War Bonds.

"I'll never forget the day they told me I was going overseas. I'd done nothing but play ball all the time I was in the navy. I was in no way prepared for any kind of combat. They gave us a duffel bag with a rifle in it. I didn't know anything about rifles. I didn't know the first thing about shooting a gun.

"They gave me a bag with all these rounds of ammunition in it and a rifle, which I gave away onboard ship. I found out I coulda been court martialed for that later on. I used to get seasick on the ferry, and the people on the ferry ship used to say, 'You're going to protect us? You're going to war?' It was very embarrassing."

• • •

In January 1944, Rizzuto was transferred to Gammadodo. There he contracted malaria.

"We had been issued Atabrine and told to take it," Rizzuto admitted, "but I was too smart. I listened to some wise guys in the barracks. They said it would turn my skin yellow. I refused to take it, and the bug got me."

While quinine had been the most popular antidote for malaria for years, Atabrine was widely offered to soldiers in this theater at this time. "A synthetic drug invented by a German researcher before the war was distributed to American troops stationed on the South Pacific islands. This drug was sold under the name of Atabrine. Complaints against the yellow pills became common. Atabrine was bitter, appeared to impart its own sickly hue to the skin. Some of its side effects were headaches, nausea, and vomiting, and in a few cases it produced a temporary psychosis," wrote World War II medical historian David Steinert. "Yet Atabrine was effective, if only the men could be made to take it. A great part of the problem was that the proper dosage had not yet been worked out. In an effort to ensure that the Atabrine was actually swallowed by the soldiers, medics or NCOs from the combat units stood at the head of mess lines to carefully watch marines and soldiers take their little yellow tablets."

"It was nothing serious. Just about everybody in the South Pacific got it at one time or another, and I guess it was as common as a cold in the nose during the winter in the United States. Anyway, they sent me to a hospital in Brisbane, Australia, for treatment," Rizzuto said.

Navy life wasn't one of Phil's favorite experiences. According to sports biographer Gene Schoor, "He also got a fungus infection and the shingles, an extremely painful disease. And then he was always seasick, to boot."

"The minute I got up on my feet in the boat, my stomach would go. I'd get violently ill," Scooter recalled.

While in the hospital, Phil met Lieutenant Commander Gerry Seidel. A former Columbia Lion gridiron star, Seidel was serving as assistant to Commander George Halas. Halas was the famed Chicago Bears coach and owner who was in charge of the navy's athletic program. Soon, Phil found himself on Seidel's staff. The ex-Yankee led classes of convalescing patients. He helped lead exercises and organize games and sports for recreation and rehabilitation.

By 1944, the first of Phil's three daughters, Patricia Ann, was born in Presbyterian Hospital, Newark, on March 8, 1944. Phil, like other soldiers of the period, would not see his daughter in person for many more months and instead survived on a steady diet of photos sent by Cora. He would not see her until she was 21 months old.

"It was 1944, and Shipfitter First Class Rodgers was aboard a ship that sailed the Pacific repairing vessels damaged by war and wear," wrote journalist Mike Cassidy. "His job was to photograph the damaged hulls before crews repaired them. He says his ship was docked either off Leyte or Morotai when he heard that some sailors were organizing a pickup baseball game."

"We played two games," Rodgers recalled. "We had a wonderful time. Brought a couple of beers from the ship. It was hot, humid, but we had a great day."

Rodgers played second base. No, not on Rizzuto's team. But he played on the same field as an All-Star shortstop and baseball legend. "He was just a wonderful, wonderful guy," Rodgers recalled.

"And when the great day was ending, Rodgers gathered a few of the guys for a picture. The photo is a window into Rizzuto's youth, Rodgers says, and he knows how meaningful that window can be from a distance of 63 years," wrote Cassidy. "It was a snapshot of nirvana.... The picture meant the world to Rodgers."

"It's a sweet photograph—five navy buddies, at ease, unwinding from war, standing in front of the scoreboard at an oasis called Halas Field. Rizzuto is second from the left, wearing shorts, an open shirt, sandals (with socks) and a big smile. Rizzuto was already a star, having played for two seasons with the Yankees before the war interrupted his career."

Other servicemen also remembered Rizzuto. One of them was his second cousin, Ernest Furone. "With a memory akin to a fisherman's, Ernest Furone lamented the image that escaped him. It was the one that got away. At the time, he was serving in the Army Air Corps during World War II," wrote journalist Bill Mitchell. "He was in Hawaii, along with Joe Pascuzzo [Phil's first cousin], who was serving with the Army's tank division, when Phil arrived. He was part of a group of major leaguers who had joined the navy and were playing exhibition games to entertain other members of the armed forces. Because Pee Wee Reese was on the same team, Rizzuto played second base."

"There we were, the three of us, and nobody had a camera," Furone said. "If I could have had a picture of us that day, I'd keep it for a lifetime."

Phil was stationed in the support forces trailing General Douglas MacArthur in the Pacific Theater. "I was in the first landing at New Guinea. Later, as the invasion moved northward from Australia, we moved to the Philippines. But they still managed to hold a World Series baseball tournament in Hawaii every year between the army and the navy. They pulled players from all over the world," Rizzuto recalled. "For example, Dom DiMaggio and I came from Australia, and Johnny Mize came from the Great

Lakes. We won seven of the nine games. The admirals won a lot of money from the generals in that series."

Dom DiMaggio and Phil were ordered to Hawaii. They were placed on a high-priority flight. Two sailors, who were supposed to be going home on furlough after fighting for many months, were bumped off the flight in order to make room for the two ballplayers.

"Imagine us getting preference over them," Phil said to Dom in disgust. "These kids have been in the fighting, and we're just ballplayers. It's a bum deal."

"Bill Dickey, who was a lieutenant commander, was our manager. He put Reese at short and me at third. Pee Wee and I are the best of friends, but I couldn't believe that Dickey would do that to me."

"I don't think it was because I was a better shortstop than Phil," Reese told Dan Hirschberg. "Maybe they thought Phil could play third base better than me. I don't know. Maybe because I had been playing there for a while and Phil was flown in. We didn't think anything about it. I know I didn't, and I'm sure Phil didn't either."

"Some of those guys bet thousands," Phil recalled. "Many of the men were loaded with dough won in crap games out in the South Pacific and no place to spend it. The ball games were good ones because every player gave out. There was no loafing or exhibition stuff. We leveled out of pride in our services and in ourselves."

"I was in Australia with Phil Rizzuto and a few other players," Dom DiMaggio recalled years later. "And the saying goes that [Admiral Chester] Nimitz and [General Douglas] MacArthur bet a case of liquor." MacArthur, believing he had the best players on the island, offered the bet to Nimitz. But Nimitz went back to his headquarters and fumed. According to DiMaggio, Nimitz was determined to win at almost any cost.

Nimitz ordered his staff, "You bring the players in, and we'll take care of the paperwork later." Bob Feller was taken off the USS *Alabama*, and Johnny Vander Meer was also brought in from the Great Lakes.

"We slaughtered the army. We slaughtered them."

Phil stayed in Hawaii a short three weeks and was ordered back to Australia. Phil was shipping out behind the front, as the war progressed. He was shipped to Finschhafen, New Guinea. Several months into his service in New Guinea, Phil was promoted to Specialist, First Class, and assigned to duty aboard a cargo ship, the SS *Triangulum*. The ship ferried goods and supplies back and forth from New Guinea to the island of Manus in the Philippines.

Phil, now a petty officer first class, was in charge of a 20-mm anti-aircraft gun. "We took a few pot shots at Jap planes that were snooping around now and then, but never hit one," he later recalled.

Mostly, Phil lived a boring life, not unlike the movie *Mr. Roberts*. From time to time he met famous men, mostly boxers. "Rizzuto used his off-duty time to write letters to Mom and Cora and play pinochle with Anton Christoforidis, the fighter who had been a prominent light heavyweight before the war," Trimble wrote. "He met up with Steve Belloise, middleweight contender, and Gus Lesnevich, who came back after the war to gain the light heavyweight title."

The ship loaded combat cargo at Manus and got underway for Hollandia on November 7 to rendezvous with a convoy proceeding to the Philippines. She arrived at Leyte Gulf on the 19th and began discharging supplies. Japanese planes frequently attacked Allied shipping, and during a raid on Thanksgiving Day, four of her men were wounded by friendly anti-aircraft fire. On December 4, the ship departed the area for Australia and, after calling at Hollandia, arrived at Brisbane, Australia, on December 17, 1944.

Phil spent Christmas aboard the *Triangulum*. In January 1945, after three months aboard ship, Phil was transferred to shore duty on the island of Samar in the Philippines. By that time, General MacArthur had reclaimed the Philippine Islands, claiming, "I have returned."

Phil was promoted to Chief Petty Officer while serving at Samar. For the rest of his time there he was in charge of all athletics. "The little guy organized softball leagues, ran handball and boxing tournaments, and supervised other recreation programs," Trimble wrote. "He was too busy to play much baseball himself, beyond a bit of pitch-and-catch now and then. In his entire nineteen months overseas, Rizzuto played only one ball game other than those in Hawaii."

The Japanese surrendered in August 1945, and Phil started his long journey back home in September 1945. As the ship made way for California, the men listened to the World Series through the Armed Forces Radio on the ship's shortwave radio. The men bet loads of cash with each other on the games. Many men sought the Scooter's sage advice before laying down their cash.

"I picked Detroit to win the Series from the Cubs, and I was right in selecting the winners of each game as it was played except one," Rizzuto recalled. "I picked the Tigers in the third game the day Claude Passeau pitched a one-hitter for Chicago. Some of the guys who followed my advice on that one looked a little mean for the rest of the day!"

By mid-October, the ship had reached San Jose, California. The first thing he did was to go see a Pacific Coast League game. The next thing he did was make his way back to Camp Shelton in Norfolk, Virginia. He was officially released from the service of his country on October 28, 1945. He had spent three years as a sailor and 19 months abroad. Now he was finally going home to see Cora and his little toddler, Patricia.

New Faces, Same Old Pinstripes

It seemed to many New Yorkers that Colonel Jacob Ruppert and his heirs would own the New York Yankees for time immemorial. The Ruppert family's ownership of the Yankees was as solid, immovable, and enduring as the Empire State Building or the Statue of Liberty.

However, serious change was about to take place. In 1945, Colonel Ruppert's heirs sold the New York Yankees and its three top farm clubs—the Newark Bears, the Kansas City Blues, and the Binghamton, New York club—to Dan Topping, Del Webb, and Larry MacPhail for the whopping price of $2,900,000. It was probably the biggest steal in the history of sports.

While the Yankees, under Barrow, Weiss, and McCarthy had created a dynasty, there was no way to know if the next generation of executives and players would bring back the trophies that previous clubs had earned.

But the real mover and shaker of the deal was Larry MacPhail. MacPhail was the one who had put the deal together. Webb and Topping were wealthy sportsmen. Topping traveled in elite circles, and his life is worthy of its own biography. Topping was an heir to a tin-plate fortune. He was a consummate socialite of his time, seen at the Kentucky Derby and other prestigious horse races, polo matches, yacht races, boxing matches, golf tournaments, and tennis matches of the day. He could be found in many society pages and columns of the era, or seen at parties and swank restaurants around the city.

Delbert E. Webb was a flamboyant American construction magnate and real estate developer. Born in Fresno, California, he dropped out of high school to become a carpenter's apprentice. By 1928, he began his career as a construction magnate in Phoenix, Arizona. He received many military contracts during World War II, including the construction of the Japanese relocation center known as Poston War Relocation Center near Parker, Arizona. He played golf with Howard Hughes, Bing Crosby, Bob Hope, and Robert and Barry Goldwater. In 1948 in Tucson, Arizona, Webb was contracted to build 600 houses and a shopping center called Pueblo Gardens. This was a prelude to his most famous construction project, Sun City, Arizona, which was launched January 1, 1960, with five models, shopping center, recreation center, and golf course. The opening weekend drew 100,000 people, ten times more than expected, and resulted in a *Time* magazine cover story. Webb also built the Las Vegas Flamingo hotel for Bugsy Siegel. He later opened his own casinos, the Sahara and The Mint.

By contrast, MacPhail was a consummate, hard-working baseball executive. MacPhail was well traveled and successful. He had managed the Cincinnati Reds and the Brooklyn Dodgers. He was known for innovations, and he would make many of the decisions going forward with the Yankees. He had helped shape this deal so he could craft and mold this franchise in a new direction. With MacPhail at the helm, the Yankees would help to usher in modern baseball.

"MacPhail was a colorful man, a man on the move, and a man who liked action," wrote sports biographer Gene Schoor. "He wasn't afraid of making changes, and he was quick to innovate. He also had a genius for making money."

MacPhail took over the Yankees in January 1945 but could not do much with the 1945 season. Baseball had been depleted of all its major stars, and the professional baseball world was turned upside-down, which was confirmed when the usually hapless St. Louis Browns won the 1944 pennant.

The Yankees finished fourth in 1945, Marse Joe's worst finish in his Yankees career. When the real players returned in 1946, MacPhail made his imprint on this club.

MacPhail didn't hesitate to make changes. He began new construction in the winter months of 1945 and 1946 and renovated the box-seat sections of the stadium. He made them larger and more comfortable. He insisted the team be the first team to travel by airplane, a concept few liked, especially Rizzuto. He was the first executive to place a bar and cocktail lounge in a Major League Baseball stadium. He installed the best and newest equipment for nighttime baseball. He saw all of these things as money-making opportunities that would swell the coffers of the Yankees organization—and they did. He would make the Yankees organization more money than it had ever made.

The other place he identified as an opportunity to realize more money, was by manipulating the spring training schedule. While at Cincinnati and with Brooklyn, MacPhail had held spring training in exotic climates. The Reds had trained in Puerto Rico, and the Bums had trained in Havana, Cuba. He did this because these teams would be seen as major draws in these new places, and he could make excellent deals with cities that would be willing to make many concessions in order to get in a major league club for six weeks during the prime vacation and tourist months. Great hotel deals, better percentages of gate receipts, and nice warm weather made for an inviting combination.

Many teams of the era used spring training and barnstorming before the season to add new revenue streams outside of regular-season baseball schedules. MacPhail would work the teams extra hard. The stadium improvements could be paid off, in part, by these little excursions. And the more exotic the location, the more press they seemed to garner. In the end, MacPhail proved right. The Yankees made more money than ever that year and became the first team in Major League Baseball to post an attendance record of more than 2,000,000 fans for the year. It was a remarkable attendance record and a testament to MacPhail's innovations.

MacPhail wanted spring training to start early. What with the players who were wartime holdovers and regular season stars from before the war, both men agreed an earlier start would help McCarthy winnow a final roster from a squad of more than 60 players. And with the previous season's disaster behind them, both men wanted a fresh new start. The beginning of spring training was scheduled for February 10, 1946. The Yankees would practice in Panama early, then return to the states for spring training.

"A lot of the boys have been away from baseball for a couple of years, and they'll need the extra weeks to get in shape," MacPhail announced to the press.

The Yankees were a hit in Panama. And Panama was a hit with the Yankees. Citizens of Panama City and U.S. nationals working in the Canal Zone flooded the ball park and thrilled to the towering home runs of DiMaggio and Keller. The fielding practice sessions of Gordon and Rizzuto, which were scheduled at the end of each session like gymnastic circus acts, were intended to dazzle the attending fans—and they did. The fielding coaches would hit balls far and wide, and Rizzuto and Gordon would practice their skillful ballet, nailing phantom runners two at a time with every hit.

"The Gordon-Rizzuto combination performed of old around second, spearing line smashes and executing imaginary double plays," wrote baseball scribe Dawson, who referred to their performance as "sparkling." Dawson also noted that Rizzuto broke his bat singling halfway through the workout. "Because of his service activity and pre-camp Florida training, he is in tip-top shape, slamming the ball and playing short like in mid-season. He is in tip-top shape."

Phil was dubbed by the local Panamanian press as "La Cucaracha," meaning "the cockroach." This was meant as a compliment because of Rizzuto's size and absolute lightning speed. Phil became a local fan favorite.

When Phil arrived in Panama, he was in great physical shape. He had rented a beachside cottage in January in St. Petersburg, Florida, where he and Cora and Patti could spend time together. Still rail thin from the effects of malaria, he rested, ate well, and worked out, gaining back 10 pounds of strength and a certain amount of mental happiness.

After months and months of boredom due to the war, many of the Yankees worked hard during the day in the scorching heat and partied hard into the night. While many players drank rum, danced the rhumba, and found romance in the tropical breezes (one married Yankee got temporarily engaged and another was found driving around in a big, beautiful, brand-new Cadillac with a General's daughter still in it), Phil remained the same.

Phil was never one much for going out at night. He did not like to stay up late or drink to excess. He was not one for nightclubs. He liked going to the movies, and throughout his career he would find friends who would join him at the movie houses.

Phil was not at ease in Panama, perhaps because he was so far away from Cora and his new little girl. Maybe he was still feeling the effects of the various and sundry illnesses that had afflicted him during his 19 months of duty abroad. Regardless, while teammates luxuriated in shopping, game fishing, sunbathing, and the indulging in the local night life, Phil started to wear down.

Rizzuto started slowing down and began to experience dizzy spells. Then he experienced sudden weight loss. Something was wrong. The malaria had returned. Once a person contracts malaria, bouts with it may occur any time that person ventures into a tropic climate.

Rizzuto was sidelined by doctors, who gave him drugs to help ward off the illness, but his strength remained sapped. He spent the rest of the team's Panamanian sojourn on the bench.

With the Panama leg of spring training behind them, the Yankees returned to Florida to compete in that season's regular schedule of spring training tune-up games. McCarthy, seeing that Rizzuto was still not fully recovered, kept him on the bench.

On the other hand, the rest of the team was in mid-season shape. They took the Grapefruit League by storm, posted 28 wins that spring, and were unanimously anointed leading contenders to take the crown. But Rizzuto still struggled, and there were soon worries. MacPhail was more nervous than McCarthy, and as a man of action MacPhail could not help himself. Just before an exhibition game against the St. Louis Cardinals, MacPhail called a press conference.

"I want to announce that the Yankees organization has acquired Bobby Brown, a shortstop who batted over .400 at Stanford University, the University of California Los Angles, and Tulane," MacPhail announced to the press. "Seven other clubs wanted him. Two of them outbid us, but we got him." The Yankees paid Brown a bonus of $50,000.

Will Wedge of the *New York Sun* asked MacPhail, tongue firmly planted in cheek, "Is it all right to write that Phil Rizzuto's job will be safe for another two weeks?"

"We don't need any more of your sarcasm, Mr. Wedge," replied the irritated MacPhail.

"I had always kept close watch on all the shortstops in the Yankee chain, looking out for the one who might someday take my job," Rizzuto admitted. "I remember the first real challenge I had was from Bobby Brown, who had two great years in Newark. Then when I saw him in spring training, I knew he'd never make a major league shortstop. Among other things, he couldn't coordinate his feet. In fact, he had to work very hard to accomplish what he did, and I have always admired Bobby for the way he worked at becoming an acceptable major league third baseman."

"When Brown showed up the next day, it was obvious Scooter had nothing to worry about," wrote sports biographer Gene Schoor.

"$50,000! Holy cow! That's a whole lot more money than they ever paid me. I sure was born too soon," Scooter reportedly said.

That was the highlight of camp. The 1946 season began with a foregone conclusion. The Yankees were winning. They had exerted themselves too soon, and it caught up to them. Some continued the partying they practiced so well in Panama. Others wore down. And more significantly, the Boston Red Sox won 40 of their first 50 games and ran away with the season.

"I was born and raised in the Bronx, just a few blocks north of Yankee Stadium. In 1946, when I was 12, I heard that you could wait around after the game and see the players leave the clubhouse. There might be eight or nine kids waiting. No police, no barricades, just players walking to the subway, signing autographs. Sad that those days don't exist any longer for kids to interact with the players, but times change," James Rielly remembered. "My distinct memory of Scooter over the four years that I showed up outside the stadium after every home game was that he always signed autographs, never said 'no,' and always stopped to chat with the people outside the Stadium. He was like a kid himself and loved the interaction. A different guy on the field…a no-nonsense, hard-nosed warrior."

By May 24, Old Marse Joe, as they called McCarthy, tendered his resignation.

"MacPhail and McCarthy were as insoluble as oil and water," wrote Arthur Daley in his Sports of the Times column. "It was a mere statement of an obvious fact.... That they'd come to a parting of the ways was absolutely inevitable." The new skipper that MacPhail named was player/manager Bill Dickey. Dickey had returned from the war, but he had left his talents elsewhere. He would go on to make more contributions to the Yankees organization, but managing the team would not be one of them. The Yankees finished abysmally, and Dickey was relieved before the end of the season. The Yankees were relieved when the season was over.

The entire team hit poorly, evidenced by DiMaggio's disappointing .290. It was the only year in his career he hit below .300. Phil hit a meager .257, but at mid-season his average had been a paltry .222, so he rebounded nicely in the later half of the season.

For Phil there were two other notable travails that season. On July 17 at Yankee Stadium, more than 30,000 fans saw St. Louis Browns hurler Nelson Potter hit Rizzuto with a pitch that sailed. It hit Rizzuto in the left temple. Rizzuto collapsed where he stood like a man who had been shot. The Stadium went silent.

"Phil was carried on a stretcher from the field to the dressing room, where examination by Dr. Robert Emmett Walsh diagnosed the injury as a concussion. Ice packs were applied until an ambulance arrived to remove Rizzuto to a New York Hospital," reported the *New York Times*. While he experienced some dizziness at the time, he recovered soon enough.

Mexico City in a Cadillac

Dashing and ambitious, Jorge Pasquel was a wealthy Mexican businessman rumored to be worth $60 million in 1946 who wanted to bring quality American major league talent to establish the Mexican Baseball League. In the early spring of 1945, Pasquel sent his brother, Bernardo, and other emissaries to engage the services of returning baseball veterans in an attempt to stockpile talent in his league.

Throughout the early parts of the campaigns, offers were made in hotel rooms or secluded restaurants where Bernardo or other Mexican businessmen proposed obscene salaries to American players to entice them to jump leagues.

"Jorge Pasquel, one of the richest men, and probably the most flamboyant in Mexico, had decided to start a new war—one in which he would pit the world's most important commodity, the American dollar, against the baseball empire of the United States. Old Jorge, a swashbuckling merchant prince, had an overpowering ambition to make the Mexican League superior to the National and American with the ultimate goal of having his native land and its league included in the World Series," Joe Trimble wrote. "Jorge and his brother, Bernardo, had amassed vast fortunes south of the border by various dealings in imports. They, through the grace of President Miguel Aleman and the Mexican government, had become multi-millionaires."

After Rizzuto's successful Panamanian debut, and being a fan favorite with New Yorkers, the Scooter became a major target for the Mexican Baseball League. Phil was making $7,500 a year. And with Brown's signing for $50,000, there is no doubt that Rizzuto was ripe for the picking. There had been rumors that Mickey Owen of Brooklyn was signed for $90,000 to jump. Rumors were rampant that other stars were also making the switch.

Major League Baseball had caught wind of the brewing scandal and had warned executives and players. Being blackballed would be the price players would pay for considering making the jump. But Rizzuto decided to listen.

"Was it serious? Man, I practically was right in the Mexican League, and if that Bernardo Pasquel had kept his trap shut and had not announced that he had signed me up while I was still in New York, I would have undoubtedly gone down there—against the much better judgment of Mrs. Rizzuto. I haven't disputed that judgment since," Phil told Dan Daniel in *The Sporting News.*

On February 19, 1946, New York Giants outfielder Danny Gardella became the first major leaguer to announce that he was jumping to the Mexican League. Their generous salaries also attracted other major leaguers, including pitchers Sal Maglie, Alex Carrasquel and Max Lanier.

Time magazine reported, "The Pasquels, who own two of La Liga Mexicana's eight teams and control the others, rustled off with second baseman George Hausmann and two other New York Giants."

The Pasquel brothers vowed to bring the likes of DiMaggio, Williams, and Musial to the Mexican League. Though the Pasquels never approached DiMaggio, it was rumored at the time that they had offered Williams $500,000 to jump. This is what they told other stars, as well. But the Pasquels did not go in unarmed. They had plenty of money to throw around, and they had sage legal advice. The Pasquels' lawyers reported correctly that the "reserve clause" could be challenged in court. It was in every player's contract. But it was clear, though the league rattled it like a saber, that it was a hollow threat of lawsuits that would never materialize.

"The reserve clause bound a player to his club for the year following the contract—he could not seek other employment in baseball but could be fired on short notice," Trimble wrote. All of that was immaterial to Rizzuto.

"You will recollect the 1946 season," Rizzuto told Daniels. "McCarthy quit on May 24, Bill Dickey took his place. Things were topsy-turvy. We finished third...I was worried to death, insecure, hounded, and harassed by the fear that I was washing up. No foolin'."

"They went after George Stirnweiss and Phil Rizzuto in Panama," Gene Schoor wrote. They filled the ballplayer's heads with promises of riches and rewards and glory. "Neither Phil nor Stirnweiss said no to the proposition, but they didn't say yes, either."

Both players decided to stay with the Yankees for the short term. They would see how the season would progress, and maybe the problem would go away, or it wouldn't. Stirnweiss was the batting champion of the depleted league in 1945. Rizzuto was already a genuine star.

Spring training ended in Florida, the season opened, and the Mexican offers had been seemingly forgotten when suddenly, in the early part of the season, a man approached Rizzuto in the parking lot at Yankee Stadium. Three men were sitting in the back of a car, and Rizzuto got in. He demanded they leave the parking lot, sure that Larry MacPhail would learn of their contact, or worse, Happy Chandler, who had decreed that any players who leapt to the Mexican Baseball League would be banned by Major League Baseball for the rest of their lives.

They drove underneath the West Side Highway, and the automobile came to a stop. The spot seemed dark and gloomy—forbidding to the young Rizzuto. Bernardo got out of the car, and Phil followed him. They stood next to one of the big support pillars as the cars raced overhead. Bernardo reached into his pocket and pulled out a fat wad of bills.

"They were all thousand dollar bills. At least they were all thousand dollars bills on the top of that wad," Scooter later reported. Bernoardo shook the hand full of thousand dollar bills in Phil's face, telling him he should pack up his family today and move to Mexico. He would be a bigger star in Mexico than he was in New York or even Panama. He would make thousands and thousands of dollars. The Pasquel brothers would pay for the move. They would set him up in a beautiful home.

"Call McCarthy now, and tell him you are home in bed with a bad cold. Then we will go down the street, buy a Cadillac, drive down to Mexico, and install you in the Mexican League. Once down in Mexico, you will call up McCarthy and tell him the truth," Bernardo told Rizzuto.

Phil said he would think about it and demanded they get back in the car. On the way back to the Stadium, Bernardo offered him a $15,000 contract, twice what he was making, plus a $10,000 signing bonus. Phil said he would need to talk it over with Cora.

Cora objected immediately and steadfastly, although she understood her husband's insecurities about the season and that the high salaries were enticing. She told him that they should not respond to the Pasquels.

"I figured he was doing me a big favor. I was over 21 and able to make my own decisions, and it was no case of a man from Mexico luring a green rookie off the path," Rizzuto said later. He was 28 years old at the time, and McCarthy had not yet left the club, but rumors were swirling. "Cora opposed the scheme. She said I would do better sticking with the Yankees. She protested about uprooting the family. She made me stop and think."

Rizzuto's mother also chimed in, voting nay, saying "You'll be like a man without a country. How can you bring up the children that way? It would be a disgrace."

The next day, while Phil was not at home, two men came to the door. One was a Newark newspaper man wanting to know if it was true that Phil was jumping to the Mexican League. Cora told the man emphatically, "No!"

The second man at the door was George Weiss. He came to ask if it was true, that Phil was leaving for Mexico. Cora told him no, but that they had offered him significant money. And that a raise might be an incentive for him to stay. Weiss said he was not authorized to offer a raise. But Cora also knew that the conversation would get back to MacPhail. It was as good as talking to MacPhail himself.

Events were now moving quickly. Phil and Cora had been invited to the Waldorf Astoria, to dinner in the Wedgewood Room with both Bernardo and Jorge Pasquel. Later, court records would show as reported in the newspapers, "Pasquel's testimony told of a dinner party with Rizzuto in the Waldorf-Astoria on May 1 or 2."

"Pasquel wined and dined us at the Waldorf," Rizzuto said. "It was some dinner. Off gold plates we ate, I tell you. Champagne and thick steaks. Anything I wanted. They had orchids for Cora. And Pasquel wore a diamond the size of an egg. He caught me staring at it and he wanted to give it to me. I had a hard time shaking my head."

That evening the Pasquels got Mickey Owen on the phone for Rizzuto. "Owen told me how wonderful everything was down there. He made it sound like the greatest thing in the world. I was impressed, but I keep thinking now that maybe he had a gun to his back!" said Rizzuto years later.

The entire evening, a woman talked to Cora about how wonderful shopping was in Mexico City and what a wonderful lifestyle could be had. Then the capper to the evening was Jorge's story how he had once shot a man to death. Cora was sickened by the story and wanted to leave. The Pasquels wrote down their top offer to Phil—$100,000 over three years. Rizzuto took the menu with him.

Off to a slow start, and with the Yankees in such turmoil, Rizzuto was considering the move. "I admit that I was ready to go, right then and there. I was really afraid that this was my last year with the Yankees anyway."

Bernardo testified in pretrial hearings, according to reports that "The next day Rizzuto had telephoned to say that if he received $15,000 for signing a contract, he would go to Mexico."

However, two things bothered Rizzuto. Bernardo's insistence to lie to McCarthy, who had endeared himself to Rizzuto and vice-versa, rubbed Rizzuto the wrong way. The second thing that pushed Rizzuto to make a decision was that Bernardo forced the issue by announcing the next day that Rizzuto had signed with the Mexican Baseball League.

George Weiss paid a second visit to the Rizzuto household. Both Phil and Cora were at home. Phil and Cora listened. Weiss, knowing of the fondness that existed between McCarthy and Rizzuto, had insisted that he was there at McCarthy's insistence. Phil and Cora knew better. Weiss recounted all the reasons Phil should not leave. However, the more threats the Yankees and Major League Baseball made, the more Rizzuto leaned toward leaving.

"Do me a favor," Weiss said, "Don't leave before you see MacPhail."

From the moment Weiss left their home, Phil and Cora now knew they were in the driver's seat between the two leagues.

On May 3, Rizzuto told the Pasquels that he was "undecided." He also had a meeting with MacPhail. In his usual blustery manner, MacPhail thundered away. And Rizzuto let him until he wore himself out. "He asked me to sign a complaint against the Pasquels so that he could get an injunction," Phil recalls. "I refused. I told him that they were only trying to help me by giving me more money for playing ball and that, if he wanted to, he could do the same thing."

MacPhail insisted that Rizzuto sign a complaint the Yankees were taking the Mexican League to court. They couldn't do it without Scooter's signature. MacPhail threatened Rizzuto that if he didn't sign it, he would be suspended, or worse, banned. In that case, countered Rizzuto, he would take the Mexican offer, and end up with more money.

When MacPhail had finally finished, Rizzuto said, "I'll stay if you give me a $10,000 bonus."

MacPhail countered $5,000. Phil held firm. MacPhail finally offered $5,000 at the beginning of the season, and $5,000 at the end of the season."

Phil had won. "It was really Cora's victory," Gene Schoor wrote.

The Yankees eventually brought a suit against the Pasquel brothers, and left Rizzuto's name off the injunction to save face for both Rizzuto and the team. But word was soon out that Rizzuto had attempted to jump. All the newspapers tracked down the story, which seemed exotic and full of cloak-and-dagger dealings.

Many of the American players from the major leagues who went down to Mexico were quickly disappointed. Many of the parks were no better than stadiums they had played in during their minor-league careers. The buses were in poor shape, and the road trips were difficult. According to Sal Maglie, "The buses were driven by madmen. They used to push those old wrecks as hard as they could on those narrow, winding roads in the mountains."

In short, many ballplayers tried to get back to the majors almost immediately. Few succeeded in getting back to the majors at all.

By today's standards, the journalistic coverage of the time smacked of American Imperialism. Newspaper accounts of Jorge Pasquel often painted the international businessman as a rogue, despite his Hollywood good looks and the list of international beauties he dated. They made him out to be some kind of Mexican bandito, like a character out of *The Treasure of the Sierra Madres.*

Today, Pasquel is thought of as an innovator and a hero.

"Mexican businessman Jorge Pasquel was an innovator and an earlier version of George Steinbrenner. In the 1930s and '40s, he handed out huge contracts and brought top Negro League and Major League players to play in the Mexican League," wrote Conor Nicholl for Major League Baseball in 2007. "The genesis formed a safe haven for Negro League players, created professional baseball's first integrated league, and made Pasquel one of the most important persons in the desegregation of Major League Baseball."

"Jorge Pasquel was an extremely wealthy and ambitious entrepreneur who understood well before his counterparts in the U.S. that white, black, and Hispanic ballplayers could get along as teammates and competitors while playing brilliant and profitable baseball," wrote Bill Littlefield of NPR's *Only a Game.* "As a result of Pasquel's efforts from the late '30s through the late '40s, such worthies as Satchel Paige, Josh Gibson, Martin Dihigo, and Ray Dandridge enjoyed opportunities in Mexico that were denied them in the

U.S., where the Major Leagues were completely segregated until 1947, and partially segregated for several years after that."

Littlefield continued, "Major League Baseball's movers and shakers, among them Brooklyn Dodgers General Manager Branch Rickey, regarded Jorge Pasquel as a pest. As far as Rickey was concerned, he had every right to sign Jackie Robinson without compensating the Negro League team for which Robinson was playing."

This event was a telling one. While Rizzuto pretended to be befuddled and confused by all the back-and-forth goings on, he played the situation for all it was worth and was as adept at poker playing as Pasquel or MacPhail. And it also said a lot about Cora, who, while stunningly beautiful, had a head for business where her husband was concerned. This ability would stand them well in future years.

Seems Like Old Times

The Yankees had done poorly and ended 1946 in a mess. New York was managed in turn by Joe McCarthy, Bill Dickey, and then Johnny Neun. Neun was then replaced the next year by Bucky Harris.

Stanley Raymond "Bucky" Harris was born on November 8, 1896, in Port Jervis, New York, to Thomas Harris (who hailed from England or Wales) and Catherine (Rupp) Harris who had come from Hughestown, Pennsylvania. A second baseman by trade, he played for the Washington Senators from 1919 to 1928 and ended his playing days with the Detroit Tigers, for a total of 11 games in the 1929 and 1931 seasons. However, by 1924 Harris was one of baseball's "boy managers," becoming a player/manager of the Washington Senators. In his first season as manager, he had taken the Senators to a pennant and won a World Championship. His team took the pennant the following year, as well.

"Despite the many losing campaigns, Harris was regarded as a knowledgeable manager and was extremely popular with his players. His patient, gentlemanly manner inspired such loyalty that when the Phillies fired Harris in mid-1943, his players threatened to strike," wrote Jim Langford, a baseball historian.

"He studies baseball as a medical student studies anatomy. He seems to be able to get the best out of mediocre talent," wrote sports columnist Quentin Reynolds, who was also host of the radio show, *The Wonderful World of Sport.*

This was the first step in the right direction for the 1947 season. Things had gone so badly in 1946 that many of the big stars re-upped before Christmas, led by the usually lagging DiMaggio. With DiMaggio first in the contractual clubhouse, the rest of the team quickly followed suit behind him. According to reports, by November 29, fourteen players had already signed their contracts.

Spring training moved along without incident for Rizzuto. Harris, whose coaches included Chuck Dressen and Johnny "Red" Corriden, worked the rookies hard but went relatively easy on the veterans. While McCarthy had lots of rules, Harris was a little more player friendly in current parlance. And the veterans were a little more careful about wearing themselves out, both on and off the field.

Just after Lincoln's birthday the team took off, playing games in Puerto Rico, Venezuela, and then finally moving back to St. Petersburg for the bulk of spring training.

According to Trimble, "Rizzuto, under the Harris system, prospered. He kept his weight at 160 pounds, rested frequently, and paced himself. Phil, who never is far out of shape, took good care of himself day by day and never knew a moment of fatigue. He did have one worry, a soreness in his throwing elbow while the club was at St. Pete in late March but that disappeared after a couple of weeks."

"Bucky Harris was a great manager, too," Rizzuto recalled. "He was my second favorite. He and Mac were the same. They knew you were big leaguers. They weren't after you all the time. They knew you were entitled to a bad play. Not a *dumb* one. Then they'd get on you."

It was a good spring, and the Rizzutos were expecting another child. Cynthia Ann was born on April 19, 1947. Phil was not with his wife. He was down in Washington, D.C., warming up before the season opener when he found out about the birth of his second child.

The team finished 97–57, taking the pennant with Joe DiMaggio named MVP. Phil Rizzuto played in 153 games. He batted .273. He usually batted first in the lineup, but he still managed to drive in 60 runs. He hit 26 doubles and nine triples.

Rizzuto had several games in which he excelled to the extreme. "The Yankees favored their pitchers with errorless support, featuring a snappy double-play combination in Stirnweiss and Phil Rizzuto," Louis Effrat wrote, about a game on May 29 in which Rizzuto had three put-outs and three assists, including two double plays.

On August 20 at Briggs Stadium versus the Detroit Tigers, Rizzuto ended a three-hour, 11-inning marathon by doubling home Lindell to win the game 14–13. It was his second RBI of the night. Rizzuto had gone 3-for-6 at the plate, and had five put-outs and four assists.

That year saw something of a ritual at Yankee Stadium. After a win at the Stadium during that season, either Harris, one of the players, or one of the writers who traveled with the team, would raise a glass after all had been served at the press bar and offer a toast. They saluted the hero of the evening's victory.

And almost as regularly, Harris would raise his glass after the first toast and offer, "And don't forget little Phil!" Harris was amazed by Rizzuto's defense and speed.

"He pulls a miracle out there each day," Harris said. "I wouldn't trade him for any shortstop in baseball. I don't care if he only hits .250, it's what he does with his glove, the way he saves our pitchers, that makes him great. I don't believe I have ever seen a game in which he did not make one great play."

Corriden also piled on the praise, saying, "I've been in baseball for over 40 years, and I'll be darned if I ever knew a ballplayer with the priceless, perfect disposition of Rizzuto. Phil's a sweetheart. He means a tremendous lot to the team because everyone likes him and responds to his cheery manner and is the better for it."

Corriden continued, "Phil, you might say, is the spark plug of the Yankees. He's the happy balance wheel which keeps the team spinning along merrily and successfully. His value can't be measured in mere fielding and batting figures. It's something that goes deeper. Growls and gripes in the locker room after a bad day disappear quickly with Rizzuto around. No team can get into the dumps with Phil to pep things up. I know Reese and admire him. But I have to go for Phil because of his disposition and the way he has of binding the Yankee infield into a perfect unit."

The 1947 World Series matched the New York Yankees against the Brooklyn Dodgers. This was the first World Series to feature the sensational Jackie Robinson, the first player to break the color barrier in Major League Baseball. It was also the first Series to be broadcast on television, although the signal was limited to New York City, Philadelphia, Washington, D.C., and Schenectady, New York.

The series saw the Yankees win the first two games at the Stadium. However, the Yankees faltered at Ebbets Field. They lost Game 3, 9–8, and then lost a heartbreaking Game 4, forever known as the Cookie Game. Brooklyn's Cookie Lavagetto lined a ninth-inning base hit against Yankee pitcher Bill Bevens, who was one out away from pitching a no-hitter, scoring two runs for Brooklyn in an unlikely 3–2 victory for the Bums from Brooklyn.

"Wait a minute.... Stanky is being called back from the plate and Lavagetto goes up to hit.... Gionfriddo walks off second.... Miksis off first..." said Red Barber in his famous call of the game that day. "They're both ready to go on anything.... Two men out, last of the ninth...the pitch...swung on, there's a drive hit out toward the right-field corner. Henrich is going back. He can't get it! It's off the wall for a base hit! Here comes the tying run, and here comes the winning run! Well, I'll be a suck-egg mule!"

The next day the Yanks came back from that devastating loss and topped the Brooks in a close 2–1 game. However, the tough Dodgers team went back to the Stadium and took the sixth game, 8–6, setting up Game 7.

Game 6 featured Al Gionfriddo's famous catch. Representing the tying run, DiMaggio stood at the plate with two outs in the sixth inning. "Swung on, belted...it's a long one...back goes Gionfriddo, back, back, back, back, back, back...heeee makes a one-handed catch against the bullpen! Oh, Doctor!" Red Barber said, making the call.

As DiMaggio circled the bases, heading for second and ultimately the dugout, he kicked the dirt. The crowd and the press went wild. "Joe never showed any emotion. That was why the reporters made such a big thing of him kicking the dirt at second base after Al Gionfriddo made that catch." Rizzuto said.

Rizzuto had a great Series. He went 8-for-26 for a batting average of .308. He scored three runs and had two RBIs. But he saved his heroics for the last game. He had two put-outs and two assists, including a double play. He also had three hits, scored two runs, and tallied one RBI in the last game. In the top of the ninth with one man on, Bruce Edwards hit the ball sharply, but Rizzuto gathered it in, tossed the ball to Stirnweiss at second, who then fired to George McQuinn to end the Series. He had set a since-broken World Series mark that year for shortstops, with 19 put-outs in one Series. He also had 15 assists for the Series. On October 6, 1947, the Yankees won the game, 5–2, and took the series, 4–3.

"Phil Rizzuto could hardly be seen. With Billy Johnson, the mite shortfielder was all over the place, center of first one group then the other," wrote James P. Dawson of the *New York Times*.

"I had to go for that double play. That was it—the chance to finish it," Rizzuto said.

"He dismissed his three hits, which figured in four Yankees runs," Dawson wrote.

"I was taggin' 'em today, hey?" Rizzuto said.

During one of the games, Jackie Robinson, who always played hard, ran out of the baseline, throwing a kind of rolling block in order to break-up a double-play as Rizzuto was attempting to throw to first. After Robinson had dusted himself off, he jogged back to the dugout to the sounds of Bronx jeers.

"Later in the game, DiMaggio ran out a routine ground ball, and Robinson, who was playing first and not very experienced at it, had his foot planted on the bag. It was almost an invitation to a spiking," sports scribe Mickey Herskowitz wrote. "But Joe twisted his body sideways as he crossed the base and avoided him."

After the game, Jimmy Cannon, the well-known sportswriter, asked DiMaggio why he had not spiked Robinson in retaliation for his rolling-up on Rizzuto.

"I thought about it," DiMaggio responded. "And then it occurred to me that Phil's Italian, I'm an Italian, and Robinson is black. I didn't want anyone to think it was [done] as against the niggers. If Phil was black or Robinson Italian, I guess I would have spiked him."

As Cannon later remarked, it was a lot of thinking for three-and-a-half seconds running. It was one of the few times someone was given a pass for trying to take out Rizzuto.

The Yankees were world champions once again.

But something funny happened on the way to the championship. Larry MacPhail quit as president of the New York Yankees. He told everyone this was it, and he told the press the real architect for many years had been George Weiss, Ed Barrow's old assistant. He said this was the way he wanted to go out. Few people took him seriously. Many were taken by surprise.

"He's a sentimental fellow. I wouldn't put too much stock in what he's saying now. He's likely to change his mind," Dan Topping told the press. However, Roger Kahn, the great baseball writer, and others indicate MacPhail's drunken behavior at the victory parties led to co-owners Dan Topping and Del Webb buying out his share of the ball club. Larry MacPhail was out. And George Weiss was in.

Scooter and Yogi

The first time Yogi saw Scooter, it was from across the field. The two had played against each other in a baseball game in Virginia during the war. Lawrence Peter "Yogi" Berra was born in St. Louis, Missouri. The youngest son of immigrants, he had led a troubled childhood—troubled because school books were abhorrent to him. His classroom, even at an early age, was the ball field. He was credited with being one of the best athletes to ever come out of St. Louis and was known in his neighborhood, the famed Hill section of St. Louis, as one of the best soccer players of his generation.

As a kid, he sold newspapers, and his boyhood hero and customer was Joe Medwick, long considered the best bad-ball hitter in baseball. That was at least, until Yogi. The running joke about Berra was that his strike zone started over his head and stopped just above the top of his feet. He could turn inside out on an inside pitch, golf a home run, and for his entire career, never swung at a good pitch. Don Drysdale once joked that it was easy to strike Yogi Berra out, just throw him three straight strikes right down the middle, and he wouldn't know what to do with them. Unfortunately for most major-league pitchers, that didn't work out too well. At the end of his career, Berra retired with more records, including home runs, than any catcher who had played before (or after) him. Dickey had set the standard for Yankees catchers a generation before. With Dickey's help, Berra shattered every record Dickey ever put up, and Berra credited all his success as a receiver to Dickey. Berra is generally considered among the greatest catchers in baseball history.

Berra grew up across the street from boyhood friend Joe Garagiola. From diapers to old age, Garagiola and Berra would know each other. After seeing a movie prefaced by some short reel travelogue about India in which a swami coaxed a snake out of a basket, a childhood friend shouted out that the yogi (misnamed) looked a lot like Larry Berra—and the name stuck.

He played baseball in the navy and had played for the Newark Bears. Berra had had a tough time making it to the big leagues. He was short, with long arms and a very muscular body. When they brought him in from Newark, one of the writers said to Bucky Harris, "He doesn't even look like a Yankee."

For his part, as much as he loved Rizzuto, Harris was not enamored of Berra and would not call him by his rightful name. Instead, to his face he called Berra "Ape." Harris used this name when speaking of Berra to others, as well. Teammates, opposing players, writers, and fans took to calling him worse. They would mimic the movements of cavemen, apes, and chimpanzees, then make inappropriate noises.

"Yogi was very good at pretending he didn't hear or at least didn't care about comments made about him, both in the clubhouse and in the stands. He was not simply good, he was a master," Rizzuto said.

"You're not nearly as good looking as Rizzuto, and he's no bargain," Earle Combs once told Berra.

But he could talk with a bat in his hands, as Casey Stengel once opined. Berra, whose catching improved over the first few years, would go on to participate in 21 World Series as a player, coach, and manager throughout his career. While Harris was perplexed at his young charge's lack of skill as a fielder, his bat was immediately irreplaceable.

"Berra could move the runner, and move him late in the game like no one else I ever saw play the game," Ted Williams said. "A lot of people said their shortstop was too small, but, damn, those two guys knew how to beat you. Makes me sick."

"As our catcher, he was great at talking," Rizzuto said of Yogi's penchant for talking to batters up at the plate. "I somehow think he thought it was part of his job, like putting on the shin guards."

"We've been friends since the first days he joined the ball club when he and I used to go to work on Charlie Keller," Rizzuto remembered. Keller would come into the locker room and Yogi would holler, "Who's the strongest man in the world?"

"King Kong Keller!" Rizzuto would shout.

"Then Charlie would go over and grab me like I was a sack of potatoes," Rizzuto remembered, "and dump me in the trash can in the middle of the room."

But Berra and Rizzuto had much in common. As two of the shortest Yankees, they had two of the prettiest wives in all of Major League Baseball. Both women were shrewd, smart, powerful, and excellent counterparts for their more benign husbands. As the seasons passed, both men became endeared to their teammates. The Yankees would kid Rizzuto throughout his entire life, and the same went for Berra. But both were beloved and became institutions in one of the most successful professional sports franchises on earth. Neither were wild carousers, they were more stay-at-home types. Both loved movies and spent countless hours watching shoot-em-up westerns or whatever fare the local theaters in many baseball towns across the country offered. Many baseball players relied on their recommendations to see good movies.

And both had a sharp instinct to make money and understand situations that belied their good nature. In the future, Rizzuto and Berra would go on to make more money in their post-baseball careers than many of their teammates or contemporaries. Both would use their aw shucks personas to cover up gaffes and slip responsibility that other players could not rely on. And both would go on to become incredible favorites with the crowd.

Berra, of course, was best known for a whole series of malaprops he either said or were attributed to him (which he did not refute), such as, "It ain't over 'til it's over," (which he never actually said verbatim), "You can't hit and think at the same time," "When you come to a fork in the road, take it," and other quotes have worked their way into the current lexicon.

Berra was rough around the edges. Never having accomplished more than an eighth-grade education, Yogi needed some polishing, just as Rizzuto had. Berra was assigned to Rizzuto early in the 1947 campaign as a roommate. This did not last long. Berra did not last long with any roommate and eventually was one of the few Yankees who got his own separate room. He was neither mean nor rude, but he was an insomniac who would continue to chat with his roommates long after the lights were shut off. He went to sleep late and woke up early—and would sometimes have his teammates read to him until he fell asleep, which they would do because they valued their own shut-eye.

While rooming with Bobby Brown, who was then studying to become a doctor, the two were just about to shut out the lights. Brown had been studying a medical manual, and Berra had just finished a comic book. He commented how much he liked his story, and then said to Brown, "How did yours turn out?"

Like Gomez had done for him, Rizzuto helped smooth out some of Berra's roughest spots. And the two went blithely on their way through history.

A Different Kind of Life

In late 1947, Dan Topping and Del Webb bought out Larry MacPhail for $2,000,000 and made long-time farm-system manager George Weiss the president of the franchise. This was good for the Yankees, but not for Bucky Harris. Harris had enjoyed MacPhail's confidence during the previous season, and it was no secret that Harris and Weiss were at odds from the previous year.

Unfortunately, 1948 was not a good season. With Harris and Weiss constantly sniping at each other, the team took a nose dive. The performances were solid but not impressive except for DiMaggio, who again was superb, knocking in a league-leading 155 runs and slugging 39 home runs.

According to Trimble, "The players sided with the affable Harris out of a natural resentment for Weiss. Most of them had come up through the farm system and had come to know George as a hard man who deprecated their worth and held them to miserable salaries while they were serving their minor-league apprenticeships. The average ball player only knows two kinds of figures, batting averages and dollar signs. Weiss and Scrooge were, in their minds, carbon copies."

However, there were clearly problems on the field. The pitching corps had been depleted by retirements, and several players had off years, including Rizzuto. Phil had started off the season with an inflammation in his leg. And it really never fully healed during the course of the campaign. When it subsided, he suffered dizzy spells and headaches, and then his throwing arm suffered discomfort, as well. He batted his lowest average to date, a paltry .252

The Yankees gamely tried to stay afloat but sputtered down toward the end, and the 1948 season closed in a tie between the Red Sox and the Indians. The Yankees finished third. Bucky Harris was gone shortly thereafter.

"If Bucky hadn't had a falling out with Weiss, he would have been the manager of the great teams Stengel inherited. He just missed winning in 1948. If we had won, he probably would have hung around. Then he would have won," Rizzuto said.

On the brighter side, Phil was awarded an honorary diploma from Richmond Hill High School in 1948. It was the school's 75th anniversary, and he was among its most famous students.

That fall and winter, the Rizzuto family established themselves on Windsor Way in Hillside, New Jersey. Newark had been too crowded and small. And so here they were, spending Christmas for the first time in the New Jersey suburbs. However, they would regularly return to Queens to see his family, and Newark to visit Cora's family.

"I grew up in Newark, New Jersey, and lived next to Cora's grandparents," wrote Bob Field, a Yankees fan, years later. "I remember seeing Phil at least twice when he came to visit. He would stand outside their house surrounded by us kids and show us how to bunt. He got my family tickets to a Yankees game once. A sweet guy and a real player."

Rizzuto and other Yankees were also often seen at a trendy Newark spot, Vittorio Castle. Richie Boiardo (who was rumored to be David Chase's inspiration for *The Sopranos*) had literally built a castle in the middle of Newark's First Ward. Popular Yankees favorites Joe DiMaggio, Rizzuto, Berra, and Joe Page often ate there among other politicians and celebrities.

In the off-season, Rizzuto worked at a clothing store, the American Shop on Broad Street in Newark, New Jersey. The owner would employ local baseball players as an attraction to lure customers into the store to buy suits. And it worked. If the baseball players were in the store, word would get around, and the shop would fill up quickly.

"Phil and I had a lot in common," said Gene Hermanski, who played with the Brooklyn Dodgers. "We're both from Jersey. We lived within a couple of miles from each other. I lived in Irvington at the time, and he lived in Hillside, where he still lives. We were almost neighbors. In fact, we worked together off-season at a men's store in Newark many, many years—the American Shop. This guy that owned it was a promoter. He figured that by getting ballplayers in, it would be like advertising. We'd go in on Wednesdays and Saturdays and people would flock in. The guy was right. The place would be mobbed."

Hermanski mentioned that over the years the owner brought in lots of other players, including Joe DiMaggio, Ralph Branca, Bobby Thomson, Jerry Coleman, Yogi Berra, and many others. Hermanski continued, "He would rotate us, and the guy made millions of dollars." Rizzuto made good money doing this in the off-season and at one point considered starting his own clothing store after his baseball life ended.

"If I remember correctly, they also had artificial palm trees. I think Stan Musial worked there from time to time. It was everyone's dream to get clothes there and hope you would see a baseball star," wrote John Kelleher, who grew up in Newark in those days. "I never got to see a ball player or to buy any clothes there, but that's what dreams are made of when you are a kid."

"The American Shop clothing store was on Broad Street, and Phil Rizzuto and Gene Hermanski [of the Brooklyn Dodgers] worked there off-season. Me and my friend Phyllis used to go there all the time around 1949 and 1950 and bug them non stop. They were amazingly nice to us," remembered Rhoda Bertels, who also grew up in Newark.

Even Philip Roth remembered the American Shop. As one of his characters impressed with other well-dressed men described, "Cookie would cordially shake the hands of the two tall, skinny white sharpies all done up in their one-button-roll suits from the American Shop."

The most memorable lines were actually penned by the great poet Ogden Nash, who wrote in the September 5, 1955, *Life* magazine:

THE DIAMOND DUDE BY OGDEN NASH

In the life of this dandiest of shortstops
Fashion starts the moment sports stops.
Since he works for the Newark American Shop
Of which Mac Stresin is the Prop,
The wardrobe acquired by Phil Rizzuto
Is as tasty as melon and prosciutto.
Thirty-five suits and twenty-odd jackets
Proclaim he's a man in the upper brackets.
There are fifteen overcoats hung in line,
And twenty-five pairs of shoes to shine,
And as for shirts and ties and socks,
Philip has more than Maine has rocks.
The suits are neat and unostentatious,
But as for sports clothes, goodness gracious!
No similar sight is to be had
This side of Gary Crosby's dad.
Does this make Mrs. Rizzuto ecstatic?
No. She has to hang her clothes in the attic.

On January 20, 1949, Rizzuto was the first Yankee to come to terms with George Weiss on a contract for the upcoming season.

"Weiss firmly believed that a well-paid ball player was a lazy one. That gave him a philosophical justification to be penurious," wrote David Halberstam of Weiss in *The Summer of '49*. Weiss was well known to be a tough negotiator, and the battles that Yogi Berra and some of the other Yankees had with him were well documented in the newspapers. At one point, he and Berra almost came to blows, and Dan Topping eventually had to intervene in the negotiations.

That year, Rizzuto got one bit of bad news—Casey Stengel—the man who had dismissed him so many years before, was named the new manager of the New York Yankees. Phil could not have been any more disappointed. He did not have a good feeling about Casey.

"'The Cricket' is ready to chirp once more for the New York Yankees. Little Phil Rizzuto yesterday became the first of the 1948 Bombers to return his signed contract to play shortstop under the new Yankee manager, Casey Stengel," wrote sportswriter Roscoe McGowen.

"Casey? No, I'm not big on him. He fell into it. In the National League, with the Braves and with the Dodgers, he was considered a clown," said Rizzuto years later, after Casey had passed on. "He inherited a good team, and he started the two-platoon system with it. The reporters loved his stories. He was a funny man. Public-relations-wise, he was good for baseball. But he didn't get along with his veterans. He wanted a bunch of young players he could control."

"Let me come clean and tell you Mr. Stengel was not my cup of tea. If I were marooned on the proverbial South Sea island, Stengel would not be on a list of people I would want to help me build signal fires," Rizzuto admitted in his 1994 memoir, *The October Twelve*.

"When he became the Yankee manager in 1949, I reminded him of that [the Brooklyn tryout], but he pretended he didn't remember," Rizzuto said of Stengel. "By '49, I didn't need a shoebox, anyway. The clubhouse boy at the Stadium shined my Yankee spikes every day."

"It's no big secret Casey and I didn't get along," Rizzuto told *Daily News* sportswriter Bill Madden. "The guys who came up with Casey were his guys. Joe and I both sensed that he wanted to put his own imprint on the team and make people forget about McCarthy. The first-base thing with Joe [when Stengel asked DiMaggio to play first base in July of 1950—an abbreviated experiment that had disastrous results] was terrible. Then in '54 he started taking me out in the middle of the game. If he'd get behind in the first inning, he'd pinch-hit for me in my first at bat!"

"Ted Williams thought [Casey] was a big deal, and I did, too," Yogi Berra said. "Talking about Casey will take a little explaining. To start with, I liked him, respected him, and owed a lot to his confidence in me. I could also understand why some people, like Phil Rizzuto and even Joe D. did not feel the same way. You would never hear anybody say Casey was not interested in himself."

Phil never tired of bad-mouthing Casey, saying to *New York Times* sportswriter Joe Durso in 1977, "He had two tempers, one for the public and writers, and one for the players under him. The players were frequently dressed down in the dugout and clubhouse. He could charm the shoes off you if he wanted to, but he could also be rough. After the first couple of seasons, he began to believe he had as much 'magic' as the newspapers said he did."

While Rizzuto held rancor toward Casey for many years, Rizzuto's greatest moments as a Yankee were still ahead of him. And it was because of Stengel that Rizzuto would shine anew, and brighter, than he ever had.

During spring training, Weiss and other Yankees brass were worried about Rizzuto's arm, and rightfully so. Rizzuto had experienced problems in his throwing arm for several seasons. Weiss was particularly worried. Casey was sure a healthy Rizzuto was a better plan than any other he could devise at shortstop. In Casey's mind, Rizzuto was a weapon to be wielded properly. But health came first. Rizzuto was on the same page.

"The arm was tired," Rizzuto admitted several years later, referring to the 1948 season. "All it needed was rest. I spent the off-season doing nothing. Just that job I had in a Newark men's shop, plugging clothes. I did not have to throw anybody out."

Stengel let Rizzuto call his own number during spring training. He urged Rizzuto to come into it slowly so he didn't stress his body. Stengel preferred that Rizzuto be ready when the season started, fresh and well rested, rather than work himself into a lather in the Grapefruit League. When the squad assembled at Huggins Field, St. Petersburg, on March 1, 1949, Stengel took Rizzuto aside and told him to get into shape as slowly as he pleased.

"When you are ready to play ball, let me know," the little professor told the little shortstop. "Give that arm plenty of rest, and don't throw a ball hard for at least a month."

"Stengel moved Rizzuto from the bottom of the lineup to the top, where he usually batted second and occasionally led off. Rizzuto's bunting ability helped him lead the AL in sacrifices for four consecutive seasons. He was among the top five base stealers seven times. Gold Gloves for fielding were not given out until 1957, the year after Rizzuto retired as a player, but he likely would have won several. He led the AL in double plays and chances three times each, in fielding percentage and putouts twice apiece, and in assists once," reported the Associated Press many years later.

Casey Stengel, whether Rizzuto liked to admit it or not, was the best thing that ever happened to his career. However, the two were not regularly cordial. Few of Casey's charges were regularly comfortable around him. Stengel was not one for making players comfortable. He liked his players tight and ready for battle. He liked to keep them guessing, using his platoon system to systematically swap players. The only regular players Stengel penciled in first were Mantle and Berra. The press joked that Casey couldn't fill out a lineup card without putting in Berra's name first. That said, Rizzuto in 1949, 1950, 1951, and 1952 only played less than 150 games a year once, and that was 144 games in 1951.

In spring training, Stengel had instituted a stringent curfew, forbidding the players to be out later than midnight. As he once said, "Being with a woman all night never hurt no professional baseball player. It's staying up all night looking for a woman that does him in." The other new rule he instituted was a ban on the local dog track. This was Weiss's doing. Weiss was an inveterate dog-track fan and had run into way too many of his charges watching the puppies race in the 1948 spring training season. He felt they were chasing the dogs more than they were shagging fly balls. Stengel didn't much worry about Rizzuto. Rizzuto was known to be a homebody, and rarely went out with the boys. Rizzuto rarely ever had a beer with dinner.

On March 31, Rizzuto had his finest game of the spring.

The Yankees won, 9–7, and Rizzuto was back to his brilliant self, making three putouts from deep in the hole between third and second. He had used his full arm strength, and his last throw was as strong as the first. There was no soreness, pain, or flinching. The infielder and the manger were both very happy.

That spring, DiMaggio was sidelined by a recurring bone spur, and late in the spring training season he was flown to Johns Hopkins for surgery. DiMaggio would be out all of April and May.

"The solid man of our club is Rizzuto," Tommy Henrich told Dan Daniel of *The Sporting News* after he injured his back. In the 1949 season, the Yankees recorded 70 illnesses or injuries. "Just so long as Phil is at short, don't worry. If our injury hex should get to him, you can scratch us off the list." Henrich was a big believer in Rizzuto. He said in another interview around that time, "It doesn't make any difference if I am out of the lineup. The Yankees can lose anybody but Phil and still win the pennant. If the little guy gets hurt, we're done. He holds the team together."

Henrich commented of Rizzuto, "The game is baseball, right? Okay, then I will give you nine Ralph Kiners. You give me nine Phil Rizzutos, and I will win."

Rizzuto had a good first three months, and the Yankees managed to hold on to first place. However, the Red Sox had a great team and were not conceding anything to the Bronx Bombers. The Yankees went into Boston's Fenway Park on June 28, 1949, with a slight lead. Everyone was primed for a great series. DiMaggio, who had been sidelined until now with bone spurs, was ready to get into action for the first time that season.

It was a rough game, with each team trying to show its intensity and impose its will. The ferocity of the series showed in the first inning. Johnny Pesky, one of the Red Sox's most gritty players and one of the backbones of their great teams of that era, came in hard to second during a force play. He slammed into Rizzuto.

"Rizzuto and Pesky collided while Scooter was making a double play in the first. It appeared that Rizzuto was hurt, but after a couple of minutes he arose and continued the game," reported Louis Effrat of the *New York Times*.

Scooter played well in the field. And in the third inning led off with a single and then scored when DiMaggio cracked a homerun moments later.

"As soon as you heard that ball hit the bat, you could just tell it was gone, and I just watched in amazement as it soared over that big wall," Rizzuto recalled many years later. "Just thinking of that sound gives me goose pimples, all these years later. Holy cow. It's still hard to believe he could do something like that after sitting out the whole season."

New York won the hard-fought game 5–4.

The next morning Scooter wasn't able to eat anything because his jaw was so sore. He smacked two doubles in the second game of that weekend series and beat out a squeeze-play bunt. However, he was experiencing headaches, so he went for x-rays the next morning, which proved negative. There was no fracture. He continued to be affected by a headache but would not ask out of the third game.

"Then, in the first inning, his right arm began to quiver nervously as he went to bat. He fanned. Phil took his place in the field for the Sox half of the inning and Pesky, his nemesis, banged a ball past the pitcher's feet and on over second base. Phil tried to reach it but couldn't control his left arm, which was shaking as with palsy," sportswriter Joe Trimble wrote.

Stengel immediately lifted Rizzuto, and the little shortstop was sent to Massachusetts General Hospital. While there they used state-of-the-art electro-encephalograph readings to see if there might be a blood clot.

"They glued twenty-four wires to my hair and began to listen to what was going on in my mind," a happy Phil remarked the next morning. "They listened and listened, but they must have heard nothing because the doctor said he couldn't find any serious symptoms. Toughest part of it all was the job I had getting the glue out of my hair."

"Pesky, he's a corker!" Phil remarked at the time. "He must hit me a dozen times a season. And every time he does, he apologizes and picks me up. But the meathead wallops me again the next chance he gets. He has cut me up more often than anyone else, even Elmer Valo of the A's, the roughest slider in the league."

Pesky later said of Rizzuto that he was, "A ballplayer who just did all of the little things right. He was one of the best bunters I ever saw. He could move the runner along. A very selfless player who did things for the good of the team. Hard-nosed on the field, but one of the nicest people you'd ever meet off it."

Rizzuto was having a stellar year. Arthur Daley said in Sports of the Times that Rizzuto "was never more brilliant." And Vic Raschi, one of the most mercurial and aggressive of the Yankees pitchers of that period, once said, "My best pitch is anything the batter grounds, lines, or pops in the direction of Rizzuto."

"I grew up in the South Bronx during the 1940s," wrote Daniel Bonner, a lifelong Yankees fan, years later. "I remember being at Yankee Stadium and seeing Phil fly high in the air over second base, legs gathered up to avoid the runner, while flinging the double-play ball to first. He was an acrobat and a top-notch pro. I was a small kid, and it was reassuring to know that we all can have success in life despite size. Those who saw Phil knew that well."

The secret that year was Phil's new partner, Jerry Coleman, at second base.

"As a player, he was better than people knew," Coleman said years later. "He was brilliant…a giant at 5'6" and 150 pounds. Other Yankees always got more credit than Phil, but he was the player who pulled it together.… Phil didn't have a great arm, but he was so quick. And he was precise and accurate. No one was better at doing the right thing in a given situation than Rizzuto. Long before everything was charted, he was always in the right position on defense."

As a rookie on the 1949 team, Coleman was nervous, never really sure if he was actually going to make the team. Jerry Coleman was born in San Jose, California, and served as a Marine aviator in World War II. He had spent four years in the minors before being called up to the majors. He eventually left baseball briefly to fly again in Korea. He received numerous honors and medals during his time in the military. His nickname was colonel, the military rank he achieved while flying.

"Phil Rizzuto…knew from the very start: Coleman was a natural; his play around second was instinctive, combining exceptional grace with acrobatic skill. He also threw a soft, feathery ball, which made things easier for Rizzuto," David Halberstam wrote. "Even more important, Coleman had exceptional range; it meant that with certain right-handed hitters, Coleman could play very near second base, and that allowed Rizzuto to play deeper in the hole between short and third. Rizzuto was thrilled by the prospect of playing every day with Coleman."

"The little guy in front of me, he made my job easy," said DiMaggio, one of the game's great center fielders. "I didn't have to pick up so many ground balls." However, that didn't stop DiMaggio from commenting on Rizzuto's, or any other player's performance. DiMaggio was quiet until the crowd cleared out; once it was just the ballplayers in the room, he would relax.

"Once he was sure there were no outsiders around, he would conduct an informal seminar on the game just played," David Halberstam wrote in *Summer of '49*. He would address each player, tell pitchers not to deviate from the game plan in order that the outfield should not be crossed up. "Phil," he might tell Rizzuto, "you didn't get over quickly enough on that grounder in the third inning. I know you made the play, but that isn't what worries me. What worries me is your getting hurt. If you get hurt, this team is in trouble. We can't afford it."

Rizzuto was the apex of the team at this point. With the rash of injuries depleting the team during the course of the season, Rizzuto was stalwart, playing in almost every game. And while almost every writer that year thought Rizzuto was in fact the glue holding the team together, two other shortstops received the majority of the All-Star Game ballots. Casey Stengel genuinely felt bad for the denied shortstop, who was classy in being shutout.

• • •

It was also in 1949 that Scooter started keeping his glove with him when the side was retired and he made his way to the dugout. Major League Baseball did not require defensive players to take their gloves off the field until 1954. Many a defensive player would simply throw their glove into the short infield and jog back to the dugout. But Rizzuto had started carrying his glove to the bench in 1949.

"When we used to have a home game on a Sunday and the following day off, I used to go home to Naugatuck, Connecticut, and look for garden snakes and worms. I'd come back the next night and give them to Johnny Lindell, who used to put them in Phil's glove on the field," former pitcher

Frank "Spec" Shea explained years later. "In those days, players used to leave their gloves on the field. Lindell would come in from left field, drop his glove, pick up Phil's, and put the worms in it. Phil would go out to the field for the next inning, put his glove on, and then raise hell, saying he wouldn't play unless he had a different glove. And he meant it. He was afraid of almost everything."

As in Kansas City and Norfolk, Rizzuto continued to be the target of practical jokes. The primary reason was that the players got such a kick out of his reactions. He was admittedly and unquestionably scared of almost everything. And there's no doubt when you do some research that he was also a bit of an actor, sometimes exaggerating his responses to get laughs. But he was genuinely afraid of many things.

Another reason ballplayers liked to play practical jokes on him was that he took it so well. He was forgiving and a person people genuinely liked. Even once at Yankee Stadium, his shoes were still being nailed to the floor or glued inside his locker.

"During our last Western trip, we played a pair at Chicago," Mantle said of the 1952 season when they were on a train bound for Cleveland. "Well, alongside me sat Phil Rizzuto, who grew up in Brooklyn. So naturally he was fairly ignorant of country life. Besides, Phil had this fearful aversion to anything that crawled, especially snakes."

"Did you ever see one?" Mickey asked.

"S-n-a-k-e-s!!! Holy cow, I can't stand those things. Don't bother me with such idiotic questions, will ya?"

"Did you ever see a rattler?" Mickey asked. Rizzuto covered his head at the mere mention.

"But, Phil, it's not what you think. I owned one. Pulled out his fangs with my fingers and trained him as a house pet. Cute little bugger."

"Please, Mickey, what are you trying to do, make me blow the pennant?"

"That's Phil. A beautiful guy—not a bad bone in his body. Always trusting and so gullible it made him a pushover for all the pranks we used to play on him. One time Charlie Keller put Phil in his footlocker and locked him up. And Phil laughed it off. No one could get him mad enough to lose his temper," Mantle said.

"They knew I hated bugs and things, and they were always stuffing my locker with lizards and spiders and creatures like that. Once, Mickey and Whitey hung a dead mouse over the steering wheel of my car. I jumped when I saw that, I'll tell you."

Rizzuto loved to drive his Austin-Healey around town at spring training.

"After practice one day, I got into the car, started it, and—boom! There was an explosion, and smoke came belching out from under the hood, and I was out the door, running for dear life. Mantle had attached a giant firecracker to the starter."

What was worse for Rizzuto was that his phobias were well known around the league, and opposing players had just as much fun playing practical jokes on Rizzuto as his own teammates. Johnny Pesky said years later, "After the change, many players of the opposing teams would play practical jokes by filling their gloves with dirt or grass, or even go as far as putting a dead rat in Phil Rizzuto's glove."

• • •

Rizzuto only got hotter toward the end of the season. On August 20, 1949, Gene Woodling hit two homeruns and Rizzuto hit one to pace the Yankees to a 7–3 win over the Athletics. In an article on September 13, as the race was tightening between the Red Sox and the Yankees, Daley wrote that Father Time was the team's ally, allowing Yogi Berra's hands to heal, as well as bringing closer Tommy Henrich and Johnny Mize back in time for a pennant drive stretch. Of their impending return, Daley wrote, "It is taking the burden off the shoulders of Phil Rizzuto, whose fielding, and Joe Page, whose relief pitching, have been carrying the team."

"One day in the closing stages of last season's pennant race, the mischievous Rizzuto strolled into Stengel's office," Arthur Daley related after the season was over. "He scuffed the carpet in feigned embarrassment."

"Mister Stengel, sir?" Rizzuto asked, his face earnest. "Do you still think I'm too small to become a major leaguer?" The "Ol' Perfesser" chased the diminutive shortfielder through the clubhouse with a baseball bat. It was the first time Phil ever threw the story back at Casey—but it wouldn't be the last.

In a late September game against the vaunted Red Sox, Rizzuto experienced something that happened only once in his career. Joe Page, the Yankees pitcher, was having his best season, and he struggled against the Red Sox. Birdie Tebbetts led off the inning with a single, Lou Stringer drew a walk, and then up came Rizzuto's friend, Dom DiMaggio. Dominic hit a scorching line drive to the shortstop gap.

"I didn't even have to move," Rizzuto recalled for sportswriter Mike Vaccaro. "It went straight into my glove."

"It would have been an easy triple play, an early entry into the log of Red Sox hard luck," Vaccaro wrote. "Only there was one problem. The ball was hit so hard, it didn't just hit Rizzuto's glove. It bored its way *through* the mitt."

"Tore the webbing right off," Rizzuto said. "Only time I ever saw that happen. Ever. It was like a bad movie." The Yankees lost that game, and by early October the pennant was still up for grabs. Joe McCarthy, now leading the Red Sox, who had bludgeoned the Yankees at times during the season, would not go quietly into the night.

"Orderly, rational, and matter-of-factly, as if they had just won by 10–1 rather than by 5–4, the Yankees filed into their dressing room immediately after Phil Rizzuto threw out Dom DiMaggio for the game-ending play yesterday," reported the Associated Press after the Yankees won a must-have game on October 1. They had defied elimination, forcing the pennant to the final day of the season against their arch nemesis Boston brethren.

After the deciding game the next day, Daley wrote, "Well, they did it! Those incredible Yankees defied the law of averages and the law of possibility. They won the American League pennant in a pulse-quickening, nerve-wracking and spine-tingling showdown contest with the Boston Red Sox at the Stadium yesterday.... Little Phil Rizzuto's first-inning triple for one run was the most insecure and painfully thin cushion on which they sat for seven agonizing innings. Tension mounted until it was almost unbearable."

During the series, a letter written to Rizzuto came to light in the press. It had been written on October 2, 1949, from a sanatorium in Canada:

Dear Mr. Rizzuto,

You may not know me but I am the young boy who wrote you a few months back asking you for an autographed picture, and you kindly answered me.

Well, Mr. Rizzuto, I want to congratulate you for sparking my beloved Yankees to the pennant, for it was your out-of-this-world plays at short and your hitting that sparked the Yankees to the pennant and I know [all] will agree that you are the big gun in the Yankees pennant drive this year.

Mr. Rizzuto you are the best shortstop in the league and by far the best bunter and I hope someday to see my hero in action....

The letter was signed Jerry McDonald, a young tuberculosis patient in Newfoundland. "I want to get something off to this kid, but with this Series, a fella hardly gets a minute," Rizzuto told the press. The boy had also solicited pictures of Joe DiMaggio. Doctors at the sanatorium would not comment on the young boy's condition, but they did concede that his health did not permit him to leave the grounds.

The Yankees won the World Series in five games over the Dodgers. Rizzuto played flawless defense, but for the first time all season, his bat completely deserted him. He batted .167 during the five games. Reese had batted above .300 and played well with one miscue.

Rizzuto had a stellar season. He had helped carry the team with his bat and most of all with his fielding. He had played in 153 games, batted .275, scored 110 runs, had 65 RBIs, hit 22 doubles, seven triples, and five homeruns, and had a fielding percentage of .971.

That year the Most Valuable Player Award went to Ted Williams. It was the shock of the baseball world. Always a proverbial bridesmaid to the award, his election in 1949 was wholly unexpected. Because his vaunted Red Sox had been banished on the last day of the season, Williams seemed like a sure second-placer. The 24-member appointed committee of baseball writers gave Williams 272 points, outdistancing the second-place vote-getter by almost 100 points. That second-place vote-getter, with 175 points, was Phil Rizzuto.

"How could I be?" Phil responded, when he was asked if he was surprised. "I knew about it two weeks before. Anyway, Ted deserved it. He had all those homers and runs batted in and practically shared the batting title. A guy like me, who doesn't hit a long ball, has got to finish second to one of those sluggers. After all, I only hit .275."

"Not that I was glad to see Williams get it. I wasn't because I felt that a little guy like myself would never get another chance at the big prize. It only happens once to a fellow in my position, I figured. It was tough to come so close. I couldn't believe I'd ever have another year like that one and, even if I did, somebody like DiMaggio or Williams would have a better one!" Rizzuto continued.

The New York baseball writers cried foul!

"Phil Rizzuto, the Yankees' mighty-mite of a shortstop whose brilliant play throughout the year generally had been expected to make him a hot contender," wrote John Drebinger that November. "Rizzuto drew only five first place votes with five writers, oddly not naming him for any one of the first ten rankings."

"Practically everybody in these parts was convinced some time ago that little Phil Rizzuto of the Yankees not only was the best shortstop but the most valuable player in the American League, and backing for that belief is made official today with the release of the circuit's fielding figures," Roscoe McGowen wrote. "Scooter was top man among shortfielders with an average of .971."

Arthur Daley wrote in December after the New York Chapter of Baseball Writers Association had named Rizzuto Player of the Year, "There was so much bitterness engendered by the slight to the Scooter when Ted Williams beat him out in incomprehensively easy fashion for the Most Valuable Player distinction that typewriter pounders felt that a wrong had to be righted. Their plaque doesn't quite serve as a substitute for the MVP award but it places little Phil in rather fancy company."

"The popular Rizzuto who, for all his size, was one of the few Yanks to escape injury last summer and whose sparkling play contributed so much to the Bomber's final triumphs, joins an imposing list of diamond heroes," Drebinger added.

As Daley himself admitted, in reality, the MVP was a gimme to a talented star who had been edged out—some claimed unfairly—when he batted .406 in 1941 but lost out to DiMaggio, whose 56-game hitting streak drew more press and accolades.

According to Milton Shapiro, the disappointed Rizzuto confided to a friend after the MVP voting was announced, "The thing is, I'm 31 years old. I don't think I'll ever have as good a season again."

The odd thing was that Casey was also awarded a plaque as baseball's Man of the Year for 1949, which also went a long way as a lifetime achievement award to a man who had made New York baseball writers' lives interesting for more than a quarter century. But Daley wrote that the baseball writers realized that Stengel, "the magician, never would have been able to pluck his last couple of rabbits out of the hat with such grandiloquent flourishes if it had not been for the extraordinarily efficient play of the impish Rizzuto. They saw little Phil save game after game with impossible performances…the cement that held together the patch-up Yankee organization. Without him the Yankees would have become unstuck—and good."

On December 8, 1949, Yogi's son, Lawrence Allen Berra, was born in St. Louis, Missouri. He weighed eight pounds, nine ounces. Phil Rizzuto would be the boy's godfather.

Mr. MVP

The accolades just kept on coming, as the Newark Athletic Club named Rizzuto as New Jersey's outstanding professional athlete of 1949. "Rizzuto was generally thought to have had his greatest year in helping the Yankees to the American League championship and the World Series triumph over the Brooklyn Dodgers," opined the Associated Press.

If anything might take some of the sting away from missing out on the MVP award, it was certainly the application of salve on the wound in the form of money. At least Mr. Weiss hoped so.

"In a session that was notable for its brevity, harmony, and unmistakable atmosphere of general satisfaction, the Yankee executive signed the 'mighty mite' of the infield, Phil Rizzuto; one of the strong men of the hurling staff, Allie Reynolds; and a pitcher of potential value, Bob Porterfield," wrote James P. Dawson. While salaries were not divulged, when one of the reporters suggested that Rizzuto had signed for $50,000, all the men laughed. Indeed, Rizzuto, it was speculated, had signed for an estimated $32,500, a pay increase of $10,000.

"It was noteworthy that when the midget shortstop emerged from the conference with Mr. Weiss, he was confronted by Mrs. Rizzuto, loaded down with packages after a tour of Fifth Avenue shops. Phil wore an expression of alarm and quietly slipped his contract into a coat pocket," Dawson observed. "All Rizzuto did was lead his club in games played (he missed just two), at bats, runs, hits, two-base hits, and three-base hits."

• • •

That February, Rizzuto began a string of appearances on television. Among Rizzuto's first media appearances was on February 2, 1950, when he was the first mystery guest on *What's My Line?* Rizzuto appeared several more times as a panelist on the popular game show that ran on CBS Sunday nights for 18 years.

According to popular culture historian Rob Edelman, "The panelists on the debut broadcast were syndicated gossip columnist Dorothy Kilgallen (who stayed until her death in 1965), poet-critic Louis Untermeyer, former New Jersey governor Harold Hoffman, and Dr. Richard Hoffman, a psychiatrist. The following week, actress Arlene Francis came on board, and remained for the show's duration." The blindfolded panelists were allowed to ask questions until one could identify that episode's contestant.

"The contestants on *What's My Line?* were awesome in their variety," Edelman continued. "Over the years they included oddball inventors, tugboat captains, pet cemetery grave diggers, pitters of prunes and dates, thumbtack makers, pigeon trainers, female baseball stitchers, gas station attendants, and even a purveyor of fried chicken, who turned out to be none other than Colonel Harlan Sanders. As for the mystery guests, writer/show business habitué Max Wilk has noted that, 'it would be far more simple to list the names of the celebrities who have not appeared on the show over all these years than it would be to list those who did.'"

Among the show's most famous personalities were Yogi Berra, Ty Cobb, Carl Sandburg, Eleanor Roosevelt, Estes Kefauver, Gracie Allen, Warren Beatty, Ed Wynn, Ed McMahon, Harold Lloyd, and Howdy Doody, among many, many others.

Another of Rizzuto's appearances was on *Sports for All* on WABD Channel 5 in New York City. Jim Thorpe was the other guest. He would appear on numerous radio and television shows throughout the year—one of which was *The Show Goes On* in May on CBS.

One of his most interesting appearances was on Ed Sullivan's show *Toast of the Town*, the predecessor to his famous variety show. He appeared with Cora, Gene Hermanski, and Hermanski's girlfriend Phyllis, and John Derek and Linda Evans. It was a most unusual appearance.

The real guest that evening on Sullivan was His Lordship, Dick Buckley, whose nightclub act was kind of different. Re-enacting scripts from the famous show *Amos 'n' Andy*, "Buckley sat the participants in four chairs and used them as human ventriloquist's dummies as he knelt behind them and enacted a scene in black dialect similar to the radio show. Buckley called the style 'Mass Pantomimicism,'" wrote Buckley devotee Earl Rivers. Buckley was an Englishman born in 1906, and he would appear on stage as very distinguished, thin, and well coiffed, with white tie and black tails. He was in fact world renowned. He also appeared on many other variety television shows of the period and produced numerous hit records.

Said Buckley in later years, "I went through the various scenes and movements of show business and trios and singles and finally I achieved a thing called 'mass pantomimicism,' which is the art of voice projection through people. It's employed and controlled by a thing called 'staccato control,' which is a system of piercing touch, a lightning touch preceded by a very strong sound."

Sullivan: I'd like you to meet Mr. Hermanski, Mr. Derek, and "The Scooter," Phil Rizzuto. What are you two fellows doing since the season's over? Out with the American Shops?

Rizzuto: Yes, the clothing store in Newark.

Sullivan: You look pretty sharp there, Scooter. Gonna be over there on Monday. I want to get one gal to come up out of the audience, with the three fellows. Can I get one gal to come up out of the audience? Who is the good-looking blonde girl sitting right out here near Tony Minor?

Rizzuto: My wife.

Sullivan: Is that your wife? [Audience laughs] Judy, you want to...No?

Hermanski: The girl next to her is my girlfriend.

Sullivan: Well, then that's the one we want up here. Come on up here. [To Hermanski] What's her name?

Hermanski: Cora is his wife, the blonde.

Sullivan: No, your girlfriend.

Rizzuto: Phyllis.

Sullivan: Phyllis, will you come on up here and join your boyfriend up on the stage?

Hermanski: Come on, Phyllis. What's wrong with you?

Sullivan: I'll tell you what we'll do, while I've got them up here, while we're determining whether Phyllis will or will not come up. I want the boys to meet a very significant figure in American entertainment. And he's gonna—you're going to work for him in a second here—His Lordship, Dick Buckley. Buckley, come out here. (Musical intro) Come over here and talk with the boys.

While standing behind the seated figures of Rizzuto, Hermanski, Phyllis, and Derek, Buckley had them open their mouths and pretend to talk, while he re-enacted the script in deep, deep voices behind them. Since it was not rehearsed, which was the point of it, each time it was a participant's turn to speak, Buckley would poke them, they would jump, and start pretending to speak, at which point Buckley's booming voice would resonate behind them.

• • •

Early in the season, Joe Cronin, Boston's general manager, spoke of the Yankees organization, saying, "The pride of the Yankees did not pass with Ruth and Gehrig. It lives on in the minds and hearts of men like DiMaggio and Henrich and Rizzuto, an indefinable something which makes the word Yankee stand for something apart, the very best there is in baseball," he said. "Players like those inspire a respect for victory in the others around them; show them the enjoyment of winning. Look at those Yankees, they're living! They know that being a Yankee is goody, the tops, the best there is in this business."

There was also the story Eddie Lopat once told about Yogi Berra. Berra had failed to run out a pop fly. When he came back to the dugout and started to strap on his catcher's gear, another player came over to him and asked him if he was sick. When Yogi responded in the negative, the player suggested, not too subtly, that Berra might have cost them a run and it better not cost them a game or a pennant. When Berra appealed to DiMaggio, the Big Dago just gave him an ice-cold stare. And Lopat realized that that was what made the Yankees the Yankees. Long before a manger could chew someone out in the old Yankee organization, the players policed themselves. It was handed down from generation to generation. It was shepherded by men like Frank Crosetti, who stayed with the team for many, many years, and people like Hank Bauer, who once barked at a young and hungover Mickey Mantle, "Kid, don't be messing around with my money," referring to the World Series checks many Yankees depended upon each year.

• • •

Phil worked on his batting in spring training.

"Johnny Mize started it all—Johnny and his bat," Phil explained later in the 1950 season, as his batting average skyrocketed.

"I used to grip my bat too hard," he said. "I was so anxious to get hits that I was too tense. It made me commit myself and sock at balls that I should have let go by. Mize noticed that at batting practice one day in Florida and suggested that I loosen up my grip and relax...at Mize's suggestion, I adopted a spread stance at the plate, widening the distance between my feet. It's the same stance I used to use in the minors, when I hit with more power than I have in the American League. My hitting seemed to improve in the exhibitions, and I figured I was on the right track."

"Back when the Kansas City Blues was a Yankees farm club, the Yankees played an exhibition game against the Blues every year. In 1950, when I was 13, or maybe 1951, my father took me to the game," wrote Larry Lorenz, a Yankees fan. "When the regulars were pulled out, I went down to the door to the visitors' locker room with my autograph book. It was drizzling, and most of the Yankees hurried out the door one fellow was holding open and into waiting taxis. I especially remember Joe DiMaggio coming out that door. I took a step or two toward him, and he pushed me. I can still hear him saying, 'Out of my way, kid.' I was disappointed, of course, and I turned to the man holding the door and asked if he were a player. He was, he said, and he took the book I offered him and signed it in balloon handwriting: 'Phil Rizzuto.' He is still a hero to me because he was a kindly man, a class guy. As for DiMaggio, in my book he should have been playing for Brooklyn. He was a bum."

While Phil felt fine at the beginning of the 1950 season, he was having trouble at the plate again. Again, Johnny Mize was the one who helped out the Scooter, who had gone hitless in his first eleven times at bat.

"Try my bat," Big John suggested.

"Mize's bat started me off," Phil said. "I'm not saying that I just took John's bat and held it out and the base hits bounced off. But it was almost like that the first time I used it. We were playing Washington and I tried to duck away from a pitch. The ball hit the bat and went into center field for a line drive single! I said to myself, 'This is it!'"

Rizzuto came out swinging. In a game on April 25, 1950, against the Athletics in Philadelphia, Rizzuto shone as never before. Batting lead-off, Phil went 4-for-4 at the plate and drew an additional walk, getting on base five times, and the defense turned in three double plays as the Yankees won, 6–3.

On May 22, Rizzuto sparkled again. "With the diminutive Phil Rizzuto a positive menace and Vic Raschi celebrating his return to action with a sparkling five-hit pitching performance, the Yankees roared into their seventh straight victory tonight, humbling the Indians 7–2," James P. Dawson reported, "When he wasn't hitting the dirt at the plate to escape pitches that came perilously close to his head, Rizzuto was badgering Mike Garcia or hammering his successor, Steve Gromek, touching off two vital Yankee rallies and keeping alive a rousing four-run ninth with which the champions effectually stifled Tribe ambitions."

"Early in the game, Phil dove into catcher Ray Murray, 6'3" and 220 pounds, in a successful effort to score a run," *Daily News* writer Trimble wrote. "His left leg, already giving stable room to a charley horse, was bruised in the collision and the wind was knocked out of Phil. Stengel and half a dozen others ran out to home plate as Phil lay in anguish. They were afraid they had lost him for a long time and that was one thing they just couldn't afford."

That night, Phil broke the American League record for consecutive errorless games by a shortstop, but no one had noticed. It wasn't actually realized until a week later. He had broken the record Eddie Joost had set the previous season of 226 chances in 42 games.

"Garcia's tight pitching forced Rizzuto down a couple of times opening the sixth, and in retaliation, the mighty midget lined a shot to left," Dawson continued. Eventually, Rizzuto worked his way to third, and DiMaggio sacrificed him home. But the play at the plate was close. "The mite rolled around in agony on the ground at the plate after being called safe on a close play by umpire Bill Grieve. He limped off the field and was back at his station for the Indian half, unhurt and undismayed."

Stengel felt responsible that Joost and Stephens beat out Phil in the 1949 All-Star balloting because Stengel and the New York baseball writers had failed to ballyhoo the little infielder. However, in 1950, Stengel did not let it happen again. Once alerted, the writers joined in to promote Phil's cause.

"I've seen some great boys in the short field in my time," Stengel announced one day, "but none of them ever did anything Phil has not shown this year. In fact, I would call my boy 'Mr. Shortstop' because I cannot conceive of a better showing by Reese, [Marty] Marion, or any other shortstop in the game."

Most notable was Stengel's five-hour filibuster marathon train ride, from New York to Boston, wherein he extolled the brilliance of Rizzuto's talents on the field.

"So he won't hit the long ball like Stephens or Joost," Stengel bellowed. "But show me anything else he can't do better. He's the fastest shortstop in the league, covers the most ground, is the most accurate thrower, and has the surest hands. He can go get a pop fly better than anybody. No shortstop alive can make as many impossible plays as Rizzuto. And did you ever see a better man on the double play?"

In June, Stengel kept firing. "He's the best bunter in baseball," the manager roared to all within hearing. "He bunts with thought and precision and what a guy he is to use for the squeeze play! We won eight straight this season, and Phil squeezed home the winning run in two of those."

"The fans are nuts if they don't vote for Rizzuto," Stengel barked at Hy Turkin of the *New York Daily News*. "And tell 'em I said so!"

Even Lou Boudreau, who had played shortstop on five All-Star teams, spoke out, saying, "Rizzuto unquestionably is the best shortstop in our league," the then Cleveland manager said in New York in early June. "He always was a great fielder. Now he's becoming a great hitter. Fellows like Stephens, Joost, and Chico Carrasquel of the White Sox are good, too, but you've simply got to put Phil ahead of 'em all, the way he's playing now."

Hank Greenberg, the great slugger and then front office boss of the Indians, also chimed in, opining, "I'd like to have him on any team I had anything to do with. He can do more with his ability and equipment than any shortstop I've ever seen. About the only thing he can't do regularly is hit the long ball for you, like Cronin used to do."

After this kind of full-court press of public relations, neither Rizzuto, Stengel, nor the press needed to worry. Phil went to the All-Star Game that year. He won his position easily. He played all fourteen innings of a competitive and exciting All-Star Game won eventually by the National Leaguers, 4–3.

Veteran St. Louis Browns pitcher Tom Ferrick was traded to the Yankees on June 15. He told the press that there was a vast difference pitching in front of the Yankees defense and Rizzuto in particular.

"Well," Ferrick said, "in St. Louis when a batter smacked a hard-hit ball in the infield, by the time I turned around, the ball was in the outfield for a hit, and I had to start running to back up one of the bases. With the Yankees, I just turn around and watch Rizzuto and the other guy, Coleman, reel off a double play. Rizzuto gets the balls that go by other shortstops and that's the main reason why pitching for the Yankees is such a good deal."

On July 14, the day when yearly attendance surpassed the 1,000,000 mark, the Scooter made an audacious play that wowed the Stadium faithful. Cleveland shortstop Ray Boone, the first of three generations of All-Star Boone family baseball players, was on third base. A Tommy Byrne pitch was popped up; and Charlie Silvera threw off his mask and chased down the ball for an out. But that left the plate empty and unprotected, because Byrne did not run to cover it. So Boone alertly decided to go for the vacant home plate. Rizzuto, noticing Boone break for home, started screaming, racing Boone to the plate. Byrne alertly turned and ran to back up Rizzuto. Silvera tossed the ball perfectly to Rizzuto, who had cut off Boone's path. Boone slid and was tagged out. Unfortunately, the game was a three-hit loss to Bob Lemon that knocked the Bombers 4½ games behind first-place Detroit.

Fourteen days later on July 28, it was Hank Bauer and Rizzuto who powered the Yankees with a homer apiece to propel the Yankees to a 4–1 win over the White Sox in Chicago. Rizzuto went 2-for-4 that day, and he also had two putouts and three assists behind Yankees fireballer Allie Reynolds.

Rizzuto was looking for his 1,000[th] hit. On Saturday he took a collar and was frustrated. On August 6, the Yankees needed to take Sunday's rubber game in a three-game series with the Indians at Cleveland. But they were facing the American League's winningest pitcher at that point, Bob Lemon. Lemon was tough for Rizzuto to hit, but Phil rose to the challenge. Against the league's best fireballer, Rizzuto went a dazzling 4-for-4. He singled for hit No. 1,000 in the first inning, then doubled in the third inning with the bases loaded as the Yankees blew by Lemon. Rizzuto added a double and triple to his day's tally, knocking in 4 runs as the Yankees won, 9–0.

He was also spectacular in the field that day.

"You know, if you'd told me this morning that I was going to have this kind of day, I'd have told you that you were crazy. I've been tired lately and haven't felt well," he said. "Nothing serious. Just sort of woozy every now and then. The doctors have given me eight different tests but all they can find is a low blood count. They've been feeding me vitamin pills to build up my energy. Of course, I hadn't been hitting and you always feel bad when you don't hit," Rizzuto said. "You know, it has taken me three days to get that thousandth hit. And when I went hitless Saturday, while looking for the big one, I thought maybe I was going to have as tough a time getting that one as I did my first one when I broke in back in 1941."

Phil experienced another great moment that summer. The birth of his third daughter, Penelope Ann. "My brother has a boy, and each of my sisters has a boy," he said after Penny arrived on July 7, 1950. "Guess I'm just never going to get a ballplayer in this family."

On August 19 in Philadelphia's Shibe Park, Rizzuto ran home from first base on a double by DiMaggio. The dramatic play saw the Scooter slide into home plate with Athletics catcher Joe Tipton leaping for the throw. Rizzuto was called safe, and the photo appeared across the country.

"I'll never forget September 6, 1950. I got a letter threatening me, Hank Bauer, Yogi Berra, and Johnny Mize. It said if I showed up in uniform against the Red Sox, I'd be shot. I turned the letter over to the FBI and told my manager, Casey Stengel, about it. You know what Casey did? He gave me a different uniform and gave mine to Billy Martin. Can you imagine that! Guess Casey thought it'd be better if Billy got shot," Rizzuto recalled later.

On September 26, an article ran remarking on Rizzuto's age, the headline said, "A Stalwart Thirty-Two." "Apart from the fact that he had been hitting over .320, and fielding brilliantly all season, Rizzuto is the only Yank to play every game this year. He leads the club in hits, runs, doubles, and stolen bases, and trails Bauer by only a few points as the Bomber top batter.... Also, it might be mentioned, the Scooter needs only nine more hits to reach the double century mark." Of course it was a lie. Rizzuto was older than that. He lied about his age because he knew in baseball that age is your enemy. Yet he was playing the best baseball of his life.

Three days later, the Cleveland Indians beat the Detroit Tigers, thereby eliminating the Tigers from pennant race, and leaving the flag to the New York Yankees. A total of 2,081,380 fans witnessed their 1950 Yankees finish the season with a .636 winning percentage. The Yankees were in Boston to face the Red Sox and celebrated at the Hotel Kenmore. Glasses were raised all around.

Henrich had faded as the season wore on, and DiMaggio had struggled to get above .300 (his late-season heroics helped lift the club with 122 RBIs), yet, Rizzuto, Coleman, and Berra played more than any other players. A new generation of Yankees was beginning to emerge. Only now were names like Billy Martin, Whitey Ford, and Yogi Berra showing up on more and more headlines.

Billy Martin joined the Yankees that year and made his major league debut on April 18, 1950. Born Alfred Manuel Martin in Berkeley, California, Martin was raised almost solely by his Italian mother after she separated from his Portuguese father. He had arrived at the name Billy because his mother always called him *bello*, ("beautiful" in Italian), which on the streets of Northern California became Billy. The wiry, confrontational, hard-partying second baseman would become a stalwart of the Yankees lineup, but his troubled life would lead him into direct confrontation with Weiss.

On July 1, 1950, Edward Charles "Whitey" Ford made his debut with the New York Yankees. He was born and raised in Queens, New York, and had received his memorable nickname in the minors on account of his white-blonde hair.

"When I got there, I was expecting an older club because the guys were already heroes to me. Joe DiMaggio, Phil Rizzuto, Billy Johnson, Tommy Henrich, Yogi Berra—I always used to picture them so much older than me. But when I got there, I found out they weren't. Yogi was only three or four years older than me," Ford said.

"We'd have been dead without him," Stengel admitted of Ford.

• • •

The 1949 and 1950 seasons showed the power and expertise that guided this organization in the hands of Weiss and Stengel. That expertise was not truly appreciated until Topping and Webb fired Weiss and Stengel at the end of the decade—so that Topping and Webb could prepare the club for sale, thus extracting every dollar out of it before selling it off. Stengel and Weiss would have cried foul at the dismantling of their machinery in their efforts to secure yet another championship.

The secret of Weiss and Stengel was youth and turnover. The Yankees' farm system was rich in talent, and it cycled through hundreds of young men a year. Weiss and Stengel kept constant tabs on the hottest prospects, and new blood was constantly brought up. While a few names would not change for a decade, every year there were a few more hungry young kids to help drive the veterans. And at the end of every year, the Yankees would spend some of their hard-earned millions to bring in a wiley veteran from another club to help power the team through hitting or pitching toward another championship drive. For many years, Kansas City, even after it became a major league club, would still sell its biggest stars to the Yankees once they had outgrown the confines of the small-town organization.

Casey's platoon system provided many different things. First, it made veterans play harder, because there was always someone nipping at their heels. Job motivation among the Yankees of that era was a major issue. Second, youth brought with it hunger. Third, the youngsters saw action and were brought along, while veterans were sometimes spelled a little rest. And lastly, no one was irreplaceable in Casey's world. Very few people of the era kept their jobs in the organization for a very long period of time. Trades and replacements kept the teams fresh and hungry. In the five-year run the Yankees made between 1949 and 1954, only eight men were on all five teams.

Silvera said years later, "There were eight of us who were on the team for the entire five straight years of championship from '49 to '53—Yogi, Bauer, Reynolds, Raschi, Lopat, Rizzuto, Woodling, and me. I'm the one they always forget." That's turnover. That's motivation.

At one point near the end of the season, with the decline of Henrich and DiMaggio, it was noted by one of the writers that Rizzuto was the last of the "Old Yankees." Phil responded, "I don't belong in the same class, much less the same breath, with those guys. Jeepers, I'm lucky to be on the same team with them."

"[The Yankees] have the best shortstop in the business," Arthur Daley wrote.

"All I know is my first year in the major leagues [1950] he won the MVP award. Not bad for a guy who was only 5'6", 155 pounds," Whitey Ford said. "He also bought me my first drink as a Yankee. We were in Detroit and I was having lunch with him and he ordered a grasshopper. I looked at it, and it looked good to me, and I said, 'What is that?' And he said, 'It's a grasshopper, do you want one?' Of all of the drinks to be my first in the big leagues. A grasshopper. Then again, just to have Phil buy me a drink was equally unbelievable."

• • •

The 1950 World Series placed the New York Yankees against the exciting Whiz Kids from Philadelphia, who had finished two games ahead of the Brooklyn Dodgers to take the National League pennant.

In the first game of the Series, Raschi posted a two-hitter, blanking the Phillies in a nail-biter, 1–0, against stout pitching from reliever-turned-starter Jim Konstanty. The Yankees went on to sweep the Series 4–0.

The press celebrated the mighty Yankees and how they had demolished the Phillies in an anticlimactic Series. But the win was deceptive. "Take a look at the box scores. We didn't exactly kick the hell out of them," Berra said years later about the Yankees victory. Of course, he was right—the first three games were all tight affairs that went down to the last out, and all were decided by one run.

Phil had a lousy Series at the plate, hitting just 2-for-14, but he was spectacular in the field. With the impressive season he posted, no one was worried about him. He had been the league leader for a second year in a row as the best fielder in the game—his .982 fielding percentage set two records at the time.

"Those partisans who have been insisting for two years that Phil Rizzuto not only is baseball's best shortstop but also its most valuable player will view the American League's official fielding averages just as they did other figures previously released in a 'we-knew-it-all-the-time' spirit," read one of the articles.

"If the Scooter doesn't get the MVP this year, I'm gonna punch you guys right in the nose," Berra warned the writers covering the club.

"In 1950, I never gave the most valuable player award a thought," he said. "I figured Joe Page would win it. One day after the Series, I was playing golf when I saw all these people running up the fairway to tell me I'd won it. I couldn't believe it." Phil went home to tell Cora. "They staged a snake dance all through the house. Everyone was kissing everyone else, and Cora waltzed around with the baby in her arms."

"To the unbounded delight of Yankee adherents, who had screamed to the high heavens when he was passed over in favor of Ted Williams a year ago, Phil Rizzuto yesterday officially was proclaimed the American League's most valuable player of 1950," wrote sports scribe Joseph M. Sheehan. "The dashing little shortstop, widely hailed as the 'indispensable man' of the world champion Bombers, won in a landslide."

"Fifteen years ago, Casey Stengel, then manager of the Brooklyn Dodgers, took a quick look at a skinny little kid who claimed to be a shortstop. Casey gave the youngster a blunt piece of advice: 'Go peddle your papers, Shorty, you're too small ever to become a major leaguer,'" reported *Time* magazine. "Little Phil Rizzuto was short on size, long on determination. He was not much of a hitter, but he taught himself to be the best bunter in the business. As a shortstop, he had none of the easy, fluid grace of the Cardinals' Marty Marion, nor the rifle arm of the Red Sox's Vern Stephens. But Rizzuto learned to scoot around his short field like a hopped-up water bug, to make throws from any position short of standing on his head. Within five years after Stengel's blunt advice, the 'Scooter' had nailed down the shortstop job with the New York Yankees."

Time's article was titled, "The New Pride of the Yankees," and went on to say, "More than any other player, he sparked the Yankees to their 1950 World Championship. Yankee manager Casey Stengel, who ate his words regarding Rizzuto long ago, got another reminder last week of how they tasted going down. Phil Rizzuto, to nobody's surprise, was voted the Most Valuable Player in the American League."

"There can be little quarrel with the nomination of Rizzuto. The 32-year old Scooter, a product of the Queens sandlots, had the greatest season of his seven-year, war interrupted, major league career," Sheehan opined. Rizzuto had blown away his nearest competitor, Billy Goodman of Boston, by more than 100 points. Yogi Berra finished a distant third.

"That year I did everything I could to help myself. For example, I went to the eye doctor and worked on exercises to strengthen my eye muscles. But I never went again. When you get on a roll, you think it's automatic. I could have kicked myself later," Rizzuto said.

He had also garnered many other awards along the way. He had been selected as the "Best Dressed Athlete of 1950" by the Clothing Institute of America; named as the "Sports Father of the Year" on Father's Day in June;

and he received an Austin sedan for his selection as the "Most Popular Yankee" by the Bronx fans.

According to Joe Trimble, "On November 28, 1950, precisely at 11:00 AM, Rizzuto walked into the Squibb Building on fashionable Fifth Avenue at 58th Street, and ascended 29 floors to the plush headquarters of the Yankees. Phil was ushered into the office of George Weiss and, after a brief discussion with the club's general manager, emerged as the fourth-highest-salaried ball player in the history of the New York organization. Babe Ruth had been paid $80,000 per year, Joe DiMaggio $100,000, and Tommy Henrich $45,000." It was reported Phil signed for $50,000. But really it was $40,000. During the brief negotiations, Rizzuto argued he was as valuable as DiMaggio had been. "But Weiss laughed me off."

"People come to the ball park to see him hit homers," Weiss said. "They don't come in to see you bunt!"

John Drebinger called Scooter "perhaps the most important contract signer for the 1951 campaign…Rizzuto, looking mighty snappy in one of his own best tailored suits, was all smiles…Li'l Phil was nothing short of terrific throughout the 1950 season, offensively and defensively." There were many journalists in the room, and photos of the day show a smiling Phil surrounded by Weiss, Topping, Casey, and Roy Hamey, the new assistant manager to Weiss.

Casey winked to the throng of newspapermen, "Well, about shortstop, I just dunno. Seems as though we have quite a few likely-looking youngsters coming up from the farm clubs. May have to look over a few of them in case we need someone…that is, in about five years or so. I think this little fellow here is going to be around for quite a while now. You know, when I took over this club in 1949 they told me I had problems and that the worst one was at shortstop. A lot of people around here told me Rizzuto was through. I more or less believed 'em then. But I guess he wasn't. All this little rascal has done is miss two games in two years for me. He held my team together many a time when it should have fallen apart. I don't know but what I would have been back in the minors without the job he did for me. I told Weiss to give him a big raise, and I guess that came about. I have to be good to Rizzuto; he's been good to me."

1951

"In 1951, when I was 11 years old and was suffering, according to our family physician, from 'extreme physical exhaustion'—after what had admittedly been a tough season for our sixth grade basketball team, my mother drove me down to Yankees spring training camp," wrote Paul Gorman years later. "A NYC street kid herself, she almost immediately went up to Rizzuto. 'My son is also little and he has been worshiping you all his life and if you aren't nice to him I'm gonna put a spell on you.' 'Gee, okay lady, where's your boy?' Rizzuto asked.

"And for the next several days, he introduced me to all the other Yankees, including me in several pepper sessions; took me home for dinner with Cora and his very beautiful daughters…and, before I left, gave me the glove he used in the 1947 World Series, and scribbled, up the fifth finger, 'To Paul. You're not so little. Phil.'"

• • •

In 1950, Yogi Berra had moved to New Jersey from St. Louis in the off-season, and the one friendship the move would truly help cement was the lifelong bond between Berra and Rizzuto. In the next few years, the two would be seen everywhere together.

By 1951, the United States was involved in the Korean War. A new draft had been instituted, and men were entering the armed forces to defend South Korea from communist domination. Jerry Coleman and Bobby Brown had already been drafted and weren't likely to last the year. At 36 years of age, this was DiMaggio's last year, and Tommy Henrich had retired.

The season got off to a difficult start when Rizzuto and pitcher Allie Reynolds were sent to Johns Hopkins for examination. Reynolds had bone chips in his right elbow that needed to be removed. Rizzuto was experiencing severe back pain and traveled from spring training to Baltimore with a back brace. However, an Associated Press report stated, "A doctor's assurance that shortstop Phil Rizzuto will be ready to play opening day lifted some of the doom and gloom from the 1951 pennant prospects of the world champion New York Yankees."

"I'm okay. I'll be in there for the opener against Washington next week," Phil assured the press. "The doctor told me I could work out if there was no pain, and if there was some pain they could shoot me with novocaine, and I could still play."

In that spring of 1951, the Yankees had trained in Phoenix instead of in Florida. When Phil returned home, he brought father-daughter cowboy hats back for his eldest child.

"I put it on, and we just walked around together," Patricia Rizzuto said.

On April 23, Rizzuto homered against the Athletics in a 5–4 victory for Vic Raschi. Rizzuto was in the swing of things. He played well and hard, but teetered near exhaustion in July when Casey benched him for the first time in a long while. It was a much-needed rest.

"He says he can play, and we sure can use the little guy out there," Casey told the writers, knowing that Rizzuto was wearing down.

"I remember once, after we made a great double play," Jerry Coleman said, "and I said jokingly to him, 'Here it is Mantle and DiMaggio get all the credit, and we're carrying this team!'" But it was true. The defense was the backbone of this Yankees team.

• • •

In late June 1951, Joe Carrieri, the young Yankees batboy, was given the opportunity to travel with the team for 17 days and cover half the country. This was a rite of passage for all the Yankees batboys. It was a chance to travel on the trains with the players and coaches.

But when the traveling secretary, Red Patterson, told him about the trip, his mother flatly refused. "You're still a baby," his mother replied. Carrieri's father refused to fight the boy's mother on her edict.

"A day or two after I got the news from Red, Phil Rizzuto called me over to his cubicle before the start of a game. He reached inside and pulled out an oversized valise," Carrieri recalled.

"Go home and pack, Joe," Phil said. "Seventeen days is a long time. You might want to change your shirt."

"I don't know if I'm going to make it, Phil. My mom's against the idea."

"Thinks you're not old enough? I can appreciate that. Say, how about telling her that I'll keep an eye on you."

Carrieri told Rizzuto he didn't think his mother would budge.

"We'll think of something," Rizzuto tried to assure the young batboy.

"When I got home and opened up my new suitcase from Phil, there was another surprise inside—$28 in singles, a gift from all the players and coaches, and a $20 check from Casey Stengel," Carrieri wrote.

As the boy was marveling over his booty, the phone rang. It was Phil Rizzuto. Phil wanted to talk with his mother.

"Mom, it's for you. It's Phil Rizzuto," Carrieri told his mother.

"Sure, it's Phil Rizzuto. Who is it really? It's Aunt Nettie, right?"

"No, Mom. It's Phil. I'm not kidding."

"Oh hi, Phil. It really is you," Carrieri's mom blushed.

"She sounded like a school girl. My mother's face turned all red," Carrieri remembered. It was the first time he'd seen his mother like this.

Phil promised the boy could room with him, and that he would personally keep an eye on him. And then he flattered her with all kinds of compliments on Carrieri, and what good young men she had brought up—Carrieri's brother had been a Yankees batboy before him.

Rizzuto had taken many a batboy under his wing and had chastised Yogi for his shabby treatment of the young men. Arthur Daley even quoted Rizzuto's chiding in the *New York Times*.

Carrieri was in, and when he boarded the train a week later, Billy Martin went to him and told him to find Phil and make sure to check in with him. Rizzuto and Berra bought him his first meal on the train. It was a big deal. Food on the trains in those days was well prepared. Carrieri also learned about the baseball pecking order. His berth on the train was situated at the end of the car, over the wheelwells. Batboys and rookies slept over the wheel wells, DiMaggio, Vic Raschi, and Allie Reynolds slept in berths in the middle of the car where the ride was quietest and smoothest.

On the train in those days, Rizzuto and Berra were tight. They liked to watch movies together on the road, and they liked to play practical jokes on each other, like taking turns hiding each others' shoes. They golfed and bowled together often.

"We had a lot of fun," Berra said.

"We rode the trains, sat around the hotel and listened and talked baseball. We learned by playing, but we also learned a lot by listening," Rizzuto recalled. "The Yankees gave DiMaggio a roomette on the train, and it was the place to gather. I learned more in that room from Joe and Tommy Henrich than I learned in any other single place."

Carrieri recalled that Rizzuto never took the team bus when a cab was also available and ordered, at his own expense when he had to, a television when they were not part of the room fee. Phil would play cards for a quarter a hand and rarely drank, and when he did it was only in moderation. He often turned in early, and he insisted Joe follow his example. Phil loved movies and prize fighting, especially rooting for the Italian-American boxers of the day, whom he would watch on television in his room.

• • •

"The only time I got to play alongside him was in the 1951 All-Star Game," said Red Sox second baseman Bobby Doerr. "I remember there was a line-drive hit right at him with a man on second base, and one of the hardest things to do as a second baseman is get over to the bag quickly to try and get the double play. Well, as soon as Phil caught it, he flicked it toward the bag and the ball seemed to stay in mid-air, almost as if it was on a string. It was waiting for me when I got there. We made the double play, and I'll always remember that because I never saw a shortstop be able to do that. Joe DiMaggio thought of Scooter as the glue on all those nine Yankee championship teams because he played behind him and got to see things that no one else could—just how good Phil was."

When the Yankees needed him, Phil responded. The Yankees were tied for first place with the Cleveland Indians. On September 17, Phil experienced the single greatest moment in his career.

"Talking about the little things we used to do to win games," Phil recalled. "In those days we didn't need a sign from the manager. I had a signal with anyone who was on third base. We worked on hit-and-run plays and squeeze bunts. I would take a pitch and hope the umpire would call it a strike. Then

I'd argue. While I was complaining, I would hold the bat at both ends. That was the signal."

With two outs, DiMaggio was on third in a tie ballgame against the Cleveland fireballer Bob Lemon. "Against the Indians I looked at Joe, who was on third base. He tipped his cap, so I knew he had the sign. Joe started late, the way you should. But somehow Lemon knew anyway. He threw at my head. I could bunt any pitch, though. I worked so hard at it. I put the ball down the third-base line, and Joe scored the winning run. Lemon was so mad he threw the ball up on the screen. I ran to first base, though. I wanted the base hit."

The Yankees won the game, 2–1, and knocked the Indians out of first place.

Stengel called it "the greatest play I ever saw."

"That squeeze play with DiMaggio on third really hurt," Lemon recalled. "I knew it was coming. DiMaggio gave it away. He broke too soon. I threw the ball right behind Phil's head, and he still laid down the perfect bunt. I tried to pitch it where he couldn't bunt it, but he laid down a blueprint and the game was over. It felt just like when you throw a good pitch and somebody hits a home run to beat you. It was the same feeling. You did everything you could, but it wasn't enough."

"I remember how great a bunter he was," Pee Wee Reese told sports editor Dan Hirshberg. "He didn't bunt the orthodox way. He'd flip the bat out. It was kind of like a chop. He didn't run around or anything. He'd just flop the bat down. I ended up doing the same thing. I aped him a little bit there. I would watch him and I finally perfected—well, I was never as good a he was—the bunt. But I got a lot of base hits that way."

Again, Rizzuto played in more games than any other Yankee. That year, Rizzuto played in 144 games, batted .274, scored 87 runs, and had 148 hits, including 21 doubles and six triples.

The Yankees won the American League race and found themselves in the World Series playing the New York Giants. The Giants were tough and battle-tested. They had beaten the Dodgers in a three-game playoff, wherein Bobby Thomson had hit the "Shot Heard 'Round the World" against Ralph

Branca. That moment would go on to become a seminal moment in Rizzuto's life, though he did not know it.

This World Series would be a tough challenge for the Yankees. It was yet another team Leo "The Lip" Durocher had fashioned. The Giants were tough as nails and shocked the Yankees, taking Game 1. The Yankees responded in Game 2, winning behind Eddie Lopat. However, the Yankees lost Mantle to a storm drain in the outfield when his cleats caught in it and his knee buckled.

Through four-and-one-half innings, Game 3 was a tight 1–0 affair with the Giants holding the tenuous lead. "With one out in the fifth, Eddie Starky managed to coax a walk off of Series veteran Vic Raschi. The Yankees, thinking the Giants were about to play a 'hit-and-run,' 'run-and-hit,' or 'straight steal,' called for a pitchout, and catcher Yogi Berra responded with a perfect throw to shortstop Phil Rizzuto in plenty of time to catch Stanky," reported the *Baseball Almanac* website. "However, the determined veteran kicked the ball out of Rizzuto's hand on the slide and scrambled up and onto third. Instead of two out and nobody on, Stanky was standing firm on third with only one out." Alvin Dark drove him in with a single, and Whitey Lockman belted a three-run homer, giving the Giants the 6-2 victory at the Polo Grounds.

"No, I'm not angry," Rizzuto told Rud Rennie for the *Herald Tribune*. "At myself, maybe, but not at Stanky. It was the first time in my life such a thing ever happened to me. Sure, he deliberately kicked the ball out of my glove. It was a smart play."

But Casey was having none of it. "Rizzuto should have tagged him in the teeth," fumed the Ol' Perfesser. "We've been too complacent, standing around waiting for them to lose. Now we're going to go out there and take it right away from them."

"Stanky? He was very easy to dislike. I played against him in the minors from 1938 to 1940. I also played against him in two World Series," Rizzuto remembered.

This was a rough-and-tumble period in baseball. "Casey always liked a lot of chatter, 'Let 'em know you're there,'" Rizzuto recalled of the era. "When I played years ago, it used to get mean. Dick Williams was mean. He would call out, as loud as can be, 'Stick one in his ear!' and believe me, it was no joke. Stanky was no shrinking violet, either. He discovered a skeleton in your closet, and that was the end. As I recall, he had a high, shrieking voice that carried all over the field."

"He did succeed in kicking the ball out of my glove in the 1951 World Series. I felt terrible. It cost us the game. I don't feel bad about it now. Ironically, it turned out to be the turning point of the Series. The guys got mad."

"I remember the next game. I'm sitting on second base after I hit a double. And Stanky's calling me a string of bad words. But he did it for a reason. I yelled back at him. So he succeeded in distracting me. That was his plan. He had a sign on with the catcher, Wes Westrum, who proceeded to pick me off. They got me in a rundown. But I was pretty good at getting out of them. Stanky's throw hit me in the head, and I ended up scoring on his error. How about that for poetic justice!" Rizzuto beamed many years later.

Rizzuto admitted, "I was nonchalanting it; I was looking at the TV camera. I almost lost the game. I almost lost the World Series."

The Yankees went on to take Games 4 and 5 and a nail-biter in Game 6 to take the World Series. Rizzuto batted .320 in the 1951 World Series, for which the New York chapter of the Baseball Writers Association of America later voted him the Babe Ruth Award as the Series' top player.

Ed Lucas

Edward Lucas grew up in the Lafayette Gardens housing project in Jersey City. "On October 3, 1951, Ed Lucas raced home from school in Jersey City to see, on the family's new Philco, Bobby Thomson win the pennant for his beloved New York Giants," wrote Steve Rushin of *Sports Illustrated*. "The 12-year-old then ran outside to celebrate on the sandlot, where he was promptly hit between the eyes by a line drive, a blow that detached both retinas and left him permanently blind." Both of his retinas were destroyed, and little Ed Lucas was devastated.

"Initially, when Ed lost his eyesight, he thought it was the end of the world. The image of blind people that he had in his mind was that of a panhandler on the streets of New York or New Jersey, selling newspapers or pencils. Ed did not know what would happen to him or what a blind person could do. Several things transpired that helped bring meaning back to his life," wrote New Jersey journalist Laura Nist. "Ed was a Giants fan and, much to the chagrin of his father, he also loved the Yankees."

"Ed's mother, he likes to say, was a professional boxer. [She boxed apples and oranges at the A&P warehouse]," Rushin continued. "That winter Rosanna Lucas marched her deeply depressed son to the American Shop, a Newark men's store, where she introduced him to part-time employee Phil Rizzuto, a Yankees star who befriended the boy."

"To cheer him up, his mother wrote a letter to Leo 'The Lip' Durocher. Durocher invited him to the Polo Grounds in 1952. He met Monte Irvin, Bobby Thomson, and Alvin Dark. It also kindled the baseball spirit in Lucas that he carries to this day," wrote James Hurst, a metropolitan-based writer. "Lucas became steadfast friends with Rizzuto, a friendship that lasted 55 years. Ed attended St. Joseph's School for the Blind to complete his elementary school education. He went on to finish high school in the Bronx."

"Phil Rizzuto took a liking to this young boy with no eyesight, who loved the game, and that is where their friendship began," journalists Tania Mitrione and Dominic Campanile continued the story. "From then on, Phil invited Ed to many games at Yankee Stadium, and their friendship continuously grew stronger. Phil always encouraged Ed to work hard, even though he had difficulty due to his loss of sight."

"Back when Ed was young and attending St. Joseph's, the institution would often take trips around the country by airplane," wrote Mitrione and Campanile. "Being young and blind, Lucas was iffy on the thought of getting on an airplane. Ed told Phil about the trip and without hesitation, Phil told Ed it would be no problem and he would accompany him on the flight. It wasn't until many years later that Ed Lucas found out that Rizzuto was absolutely frightened by the thought of airplanes. The point being that Phil went completely out of his way; stopped his eventful, hectic life, and did what frightened him most to support someone else in their time of need."

"While in High School, Lucas established a club called 'The Diamond Dusters.' The purpose of the club was to promote baseball. Lucas was able to snag special guests to his meetings," Hurst wrote.

"We had Hank Aaron, Jackie Robinson, Gil McDougald, and Phil Rizzuto to our meetings, to name a few. Rizzuto was the one who really encouraged me to stay with baseball." Lucas later received a degree in communications when he graduated from Seton Hall University. For four years Lucas worked at a local radio station. Eventually he had his own show "Around the bases with Ed Lucas."

Ed Lucas didn't miss an opening day at Yankee Stadium for another 52 years. He continues as a sports reporter covering a game he cannot see. Phil and Ed went on to become lifelong friends.

"Mr. Lucas simply said that Phil encouraged him in every aspect of his life," Mitrione and Campanile added. "That encouragement is what made it possible for Ed to graduate from Seton Hall University, become a sports writer, raise funds for St. Joseph's School for the Blind in New Jersey, and become an inspirational speaker. To Ed, Rizzuto was like a second father and was a major part of his life for 56 years. The generosity that Phil expressed during his life is what amazed Ed, along with the fond memories of spending time with Phil and other Yankee players as a young boy. What also astonished Ed is that Phil never wanted recognition."

Rizzuto never did seek any publicity for the story and only assented to small amounts of publicity to help Ed when he needed help. Ed used his connection with Phil, and Phil went along knowingly, whenever Lucas needed to raise awareness for fundraising or personal reasons. Most of the stories about Ed Lucas and Phil Rizzuto came out long after the Scooter had retired from public life.

However, Rizzuto did lend his name to St. Joseph's and helped the school raise millions of dollars over the course of his lifetime.

"I was fortunate to have seen the Scooter play at the tail end of his career but even luckier to have met him during one winter, I believe, in 1960," wrote Patrick Kielty in the *New York Times*. "My uncle Bill, a Port Authority policeman at Newark Airport, brought me along to meet Phil, who was attending a Christmas party given by the PA for the children at St Joseph's School for the Blind in Jersey City. He did this every year without any publicity, with nothing more than his unbelievable generosity. He was fabulous with those kids and endlessly kind to me, a sixteen year old in love with the Yankees and baseball in general. I still have the photo taken of him and me and my uncle. His wife Cora was just as wonderful, kind, caring, and sharing."

The New Yankees

In January 1952, Rizzuto appeared on the NBC television show *We, the People*, along with Berra, Hodges, Gil McDougald, and several others. McDougald was the young Yankees phenom who had won Rookie of the Year that year.

That off-season, Rizzuto convinced Berra to come work with him at the American Shop in Newark, selling clothing. Berra received quite a shock on his first day at work, when he looked up to see huge banners emblazoned with his name and face hung above the storefront. His first day in the store, he was mobbed by gawkers and well-wishers. Rizzuto himself was smiling ear to ear, proud he had been able to help his friend and to help the store's owner by bringing in such a local hero.

"This is just the beginning," Rizzuto said. "Wait 'til you see what's lined up for you on TV and endorsements…man, oh, man."

At one point a young customer piped up while Berra was fitting him for a suit, saying, "Be careful, Yogi. Don't misjudge this like you did that foul ball on Ted Williams," referring to a dropped foul pop that would have ended Allie Reynold's no-hitter versus the hated Red Sox.

Berra glared at him and shot back, "But I caught the next one, didn't I?" And the kid backed off.

In 1952, Rizzuto was Berra's roommate. And even more than the classy Bobby Brown, the savvy, older Rizzuto became Berra's friend and mentor. Berra found in Rizzuto someone in whom he could confide. Rizzuto, who could be just as funny as the other players when needling him, never conveyed the menace or nastiness some of the other players had toward Berra. Rizzuto was friendly. If he chided or joked with Berra, he did not ridicule or haze him. They were becoming good friends, and that friendship was growing more and more.

Sports historian Kerry Keene wrote, "Berra said his roommate Phil Rizzuto taught him many things, such as how to act in hotel dining rooms, how to handle the press and the fans, how to conduct himself socially. He even convinced Yogi—though apparently not with complete success—to stop reading comic books and start reading novels and detective stories."

In fact, it was Rizzuto who had convinced Berra to move East and settle down, both for family reasons and for business reasons. Now the two would begin working in earnest to set up financial security, which was immensely important to both of them, which set them up well for the years after baseball. Rizzuto was smart, and he knew that the two of them together were a good team and a good draw for businessmen.

"Berra and the Scooter got along very well as roomies except for one thing: Yogi never liked being alone, and he didn't like to sleep," wrote Rizzuto biographer Gene Schoor. "He wanted to talk to Phil all night and would get angry when the Scooter shut off the lights. Whenever Phil went to bed early, Yogi, coming into the room, would turn on the lights and wake him up."

But when it was the other way around and Berra was ready for sleep, he had a favor to ask of his friend and roommate. "He insisted on hearing a bedtime story. In self-defense, just so he could get some sleep, the Scooter would calm the savage beast in Yogi by telling him the story of the three little pigs, Snow White, or Little Red Riding Hood," Schoor wrote.

"Yogi could be in a room with you for an hour and feel no need to say anything. He is happy with himself. He is sure you are happy with him, and if you are not, it is your problem. Yogi Berra is one of the most secure individuals I have ever known," Rizzuto said.

The year 1952 signaled a new era of Yankee baseball. Joe DiMaggio had retired. Mickey Mantle would be the new force in center field, hitting his prodigious tape-measure home runs. And Billy Martin would be the new feisty face of the infield.

Rizzuto and Berra held out for more money in 1952. With DiMaggio's $100,000 salary gone, many Yankees were looking for a payday. Only a few nicked Weiss for the extra dollars.

"Phil Rizzuto affixed his signature today to a 1952 contract to play for the Yankees," John Drebinger wrote on March 2. "He and General Manager George M. Weiss had conferred until midnight last night. When Li'l Phil awoke this morning, he decided to accept Weiss' last compromise offer." Rizzuto took $45,000.

Spring training was held back in St. Petersburg after being in Arizona the previous year, and the press dubbed it "Casey basic training camp." With lots of new faces, but some of the old ones, too, Casey Stengel was determined to win another championship. He would drill his new squad in the basics all spring training long.

"Jerry Coleman pivoted sharply and the ball streaked out of his hand toward Phil Rizzuto at second for the start of a double play. He glanced over at the sidelines where Casey Stengel was gesturing violently to warn him not to risk getting the ball away too fast," Arthur Daley noted about Casey's vigilance during spring training.

That spring, Ty Cobb wrote an article called, "They Don't Play Baseball Anymore." In it, he lambasted the modern game, saying the game had changed too much. Cobb named Phil Rizzuto and Stan Musial as "two of the few modern ball players who could hold their own among old timers."

By 1952, Scooter was the last of the old Yankees. And he noticed, slowly, after 11 seasons of war and professional Major League Baseball, that making the big plays took a little more out of him, and it took him a little longer to recover from bruises and aches.

In the second game of the season against the Athletics, Rizzuto and Coleman showed a flash of their old brilliance.

"Ferris Fain was at bat," Rizzuto recalled, "with a runner on and Jerry playing deep. I was to take a throw at second if there was one. When Fain swung on a hit-and-run play, I broke toward the bag and had to backtrack when the guy hit the ball through the hole at short. I got the ball, but Jerry was so far over that I knew he'd never reach second in time to take my throw. But he got there. I still don't know how. Then, just as he caught the ball, the runner spilled him. I'm sure he was standing on his head when he whipped over the ball to first in time to complete the double play. It was the doggonedest thing I ever saw in my life."

"I've been in baseball a long time," Casey croaked. "But that was the greatest double play I ever saw. No man could get a ball away faster than Coleman."

In mid-April, Phil was honored by B'nai B'rith at the Hillside Avenue School. It was the lodge's seventh annual Americanism award. On April 27, the team bid Coleman good-bye as he went off to Korea.

By May, the Yankees were low on bats, just like the rest of the major leagues. The workers were on strike at the plant that manufactured Louisville Sluggers. Things got desperate for a while.

"I'm using a bat I've had in my attic for two years," Joe Collins commented.

"So you been stealing bats, too," Rizzuto chided. Looking around the clubhouse, Rizzuto commented, "Most of them are Gene Hermanski models, and that's ridiculous. Hermanski is a dear personal friend of mine and a partner in the off-season. But who wants to use that bum's bat?"

On June 12 at the Hotel Roosevelt, Rizzuto received the Gold Shoe Award as the athlete of the year. The presentation was made at the annual dinner of the shoe and allied industries.

In June of 1952, an article appeared in *Time* magazine. "Platter Chatter. Columbia Records, Inc. brought out four unbreakable 6-in., 78 rpm records for children, starring Ballplayers Phil Rizzuto, Yogi Berra, Bob Feller, and Ralph Kiner. Each star gives tips on his specialty ('Here's how to lay down a sacrifice bunt…,' 'A good pitcher never leaves anything to chance…,' etc.). Price per record: 34¢."

"When Virgil Trucks of Detroit threw two no-hitters in 1952, he benefited from an official scorer—John Drebinger of the *New York Times*—who was willing to listen to reason. In the third inning, Drebinger gave a hit to the Yankees' Phil Rizzuto when Detroit shortstop Johnny Pesky bobbled Rizzuto's ground ball, then threw too late to first," recalled the *Rocky Mountain News* in 2003. "In the seventh, with Rizzuto's hit still the only one allowed by Trucks, Drebinger called Pesky in the Detroit dugout to get his version of the play.

"I had the ball, and it squirted loose from my glove just as I reached to take it out," Pesky said. "I messed it up.

"Drebinger reversed the scoring call, charging Pesky with an error and wiping out Rizzuto's hit, a decision that made possible Trucks' second no-hitter and, when it was announced, brought a cheer even from Yankees fans."

On September 20, 1952, Phil was voted most popular player by the fans at Yankee Stadium after the Yankees had held on for a 2–0 win versus the Philadelphia Athletics. "They gave Phil Rizzuto an automobile at the Stadium yesterday for having won a popularity contest. A couple of hours later it can be taken for a certainty a roaring crowd would have voted Li'l Phil another one," John Drebinger wrote. Phil had hit a double, scored a run, and had one putout and seven assists in the field. It was radio appreciation day. An hour-long show preceeded the game, along wth radio-sponsored celebrities. "The ceremonies concluded with Phil Rizzuto being named the winner of the of the fans' poll as the Most Popular Yankee. Li'l Phil received a firey red foreign made sports car. To Mrs. Rizzuto went a platina cape jacket and both received round trip tickets for a Bermuda vacation." It was the second Austin-Healey Phil had won in three years.

Former Yankee batboy Joe Carrieri mused: "Phil Rizzuto was my favorite player. At one point I became his secretary. He would get hundreds of letters every day. He would ask me to answer them, so I would take them home and send a postcard with his signature engraved on it just so the good will public relations kept going."

Like any other older player, there were days of grace, days of brilliance, to balance out the moments of struggle. In June against Detroit, Phil felt and played like a rookie. The first time up he singled, stole second, and scored on a single by Berra. In the fifth inning, he bunted himself to first, stole second again, and scored on a single by Mantle. With Detroit in the lead, 5–4, in the ninth, he came up to bat with two men on base. He doubled and won the game. With McDougald now playing third and Martin at second, Rizzuto was now part of a much younger infield. But defense was still a cornerstone of the Stengel era—pitching and defense. Against Washington one day, he and Martin reeled off three double plays behind Allie Reynolds to help secure the win.

Rizzuto played 152 games in 1952. He struggled at the plate that season, however, and his average dipped to .254. The Yankees won the World Series in seven games against the Dodgers. Scooter played in all seven contests, but he only managed a .148 batting average against the Dodgers.

1953: End of a Career?

After the World Series in October, United Press International ran an unattributed story, quoting Rizzuto saying he was retiring at the end of the 1953 season.

"I'll be 35 years old at the end of next season, and I figure I will have had enough," it quoted the Scooter. "The last part of the season was pain and torture for me, I couldn't get to sleep at all during the World Series. I had nightmares every night. I'd wake up in the middle of the night in a cold sweat."

Always a complainer about his health, one could imagine Rizzuto saying such things at the end of a campaign. "I realize no one can go on forever, and I always thought I'd be going on until I reached 35."

In a separate piece, Stengel sang Rizzuto's praises, saying, "He's one of the few guys left who can beat you both ways—in the field and with the bat. He's one of the greatest shortstops I've ever seen. Honus Wagner was a better hitter, but I've seen the kid make plays Wagner never made."

In the article, Rizzuto threw his hat into the managerial ring, offering his services as a possible manager only in the major leagues. He refused to consider managing in the minors.

In what some thought was a cheap shot at Stengel, it was claimed that Rizzuto said, "And I wouldn't drive my men, either. I never liked it when anyone ever drove me. If I couldn't succeed as a manager my way, I'd quit in a hurry. No one would have to throw me any hints."

The next day's news carried a brief paragraph noting that Rizzuto was in the hospital for a check-up and was being examined for low blood pressure. It was also noted that he had a cyst on his throwing arm.

And a day later, Rizzuto refuted the entire story. "That report that I'm retiring after next season, why, it's ridiculous!" Rizzuto said with a thermometer between his teeth from his hospital bed.

"I figure I have three more years left in me—that is, active play. Day in and day out. After that even, I don't plan on quitting baseball. I'd like to hang around, doing utility duty, then maybe some coaching, or serving in some other capacity. But I don't think my playing days are nearly over yet."

He was at Lenox Hill Hospital for a whole week. Then doctors discovered he was suffering from a duodenal ulcer. "Smells like a funeral parlor in here," Yogi laughed when he visited Rizzuto in the hospital.

The papers reported that he would remain in the hospital under observation for another 10 days. "He'll be sent home with orders to watch his diet carefully and reduce to a minimum his off-season activities," the news report revealed.

That spring training, the Yankees were intent on grooming Andy Carey to eventually replace Rizzuto. They made Carey an understudy. A $65,000 bonus baby, he'd played third base for the Kansas City farm club in the American Association.

Stengel denied the idea that Rizzuto was being replaced and said that he would be able to play "two more years." Carey played shortstop for the Yankees versus Philadelphia on the final day of the 1952 season.

Carey liked Rizzuto. He sheepishly recalled, years later, how he had gone up to Rizzuto at spring training, and drawn a line between shortstop and third base with his cleat.

"This is my side, you stay on your side," Carey told Rizzuto. "He just looked at me and smiled," Carey said years later. "He was a great help to me. He made me feel comfortable and gave me praise after a good play."

That spring, Rizzuto's salary negotiation was a different one. He agreed to a total salary of $42,000. Of the negotiation, James P. Dawson wrote, "Rizzuto's was the strangest campaign. The club offered the Mighty Mite a raise of $1,000. But Phil didn't want money. He wanted to escape as much rigorous training as possible to conserve his energy.... Rizzuto appears lighter than last year." Dawson noted that Rizzuto's weight had not been recorded in the club's log book.

"We never weigh him in the first week or two," trainer Gus Mauch said.

Mantle recalled years later another of the numerous pranks played on Phil. "One year Phil won an Austin-Healey sports car for being the most popular Yankee. It was real small and Phil drove it down to St. Pete. A couple of veterans grabbed a hold of the car with their bare hands and wedged it sideways between two palm trees. Phil couldn't drive it out. Still, I think he sorta appreciated the joke." This was the car Phil had just won the previous September.

In the April 28 game against the St. Louis Browns, in the top of the tenth inning Rizzuto made national headlines.

Gil McDougald was on third, and Allie Reynolds hit a bouncer up the middle. The pitcher fielded it and threw to second base for the force out. While this was happening, McDougald raced for third. The second baseman threw home to catcher Clint Courtney, who had McDougald by a mile. McDougald barreled into Courtney and jarred the ball loose, scoring the go-ahead run.

The game went into extra innings. Courtney came up in the bottom of the tenth inning. He turned to Yogi Berra and said, "Someone is going to pay for that. No one is going to bowl me over and get away with it." Courtney was known as scrappy, always looking for a fight.

He hit a single, but the angry Courtney tried to stretch it into a double.

"Courtney, probably still riled by the treatment McDougald had handed him, slid high into Phil Rizzuto, but despite the impact, Phil held the ball and Courtney was out," Louis Effrat reported. "As Rizzuto limped off, spiked in two places on the right leg, the entire infield surrounded Courtney. In a flash, blows were being struck and the Brownie bench jumped into the action. Everyone it seemed was fighting."

"Collins and McDougald took a swing at Courtney. Allie Reynolds grabbed the big catcher and pinned down his arms. Billy Martin delivered the *coup de grace*," wrote sports historian Gene Schoor.

"The whole thing was disgraceful," Effrat concluded.

• • •

In June, Joe E. Brown, the famous comedian of big screen and radio, and Rizzuto stood on the steps of New York's City Hall and sold tickets to the Mayor's Trophy game to benefit sandlot ball. The game featured a mid-season exhibition contest between the Yankees and the Dodgers at the Stadium.

The 1953 World Series pitted the Yankees against the Dodgers yet again. John Drebinger wrote before the Series that the teams were fairly evenly matched but that the Yankees held the edge on defense. He wrote about the infields, "The infields, each sparked by a veteran campaigner, the Yanks' Phil Rizzuto and the Dodgers' Pee Wee Reese, are virtually a standoff, and behind the plate each side is equipped with the best catcher in its league, Yogi Berra and Roy Campanella."

On October 6, 1953, "Before the game, a man approached the Scooter and introduced himself as Dr. Marcellus Johnson of Roanoke, Virginia. At first Phil did not recollect having met the gentleman before, but when the stranger mentioned 'Bassett, 1937,' he no longer was a stranger," read a newspaper account.

It was the doctor who had operated on him when he was in the minors and left him with 37 stitches in his leg. It was the first time Rizzuto had seen the doctor since he left Bassett.

"I told Colonel Ruppert [the late Jacob Ruppert, who owned the Yankees at the time] that you would recover, but you never would be a big-league baseball player," Johnson revealed to Rizzuto for the first time.

The Yankees won the 1953 World Series, 4–2. Phil batted .316 and played well in the field. With the victory, the Yankees accomplished something neither Joe McCarthy nor anyone else ever had. The team won five straight World Championships.

"Winning five in a row means more today than it did then. We took it for granted," Rizzuto recalled.

"I don't think we sat around and talked about it," Dr. Bobby Brown said. "I think it was expected that if you were with the Yankees you were supposed to win the pennant and the World Series. If you fell short, you didn't have a very good year."

"We were used to winning. Now it means more. I've got that World Series ring that has a string of diamond chips in it. It makes a nice '5.' The kids and the grandkids like to look at it," Rizzuto said years later. "I don't think Brooklyn was a better team, man for man, than we were. In their park maybe. Ebbets Field was a picnic for them. The Stadium was different. We had better pitching, too. And pitching is ninety percent of the game."

"Ozzie Smith is the greatest shortstop I've ever seen in my entire life, but Phil fits in with all the other great ones," Gene Hermanski told sports editor Dan Hirshberg. "The guy had great range and he was with that club for many, many years. Wasn't he with the Yankees when they won all those pennants? Five championships in a row? There's your answer about Phil."

"He was very important to them even if you consider the hitting of DiMaggio and the other power hitters," Lou Boudreau said. "Phil held their defense together. Whenever there was a spectacular play needed, he would come up with it."

"He made every second baseman [Jerry] Coleman, [Billy] Martin, myself look good because he had that special gift of getting rid of the ball quickly with his hands," McDougald said. "And Phil always threw a ball that you could handle at second base and have a real good shot at turning a double play. Phil certainly made the infield successful."

Winding Down

In 1954, Rizzuto's playing time was significantly reduced. "Rizzuto lost his hold on the position in 1954 when he hit only .195 with 15 RBI in 307 at-bats, and Stengel used Willie Miranda and Jerry Coleman often at shortstop," reported the Associated Press. Miranda had arrived at Yankee Stadium in June 1953 via a cash deal with the St. Louis Browns, and Coleman had returned from the Marines in September of that same year. Rizzuto played in 127 games that year.

"You remember ever being on the bench for an important series when you weren't hurt?" *New York Post* sports scribe Milton Gross asked the benched Rizzuto.

"I can't remember a single time," Rizzuto said dejectedly. "Casey said he was resting me through the Detroit series, and I figured I'd play tonight. I didn't figure I'd be out. It's a funny feeling."

"What do you think?" Gross said. Rizzuto just shrugged. The man who had played more games in the last three years for the Yankees than any other player was relegated to bench duty.

That year, Joe DiMaggio married movie star Marilyn Monroe. "I don't know if it's good for baseball, but it sure beats the hell out of rooming with Phil Rizzuto," Yogi Berra quipped.

At the insistence of George Weiss, Rizzuto began wearing glasses, which was also seen as a sign of his age in those days. Whether or not Phil could come to terms with his new position on the team was up for determination. His struggles at the plate were obvious. By the end of the 1954 season, he had failed to hit at least one triple for the first time in his professional career. And his throwing arm was getting weak.

Andy Carey, who played third that year, told Dan Hirshberg, "There were times Phil would go deep to his right and because of his arm, he would throw the ball to me and I'd throw the guy out. He would tell me to take anything to my left and I would take a lot of balls away from him, crossing over to make that play."

"I cannot do my best under such conditions," Rizzuto told *The Sporting News*. "I'm not like Moose Skowron, who can walk off the bench cold and wallop the ball. I have to warm into a game…I am still able to play full time. But Stengel evidently doesn't think so."

That year, despite winning 103 games, the Yankees finished eight games behind the Cleveland Indians and failed to take the pennant for the first time in six years.

In 1955, yet another new shortstop was brought up by the Yankees.

"I'll admit I'm over the hill, but I'm not washed up yet," Rizzuto told sportswriter Jack Orr in St. Petersburg. "There were other shortstops who played longer than I have and were older when they quit. Look at Luke Appling. He played 142 games in 1949 when he was 40. Eddie Joost, Joe Cronin, Charlie Gehringer, Frankie Frisch—they all played at my age. Not that I'm putting myself in their class with those guys. I'm just pointing out that infielders, especially shortstops, can last a long time."

"Rizzuto's relationship, already strained, did not get better during the off-season," Dan Hirshberg wrote. "Rizzuto, in a moment of jest (he said later), had told some writer that Stengel should have taken 12½ percent of the 25 percent cut he was being asked to take, insinuating that Stengel didn't have a very good year in 1954."

"Some writers thought I was serious," Rizzuto told Michael Gaven of the *New York Journal-American*. "I have never had an open break with Stengel. No argument of any kind. There was never anything personal in Casey benching me. He simply thought he was playing the best shortstop."

"When I joined the Yankees at age 19, Phil became my first roommate. The train left spring training that season to head north and he shared the seat next to me. Later in Phil's career, [manager] Casey Stengel would sometimes pinch-hit for him late in the game, and then I would enter the game at shortstop. Can you imagine, me playing defense for Phil Rizzuto?!" Bobby Richardson said. "I learned so much about baseball and life from Phil. He was fun-loving off the field, and on the field he was the one person that kept the team together. He was deservedly recognized by the Hall of Fame, and it was an honor to be his teammate and friend."

"The little guy's right. Only don't let him kid you that he's not in the same class as 'those guys,'" said Stengel after reading those comments. "When the little guy was in his prime he could do anything anybody else ever did with a baseball. He did a lot of things better."

"Second baseman Gil McDougald suspected a change was in the works— Phil Rizzuto's playing career was winding down and somebody was going to have to succeed the enormously popular Yankee shortstop," journalist Paul Dottino wrote.

"[Phil and I] hit it off right away and no matter where I was playing we were close, especially at third base [1952–53], where I hadn't played until I got to the Yankees," McDougald said. "He certainly made me comfortable. As Phil got older and wasn't moving as quickly, he always enjoyed playing with me [at second] because I would go over and almost play shortstop sometimes, depending on the hitter. I think he felt more secure with me there because he was always afraid the writers might say he was slowing up. But he always kept himself in great shape."

New shortstop Billy Hunger was acquired in a trade with Baltimore. When a sportswriter shook his head and commented to Stengel, "He can't hit the way Rizzuto used to."

Stengel replied, "Neither can Rizzuto."

Billy Hunter (acquired at the end of 1954) actually "played more games at shortstop than Rizzuto in 1955, but Scooter started all seven games of that World Series, although he was removed for a pinch-hitter in three games," concluded an Associated Press report.

At the end of the 1954 season, the Washington Senators released Bucky Harris, and it was rumored that Rizzuto would be a candidate as a replacement. Rizzuto told reporters he would be interested in the job but that he would need to talk to Yankees brass first. Weiss, however, fumed in print, upset that their owner Calvin Griffith would even mention Rizzuto's name without first talking to the Yankees organization.

On September 18, 1955, the Yankees held Phil Rizzuto Day.

"Tomorrow will be 'Phil Rizzuto Day' at the Yankee Stadium," read the *New York Times* the day before. "It comes at an unusually opportune time, since the perennially young shortstop has just been staging one of the greatest comebacks of his career. He has belied all the gloomy sages who said he was washed up and the legs wouldn't take it any longer."

The team presented Rizzuto with a check for $6,000, which he promptly deposited in the Phil Rizzuto Scholarship Fund. Additional contributions from well-wishers swelled the amount to $8,000.

Cora, the girls, and his mother were in attendance. Phil received a color television set, a freezer full of food, assorted china, glassware, silverware, cutlery, clothes, luggage, cocktail table, rugs and paint, phonograph records, a wrist watch, fountain pens, and a year's supply of candy. He also received a commemorative plaque and tray.

"We in Hillside love you, Phil, as a neighbor, a wonderful husband and father, and as a baseball player," said Henry Goldhor, mayor of Hillside, New Jersey. Rizzuto received thunderous applause.

"No, this doesn't mean we've won the pennant," Stengel said, reminding the players and fans of the still unfinished pennant race. The Yankees were still in it with seven games to play.

In early September, Stengel said, "I think what we need to straighten out the infield is the little guy," referring to Rizzuto. Well rested down the stretch, Rizzuto responded, and the Yankees took the pennant.

In 1955, the Yankees were back in the World Series, but this time they finally lost to the Brooklyn Dodgers in seven games.

With two outs in the third inning of the deciding seventh game, Rizzuto was called out sliding into third base. He had not been thrown out, but instead, he had been struck by a grounder hit down the line.

"Phil Rizzuto simply remained seated on third base, stunned. It was unfairly ignominious. This was as classy a Yankee as there was, and he had just made the most humiliating out imaginable," recalled Washington DC commentator and journalist and lifelong Dodgers fan, Tom Oliphant. Rizzuto's out ended the inning and squashed a possible rally. "It would be wrong to second guess the slide, however, in retrospect and supported by the film, it was the correct move on his part."

"The Yankees who walked over to the dressing room to congratulate their opponents were Phil Rizzuto, Yogi Berra, and Casey Stengel (who made a beeline for Sandy Amoros)," Oliphant pointed out.

"It was a little frustrating. I don't think we went into any Series thinking the Yankees were the better ball club. The Yankees didn't create any fear among us," Pee Wee Reese said later.

Rizzuto hit .267 in the Series and established two new records, including most World Series games played by a shortstop and most by a player, eclipsing Joe DiMaggio by one.

1956

"Little Phil Rizzuto, shortstop of the New York Yankees, tonight became the father of a king-sized son," read an Associated Press report on January 17, 1956. "The child is 8 pounds, 5 ounces, and is the first-born boy to the Rizzuto family, which has three girls. The mother, Mrs. Cora Rizzuto of Hillside, is doing well at Beth Israel Hospital (Newark)." His name was Philip Francis Rizzuto Jr., and he was destined to become known as Scooter Jr.

Mantle gave a pair of cleats to Scooter to keep for his son, knowing by then, that any Mantle memorabilia would be worth something later on.

"Phil didn't make the trip to Japan [for the Yankees' postseason exhibition tour in 1955] and we were looking for somebody to play shortstop," McDougald said. "I told Casey, 'I'll fill in and play short,' because it was no big deal. We were playing exhibition games, so I didn't think it would impact the club."

"Of course, I couldn't do it as well as Phil could, but I tried my best. I really felt like it was a challenge to play short because I didn't have a great arm, so positioning was very important for me at shortstop, more so than at second or third," McDougald said.

"I'll say this, Phil was a great ballplayer…and one heck of a teammate," McDougald concluded.

Rizzuto knew the writing was on the wall, but he wanted to remain the shortstop for the New York Yankees at almost any cost.

One sports headline read, "Shortstop Derby Appears Over," in late March. "Unless something unforeseen happens, between now and opening day, it's a cinch McDougald will start at short, with Phil Rizzuto playing a role similar to last year…. As for Rizzuto, he'll again be the little guy filling the big job whenever an emergency arises."

Stengel turned to Rizzuto early in the season. Rizzuto responded on May 16, batting ninth, getting a hit, and driving in a run at Cleveland. He also played flawlessly in the field.

The next day at Chicago, Stengel penciled Rizzuto's name in the leadoff position. Rizzuto responded at the plate, going 3-for-5. He tallied two RBIs and scored a run, helping stake the Yankees to 10 runs. But he helped the White Sox with three errors in the field, which resulted in three runs. The Yankees won the game, but Rizzuto suddenly looked shaky.

The next game, Rizzuto got another hit, another RBI, and another error. Stengel pulled him for a pinch hitter in the ninth. And on May 19, dropped to eighth in the batting order, he scored a run and got a hit but was charged with another error. Stengel's little experiment was over. McDougald was the new Yankees shortstop.

At one point that season, Weiss asked Rizzuto if he might be interested in becoming a coach in the future. Rizzuto said he would consider it, and Weiss and Scooter agreed they would talk more later.

Phil played sparingly during the summer. But he made more headlines when it was revealed he had had conversations with the Gunther Brewing Company to broadcast Baltimore Orioles games for the 1957 season. Rizzuto was scheduled to tape his audition on August 13 when he would handle the play-by-play of a Dodgers-Giants game at the Polo Grounds.

"The Yankee shortstop also revealed that he had been engaged to do the Frankie Frisch postgame show at the Polo Grounds tomorrow as pinch-hitter for the ailing Fordham Flash."

Seventeen days later, the end arrived.

"It was Old Timers Day, and I was out taking pictures, as I did every year," Rizzuto remembered.

"Hey, Scooter, you should be playing with us guys today, not these youngsters you're sitting with," Allie Reynolds kidded him.

"Never mind," Crosetti said. "He beat me out of my job once. At least on the Old Timers I'm a working shortstop again. Let him stay where he is."

"The batboy came over and told me that Casey Stengel and George Weiss wanted to see me in Stengel's office. It was the last day to add a player to the roster and have him eligible for the World Series. We were trading for Enos Slaughter because Stengel said we needed another outfielder, so we had to send someone down to make room on the roster," Rizzuto said.

"They asked me to read through the list of players and to check each player's eligibility, to see who we could let go," he said. "I sat there thinking that I was a veteran and they wanted my opinion. As we read through the list I pointed out a few players who I thought could be sent down, a pitcher we had hardly used and a catcher who had been in only nine games. But each time they said, 'No, we might need him.' We started to go through the list a second time, and then half way through it dawned on me."

"We want to give you your release," Stengel finally said it out loud.

"That made me madder still," Rizzuto said. "[Slaughter] was older than I was."

"You'll get a World Series share. We'll reactivate you after September 1," Casey said. Rizzuto was numb. For Rizzuto, that the release should come at the hands of Stengel was the biggest and most galling of all slights. While he knew his time was ending, this was an awful way to end a glorious career. And to lose it at the hand of the manager who had so nonchalantly wounded him back in his teens was the last and most bitter of moments. The old wound would certainly never heal between them.

"I'll never forget that miserable day," Rizzuto said. "I dressed for the game in a state of shock." He told Jerry Coleman, who thought he was talking in jest. "Yeah, me too," he said when Rizzuto had told him he had been let go. Rizzuto set him straight, and Coleman was dumbfounded.

"He was crushed. He really was. They did it badly. Stengel was a great manager, but he was very aloof and had no real warmth to him with his players. And, you know, you came to the ballpark and looked at the lineup card, you're in or out.... We won 11 in a row once. I came out the next day and I was out of the lineup. Of course, I wasn't a good player. But with Phil, he had this great start…he started in '41, he [played] 16 years, except for a few years in the service. He was the guy. MVP in 1950. He was a great, great player. That's a tough way to do it," Coleman said.

"But in the fourth inning, I took the uniform off and walked out. As I did, I ran into George Stirnweiss," Rizzuto said. "I was walking out of the Stadium crying."

"What happened?" asked George. Rizzuto reported the news.

"Wow! Look, leave your car here. I'll drive you home. Take Cora and the kids and get out of the house. The writers will call you and you'll say something you'll regret," Stirnweiss said.

"It was the best advice I ever got," Rizzuto said. But he didn't take it.

"Phil Rizzuto's long and brilliant career with the Yankees came to a close yesterday. The 38-year-old shortstop received his unconditional release, presumably to devote full time to radio and television broadcasting," read the lead paragraph of the next day's story in the press.

"It was as a fielder that Phil chiefly distinguished himself. Marvelously agile, he had tremendous range to both sides and was a master at retreating under pop flies. He was a dazzling pivot man on double plays and his quickness in getting the ball away on his throws to first more than compensated for an arm that never was too strong," said the report. "Personable, articulate, and a close student of baseball, Rizzuto has a definite future in radio and television work if he does not chose to continue actively in baseball."

"The sports pages were sharply critical of the Yankees for the way they released Rizzuto," veteran sportsscribe Milton Shapiro wrote.

"The front office was besieged by phone calls, letters, and telegrams protesting the callous treatment," Gene Schoor, sports biographer, wrote.

All the reports also mentioned that the Yankees had made it known that they would like to find a place for Rizzuto within the organization. There was also some speculation as to whether he was in fact managerial material.

In an odd twist, Enos Slaughter told the press that he was "sick all over" about being released on waivers to the Yankees.

The next day, for the first time, Rizzuto watched a Yankees game on television.

Rizzuto admitted to the press that he was shocked. He also admitted that Weiss had said to him, "This way you can dicker for your radio and television job."

"I believe that if I were with any other team I would still have been a regular," Rizzuto told the Associated Press. But he wasn't. He had been with the perennial champion New York Yankees. And after playing baseball for almost his entire life from his youth to now, his life as a baseball player was over.

"He was such a great ballplayer," Whitey Ford said. "I'm sorry they ended his career that way. I felt sorry for him."

Years later, Berra was still upset by how Weiss (of whom he was not a fan anyway) had released his friend. "He dropped Phil for Enos Slaughter, who was even older than him. It was stunning and harsh," he said. "It just seemed real strange without him in the clubhouse, especially going into a World Series. It felt almost illegal."

"We were all surprised the way they told him and everything," Berra added.

"I felt badly for Rizzuto, but it was a classic Yankees move, signing the 40-year-old Slaughter," Mickey Mantle admitted years later.

Andy Carey said it best, "It was cut and dried. That's the way the Yankees did things."

After Slaughter joined the club, he batted .289 the rest of the season and batted .350 in the six games he played in the World Series. "The Yankees won, but Rizzuto never got over the pain of that day," wrote baseball historian Robert W. Creamer. "It was harsh but it was practical. The Yankees won the Series, and they might not have if Rizzuto had been on the roster instead of Slaughter. Casey was coldly efficient about things like that."

Phil Rizzuto (left) and Jerry Priddy were a potent double-play combination during their days with the Yankees' Kansas City Blues minor league team. This photo was taken in June 1940. (AP IMAGES)

In this August 10, 1943 photo, Yankees shortstop Phil Rizzuto (holding book) is sandwiched between two Brooklyn Dodgers—shortstop Pee Wee Reese on the left and pitcher Hugh Casey on the right. The ballplayers were stationed at the navy base in Norfolk, Virginia, at the time. (AP IMAGES)

Yankees teammates pose on the dugout steps before a game with the Boston Red Sox at Yankee Stadium on September, 25, 1948. Left to right: reserve third baseman Bobby Brown, shortstop Phil Rizzuto, second baseman George "Snuffy" Stirnweiss, and right fielder (later a first baseman) Tommy Henrich. (AP IMAGES)

Voted the American League's Most Valuable Player, a smiling Phil Rizzuto accepts his plaque from league president Will Harridge during a ceremony at Yankee Stadium on April 17, 1951. (AP IMAGES)

Phil Rizzuto takes a swing for the camera in this October 2, 1950 photo. (AP IMAGES)

Shortstop Phil Rizzuto leaps over a sliding Bobby Avila of the Cleveland Indians while completing a double play on Larry Doby's ground ball at Yankee Stadium on September 16, 1951. Umpire Bill Grieve makes the call at second. (AP IMAGES)

Known as one of the league's best bunters, Phil Rizzuto demonstrates his technique on May 13, 1952. (AP IMAGES)

Former big leaguers Phil Rizzuto (left) and Pee Wee Reese became broadcasters for the Yankees and Dodgers, respectively. Here they are in the broadcast booth at Yankee Stadium on May 8, 1960. (AP IMAGES)

Phil Rizzuto was no fan of lightning, but cold weather was no problem. In this image taken at an away game in Baltimore, Maryland, Scooter was well prepared to call the chilly April 18, 1962, game between the Orioles and Yankees. (AP IMAGES)

Yankees teammates, Hall of Famers, and lifelong friends, Phil Rizzuto (left) and
Yogi Berra walk off the field after opening night ceremonies for the minor league
Newark Bears' Riverfront Stadium in Newark, New Jersey, on July 16, 1999.
(AP IMAGES)

Phil Rizzuto (right) with one of his favorite Yankees, Derek Jeter, after delivering the ceremonial first pitch to start Game 2 of the ALCS in New York against the Boston Red Sox on October 14, 1999. (AP IMAGES)

With his wife, Cora, by his side, Phil Rizzuto makes a speech during the dedication ceremonies for Phil Rizzuto Park in Union, New Jersey, on July 21, 2004. (AP IMAGES)

III

THE
VIEW
FROM THE
BOOTH

7

IN THE BROADCAST BOOTH

In the 1930s and 1940s, radio was the largest and fastest tool of mass communication. Newspapers and magazines finished second, but television was coming up fast. On May 11, 1928, General Electric "began regular TV broadcasting with a 24-line system from a station that would become WGY in Schenectady, NY; by the end of the year, over 15 stations were licensed for TV broadcasting; Dr. Ernest Alexanderson developed the Octagon mechanical TV set with three-inch screen that was manufactured and sold by GE for home use," television historian Steven E. Schoenherr wrote. By July 30, 1930, NBC started its first TV station in New York called W2XBS.

By 1955, many of the kid's shows of the Golden Age of television had already established themselves, including *Howdy Doody*, *The Lone Ranger*, *Captain Video*, *Cisco Kid*, *Mr. Peepers*, *The Soupy Sales Show*, *Lassie*, *The Mickey Mouse Show*, and others.

Popular adult fare included *The Jack LaLanne Show*, *The Red Skelton Show*, *I Love Lucy*, *Your Show of Shows*, *Dragnet*, *The Liberace Show*, *The Tonight Show with Steve Allen*, *The Honeymooners*, *Gunsmoke*, *The $64,000 Question*, and *Father Knows Best* among many more. Popular stars including Sid Caesar, Jackie Gleason, Red Skelton, Milton Berle, Lucille Ball, Arthur Godfrey, Art Linkletter, and others garnered as much press as their silver screen counterparts.

The 1947 World Series was the first to be broadcast on television. By 1953, television had surpassed radio. Hollywood moguls witnessed the deterioration of their box office numbers, as people stayed home to watch older movies rerun on television. Second-run theaters and rerun theaters were being put out of business.

The average annual salary in the U.S. was below $3,000, and the prime rate was 1.5 percent. There were 2.5 million registered bowlers, and golf courses numbered almost 500 in the United States, a new record at the time. Spectator sports had become a $224 million business. Of those, the Yankees were the richest, and it was rumored that Topping and Webb achieved pre-tax profits of almost $20 million a year.

Cora heard the news on the radio. She and the kids were outside playing in the backyard. Phil handed a ball to his daughter, Penny. It was a ball autographed by the entire Old Timer's team that day at Yankee Stadium.

While Phil stayed at home and sat in silence, the Yankees were busy with spin control. They released information about Rizzuto's lifetime earnings, saying he had made $342,631 in his career with the Yankees, that he was well off, and he would receive his full year's pay and a Series share, if the team made the Series.

Only a couple of days passed before new opportunities arose. First was a call from Frank Lane, who was the General Manager of the St. Louis Cardinals. They asked him to come to St. Louis to finish out the season.

St. Louis was the home of another famous and accomplished shortstop, Alvin Dark. Rizzuto inquired about Dark's future.

Lane told Rizzuto that Dark was getting old and needed spelling and that Rizzuto would be just the man to do it. Rizzuto considered the offer carefully. There would be nothing better than to go to another big baseball organization, especially one like St. Louis, and prove that the Yankees brass had let him go too early. However, he found himself hesitating. Despite the Yankees harsh treatment, playing for another club almost felt disloyal to Phil.

"If I sign with anybody," Rizzuto told Lane, "I'll sign with you, but not as a player. My future is not on the field." After careful consideration in a short period of time, Rizzuto knew his playing days were behind him. While he had certainly considered that 1956 might be his last year, he had always assumed the Yankees would let him finish out the season.

Rizzuto had numerous interests outside of baseball. He was young, talented, a smooth talker, and most of all, ambitious. Ever the worry wort and always afraid of receiving the bad news that comes to all ballplayers, he had been positioning himself for just such an event during the last several years. And he was well situated.

Phil had an interest in the American Shops. The business had multiple locations, and Phil owned a percentage of one of the stores. The owner of the American Shops knew that in Rizzuto he had found a flashy, sophisticated promoter who could lure in other popular ballplayers to help sell the suits. Phil had the gift of gab, and he and Hermanski often worked their considerable charm on their pals to come to the shop to work or make appearances. He was also already scheming to open up other businesses.

Rizzuto was also drawn to broadcasting like a moth to the proverbial flame.

"In his last couple of years with the Yankees, when Casey Stengel occasionally took him out for a pinch hitter, Phil would change into his street clothes and make a beeline for the broadcast booth," sports biographer Gene Schoor wrote. "Mel Allen and Red Barber, who were doing the games for the Yankees then, had an open invitation for the Scooter, and they got him to do a half inning or so. Allen and Barber got a kick out of it, but not nearly the kick the little guy got out of it."

"I loved it," Rizzuto said. "Maybe it's the ham in me, but the more I did it, the more I loved it." Rizzuto told *The Sporting News* in the summer of 1957 that he practiced in front of the television set, even when he was still a regular player. He watched Dodgers and Giants games with the sound turned down to practice his announcing. "Announcing got my attention about five years ago as a means of staying close to the players and to the game."

He was accomplished, successful, and most importantly, beloved by the fans. As DiMaggio once said, "They come to see me play, but they come to see Phil because they love him." And Rizzuto was about to be courted.

On October 10 of that year, a *New York Times* headline pronounced, "Rizzuto to Scoot into TV and Radio."

"The former Yankee shortstop has a major deal pending and enough TV appearances scheduled this week to keep him as busy as if he were playing again in the World Series," Val Adams reported. It was either learned or leaked to the press that Rizzuto was negotiating to do the New York Giants baseball play-by-play for radio and television from the Polo Grounds. And there was an offer from the Baltimore Orioles to be considered, as well.

"Discussions are in progress with the Jacob Ruppert Brewery, sponsor of the broadcast. The outcome of negotiations was said to be dependent somewhat on several other pending business commitments by Mr. Rizzuto," Adams reported. "The former player is also preparing a half-hour weekly filmed series for television titled *Junior Sports League*."

"I got real excited about the Giants [job]. Because it was the job I wanted right at home, but the Baltimore people had been so generous that I didn't know what to do," Rizzuto told Spink in *The Sporting News*. "They asked me down there to talk it over, and I was amazed at the salary.… The hitch was that our children were established in school up here, and my family and my in-laws were up here, too."

During the World Series, Phil was invited to do a nightly segment at 7:45 PM on NBC's *News Caravan*, a popular program of the period. And on October 3, Rizzuto was back in uniform for Kraft Theatre's presentation of *The Mickey Mantle Story*, also on NBC.

In retrospect, the article published in the *New York Times* and other press outlets almost seems a subterfuge. Announcing that Phil was making a deal with the Jacob Ruppert Brewery was like a flash of gunpowder.

The sponsor of the Yankees broadcasts was Ballantine Beer. Mel Allen would bellow, "There goes another Ballantine blast!" on the radio broadcast every time a Yankee hit a home run. Carl Badenhausen was the president of the brewery, and he was a good friend of Rizzuto's. The two played golf together religiously.

"The biggest Ballantine Blast may have been the old beer company's push to place Phil Rizzuto in the broadcast booth in 1957. The move, bold at a time when few inexperienced former athletes were hired as announcers, led to a 39-year career for the most popular Yankees voice in history," Steven Marcus wrote for *Newsday*. "Rizzuto's favorite hobby was golf, and on the links he entertained many clients of Ballantine, then the Yankees' most influential sponsor. In August 1956, the Yankees released Rizzuto, whose affable demeanor had made him popular at Ballantine's golf outings."

"The Ballantine connection was strong," former Yankees public relations director Marty Appel said. "They probably would have liked to have Phil stay."

Rizzuto himself put it off to luck, according to Spink. He told Spink that while spending time with a group of Yankees executives, he joked that they should hire him for radio. "I didn't give that another thought until I got a call to do business with them. They were thinking of running a four-man staff with me as a relief man mainly at home. No traveling? Terrific. I was never keen about the road. I like it at home. Finally, they hired me as third man, full time, and after that I am a firm believer in luck," Rizzuto told Spink. But this was probably not the case. A shrew businessman, Rizzuto probably used the Orioles and Giants jobs to goad his friends at Ballantine.

"Ballantine, the story goes, told Yankees general manager George Weiss to find a spot for Rizzuto. With Red Barber and Mel Allen already New York institutions, the odd man out was Jim Woods, who was considered a very professional sidekick to the talky Allen and the consummate professional Barber," Marcus continued.

That fall Red Barber walked into Toots Shor's restaurant when his broadcast partner Jim Woods approached him, saying, "Red, I'm all shook up. George Weiss called me this morning and asked me to drop by his office this afternoon. I thought it was the routine renewal of my contract for next year with you and Mel [Allen]. When I went in, George was fussing around at his desk looking unhappy, uncertain, which, as you know, isn't like him."

"Jim, sit down," Weiss told Woods. "You've done nothing but good work for the Yankees." He then offered a litany of Woods' successes on behalf of the organization. Finally, Weiss just blurted out, "Jim, Ballantine has ordered Rizzuto into the broadcast. You are out."

Appel said Barber and Allen thought that Rizzuto, who had only a little broadcasting experience, as they well knew, was "being forced on them" at the expense of the steadfast Woods.

Marcus wrote, "If Woods felt bad about losing his job to Rizzuto, and there is no evidence that he did, he just had to recall his career announcing

Iowa football in the 1930s. That's when he replaced a future legend, though not in broadcasting. His name was Ronald Reagan."

Woods' career was star studded. He worked for numerous organizations and alongside famous announcers, such as the Giants and Russ Hodges, the Pirates and Bob Prince, and the Cardinals with Jack Buck. Along with beloved announcer Ned Martin, Woods broadcast the famous Bucky Dent home run game in 1978. Woods died in 1988.

Allen was let go after the 1964 season in a move that Allen later claimed was also engineered by Ballantine.

"Rizzuto had never done an inning of play-by-play," an embittered Barber wrote. "He has a sparkling charm when he wishes to turn it on, and no matter the jam he gets in, he gets out of it by assuming a childlike innocence he can call upon instantly."

Rizzuto was hired on December 18, 1956, by John Ferrell of the Ballantine brewery, the sponsor of the Yankees broadcasts. At the time, Mel Allen and Red Barber were considered among the best in their profession.

• • •

Melvin Allen Israel was born in Birmingham, Alabama, on February 14, 1913. He attended the University of Alabama where he was a member of Zeta Beta Tau fraternity as an undergraduate. He went on to earn a law degree from Alabama, as well. In 1935, while he was enrolled in law school, Alabama football coach Frank Thomas asked Allen to replace the team's radio announcer for $5 a game.

"My only experience was in listening to Graham McNamee and Ted Husing," Allen said, referring to two pioneer sports broadcasters.

While on vacation during Christmas 1936, after he had finished law school and passed the bar, "he stopped, on a lark, at CBS for an audition and was hired early the next year as a $45-a-week announcer, understudying Mr. Husing in sports and Robert Trout in news," according to Sandomir of the *New York Times*. "He dropped his last name when CBS felt his name was too Jewish."

During the peak of his career in the 1940s and 1950s, Allen was arguably the most prominent member of his profession, his voice familiar to millions, and he will forever be known as the one and only "legendary voice of the New York Yankees."

According to Sandomir, "Mr. Allen called Yankees games on radio and then on television from 1939 to 1964—from the last days of Lou Gehrig to the last gasp of the Yankee empire. He bled pinstripe blue and welcomed listeners with his trademark greeting, 'Hello, everybody, this is Mel Allen!'"

He coined such memorable phrases of the day as "Ballantine Blasts" and "White Owl" Wallops, according to Sandomir, "Mr. Allen may have sold more beer and cigars than any sportscaster of his time.... He introduced Lou Gehrig at his July 4, 1939, farewell and Babe Ruth at his sad 1948 adieu. Mr. Allen recalled seeing Mr. Gehrig, the stricken Yankee captain, ravaged by amyotrophic lateral sclerosis, shuffle into the dugout one day in 1940."

"Lou patted me on the thigh and said, 'Kid, I never listened to the broadcasts when I was playing, but now they're what keep me going,'" said Mr. Allen, who was then 27. "I went down the steps and bawled like a baby."

"That voice—there'll never be another like him," said Rizzuto in his days as a Yankees broadcaster. "He was the real voice of the Yankees. He was like Joe McCarthy. When you made a mistake on the field, he got to you right there. He didn't wait. Mel was like that. Right on the air, he'd correct me. At first I thought he was picking on me, but I realized later he was doing it for my benefit."

The Yankees and Ballantine asked Allen to help refine Rizzuto's delivery. Rizzuto was a rookie all over again and, as he had been placed between two big guys in the Yankees locker room, he was placed between two Hall of Fame broadcasters. They were two genuine All-Stars of radio.

"They said to me later on that I should meet with Phil before the season started." Allen said later. "We obviously talked about the mechanics of the game. It took him a while to get the mechanics. In other words, giving the count on the batter, the score, the rhythm of it, that sort of thing. It's the same way as if you're playing baseball. You don't jump right in and bat .300—you have to keep learning."

"He had already established himself as a ballplayer," Allen continued. "Now he had to get settled in. But he had to learn the mechanics of the thing.

It's a lot more than calling balls and strikes or telling the listener that it's a fly ball or a line drive."

Walter Lanier Barber was born in Columbus, Mississippi, on February 17, 1908. While attending the University of Florida, he read a scholarly paper over a campus radio station and decided that he liked broadcasting. He left college and found work as an announcer.

According to the Radio Hall of Fame, "Four years later he was asked by Powel Crosley Jr., owner of the Cincinnati Reds, to broadcast the team's games. On Opening Day in 1934, the 26-year-old redhead broadcast the first major league game he had ever seen. From 1939 through 1953, Barber served as the voice of the Brooklyn Dodgers. He was working for the New York Yankees when he retired in 1966. Barber had the distinction of broadcasting baseball's first night game on May 24, 1935, in Cincinnati and the sport's first televised contest on August 26, 1939, in Brooklyn."

Nicknamed "The Ol' Redhead," he made such colloquialisms as: "They're tearin' up the pea patch"—used for a team on a winning streak; "The bases are F.O.B. (full of Brooklyns)"—the Dodgers had loaded the bases; "Can of corn"—describing a softly hit, easily caught fly ball; "Rhubarb"—any kind of heated on-field dispute or altercation; "(Sittin' in) the catbird seat"— used when a player or team was performing exceptionally well, which was borrowed from a James Thurber story; "(Walkin' in) the tall cotton"—also used to describe success.

Barber deplored "homers," broadcasters who unabashedly rooted for the home team. He did not want to be seen cheering for his employer. He was always insistent on being a fair broadcaster. At the end of the 1953 season, Barber was pressured to become more of a homer by the new controlling owner of the Dodgers, Walter O'Malley.

According to baseball-broadcasting historian Curt Smith, however, Barber resigned from the Dodgers because O'Malley refused to back Barber in his demand that the Gillette Company pay him a higher fee for telecasting the 1953 World Series (which Gillette was sponsoring). Barber declined Gillette's fee and was replaced on the Series telecasts by Vin Scully, who partnered with the Yankees' Mel Allen. Barber was hired by the cross-town Yankees just before the start of the 1954 season.

Barber was deadpan, clear, distinct, and emotionless. He strove for straight reporting of the action. Allen was a passionate, if not talented, "homer." The two were oil and water, fire and ice.

Curt Smith, author of *Voices of Summer*, summarized the difference between Barber and Allen in these words: "Barber was white wine, crepes suzette, and bluegrass music. Allen was hot dogs, beer, and the U.S. Marine Corps Band. Like Millay, Barber was a poet. Like Sinatra, Allen was a balladeer. Detached, Red reported. Involved, Mel roared."

Scooter got a rude awakening from the two veterans. As spring training was happening for the players, it was also happening for Rizzuto.

When asked how friendly Allen and Barber were in 2007, Rizzuto said, "Not too friendly." Rizzuto told another interviewer that things had been "very uncomfortable" for about three weeks. "It took me that long to get the hang of a clear, smooth account, because I'd been hurrying and using too many words. I guess I tried too hard and pressed too much when I would listen to Mel Allen and Red Barber and hear them roll it out so easy."

"When I came on, they got on me, on the air. My mother and father were very upset because of that. I mean…I butchered a lot of words. I'd add letters. I'd say like Cuba [which he pronounces 'Cuber'], I put an 'r' on the end of it. I still do. And I'd say 'ath-a-letics.' I'd add an 'a.' And Mel would say, 'Phil, there's no second 'a' in athletics.' On the air."

"It's not pizza pie," Red Barber said. "Pizza means pie."

"How was I to know," Rizzuto lamented. "Here they were, two men who passed the law bar, and me, I hadn't even graduated high school."

"Three days into his new career, Rizzuto told his wife, Cora, that he wanted to quit," Richard Sandomir wrote years later. "But he stayed, despite occasional threats to resign, until 1996."

"Can you imagine?" Rizzuto once said about teaming with Allen and Barber, "Two guys with Southern accents speaking the king's English, and here comes this guy from Brooklyn busting up the language. It was brutal! I almost quit."

During the second week of spring training in 1957, when the Yankees and Cardinals were just about to square off with each other in an exhibition game, it suddenly began to rain. There wasn't much action to report until the rain had passed.

"I'm going for a hot dog with Red," Mel Allen told Scooter, as he got up from his chair. "We'll be right back. You take it."

And with that, Allen handed the microphone over to Rizzuto. It was a rite of initiation. Phil had to fill the dead air all by himself.

"For fifteen minutes, Mel and Red watched, out of sight from the Scooter, as Phil labored at the microphone, solo. They could see him and hear him as the Scooter filled the airways with a description of the field. But mostly he told stories about the players, and about how they felt on a rainy day, how they played the game, and so forth," wrote sports biographer Gene Schoor.

Few people thought Rizzuto would succeed.

"I remember Bill MacPhail…he was with CBS at the time, said, 'You'll never make it. You talk through your nose, you got a Brooklyn accent, you're too high, you breathe at the wrong time.' I almost quit," Rizzuto remembered.

The most famous of cutting remarks came at the hands of the infamous Howard Cosell. Cosell was a friend of Rizzuto's. In the mid-to-late 1950s, Cosell, a lawyer by trade, was wriggling his way into the broadcast profession. By hanging around Ebbets Field, Yankees Stadium, and the Polo Grounds, he had helped numerous ballplayers get liquor licenses for stores, and he dispensed other advice. On the pretext of offering legal services, while he was still a practicing lawyer, he was infamous around the office for asking, "Can you loan me ten dollars to take the Scooter out to lunch?"

"Sometimes he invited senior partners along," journalist Dave Kindred reported. Cosell offered Rizzuto this sage prediction: "You'll never last. You look like George Burns and you sound like Groucho Marx."

"Every time I start a new season behind the microphone," Rizzuto told sports journalist Allen Barra many years later, "I think of that guy. Behind the mic, who knew or cared what I looked like? I mean, Cosell wasn't exactly Cary Grant. And Groucho Marx? Both Cosell and I should have been so lucky."

Red Barber once wrote of Rizzuto, "If he fell into a ditch at midnight, it would have hot and cold running water." Barber, the consummate professional, never seemed to forgive Rizzuto. "He has not become the professional broadcaster he should be because he won't do the professional preparation."

"[Barber] didn't take to Phil because Phil was WW—wasn't watching—and he'd leave early in a game. Red, who was a very strict person in that way, felt that Phil took his broadcast job too casually, that he didn't have the proper discipline in his approach. Phil was what he was—a great personality," said Jerry Coleman, who would join the broadcast in 1963.

On his own relationship with Barber, Coleman said, "I got along great with Red. Mel got along with everybody."

"Barber hated jocks who became announcers," said Larry King to sports biographer and historian Peter Golenbock. "He liked Phil Rizzuto because Rizzuto was smart enough to go over to him and say, 'You're a great announcer. Please teach me anything you can.'"

"Mel and Red mellowed after a couple of years when they realized I wasn't trying to hurt them. I was just trying to do a job. They could see the handwriting on the wall," Rizzuto said in a 2007 interview. "It meant the ballplayers were getting a toehold in the booth, and it eventually came down to that."

"The good broadcaster reacts to the play on the field before the crowd at the ballpark," Rizzuto said. "Mel could build up the drama of a play because he sensed that it was going to be tough but playable. And quite often, with a Yankee team that grabbed everything in sight, he was anticipating great plays."

• • •

Some things, however, they could never agree on. Mel believed in never announcing that a pitcher had a no hitter going. "Mel was very superstitious," Rizzuto said. "Once I took over in the seventh and mentioned that Whitey Ford hadn't allowed a hit through six innings, and Mel almost jumped out of the booth."

"I never got better or worse. I gave birthdays and told stories, some of them were lies, but people didn't know that," Rizzuto said much later on in life.

"I loved to do birthdays. Oh, geez, I had a ball doing birthdays. I'll never forget one I did…it was the last game of the season, and I don't know if we finished last—did we ever finish last? [1966] The last out was being made, a high fly ball that Roy White hit or somebody. I went, 'Well, the season's over and before the ball is caught out in left field, Happy Birthday to Jane'…had to be an Italian name."

At first, he did two innings daily. "He'd leave in the seventh or eighth," Allen said. "Red and I'd finish." One game went into extra innings. "And now to take you into the tenth, here is…here is…" Rizzuto was already on the George Washington Bridge.

"He's a character, all right. Only Phil Rizzuto could get away with leaving the ball park early to beat the traffic across the George Washington Bridge," George Vecsey wrote in the *New York Times.*

"He became famed for leaving early," Bob Costas added. "Even when he stuck around, you'd hear him hooking the mike into the stand announcing the final score."

"He used to drive me crazy," Rizzuto's WPIX-TV director, Don Carney, said. "His talking about people's birthdays, Italian food, or some restaurant, or who got married. Once he announced a funeral. He used to take off the eighth and ninth innings, saying he had to go to the bathroom. And that was it. Gone. One of the greatest turnarounds in the history of baseball was when Rizzuto turned around on the George Washington Bridge and came back to the Stadium to do extra innings. He was afraid of lightning. I used to record giant lightning flashes, and before a storm, I'd get out those tapes and scare him half to death."

"Thunder and lightning. Lightning and I don't get along. Every time I see lightning. Actually, that's how I was able to get away in the seventh inning from all the games at the Stadium," Rizzuto joked years later.

Barber and Allen and Rizzuto worked the booth together from 1957 to 1964.

Rizzuto also started another new broadcast wherein he got a break with CBS radio. *It's Sports Time With Phil Rizzuto,* aired on more than 200 CBS network affiliate stations from 7:00 to 7:05 PM. The show was sponsored by Winston cigarettes and Val Crème. It ran six nights a week until 1973. In the early years, the man who substituted for Phil was New York Giants running back Frank Gifford.

After the football season, "Maxine and the kids went back to California while I stayed in town to do my radio show, subbing for Phil Rizzuto on CBS until Phil headed south for spring training and I could head back to California," Gifford recalled.

"He was fun to travel with, especially when he did his daily CBS Radio Network Show. The script, written by Herb Goren, would be waiting for him at the local CBS affiliate," said Marty Appel, longtime Yankees public relations and broadcast executive. "He would take a cab, run upstairs while the cab waited, read the script, and be back in the taxi on his way to play golf, in about 10 minutes."

"Don't ever tell anyone how easy this is," Rizzuto told Appel one day.

Rizzuto-Berra Lanes

Both Rizzuto and Berra were on hand for the annual screening of the World Series movie.

"I always enjoy the World Series movies," Berra said at Toots Shor's.

"Why not?" exclaimed Scooter. "You're always the star of the production. Holy smokes! I'm not even in this one!" The two were hamming it up for the press.

"Mr. Berra, sir," Rizzuto said, now officially a part of the Yankees broadcast booth, for which he was taking a razzing by his ex-teammates. "What name do I call you—Yogi or Lawrence?"

"You'll probably call me names that will get you barred from the air," Berra cracked. "Hey, Phil, how about you sneaking a mention of the chocolate drink Yoo-hoo, that I'm vice-president of?"

"Don't be so crass and commercial. Perhaps I could mention that you'd like to see all listeners at your bowling alley after it's completed," Rizzuto yukked. This was yet another instance of Rizzuto and Berra being much more sly than either of their Lardner-esque images.

Indeed, Berra and the Scooter were the proud owners of a bowling alley. Rizzuto paid half the money for the new alley that was under construction.

Berra picked up the other half. Together, they chose the site—a new, state-of-the-art shopping center called Styertowne Center near Clifton, New Jersey. Styertowne is sometimes referred to as the first suburban shopping center in America. Rizzuto-Berra Lanes was a sleek, 40-lane bowling alley that opened in May 1956.

It was not the only bowling alley Berra would own. He had another, Bowlomat, in Paramus, New Jersey, that was run by his brother, John. John would be the manager of the lanes, looking out for Berra's interests. However, Bowlomat never received the publicity that Rizzuto-Berra Lanes did.

Both Berra and Rizzuto were photographed by local newspapers as they threw the first shovels full of dirt on the new construction, even though they were not the owners of the building. Each had invested approximately $50,000. Using credit, they purchased nearly $500,000 worth of equipment and supplies. An expensive undertaking, each alley floor cost $3,500, and each pinsetter cost approximately $7,700. The equipment was purchased using time payments, and they were given a grace period of four months.

"We start making payments in September," Berra told the press. "Even on the weekends, you gotta wait for an alley a lot of times."

A glass showcase featured each of their MVP awards and their baseball gloves.

"That's the one I caught two no-hit games with," Berra pointed out. The bowling alley's cocktail lounge was shaped like the Yankee Stadium infield. "We call it the Stadium Lounge," Berra beamed. The snack bar was named the Dugout.

"Yogi is my best friend on the ball club," Rizzuto wrote. "He's the brains behind the alley; I'm the front man. In the off-season, Yogi bowls in three leagues, and he'll even come around in the afternoon and bowl. Which helps business."

Rizzuto and Berra announced on May 22, 1962, that they had decided to sell their bowling alley. The operation was sold to Lence Inc., of New York. The purchase price was not released. Lence owned and operated 23 bowling alleys in New York and New Jersey.

Comfortable in His New Life

On January 15, 1957, Phil Rizzuto appeared as himself on a new game show titled *To Tell the Truth*, hosted by Bud Collyer. One contestant and two imposters sat before a panel of celebrities, who were then charged with deducing which of the three was the real McCoy. Pat Rizzuto, Phil's daughter, was the first contestant. John Lahr and host Bud Collyer's son, Mike, posed as the imposters. Phil appeared at the end of the show to identify the real Pat Rizzuto.

Asked many years later if he used "Holy Cow!" at home, Patricia said he did so all the time. Perhaps for a B-plus on a test?

"For an A," she answered.

On March 31, 1957, Billy Meyer, Rizzuto's former Norfolk Tars and Kansas City manager, died of a heart attack at the age of 64 in Knoxville, Tennessee. Meyer was frequently troubled by ill health during the last decade of his managerial career. Once in retirement, he suffered a stroke in 1955. He had compiled a managing record of 317–452 (.412) over the course of five seasons (1948–52) with Pittsburgh. And he had a career batting average of only .236 (with one home run and 21 runs batted in). However, those accomplishments belied the amazing amount of respect the league had for Meyer. Two unique honors were bestowed upon him. For years the baseball park in his native city of Knoxville, Tennessee, was named Bill Meyer Stadium. And the Pirates retired Meyer's uniform No. 1, despite that horrible 1952 campaign when the team lost 112 games.

On June 6, 1957, Paul Bernard Krichell, the famed Yankees scout who had discovered Gehrig, Lazzeri, Rizzuto, Berra, Charlie Keller, and Vic Raschi among many more, died. He was the longest-tenured Yankees employee, and he was one of the main components in building the Yankees into the powerhouse they had become. When Krichell took over scouting, there were two scouts. By the time of his death, there were 20.

On June 15, 1957, George Weiss had all the ammunition he needed, and Stengel couldn't stop him. Billy Martin was traded to the Kansas City Athletics after the Copacabana incident proved to be the last straw for the tenacious and pugilistic Martin. A bunch of Yankees had gone to the club to see Sammy Davis Jr. and ended up in a brawl with some of the other patrons. In the end, it turns out that none of the Yankees might have had anything to do with the fight. In retrospect, the players still insist today that the bouncers actually assaulted the other patrons. But it was not the first time the New York Yankees, and Martin in particular, had been the center of bad late-night public relations.

"Every ballplayer knows how conscientious I am. Sure, I go places. I'm single and I can't sit in a hotel room, talking to the floor lamps. I roomed with Phil Rizzuto and he won the Most Valuable Player. I roomed with Mickey Mantle last year and he won everything. I can't be too bad an influence," Martin said to the press.

In October of that year, Yogi and Scooter appeared on the *Phil Silvers Show* with other Yankees in a skit about baseball as a network warm up to the World Series. It got rave reviews, with Dick Van Dyke stealing the show as a Southern country boy with two golden arms.

Rizzuto was a soft touch when it came to interviews. He was not a journalist, and he never pretended to be. A visitor to the booth, especially an old friend or player, would have no fear walking into a room with Scooter and a microphone.

An example of Rizzuto's easy interviewing manner occurred on September 25, 1960. Jackie Jensen was a former Yankee player. He had played in 108 games between 1950 and 1952 and was traded to the Washington Senators and then to the Red Sox in 1954. He was a solid all-around player with a big stick, and he made several All-Star teams during the course of his career. Jensen made his last All-Star team in 1958 when he batted .286 with a league-leading 122 RBIs. He placed second in the AL with 99 walks and fifth in home runs with 35. He won the MVP award for the 1958 season. In 1959, he again led the league in RBIs (112), won his only Gold Glove, scored a career-best 101 runs, stole 20 bases, and came in 10th in the MVP balloting. But as more teams moved to California during baseball's Western expansion, teams were now flying more and more. Jensen was phobic about flying, experiencing painful panic attacks that affected his play and psyche.

"I have only one life to live, and I'll be happier when I can spend it with my family," Jensen told the press in January 1960. "Being away from home with a baseball team for seven months a year doesn't represent the kind of life I want or the kind of life my wife and children want." Still at the peak of career, Jensen retired (although he came back in 1961 for one last season). He was one of the biggest sports stories of 1960, especially in baseball.

When he walked into the announcing booth with Phil, Scooter said, "Everybody has their own things to iron out. You have reasons for doing things. I'm not going to ask about that. But I mean…you look in great shape!"

61*

In 1956, the Yankees beat the Brooklyn Dodgers but lost a year later to the Milwaukee Braves in the fall classic. In 1958, they avenged their loss to the Braves in a rematch to retake baseball's crown. In 1960, they lost to the Pittsburgh Pirates, as Bill Mazeroski's ninth-inning game-winning home run dramatically carried defeat with it. After the loss, Stengel retired. But it was clear that he did not do so voluntarily. Stengel remarked that he had been fired for turning 70 and that he would "never make that mistake again."

Through the years, Stengel's tactical genius kept the Yankees in many games they might have otherwise lost. But toward the end of his run with the Yankees, he spurned bringing along new talent. He was always tough on rookies. And he wrestled with Yankees brass who wanted to see new players like Clete Boyer developed. Young players like Tony Kubek, Bobby Richardson, and Boyer made it known they didn't feel comfortable with Stengel. There was, in the parlance of our times, a generation gap, and he was let go. His replacement was Ralph Houk.

"I have always said that managing in the major leagues is an overrated occupation, that a good major league manager contributes no more than 10 percent to the success of a ball club," Rizzuto said. "Let me put it even stronger. I think that if Casey Stengel had managed that '61 ball club, the Yankees would not have won a pennant."

"He's got everybody loose," Yogi Berra said of new manager Ralph Houk, "and we all feel terrific. Everybody likes him, wants to play for him."

"As soon as I heard that Houk had the job, I was elated. I knew he could do it. In my last two years as a Yankee player, I spent much of my time out in the Yankee bullpen. Houk was out there, too. He wasn't out there with his cap over his eyes," Rizzuto wrote. "He was watching and picking up tips."

George Weiss was summarily fired two weeks later. It was part of Toping's supposed youth movement. Weiss had worked for the Yankees since 1931. He had been hired by Ed Barrow to create the Yankee farm system. "The minor league teams Weiss put together for the Yankees were some of the best in history, and the constant flow of talent to the parent club was testimony to his skill in finding and developing players," baseball historian Robert Creamer wrote.

The Yankees marched to the pennant in 1961. But the Yankees pennant drive was not the lead story that summer. In 1961, the main story of the day was the home run race between Roger Maris and Mickey Mantle. And Rizzuto was there for the whole thing.

"I know I was surprised watching Maris that first full season of 1960. It wasn't just his hitting that surprised me. I knew he was a good hitter," Rizzuto wrote of Maris. "But it was his all-around play that surprised me. He was the complete ballplayer."

Rizzuto marveled at the difference in the two players. "When Mantle feels the pressure, he lashes out—kicks a water cooler or a helmet or something—and it relaxes him. But Maris…bottles it up inside of him. He'd be better off if he could let off steam like Mantle and be done with it. But he can't."

Rizzuto pointed out that after Mutt Mantle's death, Mickey seemed directionless and didn't seem to care as much about anything. "Some of his failure to reach full potential has had to do with injuries he suffered over the years. He has played most of his major league career with two bad legs," Rizzuto said of Mantle. "But I also have a feeling his missed his father's counsel. In his younger days, Mutt Mantle seemed to be the only one who could work with Mickey. He'd tell Mickey what to do, and Mickey would do it."

"But there was a noticeable change in the Mantle of 1961. I played golf with him twice last season, and he seemed to be in a very, very good mood, more so than in any other year. His attitude seemed to have changed." Rizzuto gave some of the credit to Ralph Houk, the Major, as he was a called. A tough gritty catcher as a player, Houk was ready to stamp his imprint on this team. Houk was a breath of fresh air after Stengel was fired, as far as the players and especially the veterans were concerned. Houk was talking up Mantle to the press, at one point saying, "So goes Mantle, so goes the Yankees."

Mantle started off the season like a ball of fire, blasting home runs, while Maris struggled just to hit safely. But by June 22, Maris had 27 homeruns. At one point a reporter, referring to Babe Ruth, said to Maris, "I bet you lie awake thinking you're going to break his record."

"I hope you believe me when I say I never give Babe Ruth a thought. Not now or ever. I'm just thankful to be able to hit like I am."

But the press had started in on both of them. Mickey, used to years of pressure from the New York media, was able to slough off some of it. Maris was unable to. It became unbearable to him. The Yankees clinched the pennant in Baltimore on September 20, and Maris hit No. 59.

As Rizzuto called it:

"You'll forgive me if I root a little bit for Roger tonight," he told listeners late in September 1961 as the Yankees' Roger Maris chased Babe Ruth's single-season home run record. "Just tonight, that's all…2–1 pitch, drive deep to right! Way back there! Way back! And there's No. 59 for Roger Maris! Atta boy Roger, 59 home runs!"

"I remember coming back late in the season from Minneapolis to New York. Rog was still looking for No. 60. I had a long talk with him on that four-hour plane trip, and I was quite surprised at some of the things he said." Maris was discussing with Rizzuto that he was trying to calculate how many more years he would have to play baseball. He did not like his work. He was not happy in baseball.

"I figure another four or five years—five tops," Maris said. "Then I can quit and go home."

"You're kidding Rog. You'd only be 31," Scooter said.

"I'm not kidding," Maris said.

"Then you're crazy," Rizzuto said.

"I'm not crazy, either."

While Rizzuto was shocked to hear Maris say these things, he also knew Roger was tired of the circus that the summer had become and he was loathsome of the press, who seemed to know no boundaries that season. But as Rizzuto also wrote, "Despite any feelings he had, he never let up on the field. He was always the team man."

On September 26, in a game against the Baltimore Orioles at Yankee Stadium, Roger Maris tied the record of 60 home runs in a season. Around the packed venue, 19,401 fans witnessed the historic event.

On the last day of the season, October 1, 1961, against the Red Sox, more than 23,000 fans came out in the warm Indian summer weather to see if Maris could do it. Tracy Stallard, a young, big, right-hander, was the pitcher for the Red Sox. When asked how he would approach Maris, Stallard said, "I just throw the ball. I put my hard stuff against his hard stuff."

Maris came up to bat in the fourth inning with the score 0–0. There was one out. Stallard threw two balls and the fans began to boo.

"Tracy must have heard them because his next pitch was a fastball, coming in waist high, straight down the middle. Maris uncoiled, flashing that graceful, fluid swing," Rizzuto wrote.

Rizzuto's call.

"Here comes Roger Maris, they're standing up, waiting to see if Roger is going to hit number 61, here's the windup, the pitch to Roger, WAY outside, ball one. The fans are starting to boo, low, ball two. That one was in the dirt and the boos get louder. Two balls, no strikes on Roger Maris, here's the windup, fastball, hit deep to right, this could be it, way back there, holy cow he did it, 61 for Maris!"

The team rushed Roger. Even after a lucky fan had caught the ball, others in the stands tried to punch him and take the ball away. Said Rizzuto:

"Holy Cow! Look at the fight for that ball!"

"It was one of the most exciting moments of my life, watching Maris hit that ball and watching the crowd scene," Rizzuto said later.

"[Mantle] was, I think, the most valuable player on the Yankees and in the league," Rizzuto said about the 1961 season. "And this is taking away nothing from Roger Maris, who actually won the award."

October '64

"The first time I came back, I'd been out of the country for about three and a half years in the Congo and in Vietnam, and I hadn't seen the changes in baseball," journalist David Halberstam said, referring to his travels in the early Sixties. "The Mickey Mantle era was coming to an end in '64. The Yankees had gone from DiMaggio to Mantle, lasting from the Thirties all the way into the Sixties, but it was coming to an end."

While there was lots of drama on the field that year with new manager Yogi Berra, there was plenty behind the scenes, as well.

"Phil and I had a very warm relationship playing and broadcasting. He was a delightful guy…. He could hit, he could field, he could steal bases. He was a great player," wrote Jerry Coleman, who became a broadcast partner on Yankees games in 1963. "For Mel Allen, and I am sure with Red Barber, working with Phil and me had to be a problem. They were professional broadcasters. We were a couple of ex-jocks."

Berra was now field manager for the Bombers in a controversial year whose nadir was highlighted in the Phil Linz harmonica-slapping incident on the team bus following a dreadful series at Chicago. The team pulled itself together and ended up winning the pennant by a game over the White Sox and two games over the Orioles.

• • •

Mel Allen sat in the announcer's booth just staring at the baseball field in Cleveland when Red Barber arrived. Allen was deep in thought. He looked "numb" to Barber. He didn't seem to hear Red's arrival, he just kept staring out. "He has protruding dark eyes. They were bulging out so far they looked like Concord grapes. He was the saddest looking man I had ever seen," remembered Barber. "He was desolate and stricken." Barber touched his friend gently on the shoulder when it was airtime, and Mel sprang up, "Hello everybody, this is Mel Allen."

"How he did his work, I don't know," Barber said.

What had numbed Allen was that word had leaked out that Rizzuto, not Allen, would be broadcasting the 1964 World Series when the Yankees would face the St. Louis Cardinals.

"Bob Fishel told me he dreaded each day," Barber remembered. "Because Mel was on the phone with either Topping or him—all the time. Mel could not believe he would not be on the Series, could not accept he wasn't the Voice of the Yankees, until he wasn't."

"A move that so infuriated Allen to the extent that he went to the commissioner to demand reinstatement," Peter Golenbock wrote after the Series. Allen was released outright.

"In fall 1964, Allen expected the Yankees to extend his contract. Instead, in December they released him without even an announcement, ignoring Mel's honor, cheery tenderness, and reluctance to offend. To America, Allen vanished overnight, ceasing to exist for reasons he never grasped nor understood," broadcasting historian Curt Smith wrote.

"The Yankees never held a press conference," Smith said. "They left people to believe whatever they wanted—and people believed the worst."

Lacking any explanation, *Sports Illustrated* wrote, "Allen became a victim of rumors. It was as if he had leprosy." There were rumors of homosexuality, of drug abuse, of drinking, and mental instability.

"You can't name one time he got loaded," ex-partner Jerry Coleman dissented angrily. "That's garbage."

New York Times columnist George Vecsey recalls Allen at Yankee Stadium's bar "with a couple beers. Possibly he'd overdo it, not much."

By the 1980s, "Maybe he'd nurse a glass of wine for an entire hour," said *This Week In Baseball* executive producer Geoff Belinfante. "That was it. I don't think he had a problem."

"As Allen got older, he grew increasingly prolix. Some say he belabored the obvious and qualified his explanations to death," wrote J. Anthony Lukas, the Pulitzer Prize–winning journalist, who was an ardent Allen fan from his youth. "Dissatisfaction grew, first apparently among officials at Ballantine, then in the Yankee organization."

According to Curt Smith, newspaperman Maury Allen cites September 8, 1964, in Bloomington, Minnesota. "The pressroom fills before a game. In one corner, general manager Ralph Houk and a Twins attendant kibitz. In another, The Voice—'his big voice starts booming, it's loud, it dominates'— recalls Murderers Row."

Disgusted, Houk shouts an obscenity, walks out, and phones owner Dan Topping. "He'd had it," Maury said. "Mel was gone. Ralph won't talk about it, even now."

In 1971, Lukas asked Allen why he was fired, "I still don't know today. It's hard to live with." Said Mike Burke of the Yankees, "He wasn't what he used to be."

According to Smith, people were still asking in 1995. "****, that's thirty years ago, and I'm still working," Allen said. "If I knew why, I'd be glad to tell 'em, so I could get people off my back."

In short, writer Peter Golenbock summarized it best. He pointed out that over the years Allen's relations with the Yankees front office and with Ballantine's public relations officials were what really ended his reign as the voice of the Yankees. Allen consistently overbooked himself with personal appearances to make more money. He expected the Yankees traveling secretaries and back office to continue to schedule these events, to the point where he suffered almost total physical and mental exhaustion.

Allen was also known for staying up late and getting up early while on the road, and often put in messages with the hotel desks with orders not to ring him, making him inaccessible event to Topping or Webb. Topping and public relations head at Ballantine, Ed Fishel, both decided they'd had enough.

"They hired me to help keep Mel off the air a little bit because they were getting complaints that he talked too much, that he never shut up," Jerry Coleman recalled. During a rain delay in Baltimore once, they decided that instead of sending it back to New York, they would do interviews in the booth. Mel signaled for Coleman to throw him the mike.

"What do you think, Mel?" Coleman asked on air.

"And two hours and 20 minutes later, he stopped talking," Coleman remembered. "He talked through an entire rain delay, and I think that was the straw that broke the camel's back." Coleman also mentioned that during the 1963 Dodgers-Yankees World Series, "They had to take him off the air because he couldn't talk. It wasn't his voice—it just wouldn't come. That finished him professionally."

Rizzuto and Joe Garagiola would broadcast the 1964 World Series, and Barber would do it for Armed Services Radio. Harry Caray announced for the St. Louis team.

"Phil knew how to talk. He had a knack for saying things excitable. But he knew what he wanted to say, so he'd say it that way. He was funny with all his fears and superstitions, and he was serious too," Yogi Berra said. "Announcing-wise, what can you say? You'll never hear a guy who calls a game like Phil."

"In 1964, I was broadcasting the World Series between the Cardinals and the Yankees. During the second game in St. Louis, I remember looking down at the dugout, and it really hit me: Yogi was managing the Yankees in the World Series and I was broadcasting it for NBC," wrote Garagiola years later. "That we could be the same two kids who spent so many nights sitting underneath the lamppost barely seemed possible."

Joseph Henry "Joe" Garagiola Sr. was born February 12, 1926, on Elizabeth Avenue in St. Louis, Missouri, across the street from Lawrence Peter Berra—better known as Yogi. The two knew each other from the time they were in diapers because their families had been friends for decades.

As a young man Garagiola was handsome with a shock of dark black hair and an athletic body. He broke into professional baseball a year before Berra and started playing major league ball in 1946, a year before Berra caught on with the Yankees. He was an instant star in his first year with the Cards, who won the 1946 Series, and he became a celebrated hometown hero. His career as a baseball player went south after that, along with his hairline.

Garagiola always made for good copy with the writers and the banquet circuit for his gift of gab, and his inexhaustible bag of jokes, stories, and endless quotes of Yogi Berra. They afforded him success in the publishing world where several of his books became *New York Times* bestsellers. More importantly, he found his way into the announcing booth, where he enjoyed much fame and success. He went on to have 30-year association with NBC television, broadcasting many different baseball games, sports shows, and World Series, as well as being a host of *The Today Show*. In 1991, he was honored by the Baseball Hall of Fame with the Ford Frick Award for outstanding broadcasting accomplishments.

Garagiola joked about himself, "I went through baseball as 'a player to be named later.'" And his explanation of baseball was always with a twinge of humor. "Baseball is a game of race, creed, and color. The race is to first base. The creed is the rules of the game. The color? Well, the home team wears white uniforms, and the visiting team wears gray."

Garagiola was baseball's new funny man who actually knew something about the game. He was a fresh, new presence in the booth and on the screen. And his career took off like a juggernaut. However, some announcers weren't enamored with Garagiola's outlandish stories and gags, especially the journalistic Barber.

"He was a quick sensation as a funny man, but he was a strongly disruptive influence on the announcer he was paired with. Or paired against, as it sounded," Barber wrote of Garagiola. "I admire the laughs he gets as an after-dinner speaker, although he and I differ about how play-by-play should be conducted."

In 1964, it would be Yogi Berra's comeback Yankees, the powerful, perennial standard bearer of the American League, against Johnny Keane's upstart St. Louis Cardinals, as storied a franchise in the National League as there was.

"There was this surging Cardinal team with these great young black ballplayers. I hadn't followed the National League—I'm kind of an American League guy—so I watched that Series and I'm thinking, *Who is Bob Gibson? Who is Lou Brock? Who is Curt Flood? Who is Bill White?* This is a really good baseball team. They beat the Yankees in the seventh game, and I thought, 'Oh boy, something's happened. The Cardinals were ascending and the Yankees were unraveling and getting old,'" Halberstam remembered.

Caray, Garagiola, and Rizzuto were in the booth for NBC. Of course, the irony for Berra was that he had two homers in the booth—Garagiola, a close friend since boyhood, and Rizzuto, his closest friend on the Yankees.

• • •

"Phil and Harry Caray used to go around about who said it first," Jerry Coleman said. "I don't know, but Phil was born in Brooklyn and lived his entire life in New York. How'd he know what a cow looked like?"

"I never knew who Harry Caray was when I was saying 'Holy Cow,'" Rizzuto said. "My high school teacher and coach of the baseball team told me he had tried to become a baseball player and he said, 'You know, you don't want to argue with the umpire.' And I always said, 'Holy Cow,' from when I was a kid. I can't stop doing something that keeps me out of trouble."

Barber and Jerry Coleman did the Armed Forces Radio broadcast in a studio with a live television feed. Producer Gordon Bridge had the feed live in the other room with the volume up. From time to time they would listen to the broadcast while they were temporarily off the air.

"As we sat in that New York studio, listening to and working that 1964 World Series, we began to get embarrassed, and then we got angry. Garagiola kept interrupting Rizzuto on the air, cutting in on him, taking the mike away," an angry Barber recalled. "Then we got doubly mad because Rizzuto sat there and took it like a sweet little lamb. Rizzuto just let Garagiola cut in on him." For his part, Rizzuto, when Garagiola did the play-by-play, let Garagiola take the whole thing, according to Barber.

"Listen to Garagiola cutting in on Phil," Barber said to Coleman and Gordon. "Coleman said that he thought it was terrible."

"Joe does it all the time to everybody he works with…had trouble in St. Louis with Harry Caray about it…Caray stopped him…they don't like each other," Gordon reported.

Still, neither Rizzuto nor Coleman seemed to have any bad things to say about Garagiola. Coleman wrote in his autobiography, "Joe did talk a lot, there's no question about it. But at the same time, you understand what your partner does, and you work around it…Joe was good and he was probably the most underrated broadcaster in the business. He was kind of a folksy guy, but sharp as a tack. You want to know what goes on in baseball? Joe can tell you. And he always left with a humorous tone."

After Garagiola had moved on to network television, Jack Buck was once again paired with Caray. The pairing didn't work out so well the first time. "Caray treated me better than he did the first time we worked together. I was older and more experienced, and he and Garagiola had become enemies. Caray didn't view me as a rival," Jack Buck Sr. recalled many years later.

Not long after the Cardinals beat the Yankees in the World Series, the Yankees hired Perry Smith, the No. 2 man at NBC Sports. He was appointed vice president of the Yankees in charge of radio and television.

"The coming of Perry Smith was a warning bell," the embittered Barber wrote. A few weeks later, Garagiola was officially announced as Barber's and Rizzuto's new partner.

"It was the first time in my life that I had sat in a radio booth with a fellow who moved in on my broadcast. I couldn't finish what I was saying," Barber complained of Garagiola. In 1964, Barber knew his days were numbered. He noticed how his pre-game pieces were becoming fewer and fewer. Perry Smith was spending a lot more time with Garagiola—the two were old friends from NBC. By 1966, Barber was hanging on by a thread.

In 1966, the Yankees finished in 10th place in the American League. Dead last. Now under the ownership of CBS, it was the first time the franchise had finished last since 1912. On September 22, 1966, a paid attendance of 413 was announced at the 65,000-seat Yankee Stadium. Barber asked the TV cameras to pan the empty stands as he commented on the low attendance.

"The Yankees had two weeks to go in the saddest season in their history," Barber said. Barber insisted that the television cameras pan the stands to show how empty the stadium was. Even White Sox manager Eddie Stanky before the game said he could count the people in the stands from the visitor's dugout.

Although denied the camera shots on orders from the WPIX-TV director, Don Carney, Barber said on air, "I don't know what the paid attendance is today, but whatever it is, it is the smallest crowd in the history of Yankee Stadium, and this crowd is the story, not the game."

He was right. *The New York Daily News* had a photo of Mike Burke, the newly installed president of the Yankees, sitting alone in the deserted stands, yawning. A week later, Barber was invited to breakfast, where Burke told him that his contract wouldn't be renewed.

"I fired Barber personally because he was giving us a terrible time in the broadcast booth. Squabbling with Rizzuto, going out of his way to make embarrassing remarks about Garagiola on the air and make him look stupid," complained Mike Burke to the press. CBS was now in charge.

Through it all, Rizzuto stayed out of the fray. He knew what Allen and Barber thought of him. And he and Garagiola were friendly. As Marty Appel once said, Phil got along with everyone. In fact, Phil was just as popular as ever, and was a much in demand guest at parties and dinners.

"Selma, my wife, was excited that a baseball celebrity would be our guest. So she went about planning a menu that she thought would appeal to him," recalled famed New York Knicks basketball coach Red Holzman. "Phil arrived. We had drinks. We settled down at the table. Selma served her appetizer—tomato juice."

"This stuff is thirst quenching," Selma said, "It's a good way to start a meal."

"Phil agreed and then went along as he was served a Spanish omelet stuffed with tomatoes and then tomato soup. Rizzuto good naturedly ate everything up—his only complaint: 'I just hope you don't have tomato pie for dessert.'"

The New Yankees

"What has happened since 1964 is the sickening collapse of the Yankee behemoth that won 18 pennants in the 25 years Allen was with the team. In those balmy years, Yankees fans tuned in not so much for the play-by-play as for confirmation that all was still right in the best of all possible worlds. But in recent years, Yankees announcers have been a bit like classic messengers bearing bad news—and have often met the same fate," wrote J. Anthony Lukas in 1971.

Seven years of losing Yankees baseball.

"Of late, all four have been horrible," Dan Topping's desperate memorandum read, regarding the Yankees' crew of announcers in the 1970 season (Bob Gamere joined the broadcast booth for one season in 1970). "I realize it was a mighty tough job during our losing streak to give an interesting broadcast. But certainly the way the club has been doing recently, there is no excuse for all the talk about everything but reporting the game…. The club is coming out of the slump, tell the four in the booth to get going, too."

"When I covered the Yankees in the '60s, they had players like Horace Clarke, Ross Moschitto, Jake Gibbs, and Dooley Womack. It was like the first-team missed the bus," Garagiola of those awful teams.

"Caught in this dilemma, announcers often talk about everything but the dismaying events on the field," Lukas wrote.

"Rizzuto was an urban everyman. His narrative of ball game was a tapestry of present tense interwoven with scraps of the past," Robert Siegel of *All Things Considered* on National Public Radio explained Rizzuto's popularity. "I remember listening to Rizzuto during a rain delay one night in the '60s. It was storming, and the Scooter was afraid of lightning, much to the amusement of his partner that season, Joe Garagiola. I don't think I've heard anyone else, no less a sports hero, admit to such uncontrollable anxiety on the air. He was one of the most real people you could hear on radio."

"It was different," said Joe Garagiola, who broadcast Yankees games with Rizzuto from 1965–67. "He was a delight, though. He was like the kid who got in on the pass. He enjoyed everything. How can you not like working with him? How can you not like him?" Garagiola had everyman's touch. As if in response to Barber, he was quoted as saying, "Some guys make you think it's high math. It's not. It's a baseball game."

"First thing that comes into my head I say without really thinking about it," Rizzuto admitted. "Of course, my wife has told me many times that everybody's got a little trap door in the back of their head and you get an idea and it sits there, and then if you think it's all right to say it, the trap door opens and it comes out. And she says my trap door is constantly open."

"Announcers for a loser can't do anything right," Lukas continued. "If they report straight, call the errors, sloppy base-running and missed opportunities as they see them, they quickly hear repercussions from the players, whose wives listen at home and tell their husbands after the game, 'You know what so-and-so said about you today?'"

Phil Rizzuto was not immune to this kind of remarking and backlash. Hank Bauer almost punched out Scooter on the basis of one of Mrs. Bauer's reports. Mrs. Bob Turley, wife of the former Yankees fireballer, was infamous for her complaints about the broadcasters.

"If the announcers go to the other extreme—excusing errors, boosting the home team no matter what—the fans at home quickly peg them as phonies," Lukas wrote.

No matter, if CBS did nothing else right, and they didn't, they did pair Garagiola and Rizzuto. While the games were unwatchable by and large, the announcers were amusing and often hilarious. While they may not have been the best baseball announcers for purists, they were trying to sell beer and whatever else they could. And they held up pretty well.

Rizzuto, of course, continued to make new fans.

"I was born in Brooklyn and remain a Dodger fan, but I grew up in Jersey. In the early '60s, I lived in a foster home in Elizabeth, New Jersey, and one of my memories was when Mr. Rizzuto took a number of us to attend a Yankee game," Stuart Greenfield wrote. "I don't remember the outcome of the game, nor do I have the ball he gave each of us, but I have always cherished the kindness of Mr. Rizzuto."

"In August 1967, I had been given some tickets which were two rows behind the Yankee announcers," Jeff Kahn recalled. "It was one of the rare games that wasn't televised, and Phil and Joe Garagiola were doing the radio. The Yanks were down by two going into the ninth, and Garagiola left early. When Bill Robinson homered in the bottom of the ninth to tie it for the Yanks, Scooter turned around to us [the people in front of us had left] and said, 'That huckleberry, Garagiola, he'll hear this in his car and have to come back.' Ironically, it was Phil who later got the reputation for leaving games early, but that night he was there for all 14 innings, chatting with us occasionally between the extra innings. It was always enjoyable listening to Phil, even for a diehard fan during the lean years."

"In 1967, I was at a Saturday afternoon game at Yankee Stadium," remembered another fan of the period. "Late in the game, a group of us kids snuck into the Mezzanine and sat behind the broadcast booth. Joe Garagiola cheerily made the final call and sign-off. As soon as the mic was off, his smile devolved into a sneer at the sight of a bunch of kids pleading for some attention. Garagiola looked us over, slowly put on his sunglasses, and hissed out a 'No' to all of us. Not Phil. 'Hiya kids, how ya doin'?' Scooter signed autographs for anyone who asked and answered any and all questions with the same cheer and humility always present in his broadcast persona." The fan also added, "Initially stunned by the icy brush-off by Garagiola, we recovered soon enough to hoot the hell out him with a vengeance worthy of his contempt."

• • •

As far as NBC was concerned, Garagiola was being wasted on the Yankees broadcasts, and he was called up to do bigger and better things on the national stage. Between 1963 and 1969, Jerry Coleman was also working alongside Scooter in the booth.

In his second year in the majors, Coleman earned a selection to the All-Star team in 1950. In the World Series, Coleman's sparkling defense continued to define him, earning him the BBWAA's Babe Ruth Award as the Series' most valuable player.

Coleman's career declined after he was injured, relegating him to a bench role. He was forced to retire after the 1957 season, but he left on a good note, hitting .364 in a World Series loss against the Milwaukee Braves.

Coleman became a broadcaster in 1960 for the CBS Radio Network, and in 1963 he began a seven-year run calling New York Yankees games on WCBS and WHN Radio and WPIX-TV. For the second time in his career, he was now working side-by-side with Scooter.

"He was probably better at both jobs than anyone I have ever known," Coleman said. "It was an honor to play next to Phil on the field and be with him in the booth...I learned from Phil in the booth as well as on the field."

Coleman was known for his own malapropisms, but he was a fan favorite nevertheless. Coleman was known for some of his own catchphrases, including "Oh Doctor!," "You can hang a star on that baby!," "And the beat goes on" and "The natives are getting restless."

"My favorite broadcast story was when the Yankees were playing Cleveland in a doubleheader. Before the game, we were told [Sam] McDowell and [Jack] Kralick were pitching for the Indians," Coleman said of the mid-1960s broadcast.

"Phil and I were going on and on about how McDowell's control had gotten so much sharper. I think I said something about McDowell looking like a different pitcher. In about the fourth inning, the station called to say it was Kralick pitching the first game."

According to Coleman, they looked over to see Mel Allen, sick with disgust, his forehead resting on the console.

"He didn't come up for two minutes," Coleman remembered. "He realized what a disaster it was."

One of Coleman's most notable WPIX calls came when it was his turn to broadcast when ex-teammate Mickey Mantle hit his 500th career home run in 1967. Coleman's call was brief and emotional:

> *Here's the payoff pitch... This is IT! There it goes! It's out of here!*

One of Coleman's most outrageous memories came from a mid-summer game.

"On a very hot afternoon, we would take our pants off to stay somewhat cool," Coleman admitted. They did this during a weekend series in Kansas City. It was sizzling and humid. And since the broadcast team was never shot below the waist, the entire cast took off their pants, and ran back and forth on a catwalk with their announcers' jackets, shirts, and ties, but with only their underwear on below. However, the catwalk was 20 feet long between the TV and radio booths. The fans looking up could see them scurrying in their underwear going back and froth. A woman in the stands complained.

"I was sitting down, happily doing a game, when all of a sudden there's a strong hand on my shoulder. It's a cop."

"Put your pants on," insisted the officer. The broadcast team complied.

• • •

On July 7, 1966, Philip Francis Rizzuto Sr. died of a heart attack. He was 74 years old. In the 1940s and 1950s, he had worked as a uniformed pier guard, working the night shift so he could see his son play ball at Yankee Stadium, or listen on the radio, or watch on television.

"'His father stayed in the house long after his son had become famous, setting up two chairs under a shady maple tree on the sidewalk every morning and waiting for neighbors to join him in conversation,' said Marie Ruppe...who moved across the street in 1962," journalist Ellen Barry wrote years later.

He had died at 78-01 64th Street in Glendale, where he had lived for 33 years. He was survived by his wife, Rose, as well as Phil and Alfred, and his daughters Mary Stoehr (and her husband John J.) and Rose Estato (and her husband Paul J.), as well as by his two brothers, Joseph and Anthony, and his four sisters Rose Pascuzzo, Julia Guarascio, Lilliam Guarascio, and Louise Gressler. Funeral services were held at St. Pancras Roman Catholic Church, and he was interred at St. John's Cemetery. At the time he had 12 grandchildren and 3 great-grandchildren. Patricia was 22 years old, Cynthia was 19 years old, Penny was 16, and Little Scooter was 10.

Rizzuto carried on. He was always very entertaining. Vic Ziegel of the *New York Daily News* remembered, "I was sitting in the press box at Yankee Stadium, the old tin press box, no roof, no windows, no heaters, and when the wind was blowing it was like being on a peak in Nepal. This was the 1968 season, when baseball got the bright idea of raising the pitcher's mound because somebody in the commissioner's office was in love with 1–0 games. A lot of people didn't like it, and I'm guessing one of them was Phil Rizzuto. The Yanks were playing a doubleheader and Phil...asked me to go on the radio between games."

"I'm gonna start off with a question about the higher mound," Scooter told Ziegel. "So get ready. The high mound, got it?"

"The high mound, I got it." Ziegel responded. Then they went on air.

"Vic, what do you think about Mickey's chances of hitting 30 homers?"

"No, I don't think he can make it, Phil, and one good reason is the new higher mound."

Rizzuto didn't hesitate. "Yeah, the high mound, let's talk about it."

"That was Phil. He broke me up almost every time we met," Ziegel remembered.

Rizzuto-Messer-White: The Three Amigos

The Golden Era of Rizzuto's broadcast career came between 1971 and 1985. This was a period of steadiness in the booth between three great working partners: Phil Rizzuto, Frank Messer, and Bill White.

A year before Coleman's departure, the Yankees brought in Frank Messer. He was yet another great partner for Rizzuto, and the broadcasting duo would remain intact for some time.

Wallace Frank Messer was born on August 8, 1925, in Asheville, North Carolina. Messer was a Marine stationed in the South Pacific during World War II. After the war, Messer announced minor league baseball in the 1950s; his longest tenure was 10 years with the Richmond Virginians of the International League. His first opportunity to work major-league games arrived when he was hired by the Baltimore Orioles and worked alongside their noted longtime voice, Chuck Thompson, and Bill O'Donnell. In 1966, the Orioles won their first world championship. Messer also called Baltimore Colts football during the 1960s.

After the 1967 baseball season, Joe Garagiola left the Yankees broadcast booth. Messer took Garagiola's place for 1968, working with ex-Yankees Jerry Coleman and Phil Rizzuto. The Yankees longtime public relations director, Bob Fishel, had urged team management to approve a traditional play-by-play sportscaster, which the Yanks had not had since the firing of Red Barber after the 1966 season.

Messer was acclaimed by both critics and fans for his straight-shooting play-calling on radio and TV and by the club for his effectiveness promoting team events.

"We call Frank 'Old Reliable' up here, because we know when we're in trouble, he is here," Rizzuto said on the final 1973 Yankee broadcast before the renovation of the original Yankee Stadium.

Messer was not known for the turn of phrase that enlivened Allen's or Barber's broadcasts, all three being southerners, though he did frequently use the phrase, "Good Golly, Miss Molly." One of his signature phrases at the end of his last inning before switching booths from radio to TV (or vice-versa) was "(Announcer) will carry you along the rest of the way. It's been a pleasure."

"At one time, I think if I had one game to be broadcast right, I'd pick Rizzuto. Back then, he didn't miss a thing, with all the instincts of a great ballplayer. But as time went on, Phil's interests got diverted," Messer said in 1995.

Phil was not above playing practical jokes himself. Never one to stay too late at Yankee Stadium, he and Messer were working a game going into extra innings.

"Want a cup of coffee?" Rizzuto asked.

"Yes," Messer said. Rizzuto disappeared…over the George Washington Bridge. Messer continued his play-by-play.

The next day, as Messer sat in the announcer's booth for the next game, Rizzuto arrived just in time for the game, as he always did. He tapped Messer's shoulder and handed him a cup. "Here's your coffee."

Once when a bad storm was approaching the old Metropolitan Stadium in Minnesota during a mid-'60s road game, Rizzuto was at the mike alternately reporting the game and plotting his escape. Yankees fan Marty Berkowitz remembered, "Finally, he gave the mike over to Jerry Coleman. In the distance, we hear the sound of thunder and lightning followed by the trailing voice of Scooter, 'So long, Jer.'"

"Messer dotes on statistics. He keeps his own records, carefully inscribed in longhand in a 'Garden State College' spiral notebook—every Yankee game with its date, opponent, score, Yankee pitcher, opposing pitcher, attendance, and home runs," J. Anthony Lukas wrote. "The book enabled Messer to produce statistics with incredible speed."

An example of this was when Jake Gibbs hit a home run, and Messer, after referring to his notes, said, "Gibbs is the first Yankee to hit a home run with as many as two men on this year." Messer was a professional.

Another *bon mot* from his notebook was, "The last time [Frank] Howard hit a home run in Yankee Stadium was on September 3, 1967, off of Bill Monbouquette."

"More than any of the other announcers, Messer makes elaborate use of the data churned out by Bill Kane, the broadcast statistician," Lukas noted.

As for Rizzuto? "Statistics bore me."

"Messer began his Yankee tenure with Phil Rizzuto and Jerry Coleman as his booth mates. But most of the time, his partners were Rizzuto and Bill White. Their zaniness and frequent sparring required Messer to provide a counterbalance, steering them back to the game's basics," wrote Richard Sandomir in the *New York Times*.

"I think that Frank, professionally, was better than Phil, and better than I, were," White said. "He had great command of his voice and knew how to use it. He could do anything. It's too bad he didn't get the credit he deserved."

William DeKova "Bill" White was the final piece of the puzzle, hired in 1971.

He was born in Lakewood, Florida, in 1934. White attended Warren G. Harding High School in Warren, Ohio, before attending college at Hiram College near Cleveland.

"White earned a reputation as an outspoken player almost from the moment he signed with his first major league team in 1953. Perhaps because he came to professional baseball after several years in college, he was quicker to address injustices than others, and more forceful in demanding that changes be made," reported the *Boston Globe*.

As *New York Times* correspondent Claire Smith wrote: "Bill White has long prided himself on being a person who cannot be easily fitted into any mold. In the early 1960s, when it was safer for one's career as well as health to acquiesce quietly to the nation's Jim Crow laws, White was among a vocal minority of black players who spoke out vociferously against inadequacies at Florida spring-training sites and in minor-league cities throughout the South."

"White originally agreed to play baseball with the New York Giants merely as a means to earn college tuition [he was enrolled in pre-med courses]. He made the Giants' roster in 1956, however, and moved with the team to San Francisco, embarking on a fine 13-year career," the *Boston Globe* said.

"Nobody wanted ballplayers in the broadcast booth when [Rizzuto] got hired. That's one reason he made it so easy for me," White said.

"Before he accepted the Yankees job in 1971, White said he called Larry Doby, the Cleveland Hall of Famer who in 1947 became the first African-

American to play in the American League," Ralph Wimbish of the *New York Post* reported.

"I called him and Elston Howard to ask about Phil," White said. "Larry told me about how Phil went out of his way to make him feel welcome even though he played for another team. Some of his own teammates wouldn't shake Larry's hand, but Phil encouraged Larry, and he did the same with Elston," White said. "I came [to New York] with a good feeling, and Phil made me feel welcome. He helped me in my broadcasting."

"White is fondly remembered by Yankees fans for the way he often would play straight man for Rizzuto's broadcast-booth antics," Wimbish wrote.

White was selected to be a Yankees broadcaster from a field of more than 200 applicants, according to the Yankees. While the Yankees were one of the last teams to integrate on the field, in choosing White, they were the first team to integrate in the booth. "We hired him," said Yankees president Michael Burke, "because he was the best man for the job."

White, 37, had never done any play-by-play; however, he still exuded a solid, dignified confidence. "When I was a ballplayer, I had a lot of faults. I couldn't hit the inside pitch, and I couldn't run that well, but I worked hard and learned. I must have succeeded. I lasted 14 years. I intend to do the same thing with broadcasting."

"After baseball, I broadcast the 6:00 PM and 11:00 PM news here [in Philadelphia] for a while before going up to New York in '71 to do the Yankees," he said years later.

"He has an easy colloquial style studded with nuggets of pithy description," Lukas wrote.

White was a consummate professional. In the beginning, he sent his tapes to people like Vin Scully for advice and pointers. He worked with a private voice coach and commuted to Yankee Stadium from a Philadelphia suburb.

"The plan was for him to do color for a few months and then ease him into play-by-play," Marty Appel recalled.

That strategy lasted exactly eight innings. In the ninth inning, Rizzuto saw DiMaggio at an exhibition game against the Orioles at the old Miami Stadium.

"White, you take it," Rizzuto said as he suddenly scooted out of the booth.

"On the first pitch, Chico Salmon hit a game-winning homer, and Bill pretty much said, 'Uh-oh.'"

However, the three got along incredibly well and played off of one another effortlessly.

"Hey, White, you know where your loyalties are? Right here. The old pinstripes. No! You never wore them. So you have a right to sing the blues," Rizzuto said during some of the lean years.

Another *faux pas* was when the Yankees were playing a doormat team. "Phil was on a roll with one of his stories about what he and his wife did that weekend. Doc Medich was on the mound, and the batter took a wicked swing," a Yankees fan remembered.

"Holy cow—he struck him out!" Phil screamed.

"Uh, no, that was strike two," White said.

"Are you sure, White?" Phil said, and promptly finished his story like nothing had happened.

"Brooksie has some soft hands," White said of a play by Orioles third baseman Brooks Robinson. Confused, Rizzuto asked White on air what he meant. "If a guy's got heavy hands, the ball just bounces off of them. But Brooksie's hands are soft, he just smothers the ball."

White tried to use his discretion so as not to ruin his credibility with the players. One time he saw Frank Howard suiting up for a game and putting on a girdle. White mentioned it to Rizzuto before the game in conversation. Then the game began and the players took the field.

"There's slim, trim Frank Howard," Rizzuto said. "I wonder what kind of diet he's on, Bill." White responded on air that he didn't think Howard was on a diet. "Oh, you mean he's wearing one of those things." White was completely embarrassed.

"I didn't want to talk about that on the air because I was afraid I wouldn't be able to get into the clubhouse anymore. The players tell me things they don't tell other people, and I don't want to abuse their confidence."

For all the times he left the booth early on so many of his partners and colleagues, there was one time he couldn't. And it was Bill White who got the last laugh. The game was on August 24, 1974, at Shea Stadium between the Angels and the Yankees. It was the bottom of the sixth inning with the game tied 1–1, and bad weather rolled in.

"Oh, oh, ho-ly cow, as they put the error sign up, a bolt of lightning," reported Rizzuto. Now you hear the thunder. Right in the back of the scoreboard. Outside, that's where I'm heading in just a moment, only there's no one here to take this microphone over."

"Nettles makes the catch," Rizzuto continued. "One out. You should have seen that bolt of lightning!" Rizzuto spotted his broadcast partner, Bill White, who either wouldn't or couldn't relieve him.

"If Bill White was any kind of buddy, he'd come over and grab this mike," said the lightning-averse Scooter. "The pitch to Alomar. Check swing and low. You saw that lightning out there, I know you did. I want to tell you. There was another bolt and another clap of thunder." White wouldn't go back in, and Scooter was terrified.

• • •

White of course found out before most people about Rizzuto's famed score-card notations.

"Scooter, let me see your scorecard," White asked. Looking at the card, it carried a notation he wasn't familiar with "WW."

"What's this?" White asked.

"Wasn't watching," Rizzuto said.

And of course, Rizzuto's partners had no first names. He was quite consistent about it. They were Coleman, Messer, and White. And so were anyone else he worked with his entire career. It was always just a last name.

One day Scooter came in and the producer, or whoever it was, who normally filled out his scorecard, wasn't there. Scooter would normally read off the lineup card and then throw it over to his broadcast partner, Bill White.

"So he says to me, 'White, can you fill out my scorecard for me, please?'"

"Sure, no problem, Scooter." White said. White knew that Phil would not look at the card until it came time to read on air. White proceeded to fill out the lineup card. As suspected, Phil never glanced at it until they were on the air. After a few opening remarks, Rizzuto went to the lineup card.

"Tonight's lineup starts with Larry White at first base; second base Phil White; shortstop Barry White....hey, White, what is this?" The two could be heard laughing together on the air.

Then there was this little ditty. WPIX showed a shot of the full moon, which took up most of the screen. The terrain was quite noticeable.

Rizzuto said, "White, look at that moon! I think I can see Texas! (Long pause) Awwwww, Texas isn't on the moon!"

"When we first started working together, we developed this banter. And we weren't faking it, you see. We weren't like some other partners who were on the air, and then didn't speak to each other once the mics went off. There were several announcing teams that hated each other."

"For all those 18 years, number one, we had a lot of fun. I learned a lot and at no point did we have a cross word for each other. It was eighteen years of fun and friendship. I had an opportunity to meet his wife. Spent a lot of time with Cora and Little Scooter. We used to go to dinner two or three times a year. It was a great association," White said. "We probably got along so well because we were never together on the road. He liked to play golf. I liked to fish and play tennis."

"I really liked it when Bill White was on with him. They had a really nice time," Yogi Berra said.

"We had to talk. If you remember, in those years, the Yankees teams were awful. We didn't want to bring up the score. They were always losing. So we'd talk about anything just to keep people listening. We had to sell a lot of beer," White said.

"But I regret that because once the team started to get really good, once they started winning, we couldn't go back. We couldn't do a straight-forward, serious broadcast. We'd gotten into such a routine we couldn't go back. That's the one thing I regret about that," White admitted.

• • •

"This was a rainy afternoon in Minnesota on a Yankees trip in the early '70s. Looking to kill a few hours, several players and writers decided to take in the popular X-rated movie of the day. Phil Rizzuto was invited to join the group," remembered Yankees beat writer and author Phil Pepe.

"Oh, no," Scooter said. "I can't be seen at something like that."

"Off we went, Scooterless, to the theater," Pepe continued. "We were sitting in the dark for about an hour when, on the screen, flashed a particularly ribald scene. Suddenly, from the back of the silent theater, a familiar shriek was heard."

"Holy Cow!"

"Rizzuto had slipped into the theater surreptitiously, wearing a raincoat with the collar turned up, a hat and sunglasses so as not to be recognized, but with two words he had blown his cover," Pepe recalled.

Another story from Pepe was from the same period.

"I remember one airplane flight late in the season. I was sitting in the row behind Rizzuto talking with a Yankees pitcher. When the pitcher left to go to the lavatory, Rizzuto turned to me."

"Who's that guy you were talking to?" Scooter asked Pepe.

"That's Larry Gura, Scooter," I said. "He joined us in June."

Lawrence Peter Yogi Berra was inducted into the National Baseball Hall of Fame on August 7, 1972. Of course, there is a famous story about Carmen and Berra driving to Cooperstown. They got lost, and when Carmen complained, Berra responded, "We're lost, but we're making good time."

Carmen had written Berra's speech for him, too.

"I guess the first thing I ought to say is that I thank everybody for making this day necessary," recalling his gaffe of 1947. The crowd laughed uproariously. He then began to read Carmen's speech.

"I want to thank Bill Dickey for polishing me up as a catcher. I want to thank George Weiss for giving me my first New York contract. I want to thank Casey Stengel, who had the confidence to play me every day. I want to thank my wife, Carmen, the perfect baseball wife," Berra said.

He read on, thanking more people. "My only regrets are that my parents are not here to enjoy this moment with me, that my brother John is not here, and that Gil Hodges is not here. I hope they are proud of me today."

Carmen, Larry, Dale, and Tim were in the audience. Joe Garagiola, as expected, was there, and he was seen wiping tears from his eyes as his friend spoke. Phil Rizzuto and Bill Dickey were also there. Berra's voice cracked.

"I want to thank baseball," he said lastly. "It has given me more than I hoped for. When I am finished, I hope I have given it something back." A well-earned applause followed his speech. By now many of his teammates had made it to the Hall. When would it be Scooter's turn?

In 1975, during spring training, Mel Stottlemyre, the veteran Yankee pitcher, had brought his 5-year-old son, Jason, into camp that day. Stottlemeyer was taking a shower when he spotted a frog that had somehow made its way into the locker room. He scooped up the frog with a paper cup and gave it to his son. His son was delighted.

"Then I saw Phil Rizzuto across the room," Stottlemeyer remembered. "So I pointed to Phil, who was sitting in a chair, and told Jason to go show him his frog…Jason ran across the room, tapped him on the leg, and as he showed Phil the cup, the frog jumped out onto the floor. Phil jumped out of the chair as if he'd seen a bolt of lightning and ran out of the room. Jason laughed and laughed over that."

Hello! I'm Phil Rizzuto for The Money Store!

"What we're amazed at is how many people think that the Money Store is wholly owned by Phil Rizzuto," said Marc Turtletaub, chief executive of the Union, New Jersey–based lender and son of Alan Turtletaub, who founded the mortgage company in 1967 with a borrowed $18,650.

The Money Store fashioned three lines of business. The first was home-equity, or second-mortgage lending, student loans, and small business administration loans.

"All three businesses were not fashionable when we first got in them," Turtletaub said after a shareholder's meeting at the Short Hills Hilton, at the peak of the company's success. At one point, the company was the largest SBA lender in the country for six years running. The company expanded to the west coast in 1979, focusing on California. And then by the 1990s, it was focusing on the Midwest.

Rizzuto started promoting The Money Store in 1972. For decades, Rizzuto told television audiences that they could get loans at The Money Store. The ad campaign identified the former Yankees shortstop so closely to the company that many consumers actually thought they were getting loans from the pitchman himself.

"There's a whole generation of people—especially those who don't live on the East coast—who don't know him as a baseball great and as the Yankees announcer but as The Money Store guy," Turtletaub said.

"Turtletaub and his father, Alan, the founder of the company, joke in an easy manner about Rizzuto's name-recognition and the fact that people think it's his company. But they know who owns The Money Store," business writer Dan Woods wrote. "Any damage to their egos seems to have been more than made up for by the fattening of their pocketbook. From virtually nothing, their 70-percent stake in the company was worth more than $64 million" by 1992. The Money Store spent $10.7 million on advertising in 1991, running ads in more than 30 states.

The Money Store was a store-front subprime home equity lender. They went from a storefront operation to a national brand, largely with Rizzuto's help. They were among the first large commercial ventures of the kind when they grew, and this subprime business eventually caught the eye of Wall Street many years later. But in the 1970s and 1980s, they were known for a one simple reason—Phil Rizzuto.

There was no mistaking the Turtletaubs were trading on Rizzuto's name and reputation. For more than 20 years they would run a series of shoddily produced commercials featuring Rizzuto standing in front a shop window emblazoned with the words, "The Money Store." Phil was obviously shot in front of a blue screen, and then the background was dropped in. Some looked even worse.

The 30-second ads ran regionally at first. Their poor production standards and obvious cheapness made them a bit of a joke. They are now considered a part of the regional cultural memory, along with Tom Carvel's Cookie Puss ads and the annoying ads for Crazy Eddie's. They were featured on local stations in the New York area like WOR (channel 9), WPIX (channel 11), and WNEW (channel 5).

"Hello! Phil Rizzuto here for The Money Store!" Scooter shouted. In the beginning, the commercials were tame enough with him standing in front of the fake store front. But then they became more elaborate and more shoddy.

However, Rizzuto was always the spokesperson with big glasses and his loud, shouting voice.

One showed a harried Rizzuto getting into a light blue Jaguar, slowly pulling out of a dimly lit driveway at dusk with the headlights on, and bright spotlights following him:

> *Holy Cow! I'm late for The Money Store's 20th anniversary dinner. Just think, they started as a small second mortgage company and now they're America's number one independent home equity lender.*

Then the image of Phil with a dark parking lot behind him. He is lit head-on by one bright, white-hot spotlight right in his eyes.

> *Celebrate this occasion. Every qualified borrower can have a special anniversary gift. A free Money Store sponsored Master Card.*

Another ad featured a cartoon Santa's Workshop. Elves are busy building toys. A phone rings and a cartoon Santa answers.

> *Santa: Santa Speaking!*

When Phil speaks, he's seated in a wingback chair with a fireplace that says "The Money Store" over it, and a fake Christmas tree is behind him.

> *Phil: Hello Santa! Phil Rizzuto here for The Money Store with great holiday news for homeowners.*

> *Santa: What is it, Phil?*

> *Phil: For a limited time, we're offering a special second mortgage and going as low as one percent below prime.*

> *Santa: As low as one percent below prime?*

Yet another ad featured Phil sitting at a desk with a huge pile of papers stacked in front of him. It has a hideous, lime-green background, and he is wearing large thick-rimmed glasses. The desk has a "Phil Rizzuto" nameplate on it.

Holy Cow! Are you as confused as I am about these new tax laws? Aghhhhhh!

The exaggerated "Aghhhh" was the groan of a B-rate actor as Rizzuto shoved two stacks of tax papers off the desk.

"There are so many levels of bad in this commercial—but this is the kind of so bad that it works very well," Mike Lear, a vice president and associate creative director at Martin Advertising, said.

"Most of these ads are poorly done intentionally, and they tend to be made for smaller firms like The Money Store and the now-defunct Rainier Beer. By putting a famous celebrity in an unlikely role, these companies stimulate buzz in a way they otherwise could not," Will Mara wrote for ABCNews.com.

"It's all about the 'shock and awe' factor and the buzz. That's what those ads are pretty much going for," Zack Below, the CEO of the advertising agency Webzack.com, said. "Littler companies love doing that sort of thing because, why not?"

"At the end of the day, you just want people to say, 'Oh my God, did you see that… That was just ridiculous,'" Lear said.

Rizzuto even received ribbing from White about his Money Store involvement, like this exchange recalled by a *New York Post* reader:

White: "Do they break your legs if you don't pay?"

Rizzuto (screaming): "You can't say that!"

"Perhaps taking the job seemed like a natural fit," Mara conjectured. "After all, the spot personified the quirky earnestness that made him so beloved on the field and in the broadcast booth."

"They chose him for a reason," said Tony Calianese, publisher of Adforum. com.

"We remember that commercial because of Phil Rizzuto, his character and his personality, the way that he talked," Below of Webzack.com said. "That commercial really portrays some of the quirkiness that he has."

These weren't the only commercials he made. For a few years he was a spokesman for Yoo-Hoo soft drinks, through the vice president of sales and marketing, Mr. Lawrence Peter Berra, better known as Yogi. In the 1980s, he would also do some commercials for Burger King.

"I was lucky enough to have worked with Phil Rizzuto in '84 on a Burger King commercial I wrote," Alan Braunstein remembered. "He was the announcer voice we used for a baseball spot where the third-base coach was mistakenly signaling runners to steal while patting his stomach in hunger."

"Phil totally got the idea of it and gave us everything we needed and then some," Braunstein said.

I Can See Phil Rizzuto by the Dashboard Light

Born Marvin Lee Aday on September 27, 1947, (some sources say 1951) in Dallas, Texas, Meat Loaf was the first child of a police officer father, Orvis, and a school teacher mother, Wilma. Orvis was a renowned alcoholic who would often stumble through drinking binges that lasted several days. As a youth, Aday was a Yankees fan.

"They were owned by CBS and Mickey Mantle was from Oklahoma, so every Saturday the game of the week in Dallas was the Yankees. So I grew up rooting for them and hating everybody else," Meat Loaf told ESPN. To a young Meat Loaf in Texas, Mickey Mantle and the Yankees were America's team. "This was before they showed all the stats for everybody, so I kept track of them myself in a notebook. I could tell you how many doubles and triples and hits all the players had."

In 1965, Meat Loaf graduated from Thomas Jefferson High School, having already started his acting career via school productions such as *Where's Charley?* and *The Music Man*. After attending college at Lubbock Christian College, Aday transferred to what is now the University of North Texas at Denton. He moved to Los Angeles in 1967.

"[He] formed a band alternately known as Meat Loaf Soul and Popcorn Blizzard, which, until its breakup in 1969, had opened shows for The Who, Iggy Pop and the Stooges, Johnny and Edgar Winter, and Ted Nugent. He then auditioned for and got a part in a West coast production of *Hair* and traveled with the show to the East coast and then to Detroit...Meat Loaf went to New York to appear in the off-Broadway gospel musical *Rainbow in New York* in 1973, and then successfully auditioned for *More Than You Deserve*, written by Jim Steinman," the *Rolling Stone Encyclopedia of Rock and Roll* reported.

"Steinman, a New Yorker who'd spent his early teen years in California, had studied classical piano. Later he wrote a play called *Dream Engine* in New York. Meanwhile, Meat Loaf had played Eddie in the hugely successful cult film *The Rocky Horror Picture Show* and sung lead vocals on one side of Ted Nugent's platinum LP *Free for All*. After meeting at *More Than You Deserve* auditions, Meat Loaf and Steinman toured with the National Lampoon Road Show," *Rolling Stone* stated. While on the tour, Meat Loaf met and befriended a young John Belushi.

"Then Steinman wrote a musical called *Never Land* (a Peter Pan update), from which would come much of the material for *Bat Out of Hell*...Meat Loaf and Steinman rehearsed for a full year before Todd Rundgren, an early supporter of the project, agreed to produce them," said *Rolling Stone*.

One of the songs on the *Bat Out of Hell* album was "Paradise by the Dashboard Light," a song about a young couple in a car, making out and using the classic language of baseball to describe the encounter.

"In the summer of 1976, Michael Lee Aday (aka Meat Loaf) spent his time listening to one New York Yankee game after another, jotting down everything that emerged from the mouth of the team's TV color commentator, Phil Rizzuto. Though Meat Loaf wasn't looking for anything in particular, he uncovered verbal gold," Jeff Pearlman wrote.

"Phil was one of the greatest storytellers baseball has ever seen," Meat Loaf said. "He would talk about the game, but he'd also talk about Billy Martin's fishing trip or a great restaurant nearby or somebody's 50th birthday. He was very unique."

"With a soft chuckle, Meat Loaf warmly remembered the first time he and Steinman reached out to Rizzuto. The future Hall of Famer was represented by former Met Art Shamsky," Pearlman wrote.

"Phil will do it, but he wants to know if people have to get high to listen to it," Shamsky told Meat Loaf.

"No," Meat Loaf replied. "You can be sober and enjoy it, too."

According to Pearlman, "Rizzuto arrived at Manhattan's The Hit Factory one day in 1976, met with Meat Loaf and Steinman and read over his lines. He initially expected to sing something...then asked why every play was so close. When he finally recorded, Rizzuto's delivery was flat and wooden."

"Just do it like it's a game," Meat Loaf advised Scooter.

"It wasn't a broadcast, we had Rizzuto do it for us in the studio. We listened to Rizzuto all summer and wrote up all his expressions into a script and had him come into the studio. But he was real flat when he did it. So I had to run around the studio like I was circling the bases," Meat Loaf said.

The second take was perfect.

"Phil was an absolutely huge part of that song," Meat Loaf told Pearlman. "Huge. You have a tempo change, then all of sudden there's this baseball play-by-play—this amazing baseball play-by-play."

The song "Paradise by the Dashboard Light," a duet, features Meat Loaf singing the male lead and Ellen Foley singing the female lead. The two passionate young people speak to one another as their session gets hotter and hotter. At one point, Meat Loaf wails out, "We're gonna go all the way tonight; We're gonna go all the way; And tonight's the night."

At this point, the relative crescendo of the song, the highly excited voice of Phil Rizzuto breaks in.

> OK, here we go, we got a real pressure cooker going here. Two down, nobody on, no score, bottom of the ninth. There's the windup, and there it is. A line shot up the middle, look at him go. This boy can really fly. He's rounding first and really turning it on now. He's not letting up at all, he's gonna try for second. The ball is bobbled out in the center. And here's the throw and what a throw. He's gonna slide in head first. Here he comes, he's out. No, wait, safe, safe at second base....

Bat Out of Hell was released on October 21, 1977. It was not an immediate success, and its initial reviews were not particularly good.

"Meat Loaf earned his somewhat eccentric name as a performer in *The Rocky Horror Picture Show*, the theatrical torture, although he had previously spent several years as a rock singer in Detroit, even recording a single or two for Motown. *Bat Out of Hell* reflects such diversity, but can't resolve it. Meat Loaf has an outstanding voice, but his phrasing is way too stage-struck to make the album's pretensions to comic-book street life real. He needs a little less *West Side Story* and a little more Bruce Springsteen," Dave Marsh wrote. "Steinman is wordy, and his attempts to recapture adolescence are only remembrances; he can't bring out the transcendently personal elements that make a song like 'Night Moves,' an obvious influence here...But the principals have some growing to do."

To support the album, Meat Loaf hit the road, opening for Cheap Trick, a popular band at the time. Several other appearances went well for the large, oversized rocker, who weighed in at a hefty 300 pounds with his long sweaty hair and the long red scarf he used to wipe his sweaty brow.

On March 25, 1978, Meat Loaf appeared as the musical guest on *Saturday Night Live*. The English horror film star Christopher Lee introduced him:

> *And now ladies and gentlemen, I would like you to meet Loaf.*
> *(pauses, looks dumbfounded) I beg your pardon, what? (listens*
> *to the director's aside) Oh! Why...why I'm sorry, yes, of course...*
> *ah... ladies and gentlemen, Meat Loaf!"*

Walter Yetnikoff, the famed music executive once related a meeting between Meat Loaf and Bill Paley, president of CBS. "Tell me about your hit song," Paley told Meat Loaf. Paley was dressed in Brooks Brothers and Turnbull and Asser, and Meat Loaf was in a black leather jacket and jeans. The two were eating jelly doughnuts.

"It's called, 'Paradise by the Dashboard Light.'"

"I'm sorry to say I haven't heard it yet. What's the theme?" asked the dignified Paley.

"Humping."

"Oh, I see."

"Phil Rizzuto is announcing a baseball game while me and this chick are getting it on. That's the paradise part."

"Paradise indeed," Paley smiled.

Soon, *Bat Out of Hell* began to capture a following, and it eventually became one of the best-selling albums of all time. And "Paradise by the Dashboard Light" became one of its three big songs. What at first seemed like a fun little thing to do for a rock and roll singer became a big problem for Rizzuto. Local parish priests and other local Catholic organizations argued that the song was encouraging promiscuity and pre-marital sex. Rizzuto tried to distance himself from his involvement. In public, he would say that no one told him what the song was about, or what his part in it was really about.

"I want to tell you about that huckleberry," Rizzuto said, years later, using his signature phrase to describe Meat Loaf. "He really tricked me into it. He said, 'Phil, I have an idea for a song, I want you to come. We just want you to say these words.'"

"I remember doing that recording," Rizzuto told the press years later. "I was with Meat Loaf and his agent and I asked where's the music, and they said, 'Don't worry about it, we're just trying something new,'" he told the *New York Post*.

"All of a sudden I started reading the paper he put in front of me, and I said, 'Wait a minute: Why is every play a close play?' Finally we got through it. A year later, my son calls me up and says, 'Dad, you're a rock star. We got your record here, "Paradise by the Dashboard Light."' He had to play it about six times before I realized what it was about."

Rizzuto said he enjoyed the recording session, terming it "a good day's pay."

"I got in trouble with some of the nuns because of some of the language," he said. "But then they forgot about it." And then, with a smile, Phil noted, "We never found out whether he made it or not."

"Phil was no dummy—he knew exactly what was going on, and he told me such," Meat Loaf said. "He was just getting some heat from a priest and felt like he had to do something. I totally understood. But I believe Phil was proud of that song and his participation."

Regardless, Rizzuto was now a rock star, and he was mobbed by a new generation of fans who knew him as a television pitchman and cool celebrity. He was eventually awarded a platinum album when the song became a huge international hit. It remains a seminal rock and roll song.

More Championships

George Steinbrenner and his investment group bought the languishing Yankees from CBS for approximately $10 million in 1973. CBS couldn't wait to unload the franchise, which it had run into the ground. Steinbrenner said he got them cheap. He was right. But if CBS had the money and power, Steinbrenner, for all his faults, had the moxie. And by sheer force of will and determination, he brought the Yankees back from death's door and returned them to a championship team.

Steinbrenner made the controversial call, along with Gabe Paul, to bring the feisty Billy Martin back to Yankee Stadium, now in the role of manager. The first person Martin hired was former Mets and Yankees manager, Yogi Berra, as his bench coach.

"It was 1976, Billy Martin's first full season as Yankee manager and the reopening of Yankee Stadium after two drab years at Shea. The first WPIX telecast was from spring training, and Phil was to interview Billy Martin in Florida about the new season. Billy came over to Phil, and Phil went 'Whoa!' dropped the mic, and dashed off camera," one avid Yankees fan remembered.

Martin had brought a fake snake and spooked Phil . The camera crew and players could be heard laughing as Billy picked up the mic and explained to the audience what had happened.

"We go back a long way...we're friends," Rizzuto told the press about Martin. "He's better than anyone I've ever seen," he said. "He's so much ahead of anyone. I recall taking plane rides with him and listening to him explain why he did this or that. He was always thinking one step ahead."

"Phil didn't exactly hang out with anybody. He didn't have breakfast with Yogi and Ellie Howard. He didn't go out to dinner. I think he had room service pretty much stayed to himself," Phil Pepe recalled. "I never saw him and Berra hanging out at the Stadium. I know they were good friends, neighbors, business partners. I know they played golf. But I don't remember the two of them at the Stadium that much.... There was a period when he watched *North by Northwest* in every city we went to. It seemed to follow him wherever we went."

But Rizzuto was around for Martin when he needed him.

After the Fenway Park incident in 1977 with Paul Blair's substitution for Reggie Jackson, and their subsequent fight in the dugout was broadcast on national television, it was Steinbrenner who tried to reach Rizzuto to get his opinion of the situation. Steinbrenner could not reach the broadcast booth, because the Fenway switchboard operators thought it was a crank caller.

Rumors abounded the next day that Martin was gone. Dick Howser and Yogi Berra were both among the names being floated as possible replacements. For his part, Steinbrenner fully intended to fire Martin.

"Rizzuto had spirited [Billy] away for a round of golf. Rizzuto tried vainly to assure Martin that the story was wrong, that Steinbrenner was too smart a businessman to fire someone so popular with the fans," journalist Jonathan Malher wrote. Martin avoided termination that season but was fired on other occasions.

Rizzuto admitted, however, that he'd seen the other side of Martin. According to baseball historian Roger Kahn, it was Rizzuto who accompanied Martin to his resignation as Yankees manager in July 1978. Martin had uttered the fateful, "One's a born liar. The other's convicted," referring to Reggie Jackson and George Steinbrenner. Rizzuto helped a visibly shaken Martin up to a small room with a camera, where Martin then uttered his first tearful farewell.

"I don't want to hurt the team's chances for the pennant with this undue publicity," said Martin, fighting back tears unsuccessfully. The writers stood mute and transfixed, their heads slightly down. "The team has a shot at the pennant, and I hope they win it." Martin went on to thank "the Yankee management, the press, the news media, my coaches, my players, and most of all the fans." Martin was visibly shaken and unsteady.

"He barely got through his statement when he began to sob uncontrollably," Phil Pepe recalled. "Phil Rizzuto moved in, put his arm around Martin, and walked him down the stairs and out the door of the hotel. Later that day, Martin left Kansas City, left the only job he ever wanted, and flew to Florida."

"When he first came up, he wasn't like this. He didn't drink. It took a while for him to be a New Yorker," Rizzuto once publicly admitted. "When he's out of uniform and has a few lollipops, he can get in trouble. He's his own worst enemy," he said.

Of Martin's numerous hirings and firings, Rizzuto said, "I couldn't believe he was hiring the guy a fifth time," Rizzuto shouted in his best Holy Cow reaction. "It's like Steinbrenner needs former players around him to take the heat off him. He fires Virdon and brings in Billy…he fires Billy and brings in Lemon…he fires Lemon and brings back Billy, etc.

"They [the Yankees] just know he's been successful with any team he's managed. Every time he's taken over in a different city he's won, except for Texas," Rizzuto told the *Albany Times-Union*. "He's great when he gets a challenge. It's after he's been in one place a while he loses interest."

Rizzuto also called the pennant-winning home run hit by Chris Chambliss off of Kansas City Royals reliever Mark Littell in the American League Championship Series on October 14, 1976, on WPIX-TV:

> *He hits one deep to right-center! That ball is out of here! The Yankees win the pennant! Holy Cow, Chris Chambliss on one swing! And the Yankees win the American League pennant. Unbelievable, what a finish! As dramatic a finish as you'd ever want to see! With all that delay, we told you Littell had to be a little upset. And Holy Cow, Chambliss hits one over the fence, he is being mobbed by the fans, and this field will never be the same, but the Yankees have won it in the bottom of the ninth, 7–6!*

• • •

On January 19, 1977, Rose Angiotti Rizzuto, Phil's mother, passed away. She left behind her children, Phil, Alfred, Mary (Rizzuto) Stoehler, and Rose (Rizzuto) Estato, 12 grandchildren, and 12 great grandchildren. She died in the Glendale house where Phil had lived as an adolescent. Services were held at St. Pancras Roman Catholic Church, and she was buried at St. John's Cemetery near her husband. By this time, Patricia Rizzuto was 22 years old.

In the early winter of 1977, Marty Appel and his partner, now freelance broadcast services agents, approached Phil with an opportunity to leave the New York Yankees. Phil was feeling underappreciated. He was not happy with his salary and was feeling ignored. Understandable given this was the first big boom of free-agency in professional baseball. In his own dramatic way during a lunch with these men, Phil counted out his list of grievances with the organization. "He was serious," Appel said. "He was very unhappy."

"We're not just testing the waters here, Phil, right?" asked Appel. "You would go for the right offer?"

"Oh, yes," Phil was emphatic. But Appel was cautious. He knew Phil.

"We were very discreet," Appel recalled. After a series of phone calls, Appel admitted years later, that the Royals were willing to make a serious financial commitment to bring Rizzuto to Kansas City.

"Step by step, we put together a multiyear deal with more money and less travel than the Yankees offered. So anxious were the Royals to have him that membership in a prestigious country club was included. At each stage of the negotiations, we kept Phil informed," Appel remembered.

Appel recalled that they were both afraid Rizzuto might be using them to improve his lot with the Yankees, getting the organization to counteroffer, which Appel felt they would do. The Royals, for their part, were astonished. They proceeded in making an offer.

Finally, the day of reckoning arrived. The offer was final and complete. Appel called Scooter.

"Phil, we are prepared to agree on this deal if you are. We all know the mixed feelings that must be going on with you. Before I make the call, are we together on this?"

There was a long pause.

"You know," said Rizzuto, "I've been thinking about how hot it gets there in the summer. I played there you know; you wouldn't believe the heat. Cora hates the heat."

Appel knew instantly, "We all knew that his heart wasn't in it."

From 1978 to 1981, Fran Healy, former Yankees catcher, joined Rizzuto, Messer, and White in the booth.

"The best radio or TV partner Rizzuto ever had? A lot of people will say it was Bill White, but for my memories, believe it or not, it was Fran Healy," Phil Mushnick of the *New York Post* recalled. "Working radio from 1978 through 1981, the two were hilarious together with Healy paying attention to the game—someone had to—while eager to push Rizzuto's buttons."

> *Healy: Did that ever happen to you, Scooter?*
>
> *Rizzuto: Did what ever happen to me?*
>
> *Healy: What just happened.*
>
> *Rizzuto: What just happened?*

"I loved working with Phil Rizzuto. We would push the envelope and probably could have gone further than most because Scooter was a doll. He was so lovable. He could do anything," Healy remembered. "I remember one time in the late '70s, I said 'crap' on the air. Back then you couldn't say that. Today, you can say anything, but not then, no way! So when it came out, I couldn't believe it."

There was a pause, then Scooter said, "There you go Healy, thinking about those crap tables again!"

"He got me off the hook. He would never leave another announcer hanging," Healy said.

"One time in Seattle at this beautiful round hotel...round rooms and everything," Rizzuto told *Inside Sports*. "Healy got on one of those kicks."

"What did you do last night, Phil?" Healy asked.

"Well, I didn't like the room I had."

"Why?" Healy asked.

"Well, it was a round room and I couldn't corner my wife," Scooter responded. "Well! You should have seen the mail I got and the calls! They all liked it, but the station didn't too much."

"We also talked a lot of baseball. Scooter was a very knowledgeable baseball guy. We talked and argued about baseball. We argued about a lot of things, but we did it without anybody feeling uncomfortable," Healy remembered.

One night, Rizzuto left the booth during a game in Chicago. Healy greeted his return:

> Healy: "Here's Scooter, back from the men's room."
>
> Rizzuto: "Healy, you huckleberry, you're not supposed to tell people that. Tell them I went to see Bill Veeck [the White Sox president]. Besides, Healy, I've been drinking coffee all day. You know what happens when you drink coffee all day?"
>
> Healy: "What's that, Scooter?"
>
> Rizzuto: "You go see Bill Veeck."

An exchange on WABC radio:

> Healy: "Next up is Toby Harrah. Harrah is one of the few players whose name is a palindrome."
>
> Rizzuto: "A whaaaa?"
>
> Healy: "A palindrome, Scooter. That means it's spelled the same backwards and forwards."
>
> Rizzuto: "Oh." [Pause.] "Oh, you mean like 'orange.'"
>
> Healy: "Orange? Scooter, orange isn't spelled the same backwards and forwards."
>
> Rizzuto: "No, but you can't think of a rhyme for it!"

"I first sat next to him in 1978 in the WPIX booth, back when I was that station's film/theater critic and my Red Sox were 14 games ahead," recalled Jeffrey Lyons, movie critic and baseball fanatic. Lyons was such a Red Sox fan that when they came to the Stadium that year on Kol Nidre, which is the day before Yom Kippur and one of the holiest days on the Jewish calendar, he attended in the broadcast booth alongside Rizzuto.

"Scooter," I said. "Don't say 'Yommmm Keepur...' as if you've never heard of it. Say it quickly and don't congratulate Jewish people or wish them a happy holiday, since it's the Day of Atonement and whatever you do, don't say I'm here, because my mother will kill me." All went along fine, until the fourth inning.

"We want to wish our Jewish friends a happy... uh oh... hey Jeffrey Lyons... is it 'Yom Kippur?' Is that how you pronounce it?" Rizzuto asked.

Rizzuto was seen at the black-tie dinner before the 1978 running of the Belmont Stakes, where he hobnobbed with George Steinbrenner (a thoroughbred owner) and Wellington Mara, owner of the New York Giants, as well as former Governor Hugh Carey.

Former Yankees pitching sensation Ron Guidry said he loved poking fun at Rizzuto regarding the nickname that Rizzuto had hung on Guidry during an 18-strikeout performance against the California Angels in 1978. As Guidry struck out one Angel after another, Rizzuto exclaimed that Guidry was "Louisiana Lightning!" The name stuck.

"It's not that I didn't like it, but I teased him," Guidry described his joking around with Rizzuto. "One day, I told him, 'Go home tonight, sit at your desk, and write the damn name about 100 times. See if you don't get aggravated signing it. Everywhere you go, that's what [fans] want, and that was not my nickname. There are five letters in Gator, and Louisiana Lightning has 18."

"It was his character," Guidry said. "You might try to watch the game and then all of a sudden, you'd get caught up in what he's talking about. You just want to see how it's going to come out, and you'd forget about the game. A few innings pass, and he didn't say anything about the game, but you still enjoyed what he was saying."

These were heady times for the announcers. Each made some famous calls.

The Yankees broke a three-game losing streak on August 5, 1978, scoring a total of three runs, which manager Bob Lemon called "a momentous occasion," when they won, 3–2, at Yankee Stadium over the Baltimore Orioles. It was then that the news came down that Pope Paul VI had died, prompting Rizzuto to say on the air, "Well, that kind of puts the damper on even a Yankee win."

"I made a mistake when [Lemon] came to manage [in 1978]," Rizzuto later admitted. "Hey, Lem, you remember that...." referring to the 1951 squeeze play bunt against him. "Oh my...he got mad."

The Yankees were in Boston in early September for a four-game set. The teams had been battling all year long for the division lead.

"In the days leading up to the game, we'd hear guys like Yogi and Scooter fool around and say, 'You know, in the old days, all we had to do was show up against the Red Sox and they wouldn't want to play us.' We thought it was funny, some old timers telling stories. And then that's exactly what happened," said third baseman Craig Nettles many years after the Yankees swept the four-game series later known as the Boston Massacre.

"I remember walking through the press room that afternoon," said Rizzuto years later, of his memories of the third game. Boston was still leading the division by two games. "I ran into a Red Sox employee I knew and he said, 'Well, if we lose today, it's over.' And I thought, 'Over?' Forget that no matter what happens there are still three weeks to go, I mean, even if they lost, they would still be in first place! But that's how demoralized everyone was!" The Yankees routed them but still needed to win in a one-game play-off versus the Sox.

On October 2, 1978, they called the American League East playoff game on WPIX-TV when the Yankees and the Red Sox squared off in Boston for one game to decide the divisional winner.

In the first inning, Reggie Jackson crushed a ball deep into the outfield, but the brutal wind was blowing from center field right at the batter, and the towering ball was simply batted down by the wind into Carl Yastrzemski's glove for a long out.

When Jim Rice stepped up to bat, the wind, always unpredictable at Fenway, suddenly changed directions and was now blowing from behind home plate, surging out to right field.

"Holy Cow!" Rizzuto said from the broadcast booth, "The Red Sox even control the wind!"

Late in that game, White authored one of baseball's most famous calls when he broadcast Yankee shortstop Bucky Dent's home run in the seventh inning:

Deep to left! Yastrzemski will not get it—it's a home run! A three-run home run for Bucky Dent, and the Yankees now lead it by a score of 3–2! "

Rizzuto's relationships with White and Messer produced numerous good-humored exchanges. Red Sox batter Bob "Beetle" Bailey, who had gained a little weight, had just stepped into the batter's box:

Rizzuto: Looks a little out of shape, doesn't he, Bill?

White: (chuckles) Well, Beetle's been around a while.

Rizzuto: Yeah.

White: Got a lot of money—from the Pirates. Put it all in California real estate. That's why he's got that big...uh...

Rizzuto (chuckles): Big what?

White: Well, big bank account. (Both men laugh.)

When the Yankees hosted the White Sox on August 11, 1980, Messer was able to call Reggie Jackson's 400th homer on WINS radio:

There she goes! Might be upper deck!

Of course, there was also this exchange between Rizzuto and White about Reggie Jackson around the same time as Jackson came up to the plate:

Rizzuto: Two balls on Reggie.

Long pause, then a kind of choking sound from Bill White. The two laughing.

A few years later, while broadcasting a game between the Yankees and Oakland Athletics, Phil Rizzuto commented to his partner on a promising Oakland shortstop named Rob Picciolo:

Rizzuto: Bill, don't you just love those infielders with names ending in vowels?

White: You mean like Shapiro or White?

"All they were doing was having a conversation," former Yankees manager Joe Torre recalled. "It was never boring. His voice itself would always keep you from really knowing who was winning and who was losing."

In 1981, there was a baseball strike in the middle of the season. The announcers took the opportunity to take some time out for themselves during the break. Phil and Cora went away for three weeks that summer, taking their usual winter round trip to see their far-flung children in the summer instead. They visited Scooter Jr. in South Carolina and their daughters in Manchester, Vermont, and Aspen, Colorado.

Phil played a lot of golf and went to the Jersey shore for the first time in the summer.

"Funny, the kids used to get on me because I never took them to the beach, but now that I finally can, they're all gone." Then it was back to baseball as the Yankees lost to the Dodgers in the World Series that year.

Messer's most famous call was probably on July 4, 1983, on WABC, noting the final out of Dave Righetti's no-hitter at Yankee Stadium against the Red Sox. Righetti threw his last pitch to Wade Boggs, who swung and missed. Messer intoned:

> *The kick, and the pitch...he struck him out! Righetti has pitched*
> *a no-hitter! Dave Righetti has pitched a no-hitter! He strikes*
> *out Boggs for the final out of the ball game, and the Yankees*
> *pour onto the field to congratulate Dave Righetti!*

White should have actually made the call. He was supposed to call that half-inning as part of the in-game rotation of announcers between radio and SportsChannel TV. While White did the whole game bouncing between WABC and SportsChannel, Messer and Rizzuto rotated between TV, radio, and the Fan Appreciation Day giveaways on the field between innings.

But according to Messer, after White saw him return to the WABC radio booth, White insisted that Messer, the senior of the two, should call the ninth.

"It was a class act," Messer said of White's gesture.

• • •

One of the most famous of all Rizzuto announcing jobs was on July 24, 1983. The Kansas City Royals were playing the Yankees at the Stadium. This was the infamous George Brett pine-tar game.

In the seventh inning, he started to talk about Cora and home, and then he said, "It's very chilly. As a matter…I'm telling you I've been freezing. My hands are cold. I have low blood pressure anyway. And arthritis. I really should be going home."

Then came the top of the ninth inning, and George Brett came up to bat against Rich "Goose" Gossage, his old rival.

"Now, I had started to tell you, when Billy Martin made the motion for Gossage to come on, that brings back some nightmares when George Brett in 1980, that year the Royals beat the Yankees in the playoffs."

And Scooter was right. Brett smashed a home run and Rizzuto went wild on the air.

> *Where's White? Bill White is in his car on the way home, not up here getting nervous and cold.…deep to right field. Holy cow I don't believe it! Home run for George Brett! I don't believe it, that lightning could strike twice!*

But Yankees manager Billy Martin came out of the dugout and urged home-plate umpire Tim McClelland to measure the amount of pine tar on Brett's bat, citing an obscure rule that stated the pine tar on a bat could extend no further than 18 inches. Brett's pine tar extended well beyond that.

> *Oh what a huddle out there. They're really…Billy Martin standing with his arms folded out there. Boy, he was quick off that bench. Well look who has returned! He made a U-turn on that bridge! Bill White is back!*

The huddle on the field continued. The conversation got more animated:

> *And this could be a momentous decision. I can't tell by the way they're walking who's going to win this argument. He's out!*

George Brett burst out of the dugout, enraged, and charged Tim McClelland.

> *Dick Howser is furious. They're holding George Brett out there, three men are holding him. He is called out and the Yankees win the game 4–3. But this is one of the most unbelievable endings I have ever seen.*

Despite his fame, Rizzuto did indeed keep his humanity. He was able to laugh at himself. And it was his common touch that made him so popular with fans.

"I was in Fort Lauderdale during early spring training in 1982 with my wife and infant son," recalled Yankees fan Bob Lukas. "At one point, I wandered out of the stadium alone and there was the Scooter, chatting with a fan."

"Could you wait here for *just* one minute so I can get my son?" an excited Lukas asked.

"Sure," Scooter replied.

"I dashed inside as quickly as I could, grabbed my wife and son with barely an explanation, and rushed back out. The Scooter was gone. Crestfallen, I began to explain to my wife what had happened when a car pulled up in front of us. The passenger door opened and out got the Scooter.

"I thought you weren't coming back," he said.

"He looked at my boy wearing his little Yankees shirt, and of course, the Scooter chuckled, 'Ho-Holy Cow!' and graciously posed for a photo. About a year later, my wife presented the photo to the Scooter at an appearance, asking for his autograph. Needless to say, he chuckled a 'Holy Cow' and signed it [to my son], 'To Foster, Holy Cow, Phil Rizzuto.'"

"In 1983, a friend and I took a trip to Boston from New York to watch the Yanks take on the Red Sox at Fenway," Yankees fan Lou DiMaggio said. "We got there early and my buddy, who was a Boston native, suggested we go up to the North end to get some good food for lunch. As we walked through the small Italian neighborhood, I recognized Phil Rizzuto sitting in a café. We went inside and said hello. We were very courteous and made sure not to interrupt his meal. Mr. Rizzuto couldn't have been more gracious but his wife Cora went him one better. 'Phil, why don't you invite the boys to have a glass of iced tea,' she said. We sat down and spent the next hour or so being regaled with old baseball stories and wonderful anecdotes. And just before we left, Phil asked, 'Do you boys have tickets to the game?' We already did, and we were floored by his generous offer."

• • •

"During a Rizzuto broadcast, Yankee fans never knew what they were going to get—or in at least one instance, who they were going to get—such as the time he opened a game standing next to his partner, Bill White," Bill Madden of the *New York Daily News* wrote. "Hello, folks, welcome to another night of Yankee baseball. I'm Bill White and with me is…[laughter in background]."

"Rizzuto beats it over the bridge to Jersey after the sixth inning, but he crowds it all into 240 innings [a year]: birthday greetings, movie reviews, golf tips, war memories, frequent psychosomatic broodings, and fearsome predictions of rain, sleet, snow, thunder, lightning, tornados, and waterspouts. It is amazing that this nervous little gent was ever able to stand at home plate and drop a perfect squeeze bunt with Henrich or Yogi bearing down on him," *New York Times* columnist George Vecsey once wrote.

"For those who knew Rizzuto only as a broadcaster, I can report that what you saw is what you got," Phil Pepe said. "Unlike many of his contemporaries in what became his second career, Rizzuto on the air was exactly what Rizzuto was off the air: the fear of flying and of things, animate and inanimate, that crawl, squiggle, or creep, the early departure from games in order to beat the traffic over the George Washington Bridge and get home to his beloved Cora, the hours spent on the road watching movies on television (his favorite was *North By Northwest* with Cary Grant, which he claimed to have seen more than a dozen times), the naiveté, the ability to poke fun at himself, and to admit ignorance of some fact or some recently arrived player."

"Phil Rizzuto…was petrified of flying," Marty Appel said. "He hated it. He would drink some hard liquor, put a pillow over his head, go to sleep, and wake up when the plane landed."

"We were in the team plane. And he was really afraid. He was holding onto the seat, white knuckles, everything," Phil Pepe recalled. "So I said to Bill Kane, the Yankees traveling secretary, 'Boy's he's really afraid of flying.'"

"If you lived the life he did, you'd be afraid of dying, too," Kane said. Meaning that he'd led such a charmed life, you'd be afraid to give it up, as well.

Old Friends and New Friends

On November 20, 1982, Ann Guthrie Smith and the 26 year-old Philip Francis Rizzuto Jr. were married in Charleston, South Carolina. Ann's father was the late William Faber Smith Jr., and her mother was Mrs. Charles Joseph Miller of Kiawah Island, South Carolina. Ann's stepfather was principal of the Porter-Gaud School in Charleston.

Ann and Scooter Jr. had met at the University of South Carolina. Ann was a registered peri-operative nurse specialist at Providence Hospital in Columbia, South Carolina. Scooter Jr. had attended the Delbarton School in Morristown, New Jersey (graduating class of 1975), and was then finishing his Bachelor of Arts in humanities and social sciences.

The two were married by the Rev. Morris J. Lent Jr. at St. Luke's Episcopal Church in Charleston, South Carolina. Laurie Jane Smith was her sister's maid of honor. Eventually Ann and Scooter Jr. ("the apple of his father's eye" according to Patricia) moved to Deerfield Beach, Florida, where they started a family. According to Patricia, everyone calls him Scooter Jr., "except Ann." Cindy eventually moved to Florida, as well.

• • •

Baseball writer Dave Buscema described Rizzuto's den: "his baseball trophies modestly lining the wall along with a picture of Rizzuto as a cut, young athlete, an Italian-American from the bushy dark hair to the rugged nose."

Phil was fond of Jaguar automobiles, and was noted for many years for owning a metallic blue Jaguar. He dressed well in suits and ties, although he did own a number of loud plaid sports coats, which seemed *de rigeur* for broadcasters of the day.

"He's like you and I, a regular-type guy," former fire commissioner and former Hillside, New Jersey, mayor Peter Corvelli said. "He lives in a regular house, he eats regular food. He eats out in the local pizza place. He doesn't even have it delivered."

Piro's Italian deli, where he loved to buy manicotti, stuffed shells, and sausage, was one of his favorite haunts on Liberty Avenue, the main street running through the town. "People stand next to him all the time and they look at him and stare at him and then all of a sudden they say, 'Hey, that's him,'" said Dominic Piro, the owner. Rizzuto's picture hung in the store.

One newspaper journal wrote years later that Rizzuto's "photograph hangs in so many stores here that he often seems the patron saint of Hillside…there were many others who gladly recounted tales of Mr. Rizzuto's friendliness and generosity, like the time he donated thousands of dollars for lights on the local little league field."

"He does quite a few things around town, from the Little League program to the health fair," said then Vice Principal Al Lordi of Hillside High School. "The Hillside High School Scholarship Fund has several contributors, one being Phil Rizzuto. Each contributor has an award named after him. His is the Phil Rizzuto Scholarship."

"Phil raises funds by signing autographs at the annual health fair," Angelo Bonanno told sports editor Dan Hirshberg. "He signs baseballs, and the residents supply pledges to the high school booster club. In addition to what he gets at the health fair, Phil usually gives a fat check himself. Phil has always been available for any community project we've needed him for, from recycling to senior citizen programs to the health fair. It's simply a matter of availability for him." If he was available, he never turned them down. "If he's in town, Phil is right there where we need him."

Bonanno also told an adorable story of his daughter walking the neighborhood, selling Girl Scout cookies. When he asked where she had been, she told him that she went as far as Rizzuto's house. A long walk, he asked how come she had ranged so far? She said she wanted to meet a celebrity. And of course, Phil answered the door and bought the cookies.

"You'll see him at the local supermarket, the local deli, eating at the Mark Twain diner in Union," Bonanno said. "You'll see him getting his gas at the Getty Gas Station on North Broad Street."

Even the mayors of Hillside had stories. Apparently, once when he was a kid, the mayor was at bat while the United Way was filming a promotional piece. Phil Rizzuto was the umpire. Looking at James Welch, he said: "Now, don't swing too close to that ball, kid, 'cause I don't want you fouling it off and hitting me."

Welch went from a peewee batsman to the town's mayor in the early 1990s. "I can honestly say that on the municipal level, whenever someone has reached out to him, he has responded," said the then mayor.

The mayor of Hillside in 1983 had a bigger claim to fame. It was the opening of baseball season and New York City Mayor Ed Koch was throwing out the first ball of the season, and White asked Rizzuto, on the air, who was the mayor of Hillside.

"He didn't know. He said they were always changing mayors, and he didn't know who it was at the time," said Lou Santagata, mayor at that time. The town policy was to elect a new mayor each year. "A few days later it was the school board elections, and he wanted to vote. One of the men, a volunteer, told him he couldn't vote because he didn't know who the mayor was. And they made a big joke of it, of course." The Rizzutos eventually had a pancake breakfast with Santagata and his wife at a local community center benefiting the historical society. And every time they saw each other thereafter, Rizzuto would make a big deal. Rizzuto even talked about Santagata on the air for several weeks.

While Cora was active in the community and the Republican local party, she shunned the spotlight and the media. Local fundraisers and community events were fine for her, but she did not like it when Phil talked about her on the air.

"She does not want me to mention her name. Once, a game was going into extra innings, and I knew she was shopping, and I said on the air, 'You know, if any of you people are walking with a radio along Fifth Avenue and see my bride, tell her I'm going to be late for dinner.' Sure enough, somebody said something to her and oh! She told me later, 'Leave my name out of it.'"

In 1980, Jerry Priddy died of a heart attack at his home in North Hollywood, California. After leaving baseball, Priddy tried his hand at professional golf. It didn't take. On June 6, 1973, the FBI arrested him in California. He was charged with trying to extort $250,000 from a steamship company. He had threatened to put a bomb aboard one of its vessels, the *Island Princess*. He was convicted and sentenced to nine months in prison. Phil Rizzuto later said the he could never believe "that whole extortion thing."

"That wasn't the Jerry I knew. He was outspoken and hotheaded... but outside of baseball he was a regular guy. He knew a lot of prominent businesspeople. It just didn't make sense. He called me when he got out of prison and told me if he'd have had to spend one more day in there he'd have been a hardened criminal," Rizzuto said.

Priddy was defended by legendary criminal defense lawyer Paul Caruso. Many people were "amazed by the array of media personalities and athletes Caruso represented, many of whom found themselves in court testifying as character witnesses, for other Caruso clients," wrote Kenneth Ofgang for the *Metropolitan News-Enterprise*. "That tactic worked for Caruso...[when] Caruso persuaded a federal judge to give ex-New York Yankee Jerry Priddy a suspended sentence for trying to hijack a steamship. Several witnesses, including popular local broadcaster Dick Whittinghill, told the judge about what a good person Priddy was and how personal hardships had affected him."

The 1980s saw a string of announcers parade through the booth, including Healy (1978–81), John Gordon (1982–84), former Yankee slugger Bobby Murcer (1983–84), Spencer Ross (1985), Jim Kaat (1986), Billy Martin (1986–87, in between his third and fourth stints as Yankee manager), George Grande (1989–90), and Tom Seaver (1989–93).

"Murcer clearly adored Rizzuto as a friend, but his book makes clear what anybody who ever suffered through Rizzuto's play-by-play knew already: He was the worst sportscaster who ever lived," Glenn Garvin of the *Miami Herald* wrote when reviewing Murcer's autobiography in 2008. "Rizzuto vanished for long stretches of games, rarely stayed until they were over, and barely watched them even when he was in the booth." However, Garvin had clearly inserted his own opinion, because there is not one story told about Rizzuto by Murcer that is not told without a twinge of affection for the old shortstop.

"Every time I think about the Scooter, I smile," Murcer wrote.

Rizzuto had gone up and introduced himself to Murcer in 1965 when the Yankees were playing the Senators. Murcer was impressed by how friendly and classy Scooter was. But Murcer saw another side of Rizzuto when Scooter decided to interview Murcer before a game in Kansas City in the mid-1970s.

It was a pregame interview. "So there we were, the Scooter and me, standing next to the Yankee dugout, live and on the air. Scooter had just asked me the first question, and as he stuck the microphone under my chin for me to answer—zap!—this big lightning bolt and clap of thunder hit really close by. Without so much as even a 'Holy Cow, Murcer!' he flipped the microphone up in the air and bolted for the dugout...Suddenly I'm standing there, mic's on the grass, the camera's red light is on, we're live, and Scooter's long gone. So, I thought, what in thunder am I going to do? So I just picked the microphone up off the grass, looked into the camera, answered the question Scooter had put to me, and said, 'Okay, folks, we'll be back right after this!'"

Murcer joined the broadcast booth in 1983. "My three partners that first season of broadcasting...couldn't have made it easier for a raw rookie. They were great teachers, mostly by example," Murcer wrote. "Technically, I was the color guy, at least at first. And when I paired with Scooter, I got some early training in play-by-play when he'd go out for coffee after the seventh inning and make a beeline for the George Washington Bridge."

"The cannolis, and the salamis, and the antipastas, and the cakes, and the cheesecakes, and the pasta with the pesto sauce," Murcer explained about Rizzuto's beloved fans and their gifts of food to the Scooter. "We never had so much food in my entire life in the booth. And always, we'd have almost at least, every day, two big trays that somebody had brought from some place, some Italian pastry shop. We had more cannolis. Sometimes I went to bed dreaming about cannolis. But Scooter loved those cannolis. And people made sure he didn't run out of cannolis."

In later years, Murcer would boast that he had lost 35 lbs. with the retirement of the Scooter because fans no longer brought food to the booth.

"Here comes Alex Rodriguez to the plate to lead off the top of the eighth— he struck out swinging with the bases loaded his last time up," Rizzuto said during one broadcast.

Murcer revealed that the Scooter didn't use an actual scorebook. Rizzuto would come in just before the first pitch of the game. On a napkin or whatever piece of paper he could find, Rizzuto would quickly scribble a few notes to himself. Maybe he would use some actual scoring notations i.e. F-7 for a fly out to left field, or 4-3 for a groundout to second base, he also used his own variations, including the famous "WW" (wasn't watching).

Once, the Scooter stepped out and went home when he was scheduled to do an interview with Washington columnist and baseball expert George Will. Murcer had to step in again. Murcer only lasted a year in the Yankees broadcast booth, but he would return for another long stint in the 1990s.

Christmas Night 1984

On Christmas night 1984, Henry Congregane, a 38-year-old agent of the Federal Bureau of Investigation, and his wife, Patricia, Phil's daughter, were looking out of the window of their brownstone at 166 West 88th Street at about 9:15 PM. It was a neighborhood in transition. According to neighbors, their was a "testy coexistence" that made their block "representative of many streets on the West Side of Manhattan [at the time]—where owners of half-million-dollar townhouses live a few doors down from tenants paying less than $100 a month rent, and where cultural differences abound," according to Martin Gottlieb of the *New York Times*.

There were other more famous local residents, that included former New York Knicks star Earl "the Pearl" Monroe; influential figurative painter Philip Pearlstein; David Mitchell, the well known set designer for such Broadway shows as *Annie* and *La Cage aux Folles*; and Peter Samton, chief architect of 1 Police Plaza, the Grand Hyatt Hotel, and many others.

According to Gottlieb, many of the tenants in the city-owned buildings toiled in a local belt factory, while others held diverse blue-collar or handyman's jobs, or were unemployed.

Upwardly mobile professionals moved into the neighborhood when the brownstones could be had at bargain-basement prices. Many of the buildings had been marked for demolition, part of the 26-year-old West Side Urban Renewal project. These fixer-uppers, which could then be bought in the neighborhood of $35,000, had huge selling points, with grand rooms and small, backyard gardens. There was one drawback—an 18-story public housing project on the corner.

Muggings, car thefts, and burglaries were not uncommon in this neighborhood.

"People were mugged every day," recalled Emily Samton, Peter's wife.

Many local residents knew Henry Congregane. They described him as "quiet" and "calm." He was well known for sitting on the front stoop of his brownstones and watching his daughter, Jennifer, play on the sidewalk and in the street. He was known as someone who was helpful to residents of all kinds. He was a special presence who kept a wary eye out for mischief of any kind. He had broken up many of the types of crimes that were afflicting the neighborhood. He had interfered in several attempted muggings and car-jackings.

On that fateful Christmas Eve, Henry and Patricia witnessed two young men attempting to break into a car. Patricia called 911. Henry grabbed his badge and a .38-caliber revolver and ran downstairs to run off the would-be burglars. He probably assumed they would run off as many had before.

Twenty-year-old Dario Vasallo Jr. lived on the same street as Congregane and had no criminal record of any kind. He was thought of by friends and relatives as "a very sweet guy." Dario Vasallo Sr. and his wife, Iris, had raised their four children at 107 West 88th Street for 20 years. Vasallo Jr. supported his family, paying $112 a month for a four-room apartment, by working as a gypsy cab driver. Their move to this block was a sign of upward mobility, as they had left Spanish Harlem. Vasallo Sr. was not keen on the crime in the neighborhood, either. The decal on the Vasallo family's front door read,

"Never mind the dog. Beware of the owner." Next to the words was a drawing of a gun barrel.

Dario Jr. and his friend, Andres Santana, 21 years old, had been drinking and were attempting to remove a window from a parked car.

According to Congregane's testimony, Henry flashed his badge, pointed his gun, and told them both to raise their hands above their heads. He then ordered Mr. Vasallo to lie on the sidewalk. Dario complied. But even after Santana was ordered to lie down, he refused, and started to approach Congregane. As Santana got closer to Congregane, Dario began to get up.

Dario moved to get up. Congregane shot him through the left part of the chest. Dario died of his gunshot wound. Congregane and Santana were both questioned. Manhattan District Attorney, Robert M. Morgenthau, convened a grand jury that heard the testimony of 12 individuals, including Congregane and Santana.

The shooting was an instant media circus. Rizzuto's name was used in almost every article, connecting him to Congregane. The friends and relatives of Dario Vasallo Jr. shouted for justice. Racism, excessive force, and class warfare were rampant themes running through the media coverage.

"He really wasn't a bad boy," said his sister, Lisa, 22. "Maybe he was trying to break into a car, but he was unarmed, so how come he was shot?"

Many neighborhood friends came to Congregane's defense.

"We've had some other people on the block I can really see going off the handle, but I've never seen Henry raise his voice," Mrs. Samton said. "He's not quick on the trigger at all. I've never seen an excitable side."

Even the usually media shy Cora Rizzuto, spoke to the *New York Times*, insisting, "He was in charge of the safety of the block. He was a very, very good person."

Andres Santana was charged with attempted grand larceny and possession of burglary tools. Dario's autopsy report revealed traces of cocaine and PCP in his system.

On May 24, 1985, the Manhattan grand jury exonerated Congregane. "The issue was justification," said Robert M. Morgenthau, the Manhattan District Attorney. "Were these two young men threatening the agent or were they not? The grand jury found they were."

Unique in the media coverage was the fact that Phil and Cora and Henry were all named, but Patricia's name was never revealed by any media outlet.

Perfecting His Style

"He didn't try to act like an announcer," Hall of Fame teammate Whitey Ford said. "He just said what he thought. It added fun to the game."

August 4, 1985, was Phil Rizzuto Day at Yankee Stadium. Tom Seaver, then pitching for the Chicago White Sox, was chasing after his 300th win. On that day, Rizzuto's uniform No. 10 was retired. They planned the event for this day and not on his birthday, September 25, for fear of the impending baseball strike.

During this ceremony, Phil was presented with a bronze plaque, later to be placed in the stadium's Monument Park. The plaque makes reference to the fact that he "has enjoyed two outstanding careers, all-time Yankee shortstop, one of the great Yankee broadcasters." During the ceremonies, Joe DiMaggio, who was on hand, remarked, "Rizzuto is my Hall of Famer."

"Of all the most famous Yankee friendships [Ted] Williams developed was with Phil Rizzuto," sportswriter Mike Vaccarro wrote. Williams said that day, "Johnny Pesky is one of my dearest friends in life, and I always loved playing with Junior Stephens. But I have to say that if Phil Rizzuto was the Red Sox shortstop all those years, I think history would have gone a little bit differently."

Phil was also presented with a live cow, which had a halo affixed to its head, a joke on his "Holy Cow" catch phrase. The cow accidentally sideswiped Rizzuto, sending him to the ground. Neither the honoree nor the cow were seriously injured. Rizzuto later said, "That big thing stepped right on my shoe and pushed me backwards, like a karate move." He then gave a small speech about how he couldn't imagine being happier, "doing something you like and getting paid for it."

"George Steinbrenner, he thinks the world of Rizzuto. George Steinbrenner has been mad at the Hall of Fame because Rizzuto hasn't been voted in yet, and George has vowed he will not let the Yankees play in the annual Hall of Fame game in Cooperstown until they put Rizzuto in there," journalist George Vecsey wrote. "Let's face it, Rizzuto is one of a kind. People either love him or hate him. Some people think he's like a lovable uncle, the life of the Thanksgiving dinner, and other people think he's off the deep end, out of touch with the current players, plugging products and wishing people happy birthday and talking about all his fears."

The Yankees showered Rizzuto with presents. They gave him a convertible, and "everybody says it's so he can cross the bridge in style," Vecsey wrote. Among his other gifts was a 45-inch television set. Mickey Mantle quipped it was so Rizzuto "can watch the last three innings at home with Cora."

When the game finally began, "the old professional, Lindsey Nelson, with his coat of many colors," was there to lend some Tom Terrific's old Mets salad days, did the play-by-play from the Yankees booth that day, while Rizzuto and his entourage of family and friends partied upstairs in Steinbrenner's box. "He's got the whole day off, that huckleberry," Vecsey wrote.

As for Seaver, Rizzuto said, "That huckleberry, he won his 300th game at Yankee Stadium on my 'day' when they retired my number and the cow they gave me stepped on my feet."

• • •

Former major-league pitcher Jim Kaat joined Rizzuto and White in the booth in 1986. The rookie broadcaster, now colorman, was stranded by Phil Rizzuto. He was initiated like so many before him. Just like Rizzuto himself had been burned by Allen and Barber that long hot spring training game so many decades ago.

"Kaat, I got to go to the men's room," said the diminutive Rizzuto to the trusting ex-pitcher.

"I know he went back to the hotel room. Phil does that all the time," producer Don Carney burned.

But Kaat was no stranger to dicey situations. He'd written *Sports Illustrated* when it had featured Steinbrenner on the cover posing like Napoleon, and the magazine printed his remarks that the cover had shown poor taste.

"There have been no problems with George," Kaat said many years later. "Over the years I have come to appreciate his style."

Kaat had relied on Bill White for advice. "Bill gave me a good foundation. He taught me how to do Yankee telecasts without being a former Yankee," Kaat said. And in dealing with Steinbrenner, White said, "He'll send notes telling you what to say. You have to take a stand."

"He kept things loose in the booth," Kaat said. "He kept the broadcast enjoyable for the fans. He was unique in the fact that very few announcers can get by with the so-called shtick that Scooter had, being a cheerleader for one team like that. That wouldn't go over too well in these days; the critics would hammer you pretty good rooting for the home team. He could do that because he was part of the Yankee organization his whole life."

"He always arrived late. I remember Sparky Anderson when he was managing the Tigers, and he said to me, 'Introduce me to Rizzuto when you get a chance,'" Pepe recalled.

Pepe was shocked. "You mean to tell me in all the time you've been in baseball, you've never met Rizzuto?" Anderson shrugged.

"Rizzuto never went down to the field. He showed up late and did the game. He was a very private guy. His whole life was Cora, his family, early days playing golf, and TV."

• • •

In the meantime, Rizzuto continued to hold court with fans. In a cinderblock hallway behind the announcing booth, there was a sign:

PHIL RIZZUTO'S OFFICE
Open 7 to 7:30 weekdays
1 to 1:30 weekends
Autographing by appointment only
Visa/Mastercard and Cannolis Accepted

It was no office, but a short hall chocked full with large, heavy tech cases from the broadcast booths. Phil would allow anyone to come by and chat baseball with him, and he'd sign autographs. He made himself available all the time, and fans were rarely disappointed.

"Although no baseball fan, my Mom loved listening to Bill White and Phil Rizzuto," wrote one adoring baseball fan to the *New York Times*. "As a present for her 80th birthday in November 1986, I sent Phil Rizzuto a blank audio cassette c/o Yankee Stadium and requested he wish her a happy birthday. Her birthday came and went and no cassette. Then about a month later, the phone rang. Without identifying himself or why he was calling, Phil Rizzuto began apologizing, telling me how sorry he was he missed my Mom's birthday because the Stadium mail wasn't forwarded in time."

"I was walking in midtown Manhattan in 1986 at lunchtime and noticed a silver Jaguar parked in the street," recalled yet another Yankees fan. "When I went over to look at it, I saw Phil Rizzuto was in the driver's seat taking a nap. Being an unassuming Bronx boy, I tapped the window and he rolled it down and we had a 20-minute conversation about the state of the Yankees. He was waiting in his car while Cora was in a bank. I continued talking to Phil until Cora came back to the car. Well at this time, I realized I did not have anything for him to sign. There was a Burger King just a couple of stores down which was handing out $1 coupons. I asked Phil and Cora to wait while I grabbed a coupon and came back with it for him to sign. He wrote: 'To Mike! Holy Cow! Phil Rizzuto.' Needless to say, it is one of my most cherished mementos."

Of course, Rizzuto could be outspoken at times. And in many of these out bursts, he made himself more popular with fans. Sometimes they were on air, and sometimes they weren't.

"White Sox operations director Ken Harrelson denied a report by Yankee broadcaster Phil Rizzuto that pitcher Joe Cowley was being waived by the Sox for the purpose of releasing him," said the first sentence in a *Chicago Sun-Times* article on April 11, 1986.

"First, he has no business saying that. The waiver list is confidential," the angry Harrelson said. "Second, it's no big deal to put players on the list (to determine interest from other teams). We've put 13-14 on it in the last few weeks. That's not even news. It's obvious why he did it. Someone on the Yankees leaked it to make the Britt Burns deal look better from their end. Well, it's going to backfire on them because we're not talking release waivers here."

He seemed more outspoken than ever, driven especially by the team's lack of success on the field despite having among the highest payrolls in baseball.

In November 1986, Rizzuto appeared alongside Len Dykstra of the World Champion New York Mets for an autograph signing session in conjunction with a baseball card show at the Polish Community Center.

"I didn't know you huckleberries would be here," Rizzuto said to the media that had been planned to draw attention to the show.

"Phil Rizzuto…can't understand the problems some modern players have with dealing with New York pressures," wrote Gene Levy in the *Albany Times-Union*.

"What pressure? To me it's a copout for a [Dave] Winfield who is making $2 million or a [Butch] Wynegar who is making almost a million to say they can't handle the pressure," said the then 69-year-old former shortstop. "You want pressure? When we played, I lived in New York and you had to answer to all the kids after you had a bad day. Now, the players all have beautiful homes in New Jersey and the other suburbs to go home to. They make all that money."

According to Levy, Rizzuto took a swipe at fellow Yankees announcers Bill White, Jim Kaat, Frank Messer, and Spencer Ross for their penchant for statistics.

"Those huckleberries sit around taking statistics. I don't like statistics," he said. "They show statistics analyzing everything. Baseball is a simple game. You can make it too complicated."

He even took pot shots at Series-winning manager Davey Johnson, saying, "Johnson was lucky the Mets won. He pulled some rocks, too," Rizzuto said.

"Rizzuto even managed to get in a dig at another celebrated manager, Martin, who last season served as part of the Yankee announcing crew. He said Martin was off base in his end-of-season blast at Yankee coaches Don Zimmer and Joe Altobelli," Levy reported.

"I roomed with Billy, and he was one of the hardest workers and one of the best managers I've known," he said. "But he's even more outspoken than I am. Billy carries a grudge. If you do something, it may take 10 years, but he's going to get you."

"Can you believe WPIX doesn't want me to announce birthdays any more?" he said. "They told me before last season not to do that, but I manage to sneak some in anyway."

"He would keep getting in trouble with WPIX for announcing birthdays and anniversaries," Patricia Rizzuto recalled.

"Phil was exasperating, with his endless birthday and restaurant plugs. John Moore, our gifted director, was out of his league trying to reign Scooter in, as was I," said Marty Appel who, as a Yankee and WPIX employee, worked with Rizzuto for years. "No one was up to it, because, in a way at least, he held the cards. No one was going to fire him over birthday plugs…. We would tell him to tone it down; he'd say he would, but he never did."

"[Bob] Fishel was one of the first to tire of Phil's on-air work, although most fans loved it. It would drive Bob crazy that Phil was always talking about 'a break for the Yankees,' as though they weren't earning their victories on merit, only on 'lucky breaks,'" Marty Appel recalled.

Rizzuto was honest. "You don't hear the score too often, or the game too often, but I think all my friends liked to have their names mentioned, and the restaurants, I get a free meal. White knows that I do it that way," Rizzuto joked many years later. But everyone knew what he was doing. He was offering free plugs for free meals. Savvy metropolitan viewers already knew what was going on, and that endeared him to them even more. He was giving away thousands of dollars worth of free advertising for free meals for himself and his family and friends.

Appel had started out with the Yankees organization opening up fan mail for Mickey Mantle. He worked with Rizzuto in the 1980s and 1990s as a television producer.

"When I first joined the Yankees, way back in 1968, I was sincerely a great fan of his. The first time I ever met him, I said, 'Phil, there are times I turn down the sound on the TV so I can continue to hear you on the radio.' And he said, 'Oh! Don't do that! You'll catch all my mistakes.'"

"As Yankees PR director, I worked and traveled with him on a daily basis, and then as WPIX producer, I was his boss. He would say a day without a cannoli was like a day without sunshine. We always felt a day without Scooter was also gloomy. He just made everyone feel good in his presence," Appel said.

"He was a terrific pro.... He had no ego and always brought out the best in his partners, a tribute to his professionalism. And although he didn't give himself a lot of credit as a broadcaster, he could read copy in one take, always nailed pre-taped items perfectly. One thing was that we always needed him to do play-by-play, not color, because if he was the color commentator, he would pay less attention, he'd be distracted by visitors to the booth, etc. So he did play-by-play all the time and was great at it. We put TV cameras on the roof at Yankee Stadium in the late '80s to get Manhattan skyline shots—that shot you see of the ball crossing home plate from high above—but we used to joke among ourselves that it was really a surveillance camera to catch him sneaking out early," Appel remarked.

"I knew him for 40 years," Appel said. "And the people who listened to him on the radio just once, they knew what he was like as well I did."

"Phil was a lot more professional than he ever gave himself credit for. The fact was, even though he never took himself seriously, he made every one of his partners—whether it was Fran Healy, Bill White, or Frank Messer—better. You'd give him a commercial slot or a promo and he'd nail it in one take," Appel continued.

"He always had a friend in every town. Someone to drive him to the ballpark. They'd play golf in the early days," Phil Pepe recalled. "I remember he had friends in Cleveland. They'd drive him around, and he'd let them come up to the booth. Come to think of it, I don't remember him ever taking the team bus."

"Now, the players would seek him out. He didn't go down on the field a lot," Appel added. "You know, he used to squirm out of doing the interviews on the field before the game. But they knew him, and they knew he was Yankees history. And he was Yankees tradition."

• • •

Barbara Klimek, the 43-year-old niece of New York Yankees broadcaster Phil Rizzuto, was struck and killed in a hit-and-run accident on the Upper West Side of Manhattan early on the morning of September 14, 1988.

"The driver of the car, Kathleen Mahon, 29, of Reading, N.J., was arrested after a brief chase by a police cruiser near the scene of the accident at

West 74th Street and West End Avenue," reported the *New York Times*. "Ms. Mahon was charged with vehicular homicide, vehicular assault, criminally negligent homicide, operating a vehicle while intoxicated, leaving the scene of an accident and not having a driver's license."

• • •

By the late 1980s, White and Rizzuto, despite a large swath of accompanying voices, had endured as a set of classic broadcast partners.

"Bill would squeeze Phil's wrist if Phil was going off on something that might turn out to be politically incorrect. The two of them had a genuine affection for each other, and I think it was apparent," Marty Appel said. But for White, the routine of 18 years, even with Rizzuto, was starting to wear thin. "I was worried about making that change," White said. "After a while, I just said it was time to move on. My motive was just to get on with my life."

Luckily, he was approached for an important position—that of National League President. Not only that, but he was the first African-American president of either league. White replaced A. Bartlett Giamatti as President of the National League. And Giamatti succeeded Peter Ueberroth as baseball commissioner on the day White took over as league president. The announcement was made on February 3, 1989.

"My first comment was, 'Are you serious?'" White said. "But in meeting with people, I found out they were dead serious. Once I knew that, we proceeded from there."

Peter O'Malley, the chairman of the search committee and the owner of the Los Angeles Dodgers, insisted there had been no specific hunt for a black president, although several African-Americans had been interviewed.

"Bill White was selected because he was the best man for the job," O'Malley said. "He was the only man who was offered the job and, fortunately, he was the only man who accepted. Race was not a factor."

"But Clifford Alexander, whose Washington consulting firm has worked to expand baseball's hiring of minority-group members, said that the importance of White's selection could not be overlooked," Dave Anderson of the *New York Times* wrote.

"This is a highly significant appointment and should be regarded that way," Alexander said. "Baseball has set a standard that others can emulate. But if we think that one appointment is the beginning and the end, it isn't."

"If I didn't think I could do this job," White said, "I would have been foolish to take it for whatever historical significance there might have been."

Hank Aaron, then the director of player development for the Atlanta Braves, told the Associated Press he was pleased by White's selection, saying, "I don't think they could have found anyone more qualified than Bill White. He knows baseball. There will be nothing that will be a surprise for him."

White told the *Philadelphia Daily News*, "The Yankees took a trip to the West Coast last summer. I worked a game in Seattle and then I flew to Alaska and fished for five days. I flew back to Oakland for a game and then fished another four days in northern California. That's the kind of thing I'm going to miss."

Among those who attended the announcement were George Steinbrenner and Phil Rizzuto. Rizzuto told the press that he did not know about the selection until the last couple of days.

"He told me he didn't feel he was qualified," Rizzuto recalled. "I said, 'What are you talking about?' He had qualms about it, like anybody would."

Later, when someone asked White why he accepted the post, he smiled and nodded toward Rizzuto. "If you'd worked with Rizzuto as long as I have, you'd know my motivation," White said in jest. "How would you like to work 18 years with a guy who still doesn't know your first name?"

It was announced February 18, 1989, that George Grande, who had broadcast baseball for CBS Radio and ESPN, had been tagged to partner with Rizzuto for Yankees telecasts on WPIX. Rizzuto was beginning his 33rd season with the Yankees as a broadcaster. The irony of it was this—Phil was already a beloved character in the metropolitan region. He was a ubiquitous pitchman, a rambling, beloved broadcaster, and a famed Old Timer. But now, without White as his straight man, his longevity was a wonder to all around, and Rizzuto was now being considered among the better announcers despite his deficiencies.

"Managers aren't the only insecure people around the New York Yankees. Of the seven announcers who regularly broadcast Yankees games, only one—

Phil Rizzuto—held the same job last year," Pete Dougherty wrote in the *Albany Times-Union*. "The Yankee broadcast booths—WPIX (Channel 11), MSG and WABC Radio—have new talent and not an overabundance of it, either. The Mets, seen on WWOR (Channel 9) and SportsChannel and heard on flagship radio station WFAN, may have baseball's best announcer in Tim McCarver, but might have two of the worst, as well."

Dougherty pinpointed Greg Gumbel as an "enjoyable" play-by-play man and Tommy Hutton as a "top flight" analyst, but he bemoaned the rareness of Gumbel's appearances and the use of Hutton in play-by-play.

Then, commenting on Rizzuto, he opined, "His talents didn't become appreciated until Bill White left to assume the presidency of the National League. He leaves out a lot of detail, he roots too much, but he is entertaining—something lacking in most New York baseball announcers."

More accolades were to come.

"When Phil Rizzuto was told to dust off his tuxedo in order to be properly attired while receiving the William J. Slocum Award for long and meritorious service to baseball at the New York baseball writers' dinner tonight, he sounded confused," wrote Dave Anderson in the *New York Times* on January 21, 1990.

"I know the 'long' part," he said, "but I don't know what 'meritorious' means. I'll have to ask White about 'meritorious.'"

"You know, meritorious, as in merit," the caller told Rizzuto, when he was notified about the award. "You know, merit, as in a Boy Scout merit badge."

"I was a Boy Scout," Rizzuto said. "I never made First Class because I couldn't start a fire without matches."

"As a shortstop and as a broadcaster, Phil Rizzuto has never started fires. He's always been content, never contentious. Maybe that's why he's entering his 54th consecutive year in the Yankee organization. And is there anybody else in baseball, or in sports, who has been with the same organization since 1937?" Anderson continued. "Especially in recent years, when Yankee employees don't go to work until they've checked whatever 'transactions' may have transpired. To have endured as a Yankee for half a century, especially for the nearly two decades of George Steinbrenner's reign, is more than long and meritorious. It's long and miraculous."

"I looked up the winners of this award and I saw where Tom Seaver got it," Rizzuto said, referring to his then-current broadcast partner. While his detractors pointed out his faults, which were many—he failed to mention important things like score, inning, which team was batting, what the pitch count was—his legion of fans followed him happily and Phil remained as popular as ever. Despite Mel Allen's moniker, "The Voice of the Yankees," it was in fact Rizzuto's voice that two generations of Yankees fans grew up listening to.

"I heard the doctors revived a man after being dead for four-and-a-half minutes. When they asked what it was like being dead, he said it was like listening to New York Yankees announcer Phil Rizzuto during a rain delay," said David Letterman on his popular *Late Night* show.

For one night, on April 30, 1990, Mel Allen returned to the Yankees broadcast booth to announce one more game. "Mel Allen marked his seventh decade as a baseball broadcaster Monday night, working 1½ innings of the New York Yankees–Oakland Athletics game," reported the *Chicago Sun-Times.*

Allen's appearance was the brainchild of Marty Appel, always and ever watchful of a publicity opportunity. Allen, who began his major league broadcasting career in 1939, joined Phil Rizzuto and George Grande on the team's telecast over superstation WPIX.

"It was a thrill to do it," Allen said. "I'm glad they asked me."

"The only voice of the Yankees," Rizzuto said, "and the greatest voice still."

WPIX's hold on broadcasting Yankees games had become tenuous. With the rise of the Madison Square Garden cable network, WPIX, the long-standing broadcaster of the Yankees, was getting squeezed out. There was never a long-term contract for WPIX, and every year they had to re-up.

"I have a terrible feeling right now," Rizzuto told the *New York Post* in late September 1990. "Fifty years have gone by, and I can't believe there's a chance I won't be coming here any more. It's kind of frightening."

"One year we thought we were doing our final telecast ever on WPIX," Appel recalled. "We hadn't renewed our contract, and speculation was that the Yankees were going all cable. John put together a terrific closing piece, with great scenes and players from the 40 years WPIX had covered the Yankees, set to Billy Joel's 'New York State of Mind.'" Scooter would do the last bit of announcing that night.

"Phil always did play-by-play, never color. If he was the color commentator, you might as well not have him there at all," Appel said. Rizzuto would chat with the fans in the stands, the passersby, anybody who brought food or cannolis. And he didn't add much about the current players, because he did not know them well enough.

"John and I always joked about Rizzuto probably never having met Don Mattingly, because he never went downstairs and he never traveled with the team," Appel remarked. "But here he was, down to one batter, Billy Joel all cued up, and it was a fly ball to left field. Perhaps on the last batter of his broadcast career."

> *"Oh, and before this ball comes down, time to get in one last birthday wish for Mrs. Viola Ferranzano out there in the Whitestone section of Queens, a great Yankee fan."*

"We all screamed in the basement of Yankee Stadium. But that was Phil," Appel recalled. That was what made him endearing.

On a similar note, Steve Wulf wrote in *Sports Illustrated* in November 1991, "Movie critic Gene Shalit publishes a monthly newsletter, and in the October issue he quotes Phil Rizzuto, the New York Yankee broadcaster. It seems that Rizzuto was telling listeners to a late-season game in Boston that he had been in Concord, Mass., that day and that 'Everything up there is named Walden. Great poet.'"

* * *

Al Kunitz died in 1991. Rizzuto had never failed to mention Kunitz's influence and contribution to his entire career, and he would even mention him for many years later, up to the time of his own death. He gave Kunitz credit for his ability to bunt, as well as his advice on language and hard play.

When Kunitz's relatives cleaned out his possessions, they discovered a page of a medical journal that described ALS, or Lou Gehrig's disease. According to Sylvia Kunitz, Al's daughter-in-law, Al Kunitz had written, on the side of the page: "Is this what I have?"

"He probably did have it," said Sylvia Kunitz, who lives in upstate New York. Sylvia's husband, Eric—Al's son—died of ALS. And Sylvia's children, Martin Kunitz and Deborah Christensen, were also both battling the disease.

• • •

Between 1989 and 1993, Tom Seaver was in the booth with Rizzuto. The two developed an instant liking for one another. Their camaraderie was apparent in 1992 when Seaver was elected to the baseball Hall of Fame.

"Tom Seaver was up on a small platform at the New York Sheraton, talking about what the Baseball Hall of Fame meant to him," Dave Anderson recalled. Then Seaver noticed "a small, gray-haired man in a camel-hair overcoat near the rear of the room. Tom Seaver glanced at his watch."

"This press conference started at 10:00," he said with a sly smile, "so I'd like to thank Phil Rizzuto for showing up at 10:15. For three years, we've worked together broadcasting Yankee games on WPIX, and for three years he's called me 'Seaver.' From now on, it's 'Mr. Seaver.'"

Eventually, the ex-Mets star was asked about winning his 300th game in 1985 with the Chicago White Sox at Yankee Stadium.

"It happened to be Phil Rizzuto Day," Seaver said.

"You huckleberry," the familiar voice called out.

"What do you know, he's still here," Seaver said.

"You huckleberry, I got to get over the bridge."

"You can call me 'Mr. Huckleberry,'" Seaver said.

Later during the press conference, Rizzuto was asked to compare Seaver to pitchers from his era. "Bob Feller was a little faster than Seaver, but his control wasn't half as good." Rizzuto also mentioned to the media how Seaver, always the pure professional, had helped him double his WPIX salary.

"You still here?" said Seaver, working his way to the back of the room.

"Not for long," Phil Rizzuto said. "Another two minutes, it's $10 more for parking."

"Seaver bonded well with Rizzuto; they looked out for each other. When I had a difficult contract negotiation with Rizzuto in 1990, one which got ugly in the newspapers and found him calling me names, I knew Seaver was coaching him on the side," Marty Appel admitted.

"They'll give you the money, Scooter, don't give in," Seaver told Rizzuto.

"That was a miserable time for me. I loved Scooter and he deserved the money, but senior management was firm that we were only going to pay him so much," Appel remembered. Things got ugly. "I received two death threats on the phone at WPIX."

Appel admitted that during the toughest weeks of the negotiation, Cora had called him when Phil was not at home, telling him that things would work themselves out. She told Appel that Phil did not consider the situation a personal one. And when it was all over, he and Phil were able to mend their differences.

Appel also remembered that year that he had arranged for an end-of-season lunch at the Hard Rock Café. But of course, Scooter never showed. Later, when they saw him at the booth, Marty asked Scooter why he didn't attend.

"The Hard Rock Café? Holy cow, I can't go in to one of those topless places!"

Bobby Murcer said about Tom and Phil, "Tom was quite a prankster. Once, just before a game, he told me, 'If Scooter asks you a question, say, 'I don't know, ask Seaver.' Well, I went along with him, and when Scooter asked me something, I'd say, 'I don't know, ask Seaver.' Scooter did, and Seaver's response was, 'I don't know, ask Murcer.' I thought we were going to dance around the floor all day."

• • •

"We have IFB [internal feedback], where from the truck, I can talk to him, or both announcers at the same time, or separately," recalled John Moore, the WPIX-TV executive producer of the Yankee broadcasts. Rizzuto regularly forgot how IFB worked when Moore was talking to him. Rizzuto assumed everyone could hear Moore's voice. Almost every game there was some kind of snafu of this kind.

Once, while announcing at Yankee Stadium in a 10-run blow-out during the bottom of the eighth inning, it happened to Seaver and Rizzuto. Seaver was announcing. Meanwhile, Rizzuto was listening to the IFB.

"Well, we try to accommodate Phil, if possible, by letting him go home a little earlier. So I said to Phil in his ear, 'At the end of this inning, you can let George [Grande] come in and you can go home.'"

"Oh, I love you!" Scooter said right out loud.

"Seaver was right in the middle of a sentence and he stopped cold what he was saying," said Moore. Seaver paused for a bit, flummoxed by the outburst. He looked at Rizzuto.

"Well Scooter, I'm fond of you, too."

• • •

"Hey, Scooter, c'mere!" shouted Mickey Mantle to Rizzuto. It was the 1992 Old Timers Day. Scooter was walking off the field with Whitey Ford.

According to the Yankees batboy, Matthew McGough, "Rizzuto, who no longer did color commentary for every Yankees game, was working as a special Old Timers' Day correspondent…Rizzuto wore a small microphone clipped to the front of his jersey and roamed the dugout interviewing the most senior of Yankee old-timers."

"Rizzuto seemed smaller than I'd imagined. In the summer of 1992 he'd turned 74, and his size seemed even further diminished by his age. But he'd lost none of his good-natured Old New York folksiness," McGough opined.

"All right, Seaver, I'm gonna go see what Mr. Mantle has to say for himself," Rizzuto said, speaking into the microphone, to Seaver up in the booth. "How ya doin', Mick?"

"That thing on?" asked Mantle, leaning forward and tapping the small microphone.

"Sure is, Mickey," Rizzuto assured him.

"Fuck, fuck, cocksucker," Mantle barked into the microphone, laughing. "Cocksucker, shitbag, fuck!"

"Mary Mother of God!" Rizzuto shouted, cupping his hand over the microphone and scurrying down to the other end of the dugout. "Holy cow, Mick!"

"The old timers in earshot—mostly teammates of Mantle, guys in their late sixties—burst into laughter," McGough recalled.

The Literary Life of Philip Francis Rizzuto

In March 1993, Scooter joined the literati with the publication of his book, *O Holy Cow! The Selected Verse of Phil Rizzuto*, edited by Tom Peyer and Hart Seely. It was published by The Ecco Press, a literary press in Hopwell, New Jersey.

"You do not read an Ecco catalogue; you peruse it. There was the latest collection of Joyce Carol Oates short stories, and not a moment too soon. There was Italo Calvino. There was Joseph Conrad. There was Dante. And there was Phil Rizzuto," George Vecsey wrote. "Yes, Phil Rizzuto. America's favorite daffy uncle. The one who has been babbling on Yankee games on WPIX-TV for four decades. The greatest shortstop not in the Hall of Fame. That Phil Rizzuto."

Hart Seely, who was then a reporter for *The Syracuse Herald-Journal*, jokingly used to insist that Rizzuto actually spoke in verse. No one believed Seely save long time friend, Tom Peyer, who edited comic books.

"Rizzuto couldn't work the first game after Thurman Munson's funeral," Seely recalled. "But we had a tape of the pregame show, it was a bad tape, all squeaky, and as I was writing it down, I thought to myself, 'Seely, you're losing it.'"

The tapes disclosed a poignant "Prayer for the Captain," which ends:

> *Faith. You gotta have faith.*
> *You know, they say time heals all wounds,*
> *And I don't quite agree with that a hundred percent.*
> *It gets you to cope with wounds.*
> *You carry them the rest of your life.*

"There is also a haunting poem titled 'The Man in the Moon,' in which Rizzuto sees the image of Captain Munson in the full moon over Yankee Stadium. And there are poems from the Bucky Dent game, Roger Maris's 61st home run, George Brett's pine-tar-bat episode, in which Rizzuto seems, dare one say it, almost relevant," Vecsey wrote.

"In those big games, he doesn't digress," Seely said. "But baseball on television, let's be honest, isn't all that complex. If he's talking about something else, movies or cannolis, I don't think it's all that bad."

"That's wacky," Rizzuto said when he was asked for permission to publish his poetry. But the authors were giving all the proceeds to charity, and so would he. "It's hard to get the poetry in it," Rizzuto insisted. "But if you give somebody a laugh in this day and age, it's worth it."

"I have been wrong all this time to conclude that there was anything wrong with me or my Phil-receptors," baseball literary giant Roger Angell wrote in his review of the slim volume in *The New Yorker* magazine that same year. "What's been coming out of that booth all these years is poetry."

The book was a big hit and put Rizzuto on the best-seller list.

To be sure, it was not his first book. Phil had participated with Joe Trimble with a book about himself after he won the MVP award in 1950. He had also a published a book on the champion Yankees of 1961 after that season was over.

In 1993, author Dan Hirshberg published another book about him. Hirshberg was the sports editor of the *Hackettstown Star-Gazette* and had written for the *Kansas City Star* and the *Florida Times-Union*. It was called *Phil Rizzuto: A Yankee Tradition*. Rizzuto cooperated, or at least tolerated the book. The book was a solid history of Rizzuto's earlier years, along with interviews of local residents, friends, and co-workers. And it reprinted a decent selection of interviews Phil had done over the years. In the book, Hirshberg made a cogent argument as to why Rizzuto should be included in the Hall of Fame.

While the book was not the success that *O, Holy Cow!* had been, it was proof that Rizzuto remained a fan favorite despite his advancing years.

• • •

In 1953, after a big Yankees win, Greg and Gerry Grummond approached a harried Phil Rizzuto after the game, seeking an autograph. Mrs. Grummond, the boys' mother, pointed to Greg, saying, "This is our 'Little Scooter'!"

"Sorry lady, I'm in a hurry," Phil responded, manifesting some distress as he glanced at the star-filled eyes of my brother and me. And then he was gone.

"Mom, still a Yankees fan, would be furious at Phil Rizzuto and his Yankees pinstripes No. 10 for the next 40-plus years!" Gerry Drummond recalled.

"Fast-forward 40-plus years to June 18, 1993. It's the Newark airport and, with our four boys, my wife and I have just seen her folks off on a flight," Drummond recalled. "Alex, 16, tells us that he has spotted Phil Rizzuto and his wife, Cora, waiting to pick up someone. Frank, 13, decides to stake out the Scooter sighting from a respectful distance. Alex, however, wants none of this, feeling that the Rizzuto family is entitled to their privacy. Luke, 11, is ready to tag along. All three boys know 'The Scooter' autograph story as part of family lore."

At that moment for the Drummond family, fate intervened. Rizzuto is parked in a no parking zone, and a tow truck pulls up with the intention of driving away with Scooter's car. "Rizzuto, now a fit white-haired grandfather and Yankees sportscaster, hustles outside as the front end of his Cadillac is being raised up.... Scooter is arguing and gesturing wildly with the tow truck operator and with a Port Authority officer. Rizzuto's wife accompanies her husband as he attempts to persuade the tow truck operator to lower and release their car back to him." Eventually, they did.

Drummond, at the right moment, then approached Cora, asking if Phil would be open to an autograph. "I am left taking a picture of a much-relieved Rizzuto standing between Luke in his worn-out Chicago Bears cap and Frank in a Georgetown T-shirt. Phil is scribbling, To Luke, HOLY COW! Phil Rizzuto."

The Rizzutos were most gracious and Drummond shook both their hands.

When Drummond called his mom with the story, she said, "It's about time!"

• • •

In 1993, Cora and Phil Rizzuto celebrated their 50th wedding anniversary at Yankee Stadium. George Steinbrenner himself honored the couple at home plate.

"True love came my way because Joe DiMaggio asked me to pinch hit for him in 1942, and I am sure he remembers the event, and it's the reason he came to Yankee Stadium when George Steinbrenner arranged to fete my wife, Cora, and me on our golden wedding anniversary," Rizzuto said. "Not only has [George] been very nice to me and my family, he has been generous to the extreme…George honored us at home plate. It was really a thrill," Rizzuto said another time. "To have Cora, our kids, and grandkids all on the field, the fans cheering, it was tears of joy to me. Cora is not the most important thing in my life; she is the reason for life itself. So standing at home plate with her was very special."

Phil and Cora were swept up into a horse-drawn carriage and paraded around the interior of the stadium. However, Yogi Berra was not present at this event, and it pained his old friend and former roommate Rizzuto.

"George Steinbrenner made that night happen, so while I know about the fights with Billy Martin and Reggie Jackson and his firing of Yogi, for that matter, I have to feel as I do. I have the right to do so, and so does anyone else," Rizzuto stated.

"I had hoped Yogi would come to the affair at the Stadium, but he didn't. I respect him for his convictions. He won't go back to Yankee Stadium as long as George owns the team. End of subject," Rizzuto said.

"Rizzuto's been going to Yankee Stadium for 53 years. And he is still trying to find a way to beat the toll on the George Washington Bridge," Berra said of his old friend Scooter.

Money Store Benches Rizzuto as Pitchman

In 1992, when asked if they were ever thinking of a replacement, the owners of The Money Store said that one day they would. "And what would the company be looking for in a replacement?" they were asked.

"The same thing that Phil has given us: credibility," Marc Turtletaub said. But the truth was that the transition, however poorly planned, was already under way.

On March 3, 1993, after 20 years of pitching loans in television commercials for The Money Store, former Yankees shortstop Phil Rizzuto was pushed aside as the company's most visible spokesman.

"Jim Palmer, 47, a Hall of Fame pitcher turned broadcaster, is replacing the 74-year-old Rizzuto, who introduced The Money Store to two generations of customers," the Union-based lender told the press.

Headlines blared, "Money Store Benches Rizzuto as Pitchman" and "For Pitchman Phil Rizzuto, How Sweet It Isn't."

"The Money Store is hoping that Palmer, who played most of his career for the Baltimore Orioles, can help attract a new cadre of customers by bringing a fresh look to its long-standing TV ad campaign," wrote Marilee Loboda Braue of *The Record* in Bergen, New Jersey.

"We think he is the right person to represent The Money Store as we enter our second quarter-century of business," said Marc Turtletaub, company president and chief executive.

"It wasn't the best parting," Rizzuto spokesman Anthony Schillizzi said of the Hillside resident's departure as The Money Store's most visible spokesman. "He didn't leave on good terms."

When The Money Store announced that Palmer would replace the 75-year-old Rizzuto in its TV commercials, it said Rizzuto would probably stay on in some capacity, perhaps making occasional personal appearances for the company. But that was news to Rizzuto, who felt he was unceremoniously dumped by a company to which he gave instant credibility, Schillizzi told the press.

"What annoyed him most was the fact that it was just turned over to Palmer," the spokesman said. "They've commercialized off him and the Yankees. Now I guess what they're saying is Palmer will do better than what Rizzuto has been doing for 25 years."

"I would see this more as a transition, not as someone being dumped," Alan Marcus, who handles public relations for the firm, tried to spin the public relations blunder. "They really feel warmly about him. They like Phil;

they're dismayed, because they thought there was an acknowledgement that a change was going to be made. Time comes, you've got to make change."

Rizzuto's contract expired March 1.

Palmer was chosen because it was thought that he would have much wider appeal, especially to younger audiences. Said David Burns, president of Burns Sports Celebrity Service in Chicago, "Palmer, of course, is more sophisticated and younger; he's very attractive, and he certainly will appeal more to women.... And he doesn't come off as a snob, either."

"The snub by The Money Store is the latest disappointment for Rizzuto, who last month was passed over again for induction into the Baseball Hall of Fame by the Veterans Committee," Marilee Loboda Braue reported. "And The Money Store's embrace of Jim Palmer doesn't mean there won't be some reconciliation with the company. Schillizzi said Rizzuto is 'disappointed,' not bitter, and did not rule out that he might go to bat for The Money Store again, if asked."

The Turtletaub family came into a considerable amount of money when First Union Corp completed its acquisition of The Money Store Inc., which was announced in 1998.

"Sub-prime lending has become a major U.S. industry in the 1990s, although The Money Store is one of the few purchased by a commercial banking company," Heather Timmons wrote for *American Banker* magazine. That week, the Turtletaub family's stake in selling the company to First Union Corp. was estimated at $710 million.

Wall Street, always hungry for a new source of cash, swooped down on the sub-prime mortgage lender. "Talk to your mother about this business," said E. Reilly Tierney, then a Fox-Pitt, Kelton analyst. "The only company she'll know is The Money Store."

"That notoriety, built most memorably in a series of ads featuring former Yankee shortstop Phil Rizzuto, is the real reason that the company was picked up by a big bank, analysts say," Timmons wrote.

"First Union is buying a brand name," Tierney said. "It's a unique animal."

Champion Mortgage, another well-known sub-primer lender renowned throughout the Northeast for its ads featuring founder Joseph Goryeb and the tag line, "When your bank says no, Champion says yes," had been purchased in April 1992 by KeyCorp for $200 million.

Wall Street's race to scoop up the sub-prime mortgage business was on. And Rizzuto had been at the heart of it.

"Marketing executives knew that 'second mortgage' had an unappealing ring. So they seized the idea of 'home equity,' with its connotations of ownership and fairness.... Marketing executives who pushed the easy money slogans of the 1980s and 1990s now say their good intentions went awry. Mauro Appezzato used to run marketing at The Money Store, now defunct, the lender whose longtime television spokesman was Phil Rizzuto, the former Yankees shortstop and announcer," wrote business journalist Louise Story in the *New York Times*. "In 1993, Mr. Appezzato helped come up with the pitch line 'less than perfect credit,' a phrase he said was meant to refer to people whose credit was only slightly problematic. But by the late 1990s, the phrase was co-opted by sub-prime lenders like Countrywide Financial, Washington Mutual, New Century, and Ameriquest."

"Since the early 1980s, the value of home equity loans outstanding has ballooned to more than $1 trillion from $1 billion, and nearly a quarter of Americans with first mortgages have them. That explosive growth has been a boon for banks," Story wrote. "However, what has been a highly lucrative business for banks has become a disaster for many borrowers, who are falling behind on their payments at near record levels and could lose their homes."

By 2001, First Union had shut down The Money Store, which cost First Union $3.8 billion. A new version of it now exists.

"Fast forward five years. MLD Mortgage, a New Jersey–based lender founded by former [The] Money Store Vice Chairman Morton Dear convinced Wachovia to sell him The Money Store brand name. The brand was then repositioned as an online loan exchange along the lines of LendingTree, brokering mortgages for 50 lenders including Washington Mutual, NetBank, and Flagstar Bank," Jim Bruene of NetBanker.com reported.

And in the meantime, Marc Turtlebtaub went to Hollywood where he produced the films *Laws of Attraction* and *Little Miss Sunshine*.

Cooperstown

"I couldn't bring myself to vote for [Willie] Stargell on the first ballot when players like Nellie Fox, Bill Mazeroski, and Phil Rizzuto aren't in the Hall of Fame even though they were more one-dimensional than Stargell," veteran sportswriter Vern Plagenhoef told Dave Anderson in 1988. "Fox, once the Chicago White Sox's second baseman, missed by only two votes in 1985, his last year on the writers' ballot. Mazeroski, once the Pirates' second baseman, finished seventh this year with 143 votes. Rizzuto, once the Yankees' shortstop in their glory years, has been discussed and rejected by the Hall of Fame Veterans Committee in recent years but his candidacy is expected to be discussed again at the committee's March meeting."

"It's a crime that Phil Rizzuto, Marty Marion, Pee Wee Reese, and Country Slaughter aren't in the Hall of Fame," Leo Durocher once told *Baseball Digest*. "An absolute disgrace."

Every year, the Hall of Fame watch is as reliable as the rising and setting as the sun and moon. And in the Rizzuto household, the spring announcements were a painful season, when sportswriters and veterans committees would hem-and-haw over the players from the good ol' days. And the Scooter would inevitably be passed over.

"The one time I thought I would make it was when Pee Wee got in (1984). All the reporters told me I would go in with Pee Wee," Rizzuto said.

The Yankees were in spring training, playing the Orioles. Rizzuto had the day off. The reporters had wanted Rizzuto to come in, regardless, to get his reaction when the news hit. Coincidentally, Rizzuto's partner called in sick, and so Rizzuto had to go in.

"I was upset. I had to take his place. Just before the game, he walked in, and I left—mad! Leaving the park in my car, I was listening to the game on the radio.

"The Hall of Fame names are coming in…Pee Wee Reese…," Frank Messer told Bill White on the air.

"I said to myself, 'I got a chance.' Then he said, 'Rick Ferrell.' I almost drove off the road. I hit as many home runs as he did. The reporters had seen me leave the park. They knew I was mad. But I was mad because I had to come to the park. They said in their stories that I was upset. I was. But they didn't report it the way it was. They made me look bad."

"It's not in the cards," Rizzuto told Mike McAlary of the *New York Daily News*, "I'll never get in now."

"The Hall of Fame? No, I'm not upset. I don't think I belong," Phil said in 1989. "I've told people that. Actually, I'm sorry to see them lower the standards. It used to be harder. That's the way it should be. My family and friends feel worse about it that I do. But I've got no regrets. I've been very lucky."

"Scooter is one of the few ex-players who didn't think he got better and better as the years passed," one of his broadcast partners, Fran Healy, said. "The only time I ever saw him bristle was when I once mentioned, 'You were reportedly one of the greatest bunters of all time.' He said, 'What do you mean, reportedly?'"

In 1990, George Will in his book *Men at Work* wrote that Rizzuto "should arguably be" in the Hall of Fame and in his subsequent book rated him "brilliant."

It got so bad, at one point Rizzuto joked, "I'd go in as the batboy."

"Phil wants to be in the Hall of Fame. I've seen his reactions prior to voting and after the voting. It's really a downer after voting is announced," Bill White said in 1993.

In 1993, Rizzuto was offered a deal to write his autobiography, but he refused. "My life is not complete," he said. "Maybe if I made the Hall of Fame this year I would've done one."

For some reason, many people didn't believe Rizzuto belonged. Some sportswriters felt it was an anti-Yankees backlash. Others wondered if it was an anti-New York backlash. Much of it was based on pure stats, citing only batting average, total hits, and RBIs. No one bothered to look any deeper. Rizzuto's possible nomination remained one of the flashpoint conversations about who was already in the Hall and who wasn't. Rizzuto's nomination would come at the hands of the Veteran's Committee, whose reputation for letting in underachievers was legendary.

"Most baseball fans are aware of the scandals involving Shoeless Joe Jackson, Pete Rose, and most recently, steroids," baseball writer Daniel Cote wrote. "However, few casual baseball fans are aware of the Hall of Fame voting scandal that involved Hall of Fame second baseman Frankie Frisch." As Cote pointed out, there was no doubt Frisch belonged. Frisch owned a gaudy lifetime batting average of .316, 2,880 hits, four World Series rings, and the 1931 MVP. He ended his career in 1937 and was inducted in 1947.

"However, it is what he did after his playing career that he seems to be most remembered for," Cote wrote. "After his playing and managing years, Frisch became chairman of the very powerful Baseball Hall of Fame Veteran's Committee. This committee's responsibility was to elect players to the Baseball Hall of Fame who may have been overlooked during the initial balloting by the baseball writers and [who] were no longer eligible for induction. This committee tended to favor 'old-time players' who played during what they believed was the most difficult era in baseball. During his tenure as chairman, many of Frisch's former Giants and Cardinals teammates, the majority of which had been retired for over 40 years, were elected to the Hall of Fame by this committee. These inductions are among the most widely criticized inductions made by the Veteran's Committee." These players came to be known as "Frisch's Friends."

So well watched was this annual ritual that the Associated Press reported on August 1, 1993, "Phil Rizzuto's chances of getting into the Hall of Fame were apparently boosted yesterday by the addition of Yogi Berra and Pee Wee Reese—both members of the Hall—and the National League president, Bill White, to the veterans committee. Both Berra and White are close friends of Rizzuto. Berra played on 14 pennant winners with the Yankees, several with Rizzuto as a teammate. White and Rizzuto shared the microphone and a friendship on TV. Reese, the former Brooklyn shortstop, is known to favor Rizzuto's election by the veterans committee."

In late 1993 or early 1994, "New York Yankees owner George Steinbrenner went to his senior media adviser, Arthur Richman, with an order: Get former Yankees shortstop Phil Rizzuto elected to the National Baseball Hall of Fame in Cooperstown, N.Y.," Thomas Heath wrote in the *Washington Post*. "Richman got in touch with his friends on the Hall's veterans' committee, men whom he had helped throughout his life: Gabe Paul, former White Sox manager Al Lopez, and others."

"I busted my cookies to get him his votes," Richman said. Richman's efforts on Rizzuto's behalf were perfectly allowable under the rules. It seemed such a silly attempt for a five-time All-Star, American League Most Valuable Player in 1950, and the anchor of the Yankees' five consecutive championships.

"But some critics question politicking in Hall of Fame selections. They say too much back-scratching or score-settling among voters for the four major sports' halls results in honoring the wrong people and leaving others out," Heath wrote.

All these men truly thought Rizzuto belonged. But there was serious pressure mounting on this vote.

"I know I'm not going to get in this year, maybe next year," Rizzuto said earlier in the week. "With Yogi, Pee Wee, and White on the committee now, it'd look bad if I got in."

Ted Williams was a vociferous proponent of Rizzuto's entry. Williams of the rival Red Sox once rated Rizzuto as "one-two in my book" among shortstops of his era, adding, "I'd give only Luis Aparicio a slight edge." Aparicio had been in the Hall of Fame since 1984.

"For 11 years, his failure to win a spot among the baseball immortals has made the eligibility of the 76-year-old Rizzuto a hot topic wherever voters met. Despite a great career in New York, including nine trips to the World Series, Rizzuto was passed over by the Baseball Writers' Association of America in his 15 years of regular eligibility, which ended in 1980. He was hurt by a general apathy of writers toward middle infielders, although contemporaries Pee Wee Reese and Red Schoendienst got support," Larry Whiteside wrote in the *Boston Globe*. "After a three-year waiting period, for the next 10 years Rizzuto was rejected by the Veterans Committee."

The sportswriters had passed him over—and now present-day columnists and statisticians like Bill James wailed in agony over the thought of Rizzuto slipping through the gatekeeper's hands and getting into the Hall. However, many veterans from that period thought he absolutely belonged there.

"In 1964, we moved to the apartments that they built where Ebbets Field used to stand. We lived on Sullivan Place and then McKeever until 1986. In 1965, some of the old Brooklyn Dodgers came back to commemorate the 1955 [World Series] championship. Don Newcombe, Duke Snider, and I think Pee Wee Reese were there," Drew Bundini Brown wrote in the *New York Post*. "I remember Snider saying Scooter belonged in the Hall. I was surprised. I had never seen Mr. Rizzuto play. I only knew him as the voice of the Yankees broadcast on WPIX-11."

"He was a hell of a player, a great little guy and a good broadcaster, too," said former Red Sox nemesis Johnny Pesky, who had once labeled Rizzuto a "crybaby." "He was the best little player I ever saw. Who else was little that played as good as he did?"

In 1984, when Pee Wee Reese, the Dodgers shortstop of that era, was elected by the Veterans Committee, he said to Rizzuto, "If I'm in, you should be in."

But as Phil Pepe had pointed out in one of his columns, during the 1980s the Veteran's Committee was made up almost solely of former National League players and four of them were ex-Dodgers. There was a bias.

Bill White, who was now the outgoing National League president, had been Rizzuto's broadcast partner. Along with Berra, they apparently represented three of at least 12 votes that Rizzuto received from the 16 voting members; Ted Williams and Stan Musial were absent from the final vote.

Yogi Berra phoned on a Friday, February 25, 1994, from Tampa, Florida, where the Hall of Fame Veterans Committee had voted Rizzuto and the late Leo Durocher into Cooperstown.

"Did Yogi call collect?" was Rizzuto's first reaction from his Hillside, New Jersey, home.

"My number has been in Yogi's phone book so long it still has letters, like Butterfield 8, or Susquehanna 5000. Yogi's number used to be Pilgrim 8. Yogi knew I would be home," Rizzuto said.

"When Yogi told me," the Scooter said Friday, "I yelled, 'Holy Cow!' and I almost fell to the floor."

"I never thought I would get in," Rizzuto said in a telephone conference call. "It was never frustrating. I didn't think I was Hall of Fame material. But Holy Cow, I finally made it."

"Induction to the Hall of Fame was the long-awaited zenith of Phil Rizzuto's baseball life. And as the moment drew near in late July 1994, Rizzuto made sure his old Red Sox rival, fellow shortstop Johnny Pesky, got to share in the moment," Jeff Goldberg wrote. "Five days before the enshrinement ceremony, Rizzuto took part in a press conference at Yankee Stadium. The Red Sox were at the Stadium for a three-game series, and Rizzuto requested that Pesky join him for the media gathering."

"He was very friendly," Pesky said. "I was at the ballpark that day. Phil knew I was there and asked me to show up. Phil was a favorite of mine."

Rizzuto used the occasion to campaign for his fellow diminutive shortstop to join him in the Hall.

"I'm very proud of going into the Hall," Rizzuto said that day. "But I think Johnny Pesky, Richie Ashburn, and Nellie Fox should be in there, too."

"The innocence of the Fifties ran head-on into the turmoil of the Nineties at Yankee Stadium on Tuesday, as an evening that started out honoring Phil Rizzuto turned into a celebration of baseball," Bob Hertzel wrote in *The Record* (Bergen, New Jersey). "The shadow of a strike that threatens to shut down the sport after Thursday's games could not deter 50,070 revelers from feting the joys of baseball when it was a game, escaping into the memories evoked by Rizzuto and friends like Joe DiMaggio, on hand to honor the newest member of the Hall of Fame."

Hertzel pointed out that one fan poignantly held aloft a sign that read: "Baseball Don't Strike Me Out." During the course of Rizzuto's rambling speech, the fans chanted, "No strike, no strike, no strike."

"But the chant was falling upon deaf ears, just as the paper airplanes made from Phil Rizzuto posters flew out of the stands and fell harmlessly to the ground," Hertzel commented.

"Rizzuto's immortalization in Cooperstown played more like a dizzying episode of *I Love Lucy* than the stuff of history. The Scooter, with his voice strained, rivaled Lucille Ball by delivering an afternoon of verbal hijinx," Laura Vecsey recalled in the *Albany Times-Union*. "All this was after Scooter let out one ringing rendition of 'Holy Cow.' That once-infuriating hallmark phrase began to grow oddly and mysteriously more endearing as Rizzuto's induction ceremony went forth…Rizzuto was great. He was light and nutty and an ambassador of goodwill for a sport that needs enthusiasts to keep it alive, to pass it along."

"Baseball, that noble national pastime, was not defamed or undermined by Rizzuto's scatterbrained rambling Sunday, just as the Hall of Fame was not cheapened by the admittance of Rizzuto, a championship shortstop who must have been doing something right all those years up there in the Bronx," Vecsey continued. "On a sunny summer Sunday, Phil Rizzuto was the perfect antidote to Major League Baseball's current state of affairs: the impending, looming strike. He said maybe the players and owners should come to Cooperstown. It might be the perfect place to work out an agreement."

"This is typical of me," Rizzuto said just minutes into his twisting and turning acceptance speech. "I start at the end and go back to the middle and then the beginning. I'm trying to get this down. When I was a kid playing in the streets of Brooklyn wanting to be a ballplayer."

"If I hadn't been a ballplayer, I don't know what would have happened to me. A lot of nights, I'd wake up in a cold sweat thinking, *If I had not been a major league ballplayer, what would I have done for a living?* Because everything I tried to do turned bad. I tried to run a snowblower, I stuck my hand in and almost cut my fingers off," Rizzuto said.

"This is going nowhere. You see how I do this? I get sidetracked, then I don't know where I was going. See, I did it again! Oh, listen, anytime you want to leave, go ahead." Berra and Johnny Bench, who were on the stage with Rizzuto at the time, both stood up and walked off the stage, but returned laughing moments later. The crowd applauded hysterically.

Rizzuto recounted his days in New York as a kid, his trip to Bassett and his years in the war. "I played with and against the greatest…I mean that era of baseball was absolutely the best…baseball, to me it's been my whole life. I mean, thank God for baseball," Rizzuto said, who received a huge ovation at this point.

After thanking so many people, and mentioning each and every member of his family, he was about to sign off, when he realized that he had not recounted his broadcast years.

"The game is so beautiful now," he said. "Everyone's making money; the owners and the players and the fans can really enjoy this game."

The Yankees held Phil Rizzuto Hall of Fame night on August 9 when they played the Baltimore Orioles at Yankee Stadium. Paper airplanes made from Scooter posters flooded the field.

"It was like being back in Shea Stadium," joked Yankees right fielder Paul O'Neill, who was not the only joker in the house.

"Also on hand was actor Jack Nicholson, who portrayed the Joker in the movie *Batman*. He was greeted warmly by the crowd as he walked to his seat behind the plate, taking high-fives. He was to meet later with Rizzuto and his wife, Cora, hugging each," Bob Hertzel wrote. "Did they come for the game, for Rizzuto, or because the end of the season seems so near?"

"Baltimore had a 6–5 advantage that stood up when the Yankees left the tying run at third base in the ninth inning against Lee Smith, who earned his 33rd save." A player's strike ended the season three days later.

Among some, Rizzuto's enshrinement drew criticism. Most notably from popular baseball statistician and historian Bill James. James was one of the most noted statisticians in the game and wrote an entire book, *The Politics of Glory*, later retitled *Whatever Happened to the Hall of Fame?* about how the Hall of Fame works. It was a polemic based almost solely on statistics. The book got mixed reviews. Some fans bemoaned the heavy use of statistics, James' bread-and-butter, while others hailed it as the acid-test for baseball Hall of Fame candidates. Two of the big targets were Rizzuto and Don Drysdale. Chapter Six, titled 'Scooter,' was devoted solely to Rizzuto.

"I am not here to convince you that Phil Rizzuto is a Hall of Famer… although I cannot write at length about those subjects without reaching some kind of conclusion," James wrote in *Whatever Happened To The Hall of Fame?* "I am here, from my own standpoint, to reinforce the truth in what other people say, and to squash the bullshit. I'm not trying to serve any other candidate for the Hall of Fame. I'm trying to serve the argument itself."

"Let's just let Bill James decide who belongs in the Hall of Fame. He's proven that he knows more about baseball than anybody in the whole world." Dan Gutman wrote in *New York Newsday*.

To be fair to James, he gives equal time to both Rizzuto's fans as well as his detractors. On October 17, 1978, Allen Ryan wrote in the *Toronto Star* that Rizzuto would probably "never be selected to the Hall of Fame, despite some rather impressive numbers."

"In the minds of those baseball writers who vote in the Hall of Fame elections, at least five old shortstops have disappeared—Luis Aparicio, Harold (Pee Wee) Reese, Phil Rizzuto, Marty Marion, and Maury Wills...each of the forgotten five certainly deserves to be enshrined," wrote *New York Times* sportswriter Dave Anderson in 1982.

In 1979, Leonard Koppett wrote in *The Sporting News* that Pee Wee Reese, Luis Aparicio, and Rizzuto all belonged, and that the voters had turned their backs on defensive shortstops for inductions.

Bill Koenig wrote in the *Rochester Times-Union* on February 17, 1979, that "the Scooter was the best of his time."

"If you're not a pitcher, the only thing they look at is power statistics...90 percent of the shortstops play because of their glove, people like Pee Wee Reese and Marty Marion, and myself," Rizzuto said. "Fielding is overlooked!"

In August 1981, Dick Young wrote that he looked forward to a Rizzuto-Reese dual election in the next year. On March 11, 1984, Bill Madden wrote an article titled "The Rizzuto Bypass: Politics, Not Ability, Key."

George Grande told *USA Today*, "Pee Wee and Phil played intangible roles for the Dodgers and Yankees. If one got in, I believe both should be in. On that basis alone, Phil deserves to be in."

Garagiola said, "I hope we don't start to make the Hall of Fame baseball's answer to the 25-year gold watch, but...Rizzuto should have already been in there."

James pointed out that Rizzuto garnered 44 votes in 1962, the highest in the years he was eligible before falling to the second phase, the veterans committee. James also pointed out that 29 other players behind Rizzuto that year eventually made it to the Hall of Fame by 1980, passing him by. This was an important distinction, pointing out that the sportswriter's enthusiasm for Rizzuto had waned. But, it must also be pointed out that the same thing happened to Pee Wee Reese and many other shortstops.

Most illuminating is that James honors Bob Considine, Grantland Rice, and Leonard Koppett, all of whom saw Rizzuto play, and who unequivocally anointed Rizzuto and Gordon the superior short-and-second combination of the era, over Reese and Billy Herman. But then he roundly ignores their opinion, pointing out that the Baseball Writers of America voted for Herman and Reese instead, saying that was the real evidence of who belonged.

James clearly states that Rizzuto had far better numbers than three similar players that were already elected to the Hall, including George Kell, Travis Jackson, and the famed Joe Tinker.

James also fails to mention that in the run between 1949 and 1953, in which the Yankees won five World Series, that Rizzuto played more games than any other Yankee in all but one of those years. He also ignores the fact that many Yankee greats, both during that run and in later years, all said Rizzuto belonged in the Hall, not because of any cronyism, but because he was the defensive star and the glue that held the team together as the more famous players waded in and out of the season with injuries, DiMaggio and Henrich chief among them.

"His criticism of the Hall of Fame's veterans committee…is right on target. This group, which deals with players passed over by the writers, often mocks the meaning of Hall of Famer with its selections. The committee's efforts, as Mr. James notes, have smacked of cronyism," sportswriter Murray Chass wrote. "Even the recent election of Mr. Rizzuto, long rebuffed by the committee, occurred only after his good friends Yogi Berra, Bill White, and Pee Wee Reese were added to the committee. The author dwells so much on Mr. Rizzuto that it almost seems the *raison d'etre* of 'The Politics of Glory' is the debate over the former Yankee shortstop's credentials for the Hall of Fame."

Concluded Chass, "The valid arguments Mr. James presents are lost in his thicket of statistical formulas. If he hadn't already done it, he takes baseball statistics to their ultimate boredom."

While James was and is one of the biggest names in baseball statistics, the book, where Rizzuto is concerned, makes James look vindictive and mean. Nonetheless, James' opinions represented a point of view, however unpopular, that Rizzuto did not belong. The book originally did not perform half as well as his other tomes, but it has since been recast and retitled.

Many people in baseball have opined that Rizzuto belongs in the Hall of Fame, regardless of whether it be as a player or announcer. He was one of the most talented, enduring, and popular men of the game, as a player and broadcaster, for more than 50 years. And he was considered the best Yankees shortstop in club history, surpassing Crosetti, until the arrival and success of Derek Jeter. His shadow will loom large over the Yankees landscape for many years.

• • •

In 1994, Rizzuto got a new straightman, Paul Olden. Olden joined Rizzuto and Murcer in the booth to do WPIX's 50 games that year.

"I'll be ready," Olden said. "Local is different. There's no urgency to get back to the center because you're talking to an audience that knows the team well. You can be loose and Phil can do the things that make Phil so popular."

John Moore, WPIX's then executive producer, acknowledged that Olden's replacing Tom Seaver was an awkward situation. "A lot falls on Phil. He dictates the feeling in the booth. He has a knack for making everybody around him better because he's so affable."

"One of the many laughs we had in the broadcast booth came in Detroit. Like Phil, I'm afraid of certain things…in this case it was a bee that came calling in our tiny booth in Tiger Stadium. As I tried to continue the play-by-play of the game, I was madly taking swats at a bee that was buzzing around my head," Olden remembered.

Phil said, "Hey, get a shot of Olden," to producer John Moore.

"And soon the both of us were on camera doing battle with the bee," Olden said. "Finally, Phil took a small bag that contained his latest batch of birthday wishes and he smashed the bee with it. Then he quickly realized he was going to hear from what he called, 'the bee lovers out there' because he killed a bee on television. He did. And when *This Week in Baseball* came out to Yankee Stadium the following week to do a follow-up feature story, he blamed me for wearing some sweet cologne."

Throughout the 1980s and 1990s, Rizzuto was still popular, appearing on television shows such as *Seinfeld* and *Arli$$*. He was also a popular attraction at card shows and collectible signings. It was big business, as people would line up for hours to get balls, jerseys, and other paraphernalia signed by former star players. For the men who had played in the 1950s and 1960s and had not reaped the millions their current playing brethren had, few fans begrudged the few dollars charged for the signatures in the beginning of this trend. In 1995, Rizzuto made numerous appearances, most notably the Yankees Legends collector's memorabilia show at the Taj Mahal in Atlantic City, New Jersey, along with Yogi Berra, Joe DiMaggio, Don Larsen, Reggie Jackson, and Mickey Mantle. Tickets were both expensive and hard to come by. People complained of the prices, but the crowd was immense nonetheless.

"I went to a memorabilia show where Scooter was signing autographs. In front of me were two kids that couldn't have been more than 7 years old. The first kid goes up to Phil with a pastry box. He opens it and it's filled with cannolis," Drew Bundini Brown remembered.

"Holy cow!" yelled out Rizzuto, who then started eating a cannoli. Then another kid approached.

"Mr. Rizzuto. Can I give you a call some time? I know your number."

"Oh yeah?" Scooter said.

"1-800-LOAN-YES!"

"Scooter almost fell off his folding chair," Brown recalled.

• • •

In 1995, Phil Rizzuto saw the future of Yankees baseball, and his name was Derek Jeter.

"I couldn't carry Derek Jeter's glove or jockstrap," Rizzuto once said. "He's the best shortstop I've ever seen. I've seen Pee Wee Reese, Luis Aparicio, Dave Concepcion, and Ozzie Smith, and I wouldn't take anybody over Derek."

"Rizzuto compared Jeter's glide to Joe DiMaggio's. He compared Jeter to all Yankees heroes, but never to Phil Rizzuto, even though DiMaggio had assured the Scooter he was an indispensable Yankee," sportswriter Ian O'Connor recalled.

"Derek is 10 times the player I was," Rizzuto insisted. In 1995, Rizzuto told then Yankees manager Buck Showalter that the young shortstop should have already been promoted to the position full-time. The usually reserved Showalter ripped into Rizzuto for inserting this unsolicited advice.

"Buck never forgave me for that one," Rizzuto repeated.

"I like what I see of this kid, Jeter," DiMaggio told the press in 1997, during Jeter's second year in the league. "He reminds me of Phil Rizzuto. And I think he's just as valuable to this Yankees team as Rizzuto was to us. I really do."

"Where's Jeter? Where's Jeter?" Rizzuto would chirp, his eyes scanning the players in uniform.

"You'd get those two together and they'd embrace," said Yankees manager Joe Torre. "Of course, he was half Jeter's size. Whether it was a shortstop connection or the Yankees, spending your whole career in the same uniform, I think there was an automatic bond there."

"You always remember how people treat you, especially when you're young and coming up," Jeter said. "He always went out of his way."

Saying Good-bye to Mickey Mantle

Mickey Mantle died on August 13, 1995, at Baylor University Medical Center in Dallas. Mantle had lived a hard drinking life both during and especially after baseball. Long after his career was over, and near the end of his life, Mantle had admitted that his reckless and wild lifestyle (including drinking and numerous infidelities) had both wrecked his family and had hurt his playing. But Mantle often pointed to the early deaths of his father, Mutt Mantle, and his grandfather, both of whom died of Hodgkin's disease. Mantle oft repeated the line, "I'm not gonna be cheated." Mantle was certain he too would die young. But he never took into account the hard life of those men who mined zinc and lead, and the affect it may have had on their health.

"If I'd known I was gonna live this long, I'd have taken a lot better care of myself," Mantle used to joke, borrowing the famous line by football legend Bobby Layne.

By early 1994, Mantle had checked himself into the Betty Ford Clinic at the urging of his estranged wife, Merlyn, and his sons, all of whom also suffered from alcoholism and who had sobered up after treatment. However, bad news hit in March when his son, Billy, died of a heart attack after years of drug abuse.

Mantle had come clean to *Sports Illustrated* in 1994, in a cover story titled, "I Was Killing Myself," that he was tired of telling the same old jokes and stories, many of which included stories of drunkenness. He realized they were offensive stories and were hurtful to his family, friends, and fans. Mantle joined fellow Oklahoman and Yankees legend Bobby Murcer in late April 1995 to help raise money for the victims of the bombing of the Alfred P. Murrah Federal Building in Oklahoma City.

Mantle was suffering from cirrhosis and hepatitis C, which had destroyed his liver. By June 1995, Mantle received a transplant at Baylor University Medical Center in Dallas. But it was soon discovered he had inoperable cancer.

"This is a role model: Don't be like me," Mantle said in a press conference at Baylor, where again he admitted that he had let people down as a role model fans looked up to. He died three months later.

WPIX offered Rizzuto the opportunity to attend the funeral. He refused, deferring to the station's decision to send Bobby Murcer as the station's representative. Murcer, who was considered Mantle's successor as a Yankee, had developed a friendship with Mantle due to their common backgrounds and upbringing in Oklahoma.

The funeral was televised and widely attended. Many Hall of Fame players were in attendance, as well as other numerous celebrities. Mantle was buried in Dallas, Texas, at Sparkman-Hillcrest Memorial Park Cemetery.

Famed sportscaster Bob Costas eulogized the fallen Mantle, an idol of his youth. Costas said, "He was a presence in our lives—a fragile hero to whom we had an emotional attachment so strong and lasting that it defied logic.... For a huge portion of my generation, Mickey Mantle was that baseball hero. And for reasons that no statistics, no dry recitation of the facts can possibly capture, he was the most compelling baseball hero of our lifetime. And he was our symbol of baseball at a time when the game meant something to us that perhaps it no longer does.... In the last year of his life, Mickey Mantle, always so hard on himself, finally came to accept and appreciate the distinction between a role model and a hero. The first, he often was not. The second, he always will be. And, in the end, people got it."

Yankee Stadium organist Eddie Layton played "Somewhere Over the Rainbow" on the Hammond organ during the first game at the Stadium after

Mantle's death. Mantle had once told him it was among his favorite songs. The Yankees played the rest of the season with black mourning bands topped by a small No. 7 on their left sleeves.

Rizzuto regretted not attending Mantle's funeral and admitted it was the worst decision of his life. Partly out of shame, partly out of anger, and partly out of exhaustion, Rizzuto quit WPIX.

Rizzuto resigned abruptly and publicly, "upset that he called the Yankees– Red Sox game…rather than asserting his desire to attend Mickey Mantle's funeral. WPIX wanted him to stay in Boston for the game, and Rizzuto denied that [WPIX general manager Mike] Eigner forbade him from going," reported the *Chicago Sun-Times*. Initially, Rizzuto told the press he was quitting "partly because WPIX-TV wouldn't let him attend former teammate Mickey Mantle's funeral in Dallas. But several days later Rizzuto revised his stance, saying he had initially agreed with the station's decision to send fellow broadcaster Bobby Murcer to represent WPIX at the funeral."

"However, after watching Mantle's funeral on television last Tuesday, Rizzuto became so upset that he had to leave the booth during a Yankees telecast that night," the *Sun-Times* continued.

"When I saw the services, I realized what a big mistake I had made [by not attending the funeral]," said Rizzuto, who turned 78 that year. "But I had nobody to blame but myself."

Publicly, Rizzuto gave the impression he was mulling over his sudden retirement.

"I've been firm all along, and I guess it's my fault if I made anyone think there's a chance I'll come back," he said on the night of August 21. He added, "It's the hardest decision I've ever had to make, and the things being written about me, the faxes, the 'Save Our Scooter' stuff is nice, but I won't come back."

Rizzuto met with Michael Eigner, the general manager of WPIX-TV/ Channel 11. Fans still held out hope Eigner might dissuade Rizzuto from leaving the broadcast booth.

"I wasn't enjoying myself as much as I'd been in the past," he told one reporter.

Rizzuto told the press he wished to absolve the station of responsibility for his abrupt departure.

"It's time for me to go. I haven't been on top of the game like I used to," Rizzuto said days later. "It's very difficult for me to break away, but I know it's the right time. I've had such great times here, whether playing ball in a Yankee uniform or broadcasting.... The fans have been so great to me."

"As the years went on, Phil's popularity was slipping. Younger fans didn't get or didn't care for his ethnic humor, and he wasn't a Yankees legend to them, either," Appel said. "But I still loved his work and came to respect him even more as a broadcaster." According to Appel, Rizzuto brought out the best in almost every one of his partners, didn't care if they hogged the mike, as he did not particularly want to hog it himself.

However, as spring training ensued, so did talks with WPIX to bring back the Scooter, no matter however brief his appearances.

"I haven't talked to Scooter," said Rick Cerone, a former three-time Yankees catcher whom WPIX quietly added to the broadcast booth in 1996.

"We're waiting to hear from WPIX," Brandon Steiner, Rizzuto's agent, said.

Cerone had worked one game with Rizzuto the previous year. "I was supposed to do two innings, but he said, 'Go ahead, do play-by-play,'" Cerone recounted. "I ended up doing six innings. He said it was the first time he'd stayed for nine innings in a long time."

Cerone analyzed two games in 1995. "I played in his golf tournament," Cerone said. "Phil had watched both games. He said in the first one I talked too much. But in the second he said, 'You had some nice things to say and picked your spots.'"

"Scooter should come back," Cerone said.

"He's right. No matter whether Rizzuto seems more concerned with nuns' birthdays. He improves his partners. Did it with Bill White, Tom Seaver, and Murcer. He would make Cerone comfortable. He would call Cerone 'Cerone.' Never 'Rick.' No first names, please," *New York Times* journalist Richard Sandomir wrote. "He returned in 1996 for a final season, persuaded by fans, Mantle's sons, and George M. Steinbrenner III, the principal owner of the Yankees. The pull of his cherished team was too strong."

A month later, Sandomir reported on April 12, 1996, that Rizzuto, "glided into the WPIX-TV/Channel 11 booth 15 minutes before game time yesterday, bundled in a camel's hair coat he did not remove. He wore shades under his glasses to protect eyes recuperating from cataract surgery. Bobby Murcer, his partner, kissed him on both cheeks."

"I appreciate your showing up," Murcer said, laughing. John Calabrese, the associate director, hugged Scooter, too. The MSG Network's Bob Page also arrived to pay homage.

"Tuxedoed waiters deliver platters of shrimp and chicken covered with aluminum foil in the bottom of the first. The aroma of garlic makes the booth smell like Umberto's Clam House," Sandomir wrote.

"Watch Duilio or we won't get any!" Rizzuto shouted. Duilio Costabile was the cameraman in the announcing booth. Otherwise, Rizzuto was exactly the same, uttering his famous "Holy Cow!" and calling Murcer by his last name, as well issuing several birthday announcements.

Rizzuto's return, after the previous summer's emotional good-bye, also came with a limousine that took him to and from home games. "When you reach that point, you're at the top of your profession, like Al Michaels and Vin Scully," Murcer said.

"They have limos?" Rizzuto asked. He then turned to Murcer, "Tell me one day, I'll stop by and pick you up."

Rizzuto broadcast for three innings, and then, rising from his chair, he claimed, "I'm done!"

"Remember. Come back in three innings!" Calabrese said. Rizzuto's silver hair was long enough to make into a pony tail, the crew joked. "You look like a hit man!" Costabile told Rizzuto.

A WPIX staffer delivered Rizzuto's mail. One of the letters had United States District Court printed as the return address. "Oh, no," Rizzuto muttered. He opened it. "Congratulations on your return," a smiling Rizzuto said, reading the letter. "Oh, he wants a favor! Whatever you want, judge."

In 1997, the MSG network announced they would attempt to woo Rizzuto, asking him to come out for a 42nd season announcing Yankees games.

"If he wants to do something, anything, we'll let him," said Mike McCarthy, the executive producer of MSG.

MSG's announcers called 100 games on the cable network. Jim Kaat, Ken Singleton, Bobby Murcer, Rick Cerone, and Al Trautwig all called games, and Suzyn Waldman and Steve Palermo, the former umpire, contributed to the pregame and postgame shows.

• • •

On January 4, 1999, Alfred Rizzuto, Phil's brother, died. He was living in New Jersey at the time.

Scooter came out of retirement in April 1999. "The 81-year-old retired Yankees broadcaster returned to action Saturday for a Wesleyan-Williams baseball game in Middletown, Connecticut. His granddaughter, Jennifer Congregane, is a Wesleyan student and talked him into talking on the student radio station," Elliott Harris More wrote in the *Chicago Sun-Times*.

"I was a sophomore at Wesleyan University and the school arranged for Phil Rizzuto to broadcast a game on our college station because his granddaughter was a student there," Dan Blumberg said. Blumberg related his story on New York's WNYC, where he was a radio journalist. "It was 1999 and he'd been out of the Yankees broadcast booth for a few years. I was really nervous about how I'd sound next to a broadcasting legend like him—it was only the second baseball game I'd ever broadcast—but he felt rusty and seemed more nervous than me."

Here's a bit of the WESU broadcast that day. It was classic Rizzuto:

> *Rizzuto: Now are we on the air now?*
>
> *Blumberg: We are on the air, broadcasting to the greater Connecticut area.*
>
> *Rizzuto: I'm doing a terrible job and I wanted to do so well up here because my granddaughter, Jennifer Congregane, who got me to do this, figured I'd be a star and I'm butchering it. Jen! I need some help.*
>
> *Blumberg: Just keep saying "Holy Cow" and everyone's happy.*
>
> *Rizzuto: Well, if he keeps throwing pitches like that…!*

"So it wasn't the greatest broadcast on Earth—believe me, I was there—but he was as friendly as can be and tried to make me feel really comfortable as we sat there broadcasting the Wesleyan-Williams game, sitting outdoors on a really cold and rainy April day," Blumberg continued.

"I felt like a rookie again," Rizzuto said after his three-inning effort. Williams won 10–6, but as per his usual, Rizzuto left when his shift was over, with the score tied at 4. "I never prepared for a game in my life," he boasted. "I'd rather just talk about whatever I want to talk about. Get a little bit of baseball in there, a few recipes, and somebody's birthday, and I've done my job."

"On the morning of September 11, Phil Rizzuto and his wife Cora were puttering about their house in Hillside, N.J., starting to pack some bags for a cruise they planned to take up the New England coast to Montreal as a celebration of the Yankee great's 84th birthday," Bill Madden wrote in the *New York Daily News.* "They were also expecting a telephone call from Rizzuto's financial adviser, Craig Richards, whose office at Fiduciary Trust was located on the 92nd floor of the south tower at the World Trade Center."

"I went over there regularly to meet with him," Rizzuto said. "I hated that elevator, how it shaked."

On a clear day, the Rizzutos could see the Twin Towers from the attic of their elaborate and beautiful home. After the terrorist attacks, "Cora Rizzuto would seclude herself up there, occasionally staring out at the empty skyline, numb with disbelief and sadness."

As news of the attack spread, Phil and Cora grew anxious—there was no word from Richards. They feared the worst but prayed for the best. That night, they heard from Richards, who called them at home. He had worked late the night before and didn't see his children. He had decided to go to work late the next day in order to see his kids. That morning, they had begged him to stay a little longer before he went to work. He happily obliged.

"Imagine that," Rizzuto said. "His young kids probably saved him. He was just parking his car at the PATH station in Jersey City when the planes struck."

Even with the note of good news for Richards, Cora decided the trip was off. There would be no cruise.

"I couldn't bear the thought of sailing out of the harbor of this beautiful city with all that pain, grief, and destruction behind," she said.

"Rizzuto was relieved because, privately, he hadn't wanted to go, either. But now, he too felt lost and in a perpetual daze. He wished there was something he could do, but at 84 he felt helpless and housebound," Madden recalled. "Then…the Rizzutos got a phone call from their daughter, Penny, who works for a crisis intervention center in Albany. She had just spent two days at Pier 94, counseling and consoling the families of the thousands of casualties, dead, and missing."

Penny and her husband, Allan Yetto, a firefighter and an emergency diver in a fire company in the Albany area, had many connections to people who had fought the building collapse and helped with rescue efforts. Penny worked at the Albany County crisis intervention team. For Penny, and Phil and Cora, there was a personal connection.

"Dad," she said, "you've got to go over there."

"Oh, Penny, I don't know," Rizzuto replied. "Let me ask your mother what she thinks."

"She's right," Cora said, her mood suddenly brightening. "That's what we should do. Tell her we're going. We'll make the arrangements right now."

On a Tuesday morning in September, Rizzuto's birthday, Phil and Cora drove across the river and down the West Side Highway.

They approached the first security check-point with trepidation. Would they be turned back? No. The police immediately recognized the Hall of Fame shortstop and directed him to the pier.

"I couldn't believe what I saw," Rizzuto said. "What a job they've done on that pier! Carpets, computers, food, everything the people there need. I guess what really got me the most, though, were all the teddy bears. There must have been thousands of them, lining the walls the entire length of the pier. They'd been shipped up from Oklahoma City that day and there were individual notes on each one from kids in Oklahoma City to the victims' kids here."

"I'm sorry," Phil apologized as his eyes filled with tears. He grew emotional. "I'm an old man and I've seen a lot, but this really got to me. It still does just to talk about it."

At first, the Rizzutos were taken aback. What were they doing there? What were they supposed to do? But the lapse was momentary. People came to them. They recognized Phil immediately, and they knew what he was there for.

"People recognized them and began thanking them for coming, that they knew. For the next 4½ hours, the Scooter, accompanied by bleary-eyed cops who had not slept in days, moved from family to family, telling his Yankee stories of huckleberries past and present and bringing smiles to faces otherwise filled with only dwindled hope and despair," the *Daily News* reported.

"The pictures on the wall of all the missing, that was the most touching and heartbreaking part of all," Cora said.

"After awhile," Rizzuto said, "I got into a groove. They briefed us not to stay too long with one group. They looked so lost, waiting there for a death certificate or a body part. Cora knew the right things to say."

At the end of the day, one of the policemen, one who had lost a friend in the collapse, presented them a rose placed inside an envelope. The inscription on the envelope read: "Thank you for your kindness. From the New York City Police Department."

"Do you believe that? They're thanking us when we were thanking them!" Cora said. She cherished the rose for a long time.

Phil pointed out the irony that Pier 94 was not far from where their cruise ship was to depart from.

"I can't imagine a more fulfilling birthday," Rizzuto said.

"I suggested we go outside to take a picture," Madden recalled. "The bright, late-afternoon sunshine was streaming through the kitchen window, and Rizzuto seemed to welcome the opportunity to take in what was a beautiful fall day. He led me through a side door into the garage where, from the back of his car, he pulled out two silver-foil birthday balloons."

"Don't tell Cora I'm doing this," he whispered. "She doesn't understand why I kept these things."

"We walked around to the back of the house where, concealing much of a large window, a visitor couldn't help but notice this tall, sprawling orange-colored bush with berries on its branches.

"I think Cora says that's a fire thorn. It's funny, you'd come here at this time any other year and those berries would all be gone, eaten by the birds. But ever since the World Trade Center attack, the birds haven't come around."

Rizzuto, for a moment, was lost in thought. He then let the balloons go. He squinted at the bright sky, and his head tilted back as he followed their ascent silently.

"I guess that's it, they're gone," he said.

"The balloons," Madden replied.

"Yeah, the balloons."

"He shook his head, as if to acknowledge the unintentional symbolism of the balloons and the towers. For more than a half-century, Phil Rizzuto had lived the greatest life a man could ever hope to live, and then in a terrifying few minutes, he was left stupefied, first in front of his TV and then at the foot of his attic window," Madden concluded, "wondering what it's really all about."

• • •

It seemed Phil was never too busy to respond to anyone who wrote him.

James Garfola and Louie Pellegrino were distant cousins who lived upstate in Massena, New York. Rizzuto had once spoken at the Italian American Club there in the 1950s. Both Pellegrino and Garfola followed Scooter's career avidly.

According to John D. Michaud III, "Rizzuto once presented a game-used baseball glove to a young child on north Main Street during one of his trips to Massena. That glove has become a local sports folklore legend."

"One time we went to Yankee Stadium for a game. Louie left his seat and said, 'I have to go use the bathroom.' He was gone forever," said Pellegrino's widow in a 1998 interview. "He finally came back. He told me, 'I was up in the announcer's booth visiting with Phil Rizzuto.' I was amazed."

"In 1998, I decided to write to Rizzuto about Garfola and Pellegrino. I never expected to get a response," Michaud admitted. "Within a few days, I received a package back in the mail from him. Inside he had enclosed several autographed photographs. I was very excited. The bulk of the photos were for Louie Pellegrino's family. I brought over the photos to his wife. One was personally inscribed in color of him posing with a 'holy cow' on Rizzuto Day at Yankee Stadium."

The family was very happy.

One of the highlights of 2003 for Rizzuto was throwing out the first pitch of Game 2 of the American League Championship Series to former teammate and friend Yogi Berra on October 9. The picture of the two Yankees legends, opening the program before the Yankees and Red Sox took the field, was carried in newspapers across the country.

"Just like the old days," Rizzuto said. "The years fly by and it's always us and those huckleberries, the Yankees and the Red Sox. It's hard to believe. They never go away. And neither do we."

In 2004, a park located a mile from Rizzuto's house was dedicated in his name by Union County.

"He's thinner now, frail," sportswriter Dave Buscema wrote that year. "His voice is as sweet as ever, but not as sharp, his 'Hoooly Cows,' are more whispers than exclamations."

The irony was that the renovated park had no baseball fields. At the dedication in 2004, Rizzuto discussed his hope for the park. "Kids who live in apartment houses, they don't have any backyard," Rizzuto said during the festivities on July 21. "Here, they can come out all they want. Now they have a place to play."

Rizzuto said he and his wife had often visited the park. It had a gazebo. And in the summer, children frolicked under a water-sprinkling tower or ran around its soccer field.

"There are no traces of the three baseball diamonds that used to be home to a local youth baseball league," wrote Charles Kuffner, a local journalist. "The park, at one of Union County's busiest intersections where Union, Elizabeth, and Hillside meet, is named after the Hall of Fame shortstop and 40-year Yankees broadcaster. With the area's growing Latino population, it was practical for the soccer field to supplant baseball diamonds at the site."

"We have the soccer field because it's what our kids need today," said Angel Estrada, chairman of the county freeholder board.

"'Children at the park are not familiar with Rizzuto's exploits, but they often stop to study the bronze tablet dedicated to the Scooter when it's time to go home,' said Lisa Freeman, 39, of Hillside, who was there with her four children and two nephews," wrote Jeffrey Gold of the Associated Press.

"They read off the plaque when they're stalling to leave," Freeman said.

In 2005, Rizzuto did an extensive interview with Mike Francesca and Christopher Russo on WFAN. During the course of the interview, Rizzuto revealed that he had an operation where much of his stomach was removed. He also admitted that he was being treated with medical steroids. He made several light-hearted jokes referring to the recent scandals about players' use of performance-enhancing drugs in professional baseball.

Rumors about his health started to circulate when he did not attend the annual Cooperstown reunion in 2005.

Letting Go of the Past

Phil Rizzuto was now a white-maned 88-year-old man, the oldest living member of baseball's Hall of Fame. He was a little frailer each year, but he was still elegant, well-dressed, and well-coiffed. Though slighter and seemingly shorter than in previous years, his smile was still bright, and he had an impish charm in his old age.

Rizzuto said he was "doing real good." One of his daughters said he still played golf, although no longer a full 18-hole round. Patricia, Penny, and granddaughter Jennifer were with him.

"I was laid out almost for six months," Rizzuto said, adding that he was doing "much better now." Family members said he is healthy, but he has good days and bad days.

"As a female photographer snaps his picture from across the table, the flash hits him in the eyes. He politely asks her to hold the camera higher. The woman responds by raising her arms and because she is wearing one of those stylish cut-at-the-waist tops, there is a flash of skin as she reaches to the sky," Kevin Kernan of the *New York Post* recalled.

"Rizzuto smiles and so does the photographer. He's no huckleberry."

"It was a little scary coming in, can you believe the traffic?" Scooter said. "It took us more than an hour to get here. Right now I'm feeling good, but coming in, I was ready to jump out the window."

On February 3, 2006, Rizzuto was appearing at Mickey Mantle's Restaurant on Central Park South, where he and his family were announcing the sale of his own personal collection of memorabilia that he had accumulated across the years. With more than 1,000 lots, it was one of the largest personal baseball collections ever assembled, and it was eventually auctioned off by Geppi's Memorabilia Road Show during the course of the summer of 2006.

The collection included "such keepsakes as his 1950 uniform and cap with a piece of gum still stuck on top, World Series rings, a Yogi Berra mitt, a 1956 Mickey Mantle Christmas card to Phil, and the platinum record for the Meat Loaf classic 'Paradise by the Dashboard Light.'"

Phil and the family kept a few mementos.

But it was also a time for a physical move. In 2006, the Rizzutos moved out of their majestic home in Hillside, where they had lived and raised their children. Phil and Cora had been married for 62 years when they sold their house.

"He's still afraid of bugs and mice," Penny said. "When he comes to our house, he still puts a towel over his shoes so mice can't get in."

Rizzuto seemed chipper as he chatted with the press, talking about Joe DiMaggio, Meat Loaf, cannolis, and Derek Jeter. "He's my favorite shortstop of all time," Rizzuto said.

"I'm very nervous here with this," he said of the microphone at the podium.

"Where's [Bill] White, that huckleberry?" And then offered his trademark, "Holy Cow!" Rizzuto explained how Billy Hitchcock hung his nickname on him. "Joe wanted to go to the movies, and the only one who was going to go with him was me," Rizzuto recalled of the great DiMaggio. "We'd go way in the back so nobody would see us. But every once in a while, the light might be getting on him. Right away we had to get out of there."

"Did you tell him about the time on the train when they gave you the grits and you didn't know what to do with them so you put them in your pocket?" asked his granddaughter Jennifer.

"That was a riot," Rizzuto laughed.

Patricia recalled Phil's answer to a reporter who asked what he'd like to be remembered for. "My father said, 'I want to be remembered as a nice guy.'"

Geppi's Memorabilia Road Show has announced a last-minute addition to the Phil Rizzuto Collection: a pair of baseball shoes, which are attributed to Mickey Mantle's rookie season of 1951.

A slumping and confused Mantle went to the minors briefly that summer. However, he was quickly recalled and took ownership of uniform No. 7 (he had been No. 6 when the season began), and returned to right field.

It is impossible to know from which portion of the season they were from. They could well have been the shoes he wore when he hit his first of 536 home runs, or scored his first run, or had his first hit. Or they could have traveled with him to the minors for his mid-season tune-up and come back with him. This scenario makes sense because both the numbers 6 and 7 appear on the shoe tongues along with his name.

Said John Snyder, Executive Vice President of Geppi's Memorabilia Road Show, "Authenticators reported back to us that there was not enough to substantiate that these came from Mantle's rookie season. Absent that, we believe that the word of Phil Rizzuto is honor enough for this great item, and a letter of authenticity from Phil accompanies the shoes. In it, Phil writes that the shoes were a gift from Mantle after the birth of Phil Rizzuto Jr., were given to him in a brown paper bag, and resided in that bag for all these years. We are satisfied that Phil, having held on to this for more than half a century, knows their origin."

In September 2006, Rizzuto's 1950 MVP plaque fetched $175,000, three of his World Series rings sold for $84,825, and a Yankees cap with a wad of chewing gum on it went for $8,190. A large portion of the money made by the Rizzutos in the auction went to St. Joseph's School for the Blind in Jersey City.

Ed Lucas Redux

"Did anyone ever describe this ballpark to you?" Rookie Ron Swoboda of the Mets asked Ed Lucas in 1965. When Lucas told him no one had ever tried to do so in detail, Swoboda walked Lucas one lap around the warning track in Shea Stadium's outfield. Lucas ran his hand along the outfield wall.

"That same year Ed married. Eventually he had two sons, Eddie and Chris. But when the boys were four and two, respectively, Ed's wife, like Ed's Giants, left him," Steve Rushin of *Sports Illustrated* wrote.

In September 1979, seven years after she left him, Lucas's ex-wife returned. She sued for full and complete custody of their children. The couple fought bitterly through the courts; all the while, he tried to maintain a normal life for his boys. Their hard-fought case thrust itself all the way up to the New Jersey Supreme Court. Witness after witness, friends and famous people alike, came forward to testify on Lucas' behalf. Phil Rizzuto was one of them.

On September 25, 1980, Ed Lucas was awarded full and complete custody of his sons. It was a historic ruling on several levels. No male in New Jersey had ever won full custody from a female. No disabled person in the United States had ever won full custody over a non-disabled spouse.

"He raised the boys as a blind single parent with superhuman powers. Or so it appeared to Eddie and Chris, who boasted at school that their father could read with the lights out," Rushin continued.

"I wanted their lives to be as normal as possible," Lucas said.

However, Eddie's and Chris's lives were anything but normal. "It was not unusual to wake up and see Billy Martin drinking coffee at their kitchen table. Yankee Stadium became the boys' second home," Rushin wrote.

"Huge stars like Mickey Mantle would tell me my dad was their hero," Chris said. "The stadium was our babysitter. It's Babe Ruth's house, but my brother and I, it's our house as well."

Many years later, while in a local flower shop in Union, New Jersey, a florist told Phil Rizzuto about her niece. Allison Pfeifle, a nurse, had a detached retina that left her legally blind and no longer able to perform her duties in a hospital.

Ever the helpful soul, Rizzuto urged Ed Lucas to give Allison a pep talk. Lucas obliged. He and Allison spoke on the phone many times for several years before finally meeting. Allison was also an avid baseball fan. So of course, their first time out together, they went to a ball game—at Shea—

where Ed impressed her with his numerous sporting friends, including Darryl Strawberry.

With the help of Phil Rizzuto, Ed Lucas and Allison Pfeifle were the first and only people married at Yankee Stadium, on March 10, 2006. When Allison walked down the aisle, she walked from the dugout to home plate. Eddie and Chris were his best men. Included in the guest list were Phil Rizzuto, Rick Cerone, Gene Michael, and movie director Penny Marshall.

"Mr. Steinbrenner has been wonderful," Lucas told Kevin Coyne of the *New York Times*, referring to the New York Yankees' principal owner. "He picked up the whole tab."

The wedding made national and international news and was covered by the *New York Times*, the *Today Show*, the Yes Network and MSNBC. The coverage of the wedding by the YES Network was nominated for an Emmy Award.

"Baseball took my sight," said the giddy groom-to-be. "But it also gave me my life."

Perhaps more importantly, over the years Lucas and Rizzuto had raised millions to build a 21st century facility at the St. Joseph's School for the Blind, the school that had helped Lucas overcome his disability as a child.

"We're friends 55 years now," Lucas said of Scooter, who hosted an annual celebrity golf tournament for St. Joseph's, which relied on donations for about a quarter of its $8 million annual budget.

• • •

During the 1980s and 1990s, no one person attended more Yankees games at Yankees Stadium than Jim Brozzetti. A resident of Scranton, Pennsylvania, Brozzetti had made the two-hour drive to more than 900 consecutive games at the Stadium. In that time, he had met and grown close to Phil Rizzuto. Brozzetti also became friends with Roy White and Don Mattingly. He was such a well-known and unwavering presence that George Steinbrenner awarded him a 1996 Championship Ring for his devotion to the team.

"Jim Brozzetti needed someone to hold his hand, because no father should ever have to attend a memorial service for his son. He needed a friend that day like never before." described sportswriter Ian O'Connor. "Brozzetti turned 60 on that wretched February day [in 2006], the day he buried his son, Jimmy, a 20-year-old Lycoming College student who had perished in a car wreck on his way back to school. Rizzuto was the one who sat next to Brozzetti, the one who gave him a birthday gift he'd never forget."

"Jim, I'm here for you," Phil Rizzuto kept whispering to him. The frail, small, withered Yankee, nearly 90, held Brozzetti's hand for an entire hour, the worst hour of his good friend's life.

"Brozzetti couldn't ever pay him back for that hour of grace," O'Connor wrote.

"Phil Rizzuto always has been a battler, the little underdog who made it all the way to the Hall of Fame...and this has been a difficult year for him and Cora. Rizzuto couldn't make it to Yankee Stadium for Old Timer's Day. He is now at a private rehab facility, trying to overcome muscle atrophy and problems with his esophagus," Kevin Kernan wrote in the *New York Post*.

Rizzuto went for daily walks through the hallways and took part in therapy classes.

"I feel good right now," he said in September 2006. He was a hit with the nurses and other staff, many of whom asked to take a picture with him. Rizzuto patiently autographed 500 poster-size pictures, part of a limited-edition 500 photo collection. There are two pictures in the collection. One photo featured the Scooter and Frank Sinatra in the Yankee dugout, and the second showed him with Derek Jeter from the night he had thrown out the first ball to Yogi Berra, the two greatest shortstops in Yankees history.

"I like to do that," he shrugged.

Yogi and Carmen Berra went to visit with him several times, and someone from Rizzuto's family was there every day—Cora or one of their four children.

"Derek just broke my father's record for games played as a Yankee short-stop," explained Rizzuto's eldest daughter, Patricia. "If it had to be somebody, we're glad it was Derek."

"Absolutely," Phil chimed in softly. Eventually Phil left rehabilitation and went back home.

In 2007, Rizzuto's health began to fail again, and this time he could not will himself beyond his body's betrayal. Berra visited his ailing friend every

Wednesday at his home in Hillside, New Jersey. Later, as Rizzuto's health further deteriorated, he was moved to a nursing home in West Orange, where he and Berra would play bingo until the Scooter fell asleep.

In the final months of his life, in the summer of 2007, Rizzuto was in a nursing home in West Orange, New Jersey. Scooter immersed himself in watching Clark Gable movies and the Yankees games on television. In that period, Brozzetti was a constant visitor, spending time with Rizzuto. They would talk about everything, but the conversation always got around to the Yankees.

"Gee, I wished they'd pick it up," Rizzuto would say. "Too bad we have so many injuries. I hope Mariano [Rivera] gets back to being the old Mariano."

Even to the end, Rizzuto loved to mimic "Jeter's option pitch to the plate to get Oakland's Jeremy Giambi in the 2001 playoffs. Rizzuto would take a few steps across his nursing home room and flick an invisible ball from his right hand toward Brozzetti, the old shortstop recalling the cheers he inspired when he performed Jeter's toss after his ceremonial first pitches…Jeter was his favorite subject in conversations with Brozzetti," O'Connor wrote.

"Every time I told Phil you were coming," Cora said to Brozzetti months later, "he had a big smile on his face." The entire Rizzuto family was so grateful to him.

Brozzetti's visits, his phone calls, and his unwavering support and love were the least he could do, O'Connor recalled. "Phil got me through my hour of greatest need," Brozzetti said.

"The last time I saw Scooter," recalled former Yankees beat writer and author Phil Pepe, "I heard he was in a nursing home, and I paid him a visit. When I walked into his room, he gave me a big smile. I stayed only a few minutes because I was told he was not having a good day. I don't think he knew me. He never called me by name (he and I were both baptized Philip Francis). I got the feeling that he recognized me as someone from his past, but he didn't seem to know exactly what our relationship was. Still, I'm glad I went, especially when I learned that every Wednesday, Yogi Berra would visit his buddy and teammate and play bingo with him."

The last visits were particularly hard for Berra.

"It was pretty bad the last month or so. He had pneumonia," Berra said. "He was gradually going down. You could tell. He wasn't awake much of the time."

Ed Lucas also visited the stricken Rizzuto. Lucas was one of Rizzuto's last visitors at the nursing home, just days before Scooter's death.

Philip Francis "Scooter" Rizzuto, suffering from pneumonia, died in his sleep on a Monday night, August 13, 2007. He was baseball's oldest living Hall of Famer at 89 years old. He and Cora had been married 64 years.

"I've lost my beautiful prince," Cora told the press.

"He died very peacefully," Patricia Rizzuto said.

Quotes from all over the nation started pouring in. The newspapers, websites, and airwaves were filled with testimonials to Rizzuto's achievements as a man and to his personality and character.

One of the first and most prominent came from George Steinbrenner, saying, "I guess heaven must have needed a shortstop. Phil Rizzuto's contributions to the Yankees and the sport of baseball were immense for a period of over 50 years. He was one of the greatest Yankees of all time and a dear, close friend of mine whose loss is enormous to me and to the entire Yankee family."

Upon the news of his dear friend's death, Berra showed up at Yankee Stadium, in the dugout, sitting close by Joe Torre. The small, chubby man who had been such a powerful player, successful manager, and business man, was obviously shaken. Never the most eloquent man, despite his many quotations, he choked on numerous words, trying to keep his composure.

"This is a sad day for Carmen and me," said Berra, who visited Rizzuto weekly at a nursing home. "Phil was a gem, one of the greatest people I ever knew—a dear friend and great teammate. He was a heck of a player, too. When I first came up to the Yankees, he was like a big, actually small, brother to me. He's meant an awful lot to baseball and the Yankees and has left us with a lot of wonderful memories."

Especially in retirement, Berra and Rizzuto saw each other on average once a week.

"Everything he did was great," Berra continued. "He could steal bases, he could bunt, he was a pretty good hitter."

"Phil was a Hall of Famer both on and off the field, and when you were in his company, he made you feel like a family friend," said then manager Joe Torre. "Every time Scooter walked into my office, the first thing he'd say is, 'Where's Jeter? Where's Jeter?' A few minutes later I'd see the two of them giving big hugs to each other in the clubhouse. That's the type of person Phil was, you just couldn't figure out how such a big heart could fit inside such a small body."

Jeter too seemed shaken. "Mr. Rizzuto serves as the ultimate reminder that physical stature has little bearing on the size of a person's heart. Nothing was ever given to Phil, and he used every ounce of his ability to become one of the greatest Yankees to ever wear this uniform."

Everyone seemed to want to comment about Rizzuto. "Phil was one of the most jovial people you'd ever come across. We were teammates for a short time, but he made a lasting impression with everyone whose life intersected his," former teammate Don Larsen said.

"He wasn't just one of the nicest people I have ever met, he embodied what it is to be a Yankee. He also symbolized why baseball is the greatest game of all," Jeffrey Lyons lamented.

The media even reached out to Meat Loaf, with whom he had become so closely aligned in popular culture.

"He has performed 'Paradise by the Dashboard Light' in concert, oh, 7,000 times since the song's release in 1977, always making certain to play Rizzuto's part over PA systems ranging from Yakima to Yonkers, Los Angeles to London, New York to Newfoundland," Jeff Pearlman wrote.

"I think that's why I feel so close to him," Meat Loaf said. "Every night I hear him. Every night I'll continue to hear him." He paused. "That is a wonderful thing."

"Scooter was a champion of the people. He always looked more comfortable mingling with the cheap-seat fans than he did mingling with the larger-than-life ballplaying greats," Ian O'Connor wrote. Many of the Garwood residents, who lined the small community's streets in hopes of getting a glimpse of many famous stars, such as there had been for Mickey Mantle's funeral, were disappointed. Bill White and Yogi Berra were the only Yankees among the 50 or so mourners to attend.

"Rizzuto never cared to be fussed over, so his wife, Cora, kept it simple and short. The church wasn't full, and the service didn't last much more than an hour," O'Connor continued. "There was a nice touch at the luncheon afterward: a painting of Rizzuto looking up in his Yankee uniform, rising to the sky."

The family communicated, several times, that in lieu of flowers, memorial gifts may be made in Mr. Rizzuto's memory to the St. Joseph's School for the Blind.

A bouquet of flowers was placed by Rizzuto's plaque at Monument Park at the Stadium. All of the flags at Yankee Stadium were flown at half-mast before Tuesday night's game against the Baltimore Orioles. There was a moment of silence before the game and a video tribute on the big screens. "Scooter, we will miss you," said longtime Stadium announcer and friend, Bob Sheppard said as the video tribute aired. That same night, even the Red Sox paid tribute to Rizzuto with a moment of silence before their game. Former Red Sox adversary Johnny Pesky said, "He was a fine man. I'll miss him. He was always a great ballplayer and really a joy to be around. He was a big part of those Yankee teams, a shortstop who could hit and field, and he stayed close to that team after he retired. He was a tremendous personality."

But there was loss on a more personal level.

"Joe Ward, who has delivered the mail to Rizzuto's house for 13 years, said he cried when he heard that Rizzuto was dead," Jeffrey Gold wrote.

"I had surgery twice. He was the first one [to offer well wishes] on my answering machine," said Ward, 44, as he walked his mail route Tuesday. "Let me tell you, he took care of me. He was good."

"For five decades, Harold Rodgers had big plans for the photo he'd taken on a South Pacific island toward the end of World War II. It was a snapshot of nirvana, a reminder of the day Rodgers got to play baseball with New York Yankees great and fellow navy man Phil Rizzuto," Mike Cassidy wrote in the *San Jose Mercury News*. "The picture meant the world to Rodgers, but he was sure it would mean more to Rizzuto. And so Rodgers was determined to one day give it to the baseball legend. Of course, that dream fell apart...when Rizzuto...died in New Jersey."

"I think I've been 50 years at least trying to find him to give him the picture," Rodgers told Cassidy. "I'd love to send them to his family." So Cassidy found the Rizzutos and contacted Patricia Rizzuto for Rodgers.

"I think the family would very much like it," Patricia said. "Very much." Patricia admitted that the family didn't know much about their father's naval years, which made the photo all that much more important to them. Patricia and Rodgers later spoke by phone.

"He's really a very sweet man," she said.

"To pass this photo on, I think, is tremendous," he said.

EPILOGUE

On June 27, 2008, Smokey Oval Park was officially renamed Phil "Scooter" Rizzuto Park. Queens Parks Commissioner Dorothy Lewandowski joined State Assemblyman Rory Lancman and Queens residents for the dedication ceremony recognizing the new name.

"Phil Rizzuto is a role model both as a baseball player and an American. He represents the values of our community," assemblyman Lancman said. "Renaming Smokey Oval Park in his honor is a fitting tribute to his legacy and will serve as an inspiration for generations of new Americans in Richmond Hill."

Cora, Patricia, and Penny were all there at the dedication of the plaque.

"Rizzuto represents what a New Yorker is all about," said Rory Lancman, who helped sponsor legislation to rename the park in Rizzuto's honor. "He had certain qualities that make for a great role model, including honesty, optimism, always having a positive outlook and being very hard-working."

"Rizzuto was a local kid who worked very, very hard," Lancman said. "The community associates striving and succeeding with Rizzuto, which is why he is a very good role model to the community."

In addition to his Hall of Fame career on the diamond, Lancman added that he was a Hall of Famer off it as well and cited Rizzuto's raising millions of dollars in donations to St. Joseph's School for the Blind as only one example of his charity work.

"A lot of successful people keep the success to themselves," Lancman said. "He generated millions of dollars for various charities."

Phil Rizzuto had gone full circle.

ACKNOWLEDGMENTS

The author must acknowledge and commend Ken Samelson, who offered up my name to Triumph some time ago. I thank him for his advice on this book, his researching assistance, and his diligent fact-checking. Without Ken, this book would not have happened, and I am grateful for his friendship and advice.

Any author of such an effort owes a great debt of gratitude to those who went before him. The works of several writers have proved invaluable, including Peter Golenbock, Roger Kahn, and Maury Allen's many works; David Halberstam's *Summer of '49* and October 1964; Jim Bouton's *Ball Four*; Robert Creamer's *Stengel*; Leigh Montville's *Ted Williams*; Richard Ben Cramer's *Joe DiMaggio*; Joseph R. Carrieri's two books, most recently *Searching for Heroes*; and of course, the memoirs of Mickey Mantle, Whitey Ford, Don Larsen, Yogi Berra, Billy Martin, and many of Scooter's other teammates from throughout the years.

Also to be thanked are the numerous biographers who have gone before me, including Joe Trimble's classic text from which so many of the Rizzuto myths have sprung, Milton Shapiro, Gene Schoor, and last but not least, Dan Hirschberg.

Of course, I poured over more than 7,000 original sources, including some 2,000 interviews with players, umpires, managers, and other assorted folks. I also examined newspaper and magazine articles from Rizzuto's youth all the way to the present. It is hard to imagine writing this work without the dedicated and hard-working beat writers who covered the team over the years, including Arthur Daley, Joe Trimble, Red Smith, Phil Pepe, Dick Young, John Drebinger, James P. Dawson, Leonard Koppett, Dave Anderson, Robert Lipsyte, Mike Lupica, Ian O'Connor, and many others. Without their dedicated coverage and investigative reporting, the book could not have been written. My apologies to anyone whose name was inadvertently left off this list—you can probably be found in the Notes at the end of this book.

As ever, I owe a debt of special thanks in all of my professional endeavors to Gilbert King for his ear, opinions, advice, general good cheer, and encouragement.

I would, of course, like to thank Tom Bast and Mitch Rogatz of Triumph Books, who helped make this book a reality. Were it not for their excitement, enthusiasm, and faith in me, I might have given up under the weight of this massive project. I also owe a huge debt of gratitude to editors Adam Motin and Karen O'Brien, who helped mold a rather large manuscript into readable shape, and to Scott Rowan.

I would also like to thank my agent and friend Edward Claflin of Edward B. Claflin Literary Agency. I thank him for his encouragement and assistance, and for his belief in me. I would also like to thank Marcus Leaver and Jason Prince of Sterling Publishing Company, Inc., for their friend assent. Without their good will this project would have passed me by. Thank you.

I would like to thank my sons, Dylan and Dawson, whom I have taken too much time away from in order to pursue not only this work, but also my other professional aspirations. I have tried to attend as many of their Little League games as possible, but there is no replacement for a catch or an ice-cream cone, many of which were robbed by my other pursuits. I vow to them to spend more time playing and less time working.

Notes

Prologue

"Welcome everyone and…, "Phil Rizzuto, the Scooter…Lancman, Rory I, Assemblyman Lancman Calls For Creating 'Phil Rizzuto' Park, YouTube, October 1, 2007 as retrieved on Dec 25, 2008 at http://www.youtube.com/watch?v=MdL3fhxVYJg

"If people in Queens…, "Mr. Lancman is also…, "It sounds like a place…Sullivan, John, "Sikhs Back Renaming of a Queens Park for Rizzuto," *New York Times*, October 1, 2007.

Introduction

"To know Scooter…Pepe, Phil. Memories of the loveable Scooter, YESNetwork.com, August 14, 2007, as retrieved March 9, 2007, http://www.yesnetwork.com/news/article. jsp?ymd=20070814&content_id=1429523&oid=36019&vkey=12

"Everyone was pretty…Barra, Allen. "Hold the innocence: Remember Phil Rizzuto as he truly was," *The Village Voice* (New York, New York), August 22, 2007.

"to enjoy the thrill…Smith, Red. *Red Smith on Baseball* (Chicago: Ivan R. Dee, 2000), p. 183.

"Rizzuto batted .273,…Vecsey, George. "A Big Day For Scooter," *New York Times*, August 5, 1985.

Section I: The View From the Booth

Chapter 1

"While a section…Mannix, James A., Brooklyn Memories…The Italians, *The Brooklyn Eagle*, c. 1940–1945, http://www.bklyn-genealogy info.com/Town/Streets/Bklyn.Memory.html, retrieved December 24, 2008.

"Only recently,…Mannix, James A., Brooklyn Memories…The Italians, *The Brooklyn Eagle*, c. 1940–1945, http://www.bklyn-genealogy info.com/Town/Streets/Bklyn.Memory.html, retrieved December 24, 2008.

"Philip and Rose married…Schoor, Gene. *The Scooter: The Phil Rizzuto Story* (New York: Charles Scribners Sons, 1982), p. 9.

"Ridgewood is a neighborhood…Ridgewood, Queens entry, Wikipedia, http://en.wikipedia. org/wiki/Ridgewood,_Queens, as retrieved December 24, 2008.

"They settled in a frame…, "They were always…, "We couldn't find…, "[The girls] would soon…, Trimble, Joe. *Phil Rizzuto, A Biography of the Scooter* (New York: A.S. Barnes & Co., 1951), pp. 7–8, 10.

"A precursor of…, "Roughly 210,000 New York City…, "Regardless, the Depression…, Tenement Museum, Home Relief, http://www.tenement.org/Virtual_Tour/vt_baldlhomer. html, as retrieved on December 24, 2008.

"From the time that…New York City Department of Parks and Recreation, Smokey Oval Park, http://nycgovparks.org/sub_your_park/historical_signs/hs_historical_sign.php?id=8291 as retrieved on December 24, 2008.

"We had a house…Buscema, Dave. *Game of My Life* (Champaign, IL: Sports Publishing LLC, 2004), p. 14.

"This is where…Rizzuto, Patricia, interview with Assemblyman Lancman, Rizzuto Family Supports Creation Of 'Phil Rizzuto Park,' October 19, 2007, http://video.google.com/ videosearch?hl=en&q=patricia%20rizzuto&um=1&ie=UTF-8&sa=N&tab=wv#, as retrieved December 24, 2008.

"In those days…, "We felt, 'Oh,…, Barry, Ellen. "The Streets of Queens Where Rizzuto Played," *New York Times*, August 16, 2007.

"One of the best…, "That was a great…, Buscema, Dave. *Game of My Life* (Champaign, IL: Sports Publishing LLC, 2004), p. 12.

"in the streets, then…Hirschberg, Dan. *Phil Rizzuto: A Yankee Tradition* (Chicago: Sagamore Publishing, 1993), p. 3.

"The Willenbuchers were a pair…United States Federal Census, 1920, Ancestry.com, as retrieved on December 30, 2008 at: http://search.ancestry.com/cgi-bin/sse.dll?rank=0&gsln= Willenbucher&f7=NY&gss=genfact&db=1920usfedcen

"What do you play?"…Schoor, Gene. *The Scooter: The Phil Rizzuto Story* (New York: Charles Scribners Sons, 1982), p. 16.

"I can see you can…, "You're all right,"…, "Look here, Phil…, "Yeah. Don't stand there…, Schoor, Gene. *The Scooter: The Phil Rizzuto Story* (New York: Charles Scribners Sons, 1982), p. 16–17.

"I was about four feet…, "Mr. Willenbucher wouldn't let…, Hirschberg, Dan. *Phil Rizzuto: A Yankee Tradition* (Chicago: Sagamore Publishing, 1993), p. 4.

Chapter 2

"If the city politicians…, "Every nickel counted…, "He never thought…, Trimble, Joe. *Phil Rizzuto, A Biography of the Scooter* (New York: A.S. Barnes & Co., 1951), pp. 14–15.

"Al Kunitz served as a…Goodwin, George, The Cruelest Twist, ALS Independence.com, as retrived on December 7, 2008 http://www.alsindependence.com/cruelest_twist.htm

"Kunitz was a precise…Gray, Walter S., "Shared Memory for a Rizzuto fan (Mount Kisco, New York)," *New York Times*, February 11, 1990.

"Fortunately, the coach…, "You'll never be…, "That said, Kunitz switched…, Madden, Bill, "One Last Meeting with Phil Rizzuto," *New York Daily News*, Sunday, September 9, 2007, 8:21 AM. http://www.nydailynews.com/sports/baseball/yankees/2007/09/09/2007-09-09_ one_last_meeting_with_phil_rizzuto-4.html?page=0

"When I made the team…Martaian, Douglas, "Phil Rizzuto Recalls Early Years as a Yankee," *Baseball Digest*, June 1983, p. 68.

"Ralph Benzenberg, who…, "He got me to practice…, Hirschberg, Dan. *Phil Rizzuto: A Yankee Tradition* (Chicago: Sagamore Publishing, 1993), p. 5.

"Let's face it. You're…Trimble, Joe. *Phil Rizzuto, A Biography of the Scooter* (New York: A.S. Barnes & Co., 1951), p. 22.

"A ballplayer has to…, "The man on first will…, Schoor, Gene. *The Scooter: The Phil Rizzuto Story* (New York: Charles Scribners Sons, 1982), pp. 21–22.

"He was as tall as…Rizzuto, Phil, Rizzuto on Huckleberry and Holy Cow, video interview, MLB.com, 2006 as retrieved on December 7, 2008, http://mlb.mlb.com/mlb/news/tributes/obit_phil_rizzuto.jsp

"Mr. Al Kunitz asked me…Hirschberg, Dan. *Phil Rizzuto: A Yankee Tradition* (Chicago: Sagamore Publishing, 1993), p. 5.

"[I]n the early part of…Quinion, Michael, Huckleberry, World Wide Words.org, as retrieved on December 7, 2008, http://www.worldwidewords.org/qa/qa-huc1.htm

"a foolish, inept…Lighter, J.E. *The Random House Historical Dictionary of American Slang* (New York: Random House, 1997).

"Kunitz kept asking…, "Phil needed more…, "I played a whale…, Hirschberg, Dan. *Phil Rizzuto: A Yankee Tradition* (Chicago: Sagamore Publishing, 1993), pp. 6–7.

"That was the first…, "In those days…, "You had a pretty…, "I never heard of…, Trimble, Joe. *Phil Rizzuto, A Biography of the Scooter* (New York: A.S. Barnes & Co., 1951), pp. 18–19.

"I'll take the little… Schoor, Gene. *The Scooter: The Phil Rizzuto Story* (New York: Charles Scribners Sons, 1982), p. 27.

"Fordham had a… Trimble, Joe. *Phil Rizzuto, A Biography of the Scooter* (New York: A.S. Barnes & Co., 1951), p. 21.

"Somebody must be …Shapiro, Milton J. *The Phil Rizzuto Story* (New York: Julian Messner, Inc., 1959), p. 26.

"I had a good…, "The story is that…, "It wasn't much…, "The first 50 to finish…, Hirschberg, Dan. *Phil Rizzuto: A Yankee Tradition* (Chicago: Sagamore Publishing, 1993), pp. 8–9.

"A big right-handed… Trimble, Joe. *Phil Rizzuto, A Biography of the Scooter* (New York: A.S. Barnes & Co., 1951), pp. 2-3.

"Fifteen years ago…Unattributed, "New Pride of the Yankees," *Time* magazine, November 6, 1950.

"I just got out of high…O'Connell, Jack, 'Scooter' Rizzuto Dies at 89, MLB.com, August 14, 2007.

"My experience with…Hirschberg, Dan. *Phil Rizzuto: A Yankee Tradition* (Chicago: Sagamore Publishing, 1993), p. 10.

"a huge man with…Trimble, Joe. *Phil Rizzuto, A Biography of the Scooter* (New York: A.S. Barnes & Co., 1951), p. 5.

"the finest judge of baseball…Trimble, Joe. *Phil Rizzuto, A Biography of the Scooter* (New York: A.S. Barnes & Co., 1951), pp. 22–23.

"By this time I was…Hirschberg, Dan. *Phil Rizzuto: A Yankee Tradition* (Chicago: Sagamore Publishing, 1993), p. 11.

"It was a good thing…O'Connell, Jack, 'Scooter' Rizzuto Dies at 89, MLB.com, August 14, 2007.

"I'll take the little…, "I thought it was pretty…, "I went to New York…, Trimble, Joe. *Phil Rizzuto, A Biography of the Scooter* (New York: A.S. Barnes & Co., 1951), pp. 24–25.

"Rizzuto cost me fifteen…Hirschberg, Dan. *Phil Rizzuto: A Yankee Tradition* (Chicago: Sagamore Publishing, 1993), p. 12.

"Rizzuto once told...O'Connell, Jack, 'Scooter' Rizzuto Dies at 89, MLB.com, August 14, 2007.

"In the late 1970s...", "A couple of the old...", "Many of the prevaricators...", "When we left Brooklyn...", Fogg, John, "Different Age, Same Old Problem," *Washington Times* (Washington, DC), February 21, 2009.

Chapter 3

"I wasn't sure it...Trimble, Joe. *Phil Rizzuto, A Biography of the Scooter* (New York: A.S. Barnes & Co., 1951), pp. 26–27.

"I'll let you try...Hirschberg, Dan. *Phil Rizzuto: A Yankee Tradition* (Chicago: Sagamore Publishing, 1993), p. 15.

"It was a beautiful...Sandomir, Richard, Phil Rizzuto, Yankees Shortstop, Dies at 89, *New York Times*, August 14, 2007.

"There was just a...Rizzuto, Phil, radio interview, MLB.com, as retrieved March 7, 2009.

"Ray, a big, imposing...Shampoe, Clay and Thomas Garrett. *Baseball in Norfolk, Virginia* (Dover, New Hampshire: Arcadia Publishing, 2003), p. 26.

"They didn't like...", "I swear to God...", Eig, Jonathan. *Luckiest Man, The Life and Death of Lou Gehrig* (New York: Simon & Schuster, 2005), p. 184.

"Each town or each...Trimble, Joe. *Phil Rizzuto, A Biography of the Scooter* (New York: A.S. Barnes & Co., 1951), p. 27.

"One thing, anyway...", "This sentiment was...", Shapiro, Milton J. *The Phil Rizzuto Story* (New York: Julian Messner, Inc., 1959), p. 34.

"I was running to...", "We had no trainers...", "An old umpire took...", "When I woke up...", Hirschberg, Dan. *Phil Rizzuto: A Yankee Tradition* (Chicago: Sagamore Publishing, 1993), pp. 16–17.

"He wound a big...", "What has happened...", "I never thought he'd...", Trimble, Joe. *Phil Rizzuto, A Biography of the Scooter* (New York: A.S. Barnes & Co., 1951), pp. 28–29.

"Will I play again?...", "The incision has...", Shapiro, Milton J. *The Phil Rizzuto Story* (New York: Julian Messner, Inc., 1959), pp. 35–37.

"Priddy, a moon-faced...", "There they began...", "Phil and Jerry became...", Trimble, Joe. *Phil Rizzuto, A Biography of the Scooter* (New York: A.S. Barnes & Co., 1951), p. 32.

"Priddy. That huckleberry...Madden, Bill. *Pride of October* (New York: Warner Books, 2003), p. 10.

"Every writer I know...James, Bill. *Whatever Happened to the Hall of Fame?* (Free Press, 1995), p. 218.

"I was eight years...Prince, Bill, The Scooter's Finest Hour, blog response 284., This was a great article. August 16, 2007, as retrieved March 3, 2009, http://bats.blogs.nytimes.com/2007/08/14/the-scooters-finest-hour/?apage=12

"It was a spectacular...Shapiro, Milton J. *The Phil Rizzuto Story* (New York: Julian Messner, Inc., 1959), pp. 48–49.

"They moved him to...Trimble, Joe. *Phil Rizzuto, A Biography of the Scooter* (New York: A.S. Barnes & Co., 1951), p. 34.

Chapter 4

"In 1939 I was promoted…, "When Rizzuto arrived…, Hirschberg, Dan. *Phil Rizzuto: A Yankee Tradition* (Chicago: Sagamore Publishing, 1993), p. 19 and 21.

"They made such a…Shapiro, Milton J. *The Phil Rizzuto Story* (New York: Julian Messner, Inc., 1959), pp. 54–55.

"Meyer broke into the…, "In spite of these two…, "Billy Meyer," Wikipedia.com, http://en.wikipedia.org/wiki/Billy_Meyer, as retrieved on February 2, 2009.

"Then forty-five years…Trimble, Joe. *Phil Rizzuto, A Biography of the Scooter* (New York: A.S. Barnes & Co., 1951), p. 35.

"Born William Clyde Hitchcock…, "He acted to reorganize…, Akin, William. "Billy Hitchcock" The Baseball Biogrpahy Project, The Society for American Baseball Research, 2003-2009, SABR, as retrieved on February 9, 2009, http://bioproj.sabr.org/bioproj.cfm?a=v&v=l&bid=289&pid=6372

"I had played shortstop…, "Oh, man, I remember…, Hirschberg, Dan. *Phil Rizzuto: A Yankee Tradition* (Chicago: Sagamore Publishing, 1993), p. 19.

"One of the most…Trimble, Joe. *Phil Rizzuto, A Biography of the Scooter* (New York: A.S. Barnes & Co., 1951), p. 54.

"You ain't runnin'…Bernstein, Adam, "Yankees Hall of Famer, Broadcaster Phil Rizzuto," *Washington Post*, August 15, 2007, B05.

"Anybody'd ask why…, "For many years…, "Good things, it is…, Hirschberg, Dan. *Phil Rizzuto: A Yankee Tradition* (Chicago: Sagamore Publishing, 1993), pp. 21–23.

"There's always something…Shapiro, Milton J. *The Phil Rizzuto Story* (New York: Julian Messner, Inc., 1959), p. 55.

"I watched Phil Rizutto…Long, Robert, Scooter's Finest Hour, blog response, No. 103., I watched Phil Rizutto…, August 14, 2007, as retrieved March 3, 2009, http://bats.blogs.nytimes.com/2007/08/14/the-scooters-finest-hour/?apage=5#comments

"The Bainbridge Apartment…Cronkite, Walter. *A Reporter's Life* (New York: Random House, 1997), p. 75.

"I think (pitcher) Johnny…Hirschberg, Dan. *Phil Rizzuto: A Yankee Tradition* (Chicago: Sagamore Publishing, 1993), p. 19.

"Here Buzz, a present from…Shapiro, Milton J. *The Phil Rizzuto Story* (New York: Julian Messner, Inc., 1959), pp. 57–58.

"The farm hands did quite…Drebinger, John, "Yankees Win 4–3, On Three in Eighth," *New York Times*, March 28, 1940.

"I guess there wasn't…, "Betty's family was…, Trimble, Joe. *Phil Rizzuto, A Biography of the Scooter* (New York: A.S. Barnes & Co., 1951), pp. 66–67.

"It never failed so…Trimble, Joe. *Phil Rizzuto, A Biography of the Scooter* (New York: A.S. Barnes & Co., 1951), p. 38.

"The split second he saw…Shapiro, Milton J. *The Phil Rizzuto Story* (New York: Julian Messner, Inc., 1959), pp. 59–60.

"Philip is developing into…Hirschberg, Dan. *Phil Rizzuto: A Yankee Tradition* (Chicago: Sagamore Publishing, 1993), p. 24.

"The way things stand…Hirschberg, Dan. *Phil Rizzuto: A Yankee Tradition* (Chicago: Sagamore Publishing, 1993), pp. 31–32.

Section 2: At Play in Ruth's House

Chapter 5

"You read the sports…Vaccaro, Mike. *Emperors and Idiots* (New York: Broadway Books, 2005), p. 177.

"In 1926 Fred Logan…Klein, Moss. "The House That Pete Kept," *Sports Illustrated*, August 26, 1985.

"The Yankees clubhouse man…Votano, Paul. *Tony Lazzeri* (Jefferson, North Carolina: McFarland & Company, 2005), p.95.

"Beat it, Sonny…, "To tell you the truth…, Trimble, Joe. *Phil Rizzuto, A Biography of the Scooter* (New York: A.S. Barnes & Co., 1951), p. 43.

Vernon Louis "Lefty" Gomez…Lefty Gomez, wikipedia.com, http://en.wikipedia.org/wiki/Lefty_Gomez as retrieved on February 9, 2009.

"Rizzuto received most…Trimble, Joe. *Phil Rizzuto, A Biography of the Scooter* (New York: A.S. Barnes & Co., 1951), p. 41.

"Among those obtained…N/A, "Yanks Acquire Nine Men," *New York Times*, September 12, 1940.

"Although baseball's bigwigs…Drebinger, John, "Medwick Is Signed," *New York Times*, October 31, 1940.

"It appears that the…Kieran, John, "Running Some Distant Bases," *New York Times*, March 11, 1941.

"I think Rizzuto and Priddy…Drebinger, John, McCarthy to Count of Two Farmhands, *New York Times*, December 26, 1940.

"I know of no…, "If Rizzuto and Priddy…, Drebinger, John, "Barrow Predicts New Yankee Reign," *New York Times*, December 28, 1940.

"He's just born to be…Hirschberg, Dan. *Phil Rizzuto: A Yankee Tradition* (Chicago: Sagamore Publishing, 1993), p. 32.

"The first people to…Trimble, Joe. *Phil Rizzuto, A Biography of the Scooter* (New York: A.S. Barnes & Co., 1951), p. 42.

"Friends and admirers…N/A, "Rizzuto to be Honored Tonight," *New York Times*, February 5, 1941.

"was advised by President…N/A, Dateline: Montgomery, Ala., Associated Press, February 14, 1940.

"Coach Art Fletcher put…Dawson, James P., "McCarthy Inspects Freshman Infield," *New York Times*, February 24, 1941.

"Crosetti is faced with a…Dawson, James P., "Yankees Sell First-Baseman Dahlgren," *New York Times*, February 26, 1941.

"I have played alongside…Hirschberg, Dan. *Phil Rizzuto: A Yankee Tradition* (Chicago: Sagamore Publishing, 1993), p. 29.

"Rizzuto make poke an…Hirschberg, Dan. *Phil Rizzuto: A Yankee Tradition* (Chicago: Sagamore Publishing, 1993), p. 30.

"Believe me, it…Hirschberg, Dan. *Phil Rizzuto: A Yankee Tradition* (Chicago: Sagamore Publishing, 1993), p. 35.

"Priddy and Rizzuto measure… Dawson, James P., "Gordon Named New Yankee First-Baseman by McCarthy After Accepting Terms," *New York Times*, March 4, 1941.

"Rizzuto Spiked in… Dawson, James P., "Rizzuto Spiked in Yankees' Game," *New York Times*, March 5, 1941.

"was known for old-school…N/A, Frank Crosetti, 1910-2002, ESPN.com, http://www.geocities.com/cyberclopedia5/memorial/crow.html, as retrieved on February 11, 2009.

"Crosetti, particularly, taught…, "If I played too deep…, "There probably wasn't…, Trimble, Joe. *Phil Rizzuto, A Biography of the Scooter* (New York: A.S. Barnes & Co., 1951), pp. 44–45.

"Crow was just great…, "Crow was a great teacher…, Madden, Bill, "Yanks Crosetti dies at 91," *New York Daily News*, February 13, 2002.

"Rizzuto obviously occupied…Carreri, Joe. *Searching for Heroes* (Mineola, New York: Carlyn Publications, 1995), p. 144.

"I was coming to…Hirschberg, Dan. *Phil Rizzuto: A Yankee Tradition* (Chicago: Sagamore Publishing, 1993), p. 35.

"Rizzuto, I saw what…Halberstam, David. *Summer of '49* (New York: Morrow and Company, 1989), p. 42.

"Their personalities became…N/A, Frank Crosetti, 1910-2002, ESPN.com, http://www.geocities.com/cyberclopedia5/memorial/crow.html, as retrieved on February 11, 2009.

"Next to the little red…Hall, Alvin, Altherr, Thomas L. et al, The Tenth Cooperstown Symposium on Baseball and American Culture convened in June 1998, McFarland.

"Imagine opening your…Baldassaro, Lawrence, "Dashing Dagos and Walloping Wops: Media Portrayal of Italian American Major Leaguers before World War II," *NINE: A Journal of Baseball History and Culture* (Lincoln, Nebraska: University of Nebraska Press, Volume 14, Number 1, Fall 2005), pp. 98–106.

"The Yankees called…Bechtel, Brad, "RIP, Joe DiMaggio," The Mail Archive, March 8, 1999, as retrieved on February 14, 2009, http://www.mail-archive.com/postcard2@u.washington.edu/msg04922.html

"The Yankees called…Dorinson, Joseph. *Jackie Robinson: Race, Sports, and the American Dream* (Armonk, New York: M.E. Sharpe, 1998), p.117.

"Another name Rizzuto had…O'Connell, Jack, "Scooter" Rizzuto dies at 89, MLB.com, August 14, 2007, as retrieved on February 14, 2009, http://www.mlb.com/content/printer_friendly/nyy/y2007/m08/d14/c2147920.jsp

"I heard…Phil Rizzuto…Giuliani, Rudolph, Remarks at Joe DiMaggio's Memorial Service, Archives of Rudolph W. Giuliani, April 23, 1999, as retrieved on February 1, 2009, http://nyc.gov/html/records/rwg/html/99a/dimaggio2.html

"After that we had…Hirschberg, Dan. *Phil Rizzuto: A Yankee Tradition* (Chicago: Sagamore Publishing, 1993), p. 53.

"Joe was simply…Gaffney, Dennis, What Made DiMaggio a Great Player? The American Experience.com, as retrieved on February 5, 2009, http://www.pbs.org/wgbh/amex/dimaggio/sfeature/essay.html

"Hey, kid, you better…Shapiro, Milton J. *The Phil Rizzuto Story* (New York: Julian Messner, Inc., 1959), p. 67.

"Everyone wonders about…Hirschberg, Dan. *Phil Rizzuto: A Yankee Tradition* (Chicago: Sagamore Publishing, 1993), p. 33.

"Inspired, no doubt...Dawson, James P., "Rizzuto Sets Pace as Yanks Win 8–2," *New York Times*, March 14, 1941.

"One of the important...N/A, "Draft Board Defers Rizzuto in Class 3A," *New York Times*, March 30, 1941.

"Priddy, suffering by...Trimble, Joe. *Phil Rizzuto, A Biography of the Scooter* (New York: A.S. Barnes & Co., 1951), p. 47.

"Rizzuto and Priddy were...Hirschberg, Dan. *Phil Rizzuto: A Yankee Tradition* (Chicago: Sagamore Publishing, 1993), p. 30.

"What's new, kid?...Shapiro, Milton J. *The Phil Rizzuto Story* (New York: Julian Messner, Inc., 1959), pp. 69–70.

"The whole season...Forker, Dom. *The Men of Autumn* (Dallas: Taylor Publishing Company, 1989), p. 45.

"After a interminable..., "Events leading up to..., Drebinger, John, "Roosevelt Sees Yankees Shutout Senators in Inaugural," *New York Times*, April 14, 1941.

"I remember going...Williams, Ted. *My Turn at Bat—The Story of My Life* (New York: Fireside Books, 1988), p. 16.

"You play hard....Vaccaro, Mike. *Emperors and Idiots* (New York: Broadway Books, 2005), p. 235.

"With Priddy still nursing...Drebinger, John, "Roosevelt Sees Yankees Shutout Senators in Inaugural," *New York Times*, April 14, 1941.

"I had driven my...Trimble, Joe. *Phil Rizzuto, A Biography of the Scooter* (New York: A.S. Barnes & Co., 1951), p. 48.

"I got the chills...Vincent, Fay. *The Only Game in Town* (New York: Simon & Schuster, 2006), pp. 123–24.

"I'll never forget how...Trimble, Joe. *Phil Rizzuto, A Biography of the Scooter* (New York: A.S. Barnes & Co., 1951), p. 154.

"Some guy is heckling... Vincent, Fay. *The Only Game in Town* (New York: Simon & Schuster, 2006), pp. 72.

"They gave me...Phil Rizzuto, Hall of Fame Induction Speech, Cooperstown, New York, July 31, 1994.

"Phil Rizzuto lost his...Daley, Arthur, "M'carthymen Take 11-Inning Game, 4–2," *New York Times*, April 24, 1941.

"The occasion was a ..., "We had a pitcher.... Mitchell, Bill, "Rizzuto Kin Keeps With Care His Memories Of Liberty Park's Yankee," *Times Newsweekly* (Glendale, New York), September, 2007, retrieved January 6, 2009, http://www.timesnewsweekly.com/common/archives/Archives2007/July-Sept.2007/082307/NewFiles/CAVALCADE.html

"After a particularly great... Marchisotto, Dr. Robert, "The Call Many Times," *New York Times*, August 19, 2007.

"The rise of Rizzuto...Kieran, John, "The Sports of the Times," *New York Times*, May 1, 1941.

"How good is he?"..., "Phil has functioned..., "Nobody had a real..., Hirschberg, Dan. *Phil Rizzuto: A Yankee Tradition* (Chicago: Sagamore Publishing, 1993), pp. 46–48.

"It will take some...Kieran, John, "The Sports of the Times," *New York Times*, May 1, 1941.

"The Yankees continued...Daley, Arthur, "14 Hits Overpower McCarthy Men," *New York Times*, May 16, 1941.

"My throwing became...Hirschberg, Dan. *Phil Rizzuto: A Yankee Tradition* (Chicago: Sagamore Publishing, 1993), p. 48.

"Joe McCarthy had...Effrat, Louis, "Ruffing's Pinch Hit Nips White Sox," *New York Times*, May 17, 1941.

"Joe McCarthy was my...Forker, Dom. *The Men of Autumn* (Dallas: Taylor Publishing Company, 1989), pp. 47-48.

"McCarthy says I'll...Trimble, Joe. *Phil Rizzuto, A Biography of the Scooter* (New York: A.S. Barnes & Co., 1951), p. 51.

"[McCarthy] would point..., "Although Rizzuto was..., Hirschberg, Dan. *Phil Rizzuto: A Yankee Tradition* (Chicago: Sagamore Publishing, 1993), pp. 49–50.

"It's not really as...Shapiro, Milton J. *The Phil Rizzuto Story* (New York: Julian Messner, Inc., 1959), p. 76.

"The Yankee Clipper..., "On June 29, DiMaggio..., "I can't say I'm..., Frommer, Harvey, "Joe Dimaggio's 56 Game Hitting Streak Began May 15, 1941," Harvey Frommer on Sports, 2008, as retrieved on February 13, 2009, http://www.travel-watch.com/jd56game.htm

"Joe never showed..., "I remember the..., "Joe and I were..., Forker, Dom. *The Men of Autumn* (Dallas: Taylor Publishing Company, 1989), pp. 45–46.

"Same time as Joe...Rizzuto, Phil, interview with, MLB.com as retrieved on March 7, 2009.

"By the way...Kieran, John, "Sports of the Times, Looking Over the Batting Order," *New York Times*, July 13, 1941.

"Keller, Rizzuto, DiMaggio...Drebinger, John, "Bomber Prevail on 4 Triples, 7–5," *New York Times*, August 5, 1941.

"In the third inning...Effrat, Louis, "Yanks Lose 5–0, But Tie Record," *New York Times*, September 29, 1941.

"Breakfast. Aren't you...Shapiro, Milton J. *The Phil Rizzuto Story* (New York: Julian Messner, Inc., 1959), pp. 76–77.

"Pee Wee helped make...Robinson, Rachel, "Rachel Robinson Recalls How The Late Pee Wee Reese Helped Jackie Robinson Integrate Baseball," *Jet*, September 13, 1999.

"Our careers kind...Hirschberg, Dan. *Phil Rizzuto: A Yankee Tradition* (Chicago: Sagamore Publishing, 1993), p. 43.

"Phil Rizzuto exhibited...Dawson, James P., "M'Carthy Points to Today's Bad Breaks," *New York Times*, October 3, 1941.

"never equaled or approached...N/A, "Odd Record for French," *New York Times*, October 6, 1941.

"Rumor had it that..., "The condemned jumped..., Gallagher, Tom, Mickey Owen, Baseball Library.com, The Idea Logical Company, Inc., 2006, as retrieved on February 13, 2009, http://www.baseballlibrary.com/ballplayers/player.php?name=Mickey_Owen_1916

"I was just as...Trimble, Joe. *Phil Rizzuto, A Biography of the Scooter* (New York: A.S. Barnes & Co., 1951), p. 51.

"It couldn't, perhaps,...Drebinger, John, "Yanks Win In 9th, Final Out Turns Into 4-Run Rally," *New York Times*, October 6, 1941.

"Ernie "Tiny" Bonham…N/A, "History of the World Series—1941," Sporting News.com, as retrieved February 12, 2009, http://www.sportingnews.com/archives/worldseries/1941.html

Chapter 6

"I sure am…, "And listen, if …, Shapiro, Milton J. *The Phil Rizzuto Story* (New York: Julian Messner, Inc., 1959), pp. 80–81.

"I was not so interested…Schoor, Gene. *The Scooter: The Phil Rizzuto Story* (New York: Charles Scribners Sons, 1982), p. 59.

"December 6, 1941…Lippman, David, "Remembering Pearl Harbor," *Time*, December 7, 2007.

The air portion of…N/A, Attack on Pearl Harbor, Wikipedia.com, as retrieved on February 20, 2009, http://en.wikipedia.org/wiki/Attack_on_Pearl_Harbor

"Phillip is in Norfolk…Trimble, Joe. *Phil Rizzuto, A Biography of the Scooter* (New York: A.S. Barnes & Co., 1951), p. 69.

"I'm coming right…Shapiro, Milton J. *The Phil Rizzuto Story* (New York: Julian Messner, Inc., 1959), p. 83.

"I didn't see her nearly…Trimble, Joe. *Phil Rizzuto, A Biography of the Scooter* (New York: A.S. Barnes & Co., 1951), p. 71.

"Joe McCarthy is confident…N/A, "M'Carthy Hopes High For Yankees of 1942," *New York Times*, January 13, 1942.

"A new style of play…, "Rizzuto is going…, Dawson, James P., "Rizzuto Tries New Fielding Style Designed to Cover More Ground," *New York Times*, March 4, 1942.

"Mayor LaGuardia…Dawson, James P., "Yankees Defeat Red Sox for Fourth Straight," *New York Times*, April 18, 1942.

"It's funny how there…, "Rizzuto isn't as good…, Kieran, John, "Sports of the Times: A Survey of Shortstops," *New York Times*, August 16, 1942.

"Putting on a show of…Drebinger, John, "McCarthy Men Set Double Play Mark," *New York Times*, August 15, 1942.

"Little Phil Rizzuto…Drebinger, John, "Chandler Wins, 3–0, as Rizzuto Excels," *New York Times*, August 29, 1942.

"Shortstop Phil Rizzuto…N/A, "Rizzuto Receives Orders," *New York Times*, September 12, 1942.

"One might assume…Chamberlain, John, "Books of the Times," *New York Times*, September 5, 1942.

"Fred Hutchinson, the…Schoor, Gene. *The Scooter: The Phil Rizzuto Story* (New York: Charles Scribners Sons, 1982), p. 66.

"It got pretty lonely…Trimble, Joe. *Phil Rizzuto, A Biography of the Scooter* (New York: A.S. Barnes & Co., 1951), p. 71.

"The transfer breaks up…Drebinger, John, "Yankees Send Priddy and Candini to the Senators in Trade For Pitcher Zuber," *New York Times*, January 30, 1943.

"An outspoken infielder…Macht, Norman L., Jerry Priddy, BaseballLibrary.com, as retrieved on February 19, 2009, http://www.baseballlibrary.com/ballplayers/player.php?name=Gerry_Priddy_1919

"They played five or…, "The raw deal was too…, "Before the party was…, "This is an air-raid drill…, Trimble, Joe. *Phil Rizzuto, A Biography of the Scooter* (New York: A.S. Barnes & Co., 1951), pp. 72–74.

"Rizzuto is currently…N/A, "Rizzuto Married at Norfolk," Associated Press, June 24, 1943.

"Hutchinson, a broad-shouldered…, "While three or four…, Trimble, Joe. *Phil Rizzuto, A Biography of the Scooter* (New York: A.S. Barnes & Co., 1951), p. 87.

"The Rizzutos lived happily…Hirschberg, Dan. *Phil Rizzuto: A Yankee Tradition* (Chicago: Sagamore Publishing, 1993), pp. 79–80.

"I'll never forget…Schoor, Gene. *The Scooter: The Phil Rizzuto Story* (New York: Charles Scribners Sons, 1982), p. 81.

"That was like a…Forker, Dom. *The Men of Autumn* (Dallas: Taylor Publishing Company, 1989), p. 45.

"A synthetic drug invented…Steinert, David, The Use of Atabrine to Fight Malaria During World War II, World War II Combat Medic, as retrieved on February 222, 2009, http://home.att.net/~steinert/wwii.htm#   The%20Use%20of%20Atabrine%20to%20Fight%20Malaria%20During%20World%20War%20II

"He also got a…, "The minute I got…, Schoor, Gene. *The Scooter: The Phil Rizzuto Story* (New York: Charles Scribners Sons, 1982), p. 81.

"It was 1944, and…, "We played two…, "It's a sweet photograph…, Cassidy, Mike, "Snapshot of Phil Rizzuto, 63 years ago," *San Jose Mercury News* (San Jose, California), August 21, 2007.

"With a memory akin…, "There we were…, Mitchell, Bill, "Rizzuto Kin Keeps With Care His Memories Of Liberty Park's Yankee," *Times Newsweekly* (Glendale, NY), September, 2007, retrieved January 6, 2009, http://www.timesnewsweekly.com/common/archives/Archives2007/July-Sept.2007/082307/NewFiles/CAVALCADE.html

"I was in the first…, "Bill Dickey, who…, Forker, Dom. *The Men of Autumn* (Dallas: Taylor Publishing Company, 1989), p. 47.

"Imagine us getting…, "Some of those guys…, Trimble, Joe. *Phil Rizzuto, A Biography of the Scooter* (New York: A.S. Barnes & Co., 1951), p. 89.

"I don't think it…Hirschberg, Dan. *Phil Rizzuto: A Yankee Tradition* (Chicago: Sagamore Publishing, 1993), p. 80.

"I was in Australia…, "You bring the players…, Vincent, Fay. *The Only Game in Town* (New York: Simon & Schuster, 2006), pp. 123–24.

"The little guy organized…, "I picked Detroit to…, Trimble, Joe. *Phil Rizzuto, A Biography of the Scooter* (New York: A.S. Barnes & Co., 1951), pp. 90–91.

New Faces, Same Old Pinstripes

"McPhail was a colorful…Schoor, Gene. *The Scooter: The Phil Rizzuto Story* (New York: Charles Scribners Sons, 1982), p. 89.

"A lot of the boys…Shapiro, Milton J. *The Phil Rizzuto Story* (New York: Julian Messner, Inc., 1959), p. 89.

"The Gordon-Rizzuto combination…Dawson, James P., "Veterans Sparkle in Yanks' Practice," *New York Times*, February 13, 1946.

"I want to announce…Schoor, Gene. *The Scooter: The Phil Rizzuto Story* (New York: Charles Scribners Sons, 1982), p. 93.

"I had always kept…Rizzuto, Phil and Al Silverman. *The "Miracle" New York Yankees* (New York: Coward-McCan Publishing, 1962), pp. 121–22.

"I was born and…Rielly, James, Rizzuto' Finest Hour, blog response No. 26, I was born and raised…, *New York Times*, August 14, 2007, as retrieved on March 3, 2009, http://bats.blogs. nytimes.com/2007/08/14/the-scooters-finest-hour/?apage=2#comments

"MacPhail and McCarthy…Daley, Arthur, "Exit Marse Joe," *New York Times*, May 26, 1947.

"Phil was carried on…Hirschberg, Dan. *Phil Rizzuto: A Yankee Tradition* (Chicago: Sagamore Publishing, 1993), p. 83.

Mexico City in a Cadillac

"Was it serious?… "You will recollect…, "Call McCarthy now…, "I figured he was doing me…, "Paquel wined and…, Hirschberg, Dan. *Phil Rizzuto: A Yankee Tradition* (Chicago: Sagamore Publishing, 1993), p. 85.

"Jorge Pasquel, one of the…Trimble, Joe. *Phil Rizzuto, A Biography of the Scooter* (New York: A.S. Barnes & Co., 1951), p. 109.

"The Pasquels, who own…N/A, "Raids over the border," *Time*, New York, April 15, 1946.

"They went after George…Schoor, Gene. *The Scooter: The Phil Rizzuto Story* (New York: Charles Scribners Sons, 1982), p. 101.

"Pasquel's testimony told…N/A, "Rizzuto Offer Disclosed," *New York Times*, June 9, 1946.

"You'll be like a man…Schoor, Gene. *The Scooter: The Phil Rizzuto Story* (New York: Charles Scribners Sons, 1982), p. 107.

"It was some dinner…, "He asked me to…, Trimble, Joe. *Phil Rizzuto, A Biography of the Scooter* (New York: A.S. Barnes & Co., 1951), p. 114.

"I admit that I…Schoor, Gene. *The Scooter: The Phil Rizzuto Story* (New York: Charles Scribners Sons, 1982), p. 107.

"that the next day…N/A, "Rizzuto Offer Disclosed," *New York Times*, June 9, 1946.

"The buses were driven…Francis, C. Philip, The Barber, chatterfromthedugout.com, as retrieved on March 1, 2009, http://www.chatterfromthedugout.com/barber.htm

"Mexican businessman Jorge…Nicholl, Conor, Pasquel was a force for integration, MLB. com, November 14, 2007, as retrieved March 1, 2009, http://mlb.mlb.com/news/article. jsp?ymd=20071114&content_id=2300489&vkey=news_mlb&fext=.jsp&c_id=mlb

"Jorge Pasquel was an extremely…Littlefield, Bill, "South of the Color Barrier, NPR.com, Only a Game, posted March 13, 2008, as retrieved on March 1, 2009, http://www.onlyagame. org/book-reviews/2008/03/south-of-the-color-barrier-2/

Seems Like Old Times

"Despite the many…Langford, James, Bucky Harris, biography, BaseballLibrary.com, as retrieved March 1, 2009, http://www.baseballlibrary.com/ballplayers/player.php?name=Bucky_ Harris_1896

"He studies baseball…Reynolds, Quentin, Bucky Harris, Baseball Hall of Fame, as retrieved on March 1, 2009, http://users.bigpond.net.au/magnetic-island/quentin_reynolds.htm

"Rizzuto, under the…Trimble, Joe. *Phil Rizzuto, A Biography of the Scooter* (New York: A.S. Barnes & Co., 1951), p. 121.

"Bucky Harris was a…Forker, Dom. *The Men of Autumn* (Dallas: Taylor Publishing Company, 1989), p. 48.

"The Yankees favored…Effrat, Louis, "Sharp Fielding Helps Shea Win 5th in a Row," *New York Times*, May 29, 1947.

"I've been in baseball…Trimble, Joe. *Phil Rizzuto, A Biography of the Scooter* (New York: A.S. Barnes & Co., 1951), p. 125.

"Joe never showed…Forker, Dom. *The Men of Autumn* (Dallas: Taylor Publishing Company, 1989), p. 45.

"Phil Rizzuto could hardly…, "He's a sentimental…, Dawson, James P., "Decision Revealed at Contest's End," *New York Times*, October 5, 1947.

"Later in the game…Mantle, Mickey & Mickey Herskowitz. *All My Octobers* (New York: Harpers), pp. 12–13.

Scooter and Yogi

"We've been friends…Rizzuto, Phil and Al Silverman. *The "Miracle" New York Yankees* (New York: Coward-McCan Publishing), 1962, p. 158.

A Different Kind of Life

"The players sided with…Trimble, Joe. *Phil Rizzuto, A Biography of the Scooter* (New York: A.S. Barnes & Co., 1951), p. 128.

"If Bucky hadn't had… Forker, Dom. *The Men of Autumn* (Dallas: Taylor Publishing Company, 1989), p. 48.

"I grew up in Newark…Field, Bob, "Scooter's Finest Hour," Blog Response No. 263, " I grew up in Newark…, *New York Times*, August 15, 2007, as retrieved March 3, 2009, http://bats. blogs.nytimes.com/2007/08/14/the-scooters-finest-hour/?apage=11#comments

"As a player, he…Center, Bill, "Coleman: Rizzuto was Yankee Catalyst," *San Diego Union-Tribune*, August 15, 2007.

"Phil Rizzuto…knew…Halberstam, David. *Summer of '49* (New York: Morrow and Company, 1989), p. 41.

"Once he was sure…Halberstam, David. *Summer of '49* (New York: Morrow and Company, 1989), p. 51.

"If I remember correctly…Kelleher, John, Newark Talks.com, as retrieved March 3, 2009.

"The American Shop clothing…eppie544, Newark Talks.com, as retrieved March 3, 2009. Interview with Rhoda Bartels.

"Cookie would cordially…Roth, Philip. *American Pastoral* (New York: Vintage Paperbacks, 1998), p. 48.

"Weiss firmly believed…Rizzuto, Phil and Tom Horton. *The October Twelve* (New York: Forge Books 1994), p. 68.

"'The Cricket' is ready to…McGowen, Roscoe, "Rizzuto Accepts Yankees Contract," *New York Times*, January 21, 1949.

"Casey? No, I'm…Forker, Dom. *The Men of Autumn* (Dallas: Taylor Publishing Company, 1989), p. 48.

"It's no big secret…Madden, Bill, "One last meeting with Phil Rizzuto," *New York Daily News*, September 9, 2007.

"When he became…Sandomir, Richard, "Phil Rizzuto, Yankees Shortstop, Dies at 89," *New York Times*, August 14, 2007.

"Ted Williams thought... Rizzuto, Phil and Tom Horton. *The October Twelve* (New York: Forge Books 1994), p. 61.

"He had two tempers...Durso, Joe, Whitey Ford, and Mickey Mantle. *Whitey and Mickey* (New York: The Viking Press, 1977), p. 163.

"The arm was tired...Hirschberg, Dan. *Phil Rizzuto: A Yankee Tradition* (Chicago: Sagamore Publishing, 1993), p. 93.

"When you are-ready...Trimble, Joe. *Phil Rizzuto, A Biography of the Scooter* (New York: A.S. Barnes & Co., 1951), p. 128.

"Stengel moved Rizzuto...N/A, "Phil Rizzuto Dies," Associated Press, CBS 880, August 15, 2007.

"The solid man...Hirschberg, Dan. *Phil Rizzuto: A Yankee Tradition* (Chicago: Sagamore Publishing, 1993), p. 95.

"It doesn't make...Shapiro, Milton J. *The Phil Rizzuto Story* (New York: Julian Messner, Inc., 1959), p. 111.

"The game is baseball...Rizzuto, Phil and Tom Horton. *The October Twelve* (New York: Forge Books 1994), p. 83.

"Rizzuto and Pesky...Effrat, Louis, "Joe In First Start as Bombers Score," *New York Times*, June 29, 1949.

"As soon as you...Vaccaro, Mike. *Emperors and Idiots* (New York: Broadway Books, 2005), p.214.

"Then, in the first...," "Pesky, he's a corker!...," Trimble, Joe. *Phil Rizzuto, A Biography of the Scooter* (New York: A.S. Barnes & Co., 1951), pp. 138–39.

"A ballplayer who just...Cafardo, Nick, "Phil Rizzuto, 89; 'The Scooter' an icon on field, in Yankee lore," *Boston Globe*, August 14, 2007.

"I grew up in the...Bonner, Daniel, Scooter's Finest Hour, Blog response No. 104, "I grew up in the..., *New York Times*, August 14, 2007, as retrieved on March 3, 2009, http://bats.blogs. nytimes.com/2007/08/14/the-scooters-finest-hour/?apage=5#comments

"When we used...Forker, Dom, Wayne Stewart, and Michael J.Pelowski. *Baffling Baseball Trivia* (New York: Sterling Publishing Company Inc., 2004), p. 117.

"During our last Western...Mantle, Mickey and Herb Gluck. *The Mick: An American Hero* (New York: Jove Publishing, 1986), p. 91.

"They knew I hated...," "After practice one...," Rizzuto, Phil and Al Silverman. *The "Miracle" New York Yankees* (New York: Coward-McCan Publishing), 1962, p. 124.

"After the change,...Pesky, Johnny, Baseball tidbit... did you know?, Johnny Pesky, myspaceblog. com, written April 18, 2006, as retrieved on March 3, 2009, http://blogs.myspace.com/index. cfm?fuseaction=blog.ListAll&friendId=67886086

"It is taking the...Daley, Arthur, "Three Weeks to Go," *New York Times*, September 13, 1949.

"One day in the closing...Daley, Arthur, "The Scooter and the Ol' Perfesser," *New York Times*, February 5, 1950.

"I didn't even have...Vaccaro, Mike. *Emperors and Idiots* (New York: Broadway Books, 2005), p. 300.

"Well, they did it!...Daley, Arthur, "How About That!!!!," *New York Times*, October 3, 1949.

Dear Mr. Rizzuto,...Berger, Meyer, "Yankee Fan, 14, Ill in Canada, Gets Photos of Idolized Team," *New York Times*, October 8, 1949.

"How could I be?"…Trimble, Joe. *Phil Rizzuto, A Biography of the Scooter* (New York: A.S. Barnes & Co., 1951), p. 144.

"Phil Rizzuto, the Yankees'…Drebinger, John, "Ted Williams Most Valuable American Leaguer," *New York Times*, November 25, 1949.

"Practically everybody in…McGowen, Roscoe, "Rizzuto Set Pace for American League," *New York Times*, December 26, 1949.

"There was so much…Daley, Arthur, "Keeping it in the Family," *New York Times*, December 21, 1949.

"The popular Rizzuto…Drebinger, John, "Rizzuto Named Player of the Year," *New York Times*, December 16, 1949.

Mr. MVP

"Rizzuto was generally…N/A, "Rizzuto Named Pro Athlete of '49," Associated Press, January 12, 1949.

"It was noteworthy…Dawson, James P., "Rizzuto, Reynolds, Porterfield All Fall in Line With Yanks," *New York Times*, January 24, 1950.

"the magician, never…Daley, Arthur, "The Scooter and the Ol' Perfesser," *New York Times*, February 5, 1950.

Among Rizzuto's first…O'Connell, Jack, Hall of Famer Phil Rizzuto passes away Served as captain of World Champion Yankees teams, later broadcaster, MLB.com, August 18, 2007, as retrieved March 3, 2009, http://www.baseballhalloffame.org/news/article.jsp?ymd=20070814&content_id=4904&vkey=hof_news

"The panelists on the…, "The contestants on…, Edelman, Rob. *The St. James Encyclopedia of Popular Culture* (Thompson Gale Group, January 1, 2000), pp. XXX.

"Buckley sat the…, "I went through the…, Rivers, Earl, The Chairs / Amos 'n Andy, Richard Lord Buckley, 1906-1960, lordbuckley.com as retrieved on March 4, 2009, http://homepage.mac.com/tomdalekeever/chairs.txt

"Johnny Mize started…, "Try my bat, Big John…, Trimble, Joe. *Phil Rizzuto, A Biography of the Scooter* (New York: A.S. Barnes & Co., 1951), p. 155.

"Back when the Kansas…Lorenz, Larry, Scooter's Finest Hour, Blog Response no. 76. Back when the Kansas City Blues…, August 14, 2007, as retrieved March 3, 2009, http://bats.blogs.nytimes.com/2007/08/14/the-scooters-finest-hour/?apage=4#comments

"When he wasn't …, "Garcia's tight pitching…, Dawson, James P., "Bombers Capture 7th Straight, 7–2," *New York Times*, May 22, 1950.

"Early in the game…Trimble, Joe. *Phil Rizzuto, A Biography of the Scooter* (New York: A.S. Barnes & Co., 1951), p. 148.

"I've seen some great…, "The fans are nuts…, "I'd like to have him…, "Well," Ferrick said…, Trimble, Joe. *Phil Rizzuto, A Biography of the Scooter* (New York: A.S. Barnes & Co., 1951), pp. 150–51.

"On August 6th, the Yankees…, "You know, if you'd…, Trimble, Joe. *Phil Rizzuto, A Biography of the Scooter* (New York: A.S. Barnes & Co., 1951), p. 153.

"Apart from the fact…N/A, "A Stalwart Thirty-two," *New York Times*, September 26, 1950.

"There were eight…" Madden, Bill. *Pride of October* (New York: Warner Books, 2003), p. 102.

"[The Yankees] have the...Daley, Arthur, "Ignoring Cassandra," *New York Times*, October 1, 1950.

"All I know, is...Madden, Bill, "As good a shortstop as ever played," *New York Daily News*, August 15, 2009.

"Those partisans...N/A, "Rizzuto with .982, again won honors," *New York Times*, December 14, 1950.

"If the Scooter...Shapiro, Milton J. *The Phil Rizzuto Story* (New York: Julian Messner, Inc., 1959), p. 125.

"'In 1950 I never gave...Anderson, Dave, "Long And Miraculous Award For Scooter," *New York Times*, January 21, 1990.

"To the unbounded...Sheehan, Joseph M., "Rizzuto of Yanks is most valuable," *New York Times*, October 27, 1950.

"Fifteen years ago...," "More than any other...," N/A, "The New Pride of the Yankees," *Time*, November 6, 1950.

"That year I did... Forker, Dom. *The Men of Autumn* (Dallas: Taylor Publishing Company, 1989), p. 49.

"On November 28, 1950...Trimble, Joe. *Phil Rizzuto, A Biography of the Scooter* (New York: A.S. Barnes & Co., 1951), pp. 159–60.

"perhaps the most...Drebinger, John, "Rizzuto Signs $50,000 One Year Pact," *New York Times*, December 1, 1950.

"Well about shortstop...Trimble, Joe. *Phil Rizzuto, A Biography of the Scooter* (New York: A.S. Barnes & Co., 1951), p. 160.

1951

"A doctor's assurance...N/A, "Shorstop is fit, Specialist Finds," Associated Press, April 12, 1951.

"I put it on...Gold, Jeffrey, "Memories of Phil from His Longtime Jersey Home," Associated Press, August 14, 2007.

"I remember once...Madden, Bill, "As good a shortstop as ever played," *New York Daily News*, August 15, 2007.

"You're still a...Carreri, Joe. *Searching for Heroes* (Mineola, New York: Carlyn Publications, 1995), pp. 146–47.

"When I got home...," "She sounded like...," Carreri, Joe. *Searching for Heroes* (Mineola, New York: Carlyn Publications, 1995), pp. 148–49.

"We rode the trains...Rizzuto, Phil and Tom Horton. *The October Twelve* (New York: Forge Books 1994), p. 194.

"The only time...O'Connell, Jack, "Peers recall Rizzuto's greatness," MLB.com, August 14, 2007, as retrieved on March 13, 2009.

"Talking about the...," "Against he Indians...," "Stanky? He was...," "I remember the next...," Forker, Dom. *The Men of Autumn* (Dallas: Taylor Publishing Company, 1989), pp. 49–50.

"That squeeze play...," "I remember how...," Hirschberg, Dan. *Phil Rizzuto: A Yankee Tradition* (Chicago: Sagamore Publishing, 1993), p. 107.

"Casey always liked...Kuenster, John. *The Best of Baseball Digest*, (Ivan R. Dee, 2006), p. 251.

"No, I'm not angry…, "Rizzuto should have…, Shapiro, Milton J. *The Phil Rizzuto Story* (New York: Julian Messner, Inc., 1959), p. 132.

"In 1951, when…Gorman, Paul, The Scooter's Finest Hour, New York Times blog, Tyler, Thanks for all the…., New York Times blog, August 16, 2007, as retrieved March 3, 2009, http://bats. blogs.nytimes.com/2007/08/14/the-scooters-finest-hour/?apage=12

"I was nonchalanting it…Anderson, Dave, "Holy Cow! The Scooter Is Going to Cooperstown," *New York Times*, February 27, 1994.

Ed Lucas

"On Oct. 3, 1951, Ed…Rushin, Ed, "A Miracle From Coogan's Bluff," *Sports Illustrated*, February 27, 2006.

"Initially, when Ed…Nist, Laura, At Home Plate, reprinted at www.edlucas.org, originally published June 25, 2003, as retrieved on March 4, 2009, http://www.edlucas.org/ artabouthomeplate.html

"To cheer him up…, "While in High School…, Hurst, James, Ed Lucas – A Baseball Fan Forever, Sportplices.blogspot.com, October 1, 2007, as retrieved March 4, 2007, http:// sportslices.blogspot.com/2007/10/ed-lucas-baseball-fan-forever.html

"Phil Rizzuto took…, "Back when Ed…, Mitrione, Tania & Campanile Dominic, Phil Rizzuto: Man Of Class, Generosity And Pride, lideamagazine.com, December 2007, as retrieved on March 4, 2009, http://www.lideamagazine.com/rizzuto32.htm

"I was fortunate to…Kielty, Patrick, The Scooters Finest Hour, New York Times Blog, Blog response No. 238, August 15, 2007, as retrieved March 7, 2009, http://bats.blogs.nytimes. com/2007/08/14/the-scooters-finest-hour/?apage=10#comments

The New Yankees

"Phil Rizzuto affixed…Drebinger, John, "Rizzuto of Yanks Signs for $45,000," *New York Times*, March 1, 1952.

"Jerry Coleman pivoted…Daley, Arthur, "Too Short a Season," *New York Times*, March 7, 1952.

"Ferris Fain was at bat…Daley, Arthur, "Farewell to Jerry," *New York Times*, April 27, 1952.

"I'm using a bat…Daley, Arthur, "Overheard at the Stadium," *New York Times*, May 8, 1952.

"Platter Chatter…N/A, "Platter Chatter," *Time*, June 2, 1952.

"When Virgil Trucks…N/A, "On Second Thought," *Rockey Mountain News*, June 13, 2003.

"They gave Phil Rizzuto…Drebinger, John, "2 in eighth decide," *New York Times*, September 21, 1952.

"I'll be 35 years…, "He's one of the…, N/A, "Rizzuto Set to End Playing Career," *New York Times*, October 16, 1952.

"That report that I'm…N/A. "Rizzuto Expects to Play Actively," *New York Times*, October 18, 1952.

"He'll be sent home…Not attributed, "Rizzuo Suffering A Duodenal Ulcer," *New York Times*, October 24, 1952.

"This is my side…Hirschberg, Dan. *Phil Rizzuto: A Yankee Tradition* (Chicago: Sagamore Publishing, 1993), p. 110.

"Rizzuto's was the…Dawson, James P., "Rizzuto, Martin, Woodling and Mize Acept Terms," *New York Times*, March 3, 1953.

"One year Phil...Mantle, Mickey and Herb Gluck. *The Mick: An American Hero* (New York: Jove Publishing, 1986), p. 91.

"Courtney, probably...Effrat, Louis, "Bombers Win, 7-6, Amid Free-For-All," *New York Times*, April 29, 1953.

"Collins and McDougald...Schoor, Gene. *The Scooter: The Phil Rizzuto Story* (New York: Charles Scribners Sons, 1982), p. 153.

"The infields, each...Drebinger, John, "Yankees Superior on Defensive Side," *New York Times*, September 29, 1953.

"Winning five in..., "We were used..., Forker, Dom. *The Men of Autumn* (Dallas: Taylor Publishing Company, 1989), p. 50.

"I don't think..., "Ozzie Smith is..., "He was very important..., Hirschberg, Dan. *Phil Rizzuto: A Yankee Tradition* (Chicago: Sagamore Publishing, 1993), pp. 113–15.

"Before the game...N/A, "Doctor Who Gave Up on Rizzuto," *New York Times*, October 6, 1953.

"As Phil got older..., "He made every..., Dottino, Paul, "McDougald followed in Scooter's footsteps," *The Record* (Bergen, New Jersey), August 15, 2007.

Winding Down

"Rizzuto lost his hold...Not attributed, "'The Scooter' was done," Associated Press, August 15, 2007.

"I don't know if...Price, Steven D. 1001 *Funniest Things Ever Said* (Guilford, CT: Lyons Press, 2006), p. 62.

"There were times..., "I cannot do my..., Hirschberg, Dan. *Phil Rizzuto: A Yankee Tradition* (Chicago: Sagamore Publishing, 1993), p. 118.

"I'll admit I'm over...Shapiro, Milton J. *The Phil Rizzuto Story* (New York: Julian Messner, Inc., 1959), p. 165.

"Rizzuto's relationship..., "Some writers thought... Hirschberg, Dan. *Phil Rizzuto: A Yankee Tradition* (Chicago: Sagamore Publishing, 1993), p. 119.

"When I joined the...Richardson, Bobby, Quotes on the Death of Phil Rizzuto, *Sporting News* and Associated Press, August 14, 2007.

"Second baseman...Dottino, Paul, "McDougald followed in Scooter's footsteps," *The Record* (Bergen), August 15, 2007.

"Tomorrow will be...N/A, "A 'Day' For Phil," *New York Times*, September 17, 1955.

"Phil Rizzuto simply...Oliphant, Tom. *Praying for Gil Hodges* (New York: St. Martin's Press, 2005), p. 92.

1956

"Little Phil Rizzuto...N/A, "First Born Son to Rizzutos," Associated Press, January 18, 1956.

"Phil didn't make..., "[Phil and I] hit it..., Dottino, Paul, "McDougald followed in Scooter's footsteps," *The Record* (Bergen, New Jersey), August 15, 2007.

"He can't hit the...Shapiro, Milton J. *The Phil Rizzuto Story* (New York: Julian Messner, Inc., 1959), p. 167.

"No, this doesn't mean...Sheehan, Joseph M., "Phil Rizzuto's 'Day' Full of Warm Tributes," *New York Times*, September 19, 1955.

"Unless something unforeseen…Not attributed, "Shortstop Derby Appears Over," *New York Times*, March 21, 1956.

"The Yankee shortstop…Not Attributed, "Rizzuto Seeks Radio Job," *New York Times*, August 12, 1956.

"It was Old-Timers Day…Not Attributed, "'The Scooter' was done," Associated Press, August 15, 2007.

"Hey, Scooter, you…Shapiro, Milton J. *The Phil Rizzuto Story* (New York: Julian Messner, Inc., 1959), p. 178.

"They asked me to…Not Attributed, "'The Scooter' was done," Associated Press, August 15, 2007.

"We want to give…, "What happened?…, Forker, Dom. *The Men of Autumn* (Dallas: Taylor Publishing Company, 1989), p. 51.

"He was crushed.…Borelli, Stephen, "From his debut to Cooperstown, a Rizzuto timeline," *USA Today*, August 16, 2007.

"I believe that…Not attributed. Rizzuto, Shocked by Release, Associated Press, August 26, 1956.

"I felt badly for…Mantle, Mickey & Mickey Herskowitz. *All My Octobers* (New York: Harpers), p. 63.

"The Yankees won…Creamer, Robert W. *Stengel: His Life and Times* (New York: Simon & Schuster, 1984), p. 274.

Section 3: The View From the Booth

Chapter 7

"In his last couple…Schoor, Gene. *The Scooter: The Phil Rizzuto Story* (New York: Charles Scribners Sons, 1982), p. 135

"Announcing got my…Spink, J.G. Taylor, *The Sporting News*, July 31, 1957.

"The former Yankee…, "Discussions are in…, Adams, Val, "Rizzuto to Scoot into TV and Radio," *New York Times*, October 2, 1956.

"The biggest Ballantine…, "The Ballantine connection…, "If Woods felt bad…, Marcus, Steven, Brewery pushed Rizzuto into broadcast booth, Newsday, Long Island, New York, August 15, 2007.

"I didn't give that…Spink, J.G. Taylor, *The Sporting News*, July 31, 1957.

"Red, I'm all shook up…Barber, Red. *The Broadcasters* (New York: The Dial Press, 1970) p. 115.

"Rizzuto had never… Barber, Red. *The Broadcasters* (New York: The Dial Press, 1970) p. 116.

"My only experience…, "Mr. Allen called…, "Lou patted me…, Sandomir, Richard, "Mel Allen Is Dead at 83; Golden Voice of Yankees," *New York Times*, June 17, 1996.

"They said to me…, "He had already… Hirschberg, Dan. *Phil Rizzuto: A Yankee Tradition* (Chicago: Sagamore Publishing, 1993), p. 137.

"Not too friendly…, "When I came on…, Rizzuto, Phil, interview, with Fran Healy, posted August 14, 2007, as retrieved on March 7, 2009, http://www.youtube.com/watch?v=kpEqA5gKdh8

"It's not pizza…Schoor, Gene. *The Scooter: The Phil Rizzuto Story* (New York: Charles Scribners Sons, 1982), p. 180.

"Three days into...Sandomir, Richard, "Mel Allen Is Dead at 83; Golden Voice of Yankees," *New York Times*, June 17, 1996.

"Can you imagine...Madden, Bill, "As good a shortstop as ever played," *New York Daily News*, August 15, 2007.

"He was the real...Sandomir, Richard, "Mel Allen is Dead at 83," *New York Times*, June 17, 1996.

"I'm going for...Schoor, Gene. *The Scooter: The Phil Rizzuto Story* (New York: Charles Scribners Sons, 1982), p. 180.

"I remember Bill...Rizzuto, Phil, interview, with Fran Healy, posted August 14, 2007, as retrieved on March 7, 2009, http://www.youtube.com/watch?v=kpEqA5gKdh8

"You'll never last...Sandomir, Richard, "Phil Rizzuto, Yankees Shortstop, Dies at 89," *New York Times*, August 14, 2007.

"Every time I start...Barra, Allan, "Hold the innocence: Remember Phil Rizzuto as he truly was," *The Village Voice* (New York), August 22, 2007.

"[Barber] didn't take...Coleman, Jerry. *An American Journey* (Chicago: Triumph Books, 2008), p. 164.

"Barber hated jocks...Kallman, Jeff, Phil Rizzuto RIP; Innocence Stolen, Sports-central. org, August 16, 2007, as retrieved March 16, 2009, http://www.sports-central.org/ sports/2007/08/16/phil_rizzuto_rip_innocence_stolen.php.

"Mel and Red...Rizzuto, Phil, interview, with Fran Healy, posted August 14, 2007, as retrieved on March 7, 2009, http://www.youtube.com/watch?v=kpEqA5gKdh8

"The good broadcaster...", "Mel was very...", Schoor, Gene. *The Scooter: The Phil Rizzuto Story* (New York: Charles Scribners Sons, 1982), p. 181.

"I never got better...Rizzuto, Phil, interview with, MLB.com, as retrieved on March 7, 2009.

"I loved to do....Borelli, Stephen, "From his debut to Cooperstown, a Rizzuto timeline," *USA Today*, August 16, 2007.

"He'd leave in...Smith, Kurt, God Bless the Scooter, and He Will, as retrieved on March 7, 2009, http://curtsmith.mlblogs.com/archives/2007/08/the_scooter.html

"He's a character...Vecsey, George, "A Big Day For Scooter," *New York Times*, August 5, 1985.

"He became famed...Sandomir, Richard, "Phil Rizzuto, Yankees Shortstop, Dies at 89," *New York Times*, August 14, 2007.

"He used to drive...Fommer, Harvery, Holy Cow! Remembering Phil Rizzuto, baseballguru. com, as retrieved, March 8, 2009, http://baseballguru.com/hfrommer/analysishfrommer45. html

"Thunder and lighting....Borelli, Stephen, "From his debut to Cooperstown, a Rizzuto timeline," *USA Today*, August 16, 2007.

"He was fun to...Appel, Marty. *Now Pitching for the Yankees* (New York: Total Sports Illustrated, 2001), p. 258.

"Maxine and the kids...Gifford, Frank and Peter Richmond. *The Glory Game* (New York: Harper, 2008), p. 236.

Rizzuto-Berra Bowling Lanes

"I always enjoy...", "Don't be so...", "Let's go to...", "We walk in...", Daley, Arthur, "Stop, Look, and Listen," *New York Times*, January 9, 1957.

"We start making…, "That's the one…, Young, Dick. "Berra Batting .221 for Yanks—300 in the Bowling Lanes," *New York Daily News*, June 10, 1958.

"Yogi is my best… Rizzuto, Phil and Al Silverman. *The "Miracle" New York Yankees* (New York: Coward-McCan Publishing), 1962, pp. 158-59.

A Tough Summer

"Every ballplayer knows…Daley, Arthur, Still a Yankee at Heart, *New York Times*, June 30, 1957.

"I have only one…Not attributed, Jackie Jensen, wikipedia.com, as retrieved March 9, 2009.

"Everybody has their…Rizzuto, Phil, edited by Tom Peyer and Hart Seely. *Holy Cow!: The Selected Verse of Phil Rizzuto* (New York: Harper Collins, Ecco edition, 2008), p. 77.

61*

"I have always…, "As soon as I…, "I know I was…, Rizzuto, Phil and Al Silverman. *The "Miracle" New York Yankees* (New York: Coward-McCann Publishing), 1962, p. 83.

"The minor league…Creamer, Robert W. *Stengel: His Life and Times* (New York: Simon & Schuster, 1984), p. 293.

"Some of his…, "But there was a…, "I remember coming…, "Tracy must have…, Rizzuto, Phil and Al Silverman. *The "Miracle" New York Yankees* (New York: Coward-McCan Publishing), 1962, p. 125.

"You'll forgive me…Borelli, Stephen, "Spending Time With Scooter," *USA Today*, August 22, 2007.

"Here comes Roger Maris, Rizzuto, Phil, Phil Rizzuto Quotes, Baseball Almanac, baseballalmanac.com, as retrieved on March 9, 2009, http://www.baseball-almanac.com/quotes/quorizz.shtml

"Holy Cow! Look…Golenbock, Peter. *Dynasty* (Englewood Cliffs, New Jersey: Prentice-Hall Publishers, 1975), p. 382.

"It was one of … Rizzuto, Phil and Al Silverman. *The "Miracle" New York Yankees* (New York: Coward-McCan Publishing), 1962, p. 116.

"[Mantle] was, I think… Rizzuto, Phil and Al Silverman. *The "Miracle" New York Yankees* (New York: Coward-McCan Publishing), 1962, p. 125.

October '64

"The first time I…Weich, Dave, David Halberstam's Hit Streak Continues, Powells.om, June 4, 2003, as retrieved on March 9, 2009, https://www.powells.com/authors/halberstam.html.

"Phil and I had… Coleman, Jerry. *An American Journey* (Chicago: Triumph Books, 2008), p. 165.

"He has protruding…, "Bob Fishel told…, Barber, Red. *The Broadcasters* (New York: The Dial Press, 1970), p. 207.

"A move that so…Golenbock, Peter. *Dynasty* (Englewood Cliffs, New Jersey: Prentice-Hall Publishers, 1975), p. 382.

"In fall 1964, Allen…, "You can't name one…, Smith, Kurt, "Why Was Mel Allen Fired, Voices of the Game," mlb.com, as retrieved on March 10, 2009, http://curtsmith.mlblogs.com/archives/2007/06/the_reason.html

"As Allen got…Lukas, J. Anthony, "How Mel Allen Started a Life Long Love Affair," *New York Times*, September 12, 1971.

"The pressroom fills…Smith, Kurt, "Why Was Mel Allen Fired, Voices of the Game," mlb. com, as retrieved on March 10, 2009, http://curtsmith.mlblogs.com/archives/2007/06/the_ reason.html

"They hired me to… Coleman, Jerry. *An American Journey* (Chicago: Triumph Books, 2008), p. 167.

"I still don't know…Lukas, J. Anthony, "How Mel Allen Started a Life Long Love Affair," *New York Times*, September 12, 1971.

"Phil knew how to…Rizzuto, Phil, edited by Tom Peyer and Hart Seely. *Holy Cow!: The Selected Verse of Phil Rizzuto* (New York: Harper Collins, Ecco edition, 2008), back cover.

"He was a quick… Barber, Red. *The Broadcasters* (New York: The Dial Press, 1970), p. 207.

"There was this…Weich, Dave, David Halberstam's Hit Streak Continues, Powells.om, June 4, 2003, as retrieved on March 9, 2009, https://www.powells.com/authors/halberstam.html.

"As we sat…, "Joe does it all…, Barber, Red. *The Broadcasters* (New York: The Dial Press, 1970), pp. 208–9.

"Joe did talk a…Coleman, Jerry. *An American Journey* (Chicago: Triumph Books, 2008), p. 167.

"Caray treated me…Buck, Jack. *That's A Winner* (Champaign, Illinois: Sports Publishing LLC, 1999), p. 105.

"It was the first…Barber, Red. *The Broadcasters* (New York: The Dial Press, 1970), p. 117.

"The Yankees had…Barber, Red. *The Broadcasters* (New York: The Dial Press, 1970), p. 214.

I fired Barber…Lukas, J. Anthony, "How Mel Allen Started a Life Long Love Affair," *New York Times*, September 12, 1971.

"Selma, my wife…Frommer, Harvey, Harvey Frommer on Sports, as retrieved on March 10, 2009, http://www.travel-watch.com/prizzuto1.htm.

The New Yankees

"What has happened…, "Of late, all four…, Lukas, J. Anthony, "How Mel Allen Started a Life Long Love Affair," *New York Times*, September 12, 1971.

"Rizzuto was an…Seigel, Robert, "New York Loses Old Friend Phil Rizzuto," *All Things Considered*, National Public Radio, August 14, 2007.

"It was different…Borelli, Stephen, "Spending Time With Scooter," *USA Today*, August 22, 2007.

"First thing that…Seigel, Robert, "New York Loses Old Friend Phil Rizzuto," *All Things Considered*, National Public Radio, August 14, 2007.

"Announcers for a…Lukas, J. Anthony, "How Mel Allen Started a Life Long Love Affair," *New York Times*, September 12, 1971.

"I was born in…Greenfield, Stuart, The Scooter's Finest Hour blog, *New York Times*, Response No. 223, August 14, 2007, http://bats.blogs.nytimes.com/2007/08/14/the-scooters-finest-hour/?apage=9#comments

"In August 1967…Kahn, Jeff, The Scooter's Finest Hour blog, New York Times, Response No. 57, August 14, 2007, http://bats.blogs.nytimes.com/2007/08/14/the-scooters-finest-hour/?apage=3#comments

"In 1967, I was…amnjr, The Scooter's Finest Hour blog, New York Times, Response No. 164,August 14, 2007, http://bats.blogs.nytimes.com/2007/08/14/the-scooters-finest-hour/?apage=3#comments

"He was probably…, "My favorite broadcast…, "Phil and I were…, Center, Bill, "Coleman: Rizzuto was Yankee Catalyst," *San Diego Union-Tribune*, August 15, 2007.

"He didn't come up…Coleman, Jerry. *An American Journey* (Chicago: Triumph Books, 2008), p. 164.

"On a very hot afternoon…Coleman, Jerry. *An American Journey* (Chicago: Triumph Books, 2008), p. 165.

"His father stayed…Barry, Ellen, "The Streets of Queens Where Rizzuto Played," *New York Times*, August 16, 2007.

"I was sitting…Ziegel, Vic, "A funny thing happened on the way to Cooperstown," *New York Daily News*, August 15, 2007.

Rizzuto-Messer-White: The Three Amigos

A year before…Not attributed, Messer, Frank, wikipedia.com, as retrieved March 10, 2009.

"We call Frank …Not attributed, Messer, Frank, wikipedia.com, as retrieved March 10, 2009.

"At one time…Sandomir, Richard, "Frank Messer, Former Yankees Announcer, Dies at 76," *New York Times*, November 16, 2001.

"Finally, he gave…Berkowitz, Marty, I'm a life long…, blog entry, *New York Post*, August 15, 2007.

"Messer dotes on…, "The last time…, Lukas, J. Anthony, How Mel Allen Started a Life Long Love Affair, *New York Times*, September 12, 1971.

"Messer began his…, "I think that Frank…, Sandomir, Richard, "Frank Messer, Former Yankees Announcer, Dies at 76," *New York Times*, November 16, 2001.

"White earned a…, "Bill White has…, "White originally agreed…, Kram, Mark & Pendergrast, Tom, Bill White, baseball player, broadcaster, league executive, Brief Biographies, as retrieved on March 10, 2009, <a href="http://biography.jrank.org/pages/2437/White-Bill.html">Bill White Biography</a>

"Nobody wanted ballplayers…Wimbish, Ralph, "Bill on Phil," *New York Post*, August 16, 2007.

"We hired him…, "When I was…, Allen, Maury, "Bill White Breaks Color Line in Baseball Booth," *New York Post*, February 10, 1971.

"After baseball…Bitker, Steve. *The Original San Francisco Giants* (Champaign, Illinois: Sports Publishing LLC, 2001), p. 216.

"The plan was…, "On the first pitch…, Appel, Marty. *Now Pitching for the Yankees* (New York: Total Sports Illustrated, 2001), p. 258.

"Phil was on a roll…mrshawn, As a kid in the '70s…, blog, *New York Post*, August 14, 2007.

"Brooksie has some…, "There's slim…, Lukas, J. Anthony, "How Mel Allen Started a Life Long Love Affair," *New York Times*, September 12, 1971.

"Oh, oh, ho-ly cow…Sandomir, Richard, "Memories of the Scooter," *New York Times*, August 14, 2007.

"Scooter, let me…, "One day scooter…, White, Bill, interview, September 11, 2008.

"White, look at….Clancy, Michael, "Phil Rizzuto, RIP," *Village Voice*, blog response, Neil Damause, August 14, 2007.

"When we first…White, Bill, interview, September 11, 2008.

"For all those…, "I really liked it… Hirschberg, Dan. *Phil Rizzuto: A Yankee Tradition* (Chicago: Sagamore Publishing, 1993), p. 143.

"We had to talk.…White, Bill, interview, September 11, 2008.

"This was a rainy…Pepe, Phil, Memories of the Lovable Scooter, YESNetwork. com, August 14, 2007, http://www.yesnetwork.com/news/article.jsp?ymd=20070814 &content_id=1429523&oid=36019&vkey=12

"Then I saw Phil…Stottlemeyer, Mel, with John Harper. *Pride and Pinstripes* (New York: Harper Collins, 2007), p. 87.

Hello! Phil Rizzuto for the Money Store

"What we're amazed…, "All three businesses…, "There's a whole…, Woods, Dan, "In The Money," *The Record* (Bergen, New Jersey), May 21, 1992.

"Holy Cow! I'm late…, "Santa: Santa Speaking!…, Rizzuto The Money Store, television ad, YouTube.com, as retrieved on March 11, 2009.

"There are so many…, "Most of these ads…, "Perhaps taking the…, Mara, Will, Phil Rizzuto's Death Takes Fans Down Advertising Memory Lane From Scooter to Fabio, Why We Love Those Terrible Celeb Commercials, ABCNews.com, August 16, 2007, as retrieved on March 11, 2009, http://abcnews.go.com/Entertainment/Story?id=3483958&page=1

"White: Do they…Rabbit, Rizzuto/Messer/White, *New York Post* Blog, August 14, 2007.

"I was lucky enough…Braunstein, Alan, I was lucky enough…, The Scooter's Finest Hour, blog response, *New York Times*, August 16, 2007, as retrieved on arch 9, 2009, http://bats.blogs.nytimes.com/2007/08/14/the-scooters-finest-hour/?apage=12.

I Can See Phil Rizzuto By The Dashboard Light

"They were owned…"In the summer…, "Rizzuto arrived at…, "Phil was an absolutely…, Pearlman, Jeff, "Phil and Meat Loaf will always have 'Paradise'," Page @. ESPN.com, August 29, 1007, as retrieved March 11, 2009, http://sports.espn.go.com/espn/page2/story?page=pearlman/070816&sportCat=mlb

"[He] formed a band…, "Steinman, a New Yorker…, "then Steinman wrote…, George-Warren, Holly, Patricia Romanowski, and Jon Pareles, *Fireside* (New York), 2001.

"Meat Loaf earned his…Marsh, Dave, "Reviews: *Bat Out of Hell*," *Rolling Stone*, December 15, 1977.

"And now ladies and…Not Attributed, Meatloaf, wikipedia, org, as retrieved March 11, 2009.

"It's called, Paradise…Yetnikoff, Walter, with David Ritz. *Howling at the Moon* (New York: Broadway Books, 2004), p. 110.

"I want to tell…, "All of a sudden…, "I got in trouble…, Kuffner, Charles, Phil Rizzuto Park, Off The Cuff.com, July 22, 2004, as retrieved March 12, 2009, http://www.offthekuff.com/mt/archives/003875.html

"I remember doing…Keran, Kevin, "Holy Cow! Rizzuto is Still Scooting," *New York Post*, February 3, 2006.

"Phil was no dummy…Pearlman, Jeff, "Phil and Meat Loaf will always have 'Paradise'," Page @. ESPN.com, August 29, 1007, as retrieved March 11, 2009, http://sports.espn.go.com/espn/page2/story?page=pearlman/070816&sportCat=mlb

More Championships

"It was 1976,... jonmouk71, It was 1976, Phil Rizzuto (1917-2007) ..., blog response, New York Post, August 15, 2007, as retrieved on March 9, 2009, www.nydailynews.com/forums/thread.jspa?threadID=545&start=50&tstart=0

"We go back...Not Attributed, Rizzuto Thinks Old Pal Martin Will Succeed, *Albany Times Union* (Albany, New York), January 14, 1988.

"Rizzuto had spirited...Mahler, Jonathan. *Ladies and Gentlemen the Bronx is Burning* (London: Picador, 1977), p. 243.

"I don't want...", "He barely got...", Pepe, Phil. *The Ballad of Billy and George: The Tempestuous Baseball Marriage of Billy Martin and George Steinbrenner* (Chicago: Triumph Books, 2008), p. 138.

"I couldn't believe...", "They (the Yankees) just...", Not Attributed, "Rizzuto Thinks Old Pal Martin Will Succeed," *Albany Times Union* (Albany, New York), January 14, 1988.

"He hits one deep...Not attributed, Phil Rizzuto, wikipedia.org, as retrieved on March 11, 2009.

"He was serious...", "Step by step, we...", "You know," said..., Appel, Marty. *Now Pitching for the Yankees* (New York: Total Sports Illustrated, 2001), pp. 236-37.

"The best radio or TV...Vasquez, Diego, "Remembering baseball's Phil Rizzuto," *Media Life*, August 15, 2007.

"I loved working...", "We also talked..., Healy, Fran, Rizzuto was one of a kind, Game On, MSG.com, August 14, 2007, as retrieved on March 12, 2009, http://blogs.msg.com/gameon/2007/08/14/rizzuto-was-one-of-a-kind/

"One time in Seattle...Hirschberg, Dan. *Phil Rizzuto: A Yankee Tradition* (Chicago: Sagamore Publishing, 1993), p. 134.

"Here's Scooter, back...Ziegel, Vic, "A funny thing happened on the way to Cooperstown," *New York Daily News*, August 15, 2007.

"Fran Healy: "Next up is....Clancy, Michael, "Phil Rizzuto, RIP," *Village Voice*, blog response, Neil Damause, August 14, 2007.

"I first sat next...Lyons, Jeffery, "The Rizzuto I Knew," WNBC, August 2007.

"It's not that I...Hoch, Bryan, Yankees say goodbye to Scooter, MLB.com, August 18, 2007, as retrieved March 18, 2009.

"I made a mistake...Buscema, Dave. *Game of My Life* (Champaign, IL: Sports Publishing LLC, 2004), p. 19.

"I remember walking...Vaccaro, Mike. *Emperors and Idiots* (New York: Broadway Books, 2005), pp. 222-23.

"Deep to left!...Allen, Maury, "Bill White Breaks Color Line in Baseball Booth," *New York Post*, February 10, 1971.

"Rizzuto: Looks a little...Not Attribute, Bill White, wikipedia.org, as retrieved on March 12, 2009.

"Rizzuto: Two balls on...ItshotinPHX, I grew up in Fair Lawn..., The Scooter's Finest Hour, *New York Times* blog response, August 14, 2007, as retrieved on March 9, 2009, http://bats.blogs.nytimes.com/2007/08/14/the-scooters-finest-hour/?apage=1#comment-15649

"Rizzuto: Bill, don't you…Hyman, Howard, "A Vowel Tip," *New York Times*, February 19, 1989.

"The kick, and…Not Attributed, Frank Messer, wikipedia.org, as retrieved on March 9, 2009.

"Funny, the kids…Rubin, Bob, "Yankee Voices split over summer vacation," *St. Petersburg Evening Independent*, July 24, 1981.

"It was a class…Not Attributed, Frank Messer, wikipedia.org, as retrieved on March 9, 2009.

"It's very chilly… Rizzuto, Phil, edited by Tom Peyer and Hart Seely. *Holy Cow!: The Selected Verse of Phil Rizzuto* (New York: Harper Collins, Ecco edition, 2008), p. 68.

"Now, I had…, "Where's White…, Rizzuto, Phil, edited by Tom Peyer and Hart Seely. *Holy Cow!: The Selected Verse of Phil Rizzuto* (New York: Harper Collins, Ecco edition, 2008), p. 64.

"Dick Howser is… Rizzuto, Phil, edited by Tom Peyer and Hart Seely. *Holy Cow!: The Selected Verse of Phil Rizzuto* (New York: Harper Collins, Ecco edition, 2008), p. 67.

"I was in Ft. Lauderdale…Lukas, Bob, I was in Ft. Lauderdale, The Scooter's Finest Hour, blog response No. 62, *New York Times*, August 14, 2007.

"In 1983 a friend…DiMaggio, Lou, In 1983 a friend…, The Scooter's Finest Hour, blog response No. 211, *New York Times*, August 14, 2007, as retrieved on March 9, 2009, http://bats.blogs.nytimes.com/2007/08/14/the-scooters-finest-hour/?apage=12.

"During a Rizzuto…Madden, Bill, "As good a shortstop as ever played," *New York Daily News*, August 15, 2007.

"Rizzuto beats it…Vecsey, George, "Sports of The Sports; 'Holy Cow, Seaver! They Made Me a Poet'," *New York Times*, March 12, 1993.

"For those who knew…Pepe, Phil, Memories of the loveable Scooter, YESNetwork.com, August 14, 2007, as retrieved March 9, 2007, http://www.yesnetwork.com/news/article.jsp?ymd=20070814&content_id=1429523&oid=36019&vkey=12

Old Friends

"his baseball trophies…Buscema, Dave. *Game of My Life* (Champaign, IL: Sports Publishing LLC, 2004), p. 9.

"He does quite…, "Phil raises funds by…, Hirschberg, Dan. *Phil Rizzuto: A Yankee Tradition* (Chicago: Sagamore Publishing, 1993), p. 153.

"He's like you….Levy, Clifford J., "Rizzuto's the talk of the town," *New York Times*, July 30, 1994.

"People stand next…, "photograph hangs in so…, Levy, Clifford J., Rizzuto's the talk of the town, *New York Times*, July 30, 1994.

"Now, don't swing…, "You'll see him at…, "He didn't know…, Hirschberg, Dan. *Phil Rizzuto: A Yankee Tradition* (Chicago: Sagamore Publishing, 1993), pp. 154–56.

"She does not…Hirschberg, Dan. *Phil Rizzuto: A Yankee Tradition* (Chicago: Sagamore Publishing, 1993), p. 134.

"That wasn't the…Madden, Bill. *Pride of October* (New York: Warner Books, 2003), p. 12.

"Priddy was defended…Ofgang, Kenneth, "Legendary Criminal Defense Lawyer Paul Caruso Dies at 81," *Metropolitan News-Enterprise*, August 16, 2001.

"Murcer clearly adored…Gavin, Glen, "Bobby Murcer tells some tales on Phil Rizzuto," *The Miami Herald*, July 15, 2009.

"Every time I think about...Murcer, Bobby. *Yankee for Life: My 40-year Journey in Pinstripes* (New York: Harper, 2008), p. 144.

"So there we were...Murcer, Bobby. *Yankee for Life: My 40-year Journey in Pinstripes* (New York: Harper, 2008), p. 144.

"The cannolis, and...Murcer, Bobby, Bobby Murcer on Rizzuto and Cannolis, video interview, mlb.com, August 15, 2007, as retrieved on March 9, 2009, http://newyork.yankees.mlb.com/mlb/news/tributes/obit_phil_rizzuto.jsp

"Here comes Alex...Gavin, Glen, "Bobby Murcer tells some tales on Phil Rizzuto," *The Miami Herald*, July 15, 2009.

Christmas Night, 1984

"representative of many...", "People were mugged...", "a very sweet...", "We've had some...", Gottlieb, Martin, "Fatal Shooting On West Side Jars An Uneasy Balance In A Changing Neighborhood," *New York Times*, December 29, 1984.

"The issue was...Chambers, Marcia, "F.B.I. Agent Cleared in Unarmed Man's Death," *New York Times*, May 25, 1985.

Perfecting His Style

"Of all the most... Vaccaro, Mike. *Emperors and Idiots* (New York: Broadway Books, 2005), p. 235.

"has enjoyed two...", "That big thing stepped...", "George Steinbrenner, he...", "the old professional...", Vecsey, George, "A Big Day for Scooter," *New York Times*, August 5, 1985.

"That huckleberry...Anderson, Dave, "Long and Miraculous Award for Scooter," *New York Times*, January 21, 1990.

"Kaat, I got to...Smith, Curt, Jim Kaat Retirement Baseball's Loss, Voices of The GameMLBlog, September 14, 2006, as retrieved on March 12, 2009.

"There have been...", "Bill gave me a...", Raissman, Bob, "XM MLB Chat," *New York Daily News*, September 10, 2006.

"He kept things...Hooch, Bryan, Old Friends...Jim Kaat, Players across generations remember beloved Hall of Famer, MLB.com, August 15, 2007, as retrieved on March 14, 2009, http://www.baseballhalloffame.org/news/article.jsp?ymd=20070815&content_id=4919&vkey=hof_news.

"Although no baseball...Donny L., Although no baseball..., The Scooter's Finest Hour, *New York Times*, blog response No. 42, New York Times, August 14, 2007, as retrieved, March 9 2009, http://bats.blogs.nytimes.com/2007/08/14/the-scooters-finest-hour/?apage=2#comments

"I was walking....Sligoboy/Mike, "I was walking..., *New York Post*, blog response, August 24, 2007, as retrieved on March 13, 2009.

"White Sox operations...Goddard, Joe, "White Sox Notes," *Chicago Sun-Times*, April 11, 1986.

"I didn't know...", "Those huckleberries...", "I roomed with Billy...", Levy, Gene, "Rizzuto Sounds Off At Card Convention," *Albany Union-Times* (Albany, New York), November 23, 1986.

"Phil was exasperating...Appel, Marty. *Now Pitching for the Yankees* (New York: Total Sports Illustrated, 2001), p. 256.

"[Bob] Fishel was...Appel, Marty. *Now Pitching for the Yankees* (New York: Total Sports Illustrated, 2001), p. 258.

"When I first joined...Appel, Marty, radio interview, MLB Radio, August 15, 2007, as retrieved on March 14, 2009, http://newyork.yankees.mlb.com/mlb/news/tributes/obit_phil_rizzuto.jsp

"As Yankees PR Director..., "He was a terrific pro..., Marty Appel, interview, April 15, 2009.

"We put TV cameras...Appel, Marty, radio interview, MLB Radio, August 15, 2007, as retrieved on March 14, 2009, http://newyork.yankees.mlb.com/mlb/news/tributes/obit_phil_rizzuto.jsp

"I knew him for...Ziegel, Vic, "A funny thing happened on the way to Cooperstown," *New York Daily News*, August 15, 2007.

"Phil was a lot...Madden, Bill, "As good a shortstop as ever played," *New York Daily News*, August 15, 2007.

"Now, the players...Appel, Marty, radio interview, MLB Radio, August 15, 2007, as retrieved on March 14, 2009, http://newyork.yankees.mlb.com/mlb/news/tributes/obit_phil_rizzuto.jsp

"The driver of the car...Not Attributed, "Hit-Run Driver Kills Woman," *New York Times*, September 15, 1988.

"Bill would squeeze...Marty Appel, interview, April 15, 2009.

"I was worried..., "My first comment was..., "Bill White was selected..., "Hank Aaron, then the..., Martinez, Michael, "Bill White a Unanimous Choice to Head National League," *New York Times*, February 4, 1989.

The Yankees took a...Kram, Mark & Pendergrast, Tom, Bill White, baseball player, broadcaster, league executive, Brief Biographies, as retrieved on March 10, 2009, <a href="http://biography.jrank.org/pages/2437/White-Bill.html">Bill White Biography</a>

"He told me he...Martinez, Michael, "Bill White a Unanimous Choice to Head National League," *New York Times*, February 4, 1989.

"Managers aren't the..., "His talents didn't become..., Dougherty, Pete, "Yankee Announcers Fall Short," *Albany Union-Times*, September 3, 1989.

"When Phil Rizzuto was..., "I know the 'long'..., "As a shortstop and..., "I looked up the..., Anderson, Dave, "Long and miraculous Award for Scooter," *New York Times*, January 21, 1990.

"Mel Allen marked...Not Attributed, "Baseball Bits," *Chicago Sun-Times*, May 1, 1990.

"The only voice...Not attributed, "Around the Majors," *Washington Post*, May 1, 1990.

"I have a terrible...Goff, Steven, "Holy Cow!" *Washington Post*, September 28, 1990.

"One year we thought..., "Phil always did..., "Oh, and before..., Appel, Marty. *Now Pitching for the Yankees* (New York: Total Sports Illustrated, 2001), p. 257.

"Movie critic Gene...Wulf, Steve, "Error on the Thoreau," *Sports Illustrated*, November 18, 1991.

"Al Kunitz died..., "Is this what I..., "He probably did..., Goodwin, George, Al Kunitz, The Cruelest Twist, ALS Independence.com, as retrieved on March 14, 2009 http://www.alsindependence.com/cruelest_twist.htm

"Tom Seaver was up..., "This press conference..., "It happened..., "Bob Feller was..., Anderson, Dave, "Sports of The Times; The Hall's Mr. Highest Percentage," *New York Times*, January 9, 1992.

"Seaver bonded well…, "That was a miserable…, "The Hard Rock Café?…, Appel, Marty. *Now Pitching for the Yankees* (New York: Total Sports Illustrated, 2001), p. 261–62.

"Tom was quite…Murcer, Bobby. *Yankee for Life: My 40-year Journey in Pinstripes* (New York: Harper, 2008), p. 155.

"We have IFB…, "Well, we try…, Hirschberg, Dan. *Phil Rizzuto: A Yankee Tradition* (Chicago: Sagamore Publishing, 1993), p. 116.

"Hey, Scooter…, "Rizzuto, who no…, "That thing on?…, McGough, Matthew. *Bat Boy: My True Life Coming of Age with the New York Yankees* (New York: Doubleday, 2005), pp. 87–88.

"This is our 'Little…, "Fast-forward 40-plus…, "I am left taking…, Drummond, Gerry, "The day we snagged an autograph from 'The Scooter'" *The Record* (Bergen County, NJ), August 22, 2007.

"True love came…Rizzuto, Phil and Tom Horton. *The October Twelve* (New York: Forge Books 1994), p. 47.

"Not only has [George]…, "George Steinbrenner made…, Rizzuto, Phil and Tom Horton. *The October Twelve* (New York: Forge Books 1994), pp. 46–47.

The Literary Life of Philip Francis Rizzuto

"You do not read…, "Rizzuto couldn't work…, "There is also a…, "That's wacky…, Vecsey, George, "Sports of The Sports; 'Holy Cow, Seaver! They Made Me a Poet,'" *New York Times*, March 12, 1993.

"I have been wrong…Rizzuto, Phil, edited by Tom Peyer and Hart Seely. *Holy Cow!: The Selected Verse of Phil Rizzuto* (New York: Harper Collins, Ecco edition, 2008), back cover.

Money Store Benches Rizzuto as Pitchman

"The same thing…Woods, Dan, "In The Money," *The Record* (Bergen, New Jersey), May 21, 1992.

"The same thing…, "The Money Store…, Marilee Loboda Braue, "For Pitchman Phil Rizzuto, How Sweet It Isn't—Money Store Ouster A Blow," *The Record* (Bergen, New Jersey), March 4, 1993.

"We think…Marilee Loboda Braue, "Money Store Benches Rizzuto As Pitchman," *The Record* (Bergen, New Jersey), March 3, 1993.

"It wasn't the…, "What annoyed him…, Marilee Loboda Braue, "For Pitchman Phil Rizzuto, How Sweet It Isn't—Money Store Ouster A Blow," *The Record* (Bergen, New Jersey), March 4, 1993.

"Palmer, of course…Marilee Loboda Braue, "Money Store Benches Rizzuto As Pitchman," *The Record* (Bergen, New Jersey), March 3, 1993.

"Subprime lending has…, "Talk to your…, "That notoriety…, "First Union is…, Timmons, Heather, "Money Store Sale: Huge Payday for Founding Family," *American Banker*, March 9, 1998.

"Marketing executives…, "Since the early 1980s…, Story, Louise, "Home Equity Frenzy Was a Bank Ad Come True," *New York Times*, August 14, 2008.

"Fast forward five…Bruene, Jim, "The Money Store's Comeback Marred by Flawed Website," NetBanker.com, October 9, 2006, as retrieved on March 14, 2009.

Cooperstown

"I couldn't bring…Anderson, Dave, "Blank Ballots by Writers Burn Bunning," *New York Times*, January 14, 1988.

"The one time…, "I said to myself…, Forker, Dom. *The Men of Autumn* (Dallas: Taylor Publishing Company, 1989), p. 53.

"It's not in the…James, Bill. *Whatever Happened to the Hall of Fame?* (Free Press, 1995), p. 59.

"I am not here… James, Bill. *Whatever Happened to the Hall of Fame?* (Free Press, 1995), p. 29.

"The Hall of Fame?…Forker, Dom. *The Men of Autumn* (Dallas: Taylor Publishing Company, 1989), p. 44.

"Scooter is one…Anderson, Dave, "Blank Ballots by Writers Burn Bunning," *New York Times*, January 14, 1988.

"Phil wants to be…, "My life is not…, Hirschberg, Dan. *Phil Rizzuto: A Yankee Tradition* (Chicago: Sagamore Publishing, 1993), p. 166.

"Most baseball fans…, "However, it is…, Cote, Daniel, Scandals surrounding players inducted into the Baseball Hall of Fame, Helium.com, as retrieved on February 11, 2009, http://www.helium.com/items/1175294-baseball-hall-of-fame-induction-scandal

"Phil Rizzuto's chances…Not Attributed, "Veterans Committee Additions Aid Rizzuto," Associated Press, August 1, 1993.

"New York Yankees…, "I busted my…, "I know I'm not…, Anderson, Dave, "Holy Cow! The Scooter Is Going to Cooperstown," *New York Times*, February 27, 1994.

"For 11 years…Whiteside, Larry, "Rizzuto Earns Fame," *The Boston Globe*, February 26, 1994.

"In 1964 we moved….Brown, Drew Buindini, "In 1964 we moved…, blog response, *New York Post*, com, August 15, 2007, as retrieved on March 13, 2009.

"He was a hell…Goldberg, Jeff, "So Long, Scooter: Sizing Up a Legend: Pesky Recalls Rival as Friend," *Hartford Courant* (Hartford, Connecticut), August 15, 2007.

"If I'm in, you…, "When Yogi told me…, Anderson, Dave, "Holy Cow! The Scooter Is Going to Cooperstown," *New York Times*, February 27, 1994.

"I never thought…, "He was very…, Goldberg, Jeff, "So Long, Scooter: Sizing Up a Legend: Pesky Recalls Rival as Friend," *Hartford Courant* (Hartford, Connecticut), August 15, 2007.

"The innocence of the…, "The shadow of a…, "Rizzuto's immortalization…, "Rizzuto was great…, "Baseball, that noble…, Vecsey, Laura, "Scooter Arrives Happily," *Albany Times Union* (Albany, New York), August 1, 1994.

"This is typical of me…, "If I hadn't of been…, "The game is so beautiful…, "It was like being…, "Did they come for…, Hertzel, Bob, "Yankees Falter in Front of Scooter's People," *The Record* (Bergen, New Jersey), August 10, 1994.

"His criticism of…, "the valid arguments…, Chass, Murray, "The Great Phil Rizzuto Debate," *New York Times*, April 10, 1994.

"I'll be ready…, "A lot falls on…, Sandomir, Richard, "A New Straight Man for the Scooter," *New York Times*, April 5, 1994.

"One of the many…Olden, Paul, One of the many…, Phil Rizzuto blog, response, New York Post.com, August 14, 2007, as retrieved March 14, 2009.

"I went to a…Brown, Drew Bundini, "Several Years Ago, Share your favorite memory of Phil 'Scooter' Rizzuto," *New York Daily News*, August 15, 2007.

"I couldn't carry…, "Derek is 10 times…, O'Connor, Ian, "Rizzuto's legacy of friendship—Favorite Uncle Phil to Those Around Him," *The Record*, (Bergen, New Jersey), August 19, 2007.

"I like what I see…Vaccaro, Mike. *Emperors and Idiots* (New York: Broadway Books, 2005), p. 173.

"Where's Jeter?…Hoch, Bryan, Jeter recalls time with Rizzuto, MLB.com, August 14, 2007, as retrieved on March 13, 2009.

Saying Goodbye to Mickey Mantle

Mickey Mantle died…Mantle, Mickey, "I Was Killing Myself," *Sports Illustrated*, April 18, 1994.

"He was a presence…Costas, Bob, "Eulogy for Mickey Mantle," *Chicago Sun-Times*, Chicago, IL, August 16, 1995.

"upset that he…,"Rizzuto met with…, "When I saw the…, Not Attributed, "Mantle Death Convinces Yanks' Rizzuto to Retire," *Chicago Sun-Times*, August 24, 1995.

"I've been firm…, "I wasn't enjoying…, Not Attributed, "Rizzuto Stands by Decision," *New York Times*, August 21, 1995.

"It's time for me…Not Attributed, "Mantle Death Convinces Yanks' Rizzuto to Retire," *Chicago Sun-Times*, August 24, 1995.

"As the years…Appel, Marty. *Now Pitching for the Yankees* (New York: Total Sports Illustrated, 2001), p. 258.

"It's very difficult…Not Attributed, "Mantle Death Convinces Yanks' Rizzuto to Retire," *Chicago Sun-Times*, August 24, 1995.

"I haven't talked…, "I was supposed to…, "He's right. No matter…, Sandomir, Richard, "Rizzuto Unplugged? Maybe It Won't Last," *New York Times*, March 10, 1996.

"Watch Duilio or…, "glided into the…, "Remember. Come back…, "Oh, no," Rizzuto…, Sandomir, Richard, "Thursday in the Park With Mr. Holy Cow," *New York Times*, April 12, 1996.

"If he wants to do…Not Attributed, "MSG Plans to Woo Rizztuo," *New York Times*, March 11, 2007.

"The 81-year-old…More, Elliott Harris, "Holy cow! There's no statue of limitations for Rizzuto," *Chicago Sun-Times*, April 20, 1999.

"I was a sophomore…, "Rizzuto: Now are…, "So it wasn't the…, Blumberg, Dan, Reporter Shares Memories of Phil Rizzuto, WNYC Radio. WNYC.com, August 15, 2007 as retrieved on March 15, 2009.

"I felt like a rookie…More, Elliott Harris, "Holy cow! There's no statue of limitations for Rizzuto," *Chicago Sun-Times*, April 20, 1999.

"On the morning of…, "Rizzuto was relieved…, "Dad," she said…, "I couldn't believe…, "People recognized…, Madden, Bill, Metro Sports Baseball, New York Daily News, September 30, 2001, as retrieved on March 15, 2009, http://www.nydailynews.com/2001-09-3…l/a-126908.asp (http://www.nydailynews.com/2001-09-30/Metro_Sports/Baseball/a-126908.asp) http://forums.nyyfans.com/showthread.php?p=230766&highlight=Scooter#post230766

"I suggested we go…, "I think Cora says…, "I guess that's…, Madden, Bill, "One last meeting with Phil Rizzuto," *New York Daily News*, September 9, 2007.

"Rizzuto once presented…, "One time we went…, "In 1998, I decided…, Michaud, John D. III, Like Many People in Upstate…, Scooter's Finest Hour, *New York Times*, August 14, 2007, blog response No. 241, as retrieved February 9, 2009, http://bats.blogs.nytimes.com/2007/08/14/the-scooters-finest-hour/?apage=11#comments

"Just like the old…Vaccaro, Mike. *Emperors and Idiots* (New York: Broadway Books, 2005), p. 25.

"He's thinner now…Buscema, Dave. *Game of My Life* (Champaign, IL: Sports Publishing LLC, 2004), p. 9.

"Kids who live in…Gold, Jeffrey, "Memories Of Phil From His Longtime Jersey Home," Associated Press, August 14, 2007.

"There are no traces…, "We have the…, Kuffner, Charles, Phil Rizzuto Park, Off the Kuff.com, July 22, 2004, as retrieved on February 9, 2009.

Letting Go of the Past

"I was laid out…, "Joe wanted to go…, Blum, Ronald, "The Scooter peddles memorabilia; Yankee icon Phil Rizzuto to auction off personal baseball items," *Albany Times-Union* (Albany, New York), February 5, 2006.

"As a female photographer…, "such keepsakes as…, "He's still afraid…, "Did you tell him…, Kernan, Kevin, "Holy Cow! Rizzuto is Still Scooting," *New York Post*, February 3, 2006.

Ed Lucas Redux

"Did anyone ever…, "That same year…, "He raised the boys…, "Baseball took my…, Rushin, Steve, "Miracle at Coogan's Bluff," *Sports Illustrated*, February 27, 2006.

"The stadium was…, "Mr. Steinbrenner has…, "We're friends 55…, Coyne, Kevin, "Baseball Stole His Eyes, but Not His Passion," *New York Times*, March 18, 2007.

"Jim Brozzetti needed…, "Brozzetti was a…, O'Connor, Ian, "Rizzuto's legacy of friendship—Favorite Uncle Phil to those around him," *The Record* (Bergen, New Jersey), August 19, 2007.

"Phil Rizzuto always…, "I feel good…, "Derek just broke…, Kernan, Kevin, "Rizzuto Fights on In His Most Recent Battle," *New York Post*, September 6, 2006.

"The last time I…Pepe, Phil, Memories of the loveable Scooter, YESNetwork.com, August 14, 2007, as retrieved March 9, 2007, http://www.yesnetwork.com/news/article.jsp?ymd=20070814&content_id=1429523&oid=36019&vkey=12

"He died very…, "Joe Ward, who…, Gold, Jeffrey, Memories Of Phil From His Longtime Jersey Home, Associated Press, August 14, 2007.

"For five decades…, "I think the family…, Cassidy, Mike, "Snapshot of Phil Rizzuto, 63 years ago," *San Jose Mercury News*, August 21, 2007.

INDEX

359